우루과이라운드

제도 및 기타 분야 협상 2

우루과이라운드

제도 및 기타 분야 협상 2

| 머리말

　우루과이라운드는 국제적 교역 질서를 수립하려는 다각적 무역 교섭으로서, 각국의 보호무역 추세를 보다 완화하고 다자무역체제를 강화하기 위해 출범되었다. 1986년 9월 개시가 선언되었으며, 15개 분야의 교섭을 1990년 말까지 진행하기로 했다. 그러나 각 분야의 중간 교섭이 이루어진 1989년 이후에도 농산물, 지적소유권, 서비스무역, 섬유, 긴급수입제한 등 많은 분야에서 대립하며 1992년이 돼서야 타결에 이를 수 있었다. 한국은 특히 농산물 분야에서 기존 수입 제한 품목 대부분을 개방해야 했기에 큰 경쟁력 하락을 겪었고, 관세와 기술 장벽 완화, 보조금 및 수입 규제 정책의 변화로 제조업 수출입에도 많은 변화가 있었다.

　본 총서는 우루과이라운드 협상이 막바지에 다다랐던 1991~1992년 사이 외교부에서 작성한 관련 자료를 담고 있다. 관련 협상의 치열했던 후반기 동향과 관계부처회의, 무역협상위원회 회의, 실무대책회의, 규범 및 제도, 투자회의, 특히나 가장 많은 논란이 있었던 농산물과 서비스 분야 협상 등의 자료를 포함해 총 28권으로 구성되었다. 전체 분량은 약 1만 3천여 쪽에 이른다.

2024년 3월

한국학술정보(주)

| 일러두기

· 본 총서에 실린 자료는 2022년 4월과 2023년 4월에 각각 공개한 외교문서 4,827권, 76만여 쪽 가운데 일부를 발췌한 것이다.

· 각 권의 제목과 순서는 공개된 원본을 최대한 반영하였으나, 주제에 따라 일부는 적절히 변경하였다.

· 원본 자료는 A4 판형에 맞게 축소하거나 원본 비율을 유지한 채 A4 페이지 안에 삽입하였다. 또한 현재 시점에선 공개되지 않아 '공란'이란 표기만 있는 페이지 역시 그대로 실었다.

· 외교부가 공개한 문서 각 권의 첫 페이지에는 '정리 보존 문서 목록'이란 이름으로 기록물 종류, 일자, 명칭, 간단한 내용 등의 정보가 수록되어 있으며, 이를 기준으로 0001번부터 번호가 매겨져 있다. 이는 삭제하지 않고 총서에 그대로 수록하였다.

· 보고서 내용에 관한 더 자세한 정보가 필요하다면, 외교부가 온라인상에 제공하는 『대한민국 외교사료요약집』1991년과 1992년 자료를 참조할 수 있다.

| 차례

정 리 보 존 문 서 목 록

기록물종류	일반공문서철		등록번호	2019090028	등록일자	2019-09-04
분류번호	764.51		국가코드		보존기간	영구
명 칭	UR(우루과이라운드) / 세이프가드 협상, 1991					
생 산 과	통상기구과		생산년도	1991~1991	담당그룹	다자통상
내용목차						

0001

전 언 통 신 문

국협 28140-7

수신 수신처 참조

제목 UR/ 세이프가드 협상 대책회의

　　　지난 브랏셀 TNC 각료회의 기간중 표제협상에 있어서 EC가 선별적용
양보의사를 표명함에 따라 새로운 협정안이 제시되고 구체적인 협의는 하지
못하였는 바, 동 협정안이 향후 협상의 기초로 사용될 것에 대비하여 우리나라
입장을 설정코자 다음과 같이 대책회의를 개최하고자 하오니 참석하여 주시기
바랍니다.

　　　　　　　　　　　　　　- 다　　음 -

1. 일서 및 장소 : 1991. 1. 9 (수) 16:00
　　　　　　　　　　상공부 무역위원회 참갈장 (3동 106-1호)

2. 참 석 범 위 : 상 공 부 산업조사관 (회의주재)
　　　　　　　　　　　　조사총괄과장, 국제협력담당관, 무역정책과장

　　　　　경제기획원 ┐
　　　　　외 무 부
　　　　　농림수산부　　　　　무역 관계자
　　　　　K I E T
　　　　　K O T R A ┘

3. 회 의 의 제 : GATT 사무국 협정안에 대한 우리입장 설정.　끝.

　　　　　　　　　　　　　　　　　통화시간 : 91.1.8. 16:45
　　　　　　　　　　　　　　　　　송 화 자 : 노 인 환
　　　　　　　　　　　　　　　　　수 화 자 : 이 급 선

0002

緊急輸入制限措置（Safeguards）

I. UR進展狀況 및 展望

1. 協商背景 및 目標

- 緊急輸入制限措置는 自由化된 品目의 輸入이 急增하여 同種 또는 直接 競爭關係에 있는 輸入國의 國內産業에 심각한 被害가 發生하거나 被害憂慮가 있을 경우, 限時的으로 關稅引上 또는 數量規制 등의 形態로 輸入을 制限하는 措置를 意味（GATT 19條）

- 同 措置 發動時 特定國家의 商品만을 選別的으로 制限하는 것은 GATT의 基本原則인 最惠國待遇（MFN待遇）原則에 違反이며, GATT에 通報, 關聯 當事國과의 協議, 同 措置에 影響을 받는 國家에 대한 補償措置 등 嚴格한 規定에 따라야 하므로 輸入 先進國들은 兩者間 輸出自律規制 協定과 같은 GATT 規定을 일탈한 措置（회색조치）로 輸入을 規制해 옴.

- 금번 協商을 통하여 safeguards措置의 實用性, 明瞭性을 確保함으로써 輸入國들이 정당한 貿易에 대하여 反덤핑, 補助金, 相計關稅 등의 措置를 남발하는 現象 및 GATT밖에서 회색조치로 處理하는 傾向을 防止하고자 하는 것임.

- safeguards는 競爭力에 의한 公正한 貿易에 대한 規制措置라는 점에서 不公正貿易에 대한 反덤핑措置와 性格上 差異가 있으며 우리나라에서는 貿易委員會가 同 措置를 産業被害 救濟制度의 일환으로 運營중임.

- 104 -

0003

2. 進展狀況

가. 제네바 協商 그룹 會議

○ '89年 7月 議長 協定案이 제시된 이후 현재까지 이를 중심으로
8次에 걸쳐 討議 및 修正하는 方式으로 協商을 進行

○ 選別適用 許容與否등 중요부분에 대한 合意가 이루어지지 못한
상태에서 議長의 9次 協定案을 브랏셀 閣僚會議의 協商基礎로
使用하기로 決定하고 閣僚들의 政治的 解決로 넘김.

나. 브랏셀 閣僚會議

○ EC의 選別適用 철회 意思表示로 小規模 非公式 會議가 開催되어
새로운 協定案이 提示되었으나 農産物 協商의 교착으로 인해
구체적인 協議는 갖지 못함.

 - 選別措置 條項을 없애는 대신, 數量規制時 旣存 國別 市場占有率의
   5% point 또는 國別 輸入量의 30%중 적은 것으로 cut-back
   할 수 있도록 함.

 - 회색조치는 3~4年 時限內에 撤廢하되, 例外的으로 特定 品目에
   대하여는 8年까지 존속 許容 可能

다. 合意된 事項(意見接近分野)

○ 회색조치는 撤廢되어야 하며 緊急輸入制限措置 發動基準을 緩和하고
일정한 條件 充足時 補償·報復을 면제해야 한다는데 대해서는 意見
接近

 - 그러나, 選別適用 許容與否에 대한 異見으로 인해 구체적인 發動
   基準, 회색조치 撤廢期間 및 補償·報復 免除期間에 대한 명시적인
   合意는 이루지 못함.

-105-

0004

3 . 爭點事項

가. 制限된 選別適用 許容 與否

　○ 大多數國家 : 무차별 原則을 준수하되 보상·보복면제등 發動要件을
　　　　　　　　現實的으로 改善

　○ E C : 現實性 不足으로 活用되지 않는 規定은 의미가 없고 회색
　　　　　조치만을 조장하게 되므로 選別適用 認定

　※ 美國과 EC의 選別適用 주장의 差異點

　　─ 美國은 妥協案으로 當事國間 合意를 전제로한 選別適用 (Con-
　　　sensual Selectivity)을 제안 (카나다가 檢討用意 表明)

　　─ EC는 合意與否에 불문하고 例外的인 狀況條件 充足時 일방적인
　　　選別適用을 許容한 것을 主張

　　　• Non-Paper (11.12)를 통해 制限된 國家로부터의 輸入急增이
　　　　總輸入量의 상당한 부분을 차지하는 例外的인 狀況條件에 해당할
　　　　경우, 3年以內 短期間 發動, 보복인정, 多者間 監視 機能등
　　　　强化된 規律이 適用되는 選別措置를 提案

나. 灰色措置 撤廢期間 및 方法

　○ E C : 撤廢時限을 設定치 말고 當事國이 協議, GATT에 提出

　○ 大多數國家 : 多者間에 合意된 3年 정도의 최대시한을 設定, 撤廢

다. 補償·報復免除期間

　○ 大多數國家 : 選別適用을 철회한 경우, 기간에 있어서는 融通性 있는
　　　　　　　　檢討 用意 表明 (美國은 4年 要求)

　○ E C : 選別性과 補償·報復 免除를 連繫, 妥協點을 摸索할 狀況이
　　　　아님 (連繫時는 5年間 免除)

0005

라. 數量規制時 쿼타 減縮 與否

   ○ 大多數國家 : 公正貿易에 대한 規制措置 이므로 과거의 平均 輸入
                   物量은 保障되어야 함.

   ○ E C : 特別한 경우 減縮의 정당성 입증을 진제로 인정 쿼타物量
              減縮許容

   ○ 美 國 : 輸出國別 市場占有率 順序가 바뀌지 않는 範圍內에서 최대
              (X %)의 쿼타 減縮 許容

마. E C (關稅同盟)의 地位

   ○ E C : 일부 會員國 또는 一部地域을 대신하거나 EC 전체 次元의
            Safeguards 措置를 발동하고 域內國間의 交易에는 適用 하지
            않을 것을 主張

   ○ 餘他國家 : EC 전체 또는 會員國別 발동중 選擇한 것을 要求하고
            SG措置對象에서 域內國家 除外는 사실상 選別適用임을
            지적

바. 構造調整 支援措置

   ○ EC, 인도, 브라질 : 構造調整 支援을 Safeguards措置의 發動 目的
                으로 許容하고 輸出補助金의 성격이 아닌 支援
                措置는 認定

   ○ 大多數國家 : 補助金 協商에서 論議되고 있는 事項임을 이유로 반대
            (우리나라는 소극적으로 對應)

사. 開途國 優待條項

   ○ 一部 開途國을 除外하고는 대부분의 國家가 例外認定에 反對

아. 其他 發動 節次上 問題

   ○ 措置 發動期間

    — 美 國 : 最初 5年, 延長 3年으로 總8年

    — 日 本 : 最初, 延長 區分없이 5年

    — 對多數國家 : 最初 3年, 延長 3年으로 總6年

0006

O 暫定措置 期間

  - 美國, EC, 카나다 등은 調査節次上 충분한 期間이 필요함을
    主張

  - 濠洲, 홍콩 등은 暫定措置의 特殊狀況을 考慮 90일 이상 許容
    反對

O 再發動 禁止期間

  - 대부분의 國家가 2年의 再發動 禁止期間에는 지지하나, 180日
    以內의 短期措置의 再發動 禁止를 위한 例外的인 條項에 대해서는
    카나다, 뉴질랜드, 브라질, 인도 등 農産物 輸出國들만 支持 表明

O 旣存의 GATT 19 條에 의한 措置 撤廢期間

  - 美國 및 카나다 : 措置發動後 8年 以內 또는 新協定 發效後 3年
                            以內 撤廢

  - EC : 新協定 發效後 3年以內 撤廢는 너무 短期間임.

O 國內産業의 範圍

  - 被害 判定時 國內産業의 範圍를 國內生産의 상당부분으로 할
    것인가 또는 通商 50%이상, 최소한 33%이상으로 計量化 與否
    問題로서 대부분의 國家가 現實的으로 計量化가 困難함을 표명
    하고 있으나 EC만이 計量化 必要性 主張

- 108 -

0007

4. 向後 協商展望

○ 새로이 提示된 協定案을 向後 協商의 基礎로 採擇하여 協商을 進行할 것으로 展望

○ 豫想되는 協商 結果는 MFN原則이 유지되면서 發動條件이 보다 緩和되는 內容으로 合意될 것으로 展望

— 選別適用에 대해 EC만이 강하게 許容 主張을 하고 있고 대부분의 國家가 이에 반대하고 있어 選別性이 採擇될 可能性은 희박(美國은 伸縮的인 자세를 보일 것으로 豫想)

— 灰色措置 發動時限(例: 3～5年, 一定條件으로 例外認定), Safeguards措置 發動期間(例: 最大8年程度) 및 補償·報復免除가 인정되는 Safeguards措置 期間(例: 3～5年)이 다소 延長되는등 措置 發動에 따르는 負擔이 緩和되어 活用 可能性이 提高됨.

— 數量規制時 쿼타 減縮問題는 實質的으로 選別適用 效果가 發生되므로 許容될 可能性은 희박함.

○ 制限된 Selectivity가 許容될 可能性도 배제할 수는 없음.

— 選別措置時에는 上記 MFA原則 適用時 許容되는 것보다 상대적으로 發動條件이 強化됨

II. 우리나라에 미치는 影響

1. 有利한 側面

o 不公正 貿易에 대한 規制措置보다 規制水準이 弱하고 規制 節次도 보다 명료화되어 輸出 豫測可能性이 提高됨.

o 主要 輸出品에 대한 VER 등으로 인해 輸出增大 및 成長 潛在力이 制約을 받아오던 회색조치가 撤廢되어 輸出增大 效果 發生

o 우리의 市場開放 擴大 및 輸入增加로 인한 國內産業 被害防止 및 구제를 위해 同 措置의 발동이 보다 용이해짐.

2. 不利한 側面

o 先進國이 自律規制, 反덤핑 등을 통한 規制에서 Safeguards 措置로 轉換하게 되어 우리의 主要 輸出商品이 規制對象에 包含될 可能性이 높아짐.

— 輸出 伸張率이 높은 有望品目에 대한 規制로 인해 輸出障碍 發生

— 특히, 數量規制時 쿼타 減縮이 認定될 경우에는 被害가 더욱 惡化됨.

1. 各國의 Safeguards 發動現況

가. 概 觀

ㅇ 19條 措置중 約 90%가 濠洲, 美國, 카나다, EC등 4個國에
   의해 발동

ㅇ 많은 開途國이 19條 발동에 의해 影響을 받고 있으나 補償 및
   보복은 先進國 특히 美國과 EC에게만 關聯되어 있음.

ㅇ 農産物 및 食品, 織物 및 衣類分野가 19條의 인기있는 發動對象이
   되고 있으며, 短期間의 措置는 거의 모두가 農産物 및 食品과
   관련됨.

ㅇ 19條 措置가 무차별적으로 適用되고는 있으나 價格帶(Price
   brackets)의 使用이 措置에 의해 影響을 받는 輸出國의 數를
   制限하고 있음.

- 몇몇 措置는 OMA, VER과 같은 兩者間 또는 複數間(Plurilateral) 協定締結로 轉換됨.

나. 國別 發動現況('87.7.31, GATT/NG 9/ W/ 2/ Rev. 1)

ㅇ GATT 에 通報된 134件중 濠洲가 가장 빈번히 19條 發動
  (總 38件 發動, 5件 進行중)

- 美國(27件, 2件 進行中), 카나다(22件, 2件 進行中)
  EC (14件, 6件 進行中)

- 開途國 發動(7件, 4件 進行中)

-111-

0010

○ 品目別로는 農産物 및 食品이 가장 빈빈함(35 件)

― 織物 및 衣類(26 件), 鐵鋼(12 件), 電氣·電子製品(9 件),

  신발(9 件)

○ 發動時期別로는 70 年代에 가장 빈빈히 發動됨(47 件)

― 60 年代(35 件), 80 年以後(33 件)

〈 國別·品目別·時期別 19 條 發動現況 〉

1987.7.31

國 別	品目								發動時期別				現在實施中
	農産物및食品	織物및衣類	鐵鋼	電氣電子製品	신발	自動車	共他	總計	1950~1959	1960~1969	1970~1979	1980~現在	
濠洲	2	9	5	3	4	5	10	38	2	15	17	4	5
美國	3	4	4	1	1	1	13	27	11	3	9	4	2
카나다	11	7			3		1	22	2	3	13	4	2
E C	8	1	1	3	1		1	14			3	11	6
그 리 스	1			1				3	2	1			
스 페 인		1	1					2		2			1
이 태 리	2						1	3		2		1	1
프 랑 스	1		1					2		2			
獨 逸							2	2	1	1			1
오스트리아	3						2	5	1	3		1	1
칠 레	3							3				3	3
남아프리카					1		2	3				3	3
핀 란 드		1					1	2			1	1	
아이슬란드							1	1			1		
이 스 라 엘				1			1	1			1		
뉴 질 랜 드		1					1	1			1		
나이지리아							1	1		1			1
노 르 웨 이		1					1	1			1		
페 루							1	1		1			
로 디 지 아		1					1	1		1			
스 위 스	1						1	1				1	
總 計	35	26	12	9	9	6	37	134	19	35	47	33	26

―112―

0011

다. 發動形態別 現況

○ 關稅 및 非關稅措置가 總發動件數의 各各 절반(67件)을 차지

— 50 年代에는 關稅措置가 압도적 (80 %)

— 70 年代에는 非關稅措置가 대다수를 차지 (70 %)

○ 최근에는 關稅措置와 非關稅措置의 比率이 大略 均衡 維持

措 置 形 態			
發 動 時 期	關 稅	非 關 稅	合 計
1950 ~ 1959	15	4	19
1960 ~ 1969	19	16	35
1970 ~ 1979	15	32	47
1980 ~ 現 在	18	15	33
合 計	67	67	134

라. 發動期間別 現況

○ 5 年以內의 措置가 約 80 % 차지

○ 一部措置는 關稅再協商後 종결되고, 一部는 OMA , VER로 代替됨.

發 動 時 期	1 年以內	1 ~ 2 年	3 ~ 5 年	5 年以上
1950 ~ 1959	3	3	3	9
1960 ~ 1969	6	7	9	9
1970 ~ 1979	7	15	17	5
1980 ~ 現 在	9	3	3	-
合 計	25	28	32	23

0012

마. 補償 및 報復

　　○ 補償은(20件) 19 措置가 關稅形態일 경우 提供

　　　─ 時期別로는 50年代(10件), 60年代(8件), 70年代(1件),

　　　　80年以後(1件)

　　　─ 補償提供은 美國(9件), 그리스(3件), 호주 및 카나다(各各 2件)

　　○ 時間이 지남에 따라 補償은 減少하고 報復措置가 增加(13件)

　　　─ 時期別로는 50年代(2件), 60年代(3件), 70年代(4件),

　　　　80年以後(4件)

　　○ 補償 및 報復은 先進國에만 關聯되고, 開途國에는 補償 및 報復이

　　　各各 단 1件씩만 關聯됨.

　　　─ 補償('59, 호주의 대 체코)

　　　─ 報復('52, 美國의 대 터이키)

2. 우리나라에 대한 Safeguards 發動現況

가. 槪 觀

　　○ '87.9 까지 發動된 Safeguards 措置중 우리나라가 主要供給國으로서

　　　規制對象이 된 事例는 15件으로 開途國중 가장 높음

　　─ 홍콩(8件), 臺灣(1件)

　　○ 우리나라의 國際規範에 대한 接近方法이나 理解가 다른 競爭國에

　　　비해 낮은 것으로 評價됨.

─ 114 ─

0013

나. 우리나라에 대한 Safeguards 發動事例

　O 現在 先進國으로부터 GATT 規定에 의한 Safeguards 措置發動으로
　　規制받고 있는 品目은 없으나 Safeguards의 가장 큰 問題點으로
　　認識되고 있는 Safeguards 發動을 留保한 狀態인 VER, OMA 등
　　Grey - Area 措置로 轉換 또는 締結에 의해 被害를 많이 당하고
　　있음.

發動國	品　目	措置內容	開　始　/　終　了
호주 (2)	신발類	數量制限 (GQ)	'74.10.1 / '82.1.1
	Sand 부츠 및 신발部品	〃	'76.5.11 / '82.1.1
美國 (4)	特殊鋼	OMA, 其他輸入制限	'76.6.14 / '80.12.13
	〔一部〕	〔수량제한 (GQ)〕	〔'83.7.20 / '89.9.30〕(OMA로 轉換)
	신발類	VER	'77.6.28 / '81.6.30
	라디오	關稅引上	'78.4.14 / '81.4.10
	법랑食器	追加關稅	'80.1.17 / '84.1.17
카나다(5)	남자용 편직셔츠	數量制限 (GQ)	'71.11.30 / '78.12.31
	아크릴絲	〃	'76.1.1 / '78.8.31
	衣　類	〃	'76.11.29 / '78.12.31
	非고무화류	〃	'77.12.1 / '81.11.30
	〔女性用신발〕	〔　〃　〕	〔'85.12.1 / '88.11.30〕
	非革靴類	〃	'81.12.1 / '85.11.30
EC (4)	錄音機	數量制限	'73.4.1 / '73.12.31
	T・V	〃	'77.7.22 / '79.6.22
	Stone ware	〃 (GQ)	'83.1.1 / '83.4.16 (VER로 轉換)
	Quartz 時計	〃	'84.4.20 / '86.12.31

3. 選別適用許容에 관한 論議經緯

가. 東京라운드時의 主要 提案內容

　○ 3個提案 모두 Selectivity 認定

　─ 適用條件에 대해서는 다소간 差異가 있으며, 韓·홍콩 共同案은

　　協議에 必要한 엄격한 前提條件 提示

項　　目	GATT事務局案('79.4)	先進 7個國案('78.6)	韓·홍콩案('78.12)
○MFN原則 下에 例外 的인 許容	○原則的으로 無差別 適用 ─심각한 被害 또는 憂慮가 명백히 존재하는 非正常的 이고 例外的인 狀況下에서 選別 適用 許容	○左　　同	○左　　同
○要　　件	○1~3個國으로부터 의 輸入急增 ○同 輸入量이 全體 輸入에서 높은 比重을 차지할 경우	○하나 내지 數個國 (one or an li- mited number) ○다른 國家로부터의 輸入에 의한 被害 가 미미하여 무시 할 수 있을 정도 (negligible)	○1~3個國 ○實質的이고 주요한 比重 (substantial & major) ○被害가 同 國家들로 부터의 輸入에 의한 것이 명백할 경우

0015

項　　目	GATT 事務局案 ('79.4)	先進 7 個國案 ('78.6)	韓・홍콩案 ('78.12)
○措置範圍	―	○同 國家들로부터의 輸入에 限定	○左　　同
○合　意	○被規制國들과 合意 ·後	○左　　同	○左　　同
- 條　件	―	―	- 同 商品 輸入의 30 % 이상을 차지하는 輸出國을 對象 - 보다 큰 輸出國이 合意에 응하지 않을 경우 보다 작은 輸出國의 合意義務 없음
- 期　間	- 60 日 以內	- 적절한 期限以內	- 60 日 以內
- 決裂時	- SG委員會에 회부	- 左　　同	- 左　　同 ·同 委員會는 지체없이 적절한 勸告案 提示

項　　　目	GATT 事務局案 ('79.4)	先進 7 個國案 ('78.6)	韓・홍콩案 ('78.12)
○緊急 　狀況時	○關聯國과　緊急協議 （10日）後，合意 失敗時　SG委員會 에　회부	○SG 措置　發動後 즉시　SG委員會에 회부	○事前協議　없이 　MFN으로　措置發動 後 즉시　SG委員會 에　회부，選別措置 로　轉換하기 위해 協議
○狀況 　變化時	○　　　─	○委員會　勸告에 따른 措置發動　後 狀況 變化로　勸告가 정당화될　수 없거나 被規制國이　他國에 비해　불리한　狀況 發生時는　언제든지 SG委員會에　再 회부가능	○左　　　同
○被規制國 　權利	○　　　─	○相互合意時　報復 不行使도　合意事項 으로　包含可能 －緊急狀況時는　즉시 　報復　可能 －規制國이　委員會 　勸告拒否時는 즉시 　報復　可能	○左　　　同

나. 過去의 우리立場('82 Work Program의 39次 GATT總會 報告 對備, '83.11)

O 原則的으로 無差別 原則을 주장하되,

O 選別適用 許容時는 選別適用이 사실상 不可能할 정도로 發動要件과 內容을 엄격히 함.

　- 例外的이고 비정상적인 狀況의 명확한 定義

　- 被規制國은 1~3個國이고 1個 國家의 市場占有率이 최소한 30% 이상을 占하고 輸入國의 産業被害가 同 國家에 의하여 基因된 경우

　- 輸入國은 選別措置 發動要件을 關聯 輸出國 및 SG委員會에 立證

　- 選別適用은 短期間(18個月以內)이이야 하고 그 期間을 明示

다. UR協商 論議事項

議長協定案	E C	美國	韓國
O 1案 : MFN原則 適用 - 단, 最貧開途國 및 占有率이 미미한 開途國의 商品은 除外하고 同 國家들이 SG措置 發動時는 融通性 賦與	O 特定狀況下에서는 일방적인 選別 適用 許容 * 議長의 2案 支持	O 相互合意에 의한 選別適用 許容 - 단, 合意失敗 時는 MFN 原則 適用	O MFN原則 遵守 - 開途國에 대한 例外 認定 不可

議 長 協 定 案	E C	美 國	韓 國
○ 2案 : 選別適用 許容 - 國內 調査機關이 被害의 主된 原因이 特定國의 輸入에서 기인하고 同 輸入이 總輸入의 상당한 부분인 것으로 判定時는 同國家의 輸入에 대해서만 SG措置 發動이 可能하나, 總 輸入의 (X)% 이하를 占하는 國家에는 不適用함 - (36)個月동안 選別 措置 可能하며 同期間동안 非規制國 으로부터의 輸入이 상당히 增加한 경우에는 모든 國家로 SG措置 擴大 可能	- 制限된 輸出國에 의해 被害가 發生하고 同 輸出國의 市場 占有率이 (X)%를 차지할 경우 - 36個月의 시한으로 選別措置를 취하며, - 同 期間中 非規制國의 輸入 急增時는 追加 選別規制 可能	○選別適用時의 disincentive - 短期間 適用 (5年) * MFN : 8年 - 措置發動後 1年後부터 强制的인 規制緩和 義務 * MFN : 3年後부터 可能한한 規制 緩和 - 補償, 報復減縮 不可 * MFN : 減縮 可能	

Talking Points (Safeguards)

1. **MFN Principle/Selectivity** (paras. 5, 8, 10a)

    A. There is no doubt that the results of the Uruguay Round negotiations should confirm that Article XIX actions can only be applied on an MFN basis - even the EC in principle, shares this view.

    It may be important to make Article XIX more usable by accommodating the realistic needs of the importing countries. However, what is more important is the reality of the political relationship between large and small countries.

    If we allow Article XIX measures to be applied selectively, only those smaller and weaker nations which have no or negligible retaliative power will be subjected to such measures.

    This would signify, at the national level, a refusal of the role of competitiveness, and at the international level a promotion of power politics, which is totally unacceptable to my government.

    B. The proposal for "consensual selectivity" has to be assessed in the same context. If the exporter is the weaker party in the transaction, prior consent by exporting countries to be subject to selective import restrictions would not be anything more than a procedure of a ritual nature.

0020

C. We also have a strong doubt as to whether "selectivity in exceptional circumstances" or the "limited selective option" (LSO) as proposed by the EC can be considered as a means to prevent grey area measures.

It is a matter of principle that no price can be paid for the elimination of grey area measures which are clearly inconsistent with the provisions of the General Agreement. The EC proposal, which seeks the recognition of selectivity as a price for the elimination of grey area measures, is not acceptable.

The origin of grey area measures lies in a lack of political will to abide by the rules, not in flaws in the legal system. The EC's assertion that Article XIX is too tight to be applicable can not be raised as an excuse.

Further, we can not shake off the apprehension that the EC proposal will prove to be discriminatory in the selection of the suppliers to be punished, in spite of the EC's effort to qualify the selection in terms of the concept of "significant proportion of total imports". This is because, in reality, only those developing countries whose exports are concentrated in certain limited numbers of items would be affected by such criteria.

We have experienced the Tokyo Round failure to quantify the term "significant proportion". I believe the situation will be the same this time because the concept of selectivity is a non-starter from the beginning.

0021

2. Grey Area Measures (Paras. 19, 24, 25)

A. In principle, no price should be paid to ensure that governments act within the rules of Article XIX.

The concept of retaliation is another pillar that sustains the GATT safeguards system, and it is also an important element for the deterence of the abuse of safeguards protection. As a small exporting country we attach great importance to the concept.

However, for the elimination of the grey area measures which have long plagued the multilateral trading system, flexibility can be sought in elements other than the MFN principle.

Waiver of retaliation can only be considered at the final stage of our negotiations if it is certain that this incentive would lead to a compromise agreement not to seek selective safeguards and to eliminate the grey area measures.

B. Concerning the coverage of the provisions on the elimination of grey area measures, we prefer drawing a broad net in order to capture measures falling outside the purview of Article XIX of the GATT. We have in mind those grey area measures of the anti-dumping nature which are, in one sense, certainly spill-overs from the safeguard situation.

C. As for the modality to eliminate or phase out the grey area measures, in general we support the format described in the draft text.

0022

That means, we attach importance to the concept of the outer limit within which all existing grey area measures should be eliminated or brought into conformity with the provisions of the General Agreement.

0023

3. Adjustment Assistance (paras. 15, 16)

A. It is our belief that in the new Safeguard Agreement only border measures should be permitted as safeguard measures. Domestic subsidies, as a means of safeguards, might give unduly expanded policy options for importing countries to the disadvantage of exporting countries.

However, we agree that, in certain cases where the origin of the injury is of a structural nature, border measures would not function as an effective remedy to the injury. In such cases, adjustment assistance measures could be permitted as safeguard measures.

B. In any case, adjustment assistance measures should be governed by the subsidy rules of the GATT. This is important because we need a Safeguard Agreement that can be applied for a short period of time, and the effect of subsidies could last longer than the time necessary to cure the injury.

0024

4. <u>Developing Countries</u> (paras. 20, 21, 22)

As a developing country participant in the Uruguay Round negotiations, we fully share the philosophy behind the proposed special clauses for developing countries.

However, our aim at these negotiations is to establish an MFN based Safeguards Agreement. An across-the-board exception is what we should avoid.

My delegation suggests use of special treatments on specific elements in the agreement, such as duration, extentions of the safeguard measures, and retaliation and compensation.

0025

5. <u>Time periods</u>

  A. Initial period (para. 9)
    ° three years

  B. Total duration (para. 11)
    ° no position

  C. Progressive liberalization (para. 12)
    ° one year

  D. Existing safeguard measures (para. 23)
    ° five years.

0026

6. Customs Union (Footnote, para. 2)

   ° When a safeguard measure is applied by a customs union on behalf of a member state, other members of the union should not be exempted from the application of the safeguard measure.

   ° If other members of the union are exempted, this would constitute a clear discrimination in terms of the source of imports, and thereby a serious derogation from the MFN principle.

0027

Talking Points (Rollback)

A. We welcome, in principle, the initiatives taken by New Zealand, Australia and others to purge all existing GATT-inconsistent measures by agreeing to commit ourselves to eliminate them or bring them into conformity with the GATT according to a time frame agreed upon in this final TNC meeting.

B. However, we might have to give careful consideration to whether or not it is desirable to establish an across-the-board time limit for all the existing measures which have been found GATT-inconsistent in Article XXIII procedures. What we are concerned about is the specificity of each panel recommendation which is the result of careful consideration of special circumstances surrounding the cases in question.

C. The same argument applies to the measures which are found to be GATT-inconsistent as a result of the Uruguay Round negotiations. The elimination of certain measures was negotiated within the overall context which is specific to each individual negotiating group.

0028

UR Safeguards GATT 사무국 협정안 검토

1. 개 요

가. 배 경

o 브랏셀 NTC 각료회의 기간중 12.5 Green Room 회의에서 EC가 여타 요소에서 댓가를 기대할 수 있다면 선별적용을 철회할 의사를 표명하자 GATT 사무국이 주요 국가들과 협의하여 새로운 협정안을 작성, 12.6 Green Room 회의에 제시

o 그러나 농산물 협상의 난항으로 인해 구체적인 토의는 하지 못함
  - 사무국안의 지위에 대한 논란이 있을것이나 협상의 기초로 사용될 것으로 전망됨

나. 새로운 협정안 개관

o 선별적용 관련 조항을 없애는 대신,

  - 수량규제시 특정수출국이 전체 피해에 미친 정도를 고려하여 시정점유율의 5% point 감축 또는, 수출량의 30% 감축중 적은 범위내에서 cut-back 가능
  - 회색조치는 3 ~ 4년 이내에 철폐하되, 예외적으로 특정품목에 대해서는 8년까지 시한을 연장할 수 있는 예외적 상황 설정
  - SG 조치 기간을 최초 4년, 연장 4년으로 하여 최장 8년간 발동 가능
  - 동일 품목에 대한 SG조치 재발동 금지기간은 2년으로 하되, SG 조치 종료이후 1년이 경과되고 과거 5년간 2회 이하 발동한 경우, 180일 조건을 이내의 SG 조치 발동을 허용하는 예외조건 설정
  - 개도국 우대조치로 시장점유율 1% 이하인 개도국 상품에 대한 SG 조치 발동금지와 개도국이 SG 조치를 발동할 경우 최대 10년간 발동 및 동일 품목에 대한 재발동 가능시점을 2년의 최저 기간은 유지하되, 과거 SG 조치 기간의 절반이 경과된 후로 완화

0029

다. EC의 선별적용 철회에 대한 주요국 반응

o 대부분의 국가가 EC측의 전진적인 협상자세에 고무되었음을 밝히고 MFN
  원칙에 기초한 Safeguards 협정에 합의할 수 있기를 기대한다고 표명하면서
  EC가 GATT 체제하에서 당연히 부담해야할 의무를 수락하면서 어떤 댓가를
  요구하는 것은 부당함을 주장

  - MFN 원칙 적용시 보상·보복문제, 회색조치 철폐시한, SG 조치 발동시한
    등에 융통성 표명

2. 변경된 주요 협상 요소 검토 : 별첨 참조

3. 협상 대책(안)

o 회색조치 철폐기간, 보상·보복 면제기간, 조치발동 기간의 연장등을
  선별적용 철회의 조건으로 제시 (MFN 원칙 견지)

  * 하기 cut-back 조항의 포함이 강하게 대두될 경우에는 과거 평균수출
    물량이 보장되고 degressivity가 인정되는 등의 전제하에 예외적인
    선별적용을 선택하는 문제 검토

o 수량규제시 쿼타 감축은 반대 : 평균 수출물량 보장

  - SG 조치는 불공정 수출에 대한 규제가 아니므로 쿼타감축은 과도한 규제

  - 명목적으로는 MFN 원칙이 유지되나 우리나라등 수출구조상 시장점유율이
    상대적으로 높은 국가에는 사실상 실질적인 선별적용 효과 발생

o 기타 협정 요소는 융통성 있게 대처, 협상 타결 유도

  - 선별적용 철회조건으로 회색조치 철폐기간 (최대 8년 이내), 보상·보복
    면제기간 (최대한 최초 발동기간), 총 SG 조치 기간 (최대 10년), 재발동
    금지기간의 예외, 개도국 우대조치 등에 대해 융통성 있는 입장으로
    대처

0030

변경된 주요 협상 요소 검토

1. EC (관세동맹)의 지위 : 2항 주석

가. 내 용

의 장 안	사 무 국 안
- 관세동맹은 동맹단위로 또는 특정 회원국을 대신하여 SG 조치 발동가능. 관세동맹 단위로 동 조치 발동시는 심각한 피해를 결정하는 모든 조건은 관세동맹 전체에 존재하는 여건에 기초해야 하며, 특정 회원국을 대신하여 발동할 경우에는 특정 회원국의 여건에 기초하고 SG 조치도 동 특정 회원국으로 한정됨	- 동 일
- 특정 회원국을 대신하여 SG 조치 발동시에는 [여타 회원국으로부터의 수입급증은 피해 판정 요인에서 제외되는 것으로], [동 조치는 관세동맹내의 여타 회원국으로 부터의 수입에도 적용되는 것으로] 이해됨	- 본 협정은 GATT 19조와 24조 8항간의 연계성에 대한 해석을 침해하지 않음

나. 검 토

o 현재까지 EC만이 일부 회원국 또는 일부지역을 대신하여 EC 전체차원의 SG 조치를 취하고 이 경우에도 역내국간의 교역은 피해판정 및 규제 조치에서 제외할 것을 주장하고 있고 여타국가는 SG 조치 대상에서 역내국가의 제외는 사실상 선별적용임을 들어 반대하고 있음

o '93 이후의 EC의 GATT상 지위는 Safeguards 뿐만 아니라 GATT 전체의 문제이므로 사무국안에서는 관세동맹의 지위를 명시한 24조 8항의 해석에 따르는 것으로 하여 명확한 해석을 회피하고 있음

o 따라서, 우리나라로서는 역외국가에 대한 차별 방지를 위해 EC를 단일 주체로 인정해온 기존입장을 유지하되, 협상 타결의 장애요소가 되지 않도록 GATT 전체 차원의 문제로 명시한 사무국안에 대해 특별히 반대할 필요는 없음

0031

2. 예외적인 선별적용 관련 조항 : 5항

가. 내 용

의 장 안	사 무 국 안
- SG 조치는 [개도국 우대 조항을 적용 하면서] 수출국에 관계없이 수입되는 모든 물품에 적용 되어야 함	- SG 조치는 수출국에 관계없이 수입되는 모든 물품에 적용되어야 함
- [예외적으로 수입국은 제한된 수출국에 대하여 선별적으로 조치할 수 있음. 동 예외는 수입 국의 권위있는 기관이 ① 심각한 피해가 제한된 수출국으로부터의 급격하고 실질적인 수입증가에 기인하고 또한 ② 동 수입이 총 수입량중 상당한 부분을 점유하고 있는 것으로 판정할 경우에만 가능함. 선별적 조치는 총 수입량의 최소 점유율이 (X%) 보다 적은 국가에는 발동하지 않음]	- 삭제

나. 검 토

o 우리나라의 기본입장과 같이 선별적용이 허용되는 예외적인 상황을 제거하고 MFN 원칙하에 SG 조치를 발동하는 내용이므로 지지

0032

3. SG 발동시의 규제조치 (쿼타감축) : 8항, 9항

가. 내 용

의 장 안	사 무 국 안
- SG 조치는 심각한 피해를 예방 또는 구제하거나 구조조정을 용이하게 하기 위한 필요한 범위내 에서 발동되어야 함 - 동 조치는 관세인상 [또는, 구조조정 지원조치] 의 형태이어야 하나 수입수량 제한 형태도 가능함 - 수량제한 형태의 SG 조치가 취해지는 경우에도 수입물량을 통계가 가용한 통상 과거 3년간의 평균 수입 수준인 최근 대표적인 기간의 수입 수량의 수준 이하로 감소시켜서는 안됨	- 동 일 - 체약국은 상기 목적달성에 가장 적합한 형태의 조치를 선택할 수 있음 - [수량제한 조치는 통계가 가용한 통상 과거 3년간의 평균 수입 수준인 최근 대표적인 기간의 수입수량 수준 이하로 감소 시켜서는 안됨] - [수출국별로 쿼타를 할당할 경우 관련 수출국과 합의가 이루어 지지 않았을시는 수입국의 과거 대표적 기간동안의 수출물량과 동등한 비율로 쿼타를 할당하되, 특정 수출국이 전체 피해에 미친 정도를 고려하여 피해구제에 필요한 정도 내에서 개별국의 쿼타 할당을 대표적 기간동안의 시장점유율 5% point 감축 또는 30% 감축량중 적은것을 초과하지 않는 범위내 에서 쿼타량을 조정할 수 있음. 동 쿼타조정은 해당품목의 시장 점유율이 1% 미만인 국가에는 적용되지 않으며, 수입국은 동 쿼타 조정시 그 이유를 정당화 해야 함

나. 검 토

o SG 조치는 공정무역에 대한 규제이므로 과거의 평균 수입물량을 보장되어야
한다는 대다수 국가의 주장에 반해, EC는 특별한 경우 쿼타 감축의 정당성
입증을 전제로 일정량의 쿼타 감축허용을, 미국도 수출국별 시장점유율의
순서가 바뀌지 않는 범위내에서 최대 X%의 쿼타량 감축 허용을 요구하고
있음

0033

o 상기 쿼타 감축안은 선별적용 철회 조건으로 제시된 것이나, 발동대상 선정시에 MFN 원칙이 지켜지더라도 규제조치시에 시장점유율 1% 미만 상품 수출국을 제외하고 수출국별 쿼타량을 수입국의 자의적 판단에 따라 조정, 감축할 경우에는 사후에 정당성 입증 의무만을 지면서 사실상 선별적용 효과를 발생시키게 되어 효과면에서는 선별적용보다 강한 규제 결과가 됨

o 따라서, 수출구조상 선진수입국과의 경쟁이 불가피하고 SG 조치 규제대상이 될 가능성이 높은 우리나라로서는 동 조치허용은 MFN 원칙이라는 명분하에 제한된 조건하에 선별적용을 허용하는 것 보다 강한 규제 효과가 발생되는 불이익이 예견되므로 반대

  - 또한, 쿼타감축은 과거 3년간의 평균 수입물량을 보장하고 이를 국별로 할당시 수출국과의 합의가 없을 경우에는 과거 3년간의 평균 점유율을 적용하여 쿼타를 배분하도록 하고 있는 GATT 규정 (13조 2항 (b))과 어긋나게 됨

  * 동 조항 포함 보다는 평균수출 물량 보장 및 degrssivity 가 인정되는 예외적인 선별적용을 수용하는 방안 검토

o 관세, 비관세, 구조조정 지원조치등 조치형태의 발동국 선택은 현실적으로 별다른 변동이 없으므로 수용 가능

4. 개도국 우대 (예외) : 19항, 20항

가. 내 용

의 장 안	사 무 국 안
- [최빈개도국의 수출에 대하여는 당해 최빈개도국이 개별적으로 또는 집합적으로 주요 공급국 여부에 관계없이 SG 조치가 발동되지 않음] - [수입국내에서 당해물품의 시장점유율이 1% 이하이거나 당해물품이 최근 대표적 기간동안 관련 개도국의 총 수출의 (X%) 이상인 개도국으로부터의 상품에는 SG 조치가 발동되지 않음] - [개도국 및 최빈개도국은 각국의 발전, 재정 또는 무역환경에 따라 본 협정에 규정된 SG 조치 발동요건에 있어서, 특히 SG 발동기간 및 연장, 또는 SG 조치 재발동에 있어서 융통성을 보유하며, 동 국가들에게는 보상.보복 관련 조항이 적용되지 않음]	- 삭 제 - [당해물품의 시장점유율이 1% 이하인 개도국 상품에 대해서는 SG 조치가 발동되지 않음] - 개도국 및 최빈개도국의 SG 조치 발동시에는 본 협정의 최대 발동 시한에 2년을 추가 할 수 있으며 본 협정 발효이후 SG 조치가 적용된 동일한 물품의 수입에 대하여는 기존의 SG 조치가 취해졌던 기간의 ½ 기간이후에 재차 SG 조치를 발동할 수 있으나 최소한 2년이 경과되어야 함

나. 검 토

o 개도국 우대조치 이므로 반대할 명분은 없으나, 이들국가의 제외시 상대적
   으로 우리나라에 대한 불이익이 발생되므로 기존의 소극적 반대 입장을
   유지

   - 개도국의 SG 조치 발동에 대한 2년의 발동기간 연장 및 재발동 금지기간
     단축은 지지 가능하나,

   - 1% 이하의 시장점유율 국가의 제외는 지지 곤란

5. 특정 회색조치의 철폐시한 연장 : 23항

가. 내 용

의 장 안	사 무 국 안
- 모든 회색조치는 본 협정 발효후 180일 이내에 관련당사국에 의해 SG 위원회에 제출되는 시간계획 (timetables)에 따라 철폐되며, 동 시간계획은 모든 회색조치가 본 협정 발효후 [3년]을 초과하지 않는 기간이내에 철폐되거나 본 협정에 일치되도록 하는 것이어야 함]	- .... [부록 1에 설정된 최대 8년까지의 예외를 인정하면서], [3년] 또는 [4년] 이내에 철폐하거나 본 협정에 일치되도록 하는 것이어야 함 * 부록 1의 예외적 상황은 미제시

나. 검 토

o EC의 선별적용 철회에 따라 여타국이 융통성의 하나로 제시한 회색조치
   철폐시한 연장을 반영한 것임

o 우리나라도 MFN 준수시 회색조치 철폐시한에 대한 융통성을 표명한 바
   있으므로 3 ~ 4년의 철폐원칙과 예외적인 8년 시한을 수용함

   - 단, 확고한 철폐원칙과 예외적 상황 설정시 수출국과의 협의가 전제
     되어야 함을 주장하여 철폐시한 까지의 규제하 수출물량의 증대등
     양자협상 입장을 강화시키는 효과를 기대할 수 있도록 함

0035

6. 기타 협상 요소

가. 국내산업의 범위 (6항 (b) : 미결요소)

　(1) 내　용

　　　o 피해판정시 국내산업의 범위를 국내생산의 "상당한 부분"으로만 할 것인가
　　　　또는 "통상 50% 이상, 최소한 33% 이상"을 추가시켜 계량화 하는지 여부

　(2) 검　토

　　　o 우리나라로서는 대외무역법상 "상당한 부분"을 차지하고 있는 국내생산자
　　　　등으로 규정하고 있고 대부분의 국가가 현실적으로 계량화가 곤란함을
　　　　표명하고 있는 점을 감안, 기존입장 (계량화된 표현 삭제) 유지가 바람직

　　　o 단, 계량화 할 경우 선진국과의 상대적인 시장규모의 차이로 인한 유리점,
　　　　반덤핑 협상에서의 우리나라 입장(50%)등을 고려, 소극적으로 대처

나. 조치 발동기간 : 10항, 12항

　(1) 내　용

의　장　안	사　무　국　안
- 최초 발동기간 : 3년 또는 5년 - 총 발동기간　: 5년 또는 8년	- 4년 - 8년

　(2) 검　토

　　　o 대외무역법상 최대 10년 (5년 + 5년), 발동국 입장 고려, 여타국의
　　　　융통성 있는 입장, 선별적용 철회 조건등을 감안하여 "최소한 6년
　　　　이상"의 기존 입장에 따라 융통성있게 대처

0036

다. 재발동 금지기간 : 14항, 15항

(1) 내 용

   o 동일 품목에 대한 SG 조치 재발동은 기존의 SG 조치 기간과 동일한
     기간이 경과된 후에만 가능하며 최소한 2년 경과후에만 재발동 가능

   o 단, 1년이 경과하고 과거 5년간 3번이상 발동되지 않았을 경우에는
     180일 이내의 SG 조치는 발동 가능

(2) 검 토

   o 규제국의 빈번한 SG 조치 발동억제를 위해서 재발동 금지기간을 설정하고
     이에반해 보다 융통성 있는 규제근거를 확보하기 위해 180일 이내의
     예외적 조치를 허용하는 타협안 성격임
     - 예 : 20년을 기준할때 1년 단위의 SG 조치는 7회, 2년 단위는 5회가
            가능하나, 예외조항으로 인해 6개월 단위의 SG 조치를 각각 2회,
            3회 추가 발동할 수 있게 됨

   o 우리나라의 경우, 수출국 입장에서의 2년의 규제 금지기간과 함께
     수입국 입장에서의 규제 필요성을 고려할 때, 2년의 원칙과 180일의 예외조항의
     설정에 반대할 필요는 없음

라. 기존의 SG 조치 철폐시한 : 21항

(1) 내 용

의 장 안	사 무 국 안
- 각국은 GATT 19조에 의해 발동된 현존하는 모든 SG 조치를 발동된후 [8년] 이내, 또는 본 협정 발효이후 [5년] 이내중 늦은기간 이내에 철폐함	- 기존 조치발동후 8년 이내 또는, 본 협정 발효후 [5년], [6년] 이내중 늦은기간 이내에 철폐함

0037

(2) 검　토

o 우리나라는 현재 GATT에 통보된 19조상의 SG 조치를 발동하거나 규제받고
   있지 않은 상황이므로 특별한 의견 제시 불필요

마. 구조조정 지원조치 : 삭 제

(1) 내용

의　장　안	사　무　국　안
- [본 협정 2조의 관련 규정과 일치된 심각한 피해 판정을 할 경우, 체약국은 국경조치의 대안으로써 기업이나 노동자에 의해 행해진 구조조정을 지원하기 위하여 구조조정 지원 조치를 택할 수 있음. 이러한 근거에 의한 모든 구조조정 지원조치는 본 협정 8항 ~ 13항의 규정과 일치되어야 함	- 삭 제
- [구조조정 지원조치는 수출보조금의 형태 이어서는 안됨]	- 삭 제

(2) 검　토

o SG 조치의 형태로 구조조정 지원조치 허용문제, 정부 지원조치가 주로
   보조금 성격을 갖게됨에 따른 보조금 협상 결과와의 연계문제 등으로
   인해 SG 조치에 따른 구조조정 문제를 별도로 논의하는 것 자체에 대한
   논란이 지속되자 동 조항을 삭제하고 SG 조치 형태의 선택을 발동국에
   위임한 것으로 판단됨

o 따라서, 구조조정 문제는 지원형태에 따라 GATT 규정, 특히 보조금 협상
   결과에의 부합여부등 특정국가의 이의 제기시 SG 위원회 또는 일반 GATT
   분쟁해결절차에 따라 해결되게 됨

o 우리나라로서는 실질적으로는 정부 지원조치의 예외 설정이 필요하나
   명분이 없는 관계로 소극적으로 대응해 온 바, SG 협상으로 부터 GATT상의
   문제로 처리한 동 조항의 삭제에 대해 이의 제기 불필요

0038

UR/ Safeguards 관계부처 회의 결과

91. 1. 10.
통상기구과

1. 일시·장소 : 91.1.9 (수) 16:00 상공부 무역위원회 회의실

2. 참석범위

   ° 상공부 산업조사관 (회의 주재)

   ° 경기원, 외무부, 농림수산부, 상공부 및 무역협회, KOTRA 담당과장 또는 실무자
     - 당부는 통상기구과 조현동 사무관 참석

3. 회의안건 : 브랏셀 각료회의시 제시된 새로운 협정초안 검토 및 아국입장 수립

4. 논의내용

   가. 검토내용

   ° 수입측면

     - 국내시장의 급격한 개방추세에 따라 향후 예상되는 국내산업 피해구제
       차원에서 초안상의 Cutback 조항은 유용한 수입규제 수단이 될 수
       있음 (상공부 무역위원회)

     - 중국등으로 부터의 저렴한 농산물 수입 급증에 대비 발동요건의 대폭
       완화가 필요함. 다만 현실적으로 농산물의 특성상 일반
       Safeguards 제도의 적용이 어렵고 농산물 협상에서 Special Safeguards
       도입이 논의되고 있기 때문에, 농산물과 관련해서는 동 협정 초안이
       큰 문제가 없을 것으로 봄. (농림수산부)

   ° 수출측면

     - 새로운 초안을 통해 일단 원칙적으로 Selectivity 가 철폐된 것은
       바람직하나, 시장점유율 5% Point 또는 수출불량이 30% 범위 내
       Cutback 허용은 사실상 Selectivity 와 같은 효과를 초래 할 것임

공람	통상기구과	91년 1월 10일	담당	과장	국장	차관보	차관	장관

0039

- 특히 과거 대표적 기간 수출물량의 30% Cutback 은 수출업자 입장에서 볼 때 그 보다 훨씬 더 큰 피해를 의미하는 것이 되므로 수용할 수 없음. (상공부 상역국)

o 협상측면

- EC가 Selectivity 를 철회하는 양보를 하였으므로 Cutback 에 있어 자의성 범위를 보다 제한할 수 있다면 동 초안은 수용 가능하다고 봄 (경제기획원)

- 브랏셀 회의시 Cutback 조항이 사실상 Selectivity 효과를 갖는다는 이유로 아국 외에도 많은 수출국들이 강력히 반발하였으므로, 현 초안대로 채택되기는 어려울 것이며, 전체협상이 교착상태 이므로 일단 아국 기본입장 (Cutback 수용 가능여부등)을 결정하고 향후진전 추이를 보아가며 협상에 대처함이 바람직 할 것임. (외무부)

나. 결론

o <u>Cutback 조항 수용 불가</u>

- SG 조치는 불공정 수출에 대한 규제가 아니므로 물량감축은 과도한 규제 (수출국에 일방적으로 불리)

o 대신 <u>기타 협정요소에서 보다 유연성 부여</u>

- Selectivity 철회 조건으로 장기간의 회색조치 철폐 시한 인정 (최대 8년)

- 장기간의 보상·보복 면제기간 인정 (최대 최초 발동기간)

- 장기간의 총 발동기간 인정 (최대 10년)등

o 단. 대외 협상 차원에서는 여타 수출국들이 Cutback 조항에 강력히 반대하고 있으므로 <u>적극적인 반대 입장은 상황에 따라 표면</u>

- EC의 Selectivity 철회 평가, 여타요소 유연성 표시등 긍정적 측면의 입장표명이 바람직.   끝.

0040

발 신 전 보

WUS -0112   WEC -0020

번   호 : WGV-0065   910112 1206 FK 종별: 암호송신

수   신 : 주 제네바, 미국, EC 대사. 총영사

발   신 : 장 관 (통기)

제   목 : 수입급증에 의한 산업 피해조사 관련 사항 파악

1,   상공부 무역위원회는 90.11.16. 농협중앙회의 신청에 의거 조제 팝콘 옥수수의
       수입급증에 따른 긴급수입제한 조치 (Safeguards)발동 여부 판정을 위한 국내
       산업 피해조사를 개시키로 결정(90.12.12) 하였음.

2,   이와 관련 미국은 90.12.27. 주한 미국대사관을 통해 미국정부, 이해관계가
       있는 미국내 기업 및 미국 제품을 수입하는 한국내 수입상들이 본 조사
       과정에 이해관계인 자격으로 참가할 수 있도록 무역위원회에 공식 요청하여
       왔음.

3,   동 사안에 대한 무역위원회의 방침 결정에 참고코자하니 관련된 GATT의 사례
       및 미국, EC의 관련 국내 규정과 선례를 조사하여 아래 사항 파악 보고 바람.

       가.   수입급증에 의한 산업 피해조사시 이해관계인의 범위

              ㅇ   수출국 정부도 이해관계인에 포함되는지 여부

              ㅇ   산업피해 조사과정에 수출국 정부 및 수출업자가 이해 관계인으로
                   참가 신청한 사례 및 이에 따른 해당 수입국의 조치 내용

       나.   덤핑, 보조금 지급에 대한 반덤핑, 상계관세 조사 및 불공정 수출입
              조사의 경우등에 있어 이해 관계인의 범위.   끝.

                                    (통상국장 김삼훈)

대 한 민 국
상 공 부

국 협· 28140- 9   (503-9446)   1991. 1. 9.
수 신   외무부 장관
제 목   산업피해조사시 수출국 정부 및 수출자의 이해 관계인 참가 여부

1. 조제 팝콘 옥수수의 수입급증에 따라 농업협동조합중앙회가 '90.11.16 신청하여 동년·12.12 조사개시 결정된 산업피해조사 (Safeguards)와 관련입니다.

2. 상기건과 관련하여 주한 미국 대사관에서는 "미국정부 및/또는 (and/or) 이해 관계가 있는 미국내의 개인회사 및/또는 미국 제품을 수입하는 한국 수입상들"이 본 조사의 이해 관계인 자격으로 참가할 수 있기를 90.12.27 당부 무역위원회에 공식적으로 요청하여 왔읍니다.

3. 이와 관련하여 다음 사항에 관한 GATT및 미국, EC의 규정 및 선례를 제네바(GATT), 미국, 브랏셀 (EC집행위) 주재 한국 대사관으로 하여금 파악, 그 결과를 지급 회신되도록 협조하여 주시기 바랍니다.

= 다   음 =

가. 수입급증으로 인한 산업피해조사 (Safeguards)시 이해 관계인의 범위
   ㅇ 수출국 정부도 이해관계인에 포함되는지 여부

/계속/

0042

국 협· 28140-   1991. 1. 9.

　　　o 산업피해조사 과정에 수출국 정부 및 수출자가 이해 관계인으로

　　　　참가 신청한 사실 유무와 이에 따른 해당국의 조치 내용

　　　　(이러한 조치가 당해 수입국의 재량 사항인지, 거절한 경우가

　　　　있는지, 또 이와 유사한 사례에 대한 논의가 있었는지의

　　　　어부 등)

　　나. 덤핑수입 또는 보조금 지급에 따른 반덤핑.상계관세 조사의 경우 및

　　　　불공정수출입 조사의 경우등에 있어서의 이해 관계인의 범위　　　끝.

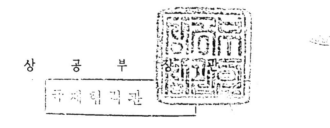

상　　공　　부

0043

외 무 부

종 별 :

번 호 : GVW-0075   일 시 : 91 0114 1830

수 신 : 장 관(봉기, 상공부)

발 신 : 주 제네바 대사대리

제 목 : 수입급증에 의한 산업피해 조사 관련

대: WGV-0065

대호 상공부 무역 위원회의 팝콘 옥수수의 SAFEGUARDS 조사 절차와 관련 당관 김상무관보가 갓트 사무국 LIU SAFEGUARDS 담당을 접촉 파악한 내용 하기 보고함.

1. 미국의 아국 SAFEGHUARDS 조사 절차에의 참여가능 문제

가. 현행 갓트 19조의 SAFEGUARDS 규정에 의하면 SAFEGUARDS 발동을 위한 피해조사 과정에 특정이해 관계국을 참여시킬 의무는 없음.

나. 갓트 19조 2항의 이해 당사국과의 협의 절차 (CONSULTATION) 는 피해 조사를 완료한후 최종적으로 SAFEGUARDS 조치를 발동하기에 앞서 주로 보상 및 쿼타 배정문제등 사후 조치를 협의코자 함이 주목적이며 조사 절차의 공정성여부를 협의코자 함은 아님.

다. 따라서 19조의 피해조사 자체는 수입국의 고유권한으로서, 수출국 정부 또는 기업의 조사과정에의 참여 요청을 수락할지 여부는 수입국의 결정에 달려 있으며, 따라서 이경우 수출국의 참여요청이 단순히 수입국의 피해 조사에 필요한 통계및 자료 제공등 조사 진행에 도움이 된다고 판단하면 수입국이 수락할수도 있겠으나, 조사절차 자체에의 관여 또는 영향을 미칠 소지가있다고 판단될 경우에는 거절할수 있다고 봄.

2. 과거 유사한 사례

O 갓트 사무국으로서는 과거에 조사 절차에의 참여문제로 인한 분쟁사례가 없었으므로, 실제로 수출국 정부또는 업자가 조사절차에의 참여를 신청한 경우가 있었는지 여부 및 이에 대한 수입국의 조치 내용에 대한 정보는 알수 없다고함.

③ 덤핑 및 상계관세 조사 절차의 경우

O 덤핑 및 상계관세 조사 절차의 경우에는 협정상 명문으로 관련 수출입업자 및 수출국정부에게 참여 기회가 주어져 있음. 끝

통상국   2차보   상공부

PAGE 1   91.01.15   09:16 WG

관리
번호 91-85

외 무 부

종 별 :

번 호 : ECW-0048   일   시 : 91 0117 1200

수 신 : 장관 (봉기,봉이,상공부)

발 신 : 주 EC 대사

제 목 : 수입급증에 의한 산업피해조사 관련사항 파악

대: WEC-20

연: 이씨상 20646-387(90.10.17)

대호 지시에따라 당관 박상무관이 1.16. EC 집행위 STEWART 수석조사관을 접촉, 파악한 내용을 다음 보고함

　　1. 수입급증에 의한 산업피해조사시 이해관계인의 범위

　　O EC 이사회 공동수입규정 (COMMON RULES FOR IMPORTS NO 288/82) 제 6 항 COMMUNITY INVESTIGATION PROCEDURE 는 이해관계인의 범위를 직접 규정하고 있지는 않으나 제 2 조에서 EC 집행위는 수입업자, 중개업자, 생산자및 관련단체들로 부터 조사에 필요한 정보를 파악할수 있도록 규정하고 있음

　　O 또한 제 4 조에서는 EC 집행위로 하여금 조사의 결과로 영향을 입게 됨을 소명하는 관련 자연인 또는 법인으로 부터 서면 또는 구두로 청문할수 있도록 규정하고 있음

　　O STEWART 담당관은 이해관계인의 범위에 수출국정부가 포함된다는 규정은 없으나, 산업피해조사에 수출국 정부가 직접적인 이해당사자는 아니라 할지라도 당해 정부가 동 조사에 간접적으로 영향을 받는점, 산업피해조사의 결과에따라 규제 조치를 취하기전에 당해정부와 사전에 협의하게 되어 있는점등을 고려할때 수 출국정부도 이해관계인으로 볼수 있을것이라고 하였음

　　O EC 산업피해조사 과정에 수출국정부가 이해관계인으로 참가 신청한 사례에 대하여 동인은 공식적인 참가신청이라기 보다는 관례적으로 수출국정부가 서면 내지 면담등을 통해 산업피해 조사에 수출국의 의견을 표시해올 경우 이를 접수하고 필요시 고려해오고 있다고 하였음

　　2. 반덤핑, 상계 관계조사및 불공정 수출입조사등에 있어서 이해관계인의 범위

　　통상국   차관   2차보   통상국   정와대   상공부

O EC 이사회 반덤핑, 상계관세규정 (NO 2423/88 연호첨부물 참조) 제 7 항 1조(A)에 의하면 조사개시 공고시 조사의 진행으로 영향을 받게될 이해관계인으로 하여금 서면 또는 구두로 그들의 견해를 개진할수 있는 기간을 명시하도록 하고, 제 5 조에는 이들로부터 서면 또는 구두로 견해를 청취하도록 규정하고 있으며, 1 조 (B) 에는 숫루업자, 수입업자및 수출국 정부대표에게 동 조사개시 내용을 알리도록 규정하고 있음

O 또한 제 2 조는 EC 집행위로 하여금 관계수출국및 수출회사의 동의하에 직접 조사할수 있고 수입업자, 수출업자, 중개업자, 생산자및 관련단체들의 기록을 조사할수 있도록 규정하고 있음

O 제 4 조 (A) 는 제소자, 수출업자, 수입업자및 수출국정부의 대표자는 EC 집행위나 회원국의 대외비 또는 내부자료가 아닌 경우 그들의 이익을 방어하는데 관계되는 자료들을 검토할수 있도록 규정하고 있음

O STEWART 조사관은 EC 규정에는 수입급증에 의한 SAFEGUARD 조사와 마찬가지로 수출국정부가 이해관계인에 포함된다는 직접적인 규정은 없으나 상기 규정들로 보아 수출국정부를 이해관계인으로 볼수 있을것이라 말하고 정부보조가 문제가 되는 상계관세 조사의 경우는 더욱 그러할 것이라고 하였음

3. 결론

O EC 규정상 SAFEGUARD, 반덤핑, 상계관세 조사시 이해관계인의 범위에 관한 직접적인 규정은 없으나 EC 집행위는 관례적으로 수출국정부를 이해관계인으로 인정하고 있다고 볼수있음

O 그러나 수출국정부를 이해관계인의 하나로 간주한다 하더라도 조사의 전과정에 참가하는 것이 아니라 당해국 정부의 의견과 관심을 개진하는 정도이며, 특히 업계의 비밀사항이 많은 조사과정에는 제한적으로 적용해야 할것으로 생각됨

O STEWART 담당관에 의하면 EC 집행위가 일본산 제품의 반덤핑 현지조사를 할 경우 일본 봉산성으로 부터 직원이 동조사에 파견되는것이 보통이라고 말하고, EC 가 이를 허용하는것도 수출국 정부를 넓은 의미에서 이해관계인으로 보기 때문이라고 하였음. 산업피해, 반덤핑제도가 일천한 우리나라의 경우 선진국의 한 국내에서의 반덤핑 현지조사시 상공부 직원을 현장에 입회토록 함으로서 동조사에대한 정부의 관심을 보여주고 한편으로는 조사기법을 익힐수 있는 기회가 될것으로 판단되는바 제도수립에 참고바람. 끝

PAGE 2

0046

(대사 권동만-국장)
예고: 91.12.31. 까지

장관

대 한 민 국
상 공 부

국 협· 28140-꺼   (503 - 9446)   1991. 1. 31.

수 신   외무부 장관

참 조   통상국장

제 목   UR/세이프가드 협상안에 대한 검토

1. GW-0178 (90.1.28)과 관련임

2. 지난 브랏셀 회의 (90.12.6)에서 사무국이 제시한 새로운 세이프가드
협상안에 대한 당부 검토의견을 별첨과 같이 송부하오니 조치하여 주시기 바랍니다.

첨 부 : 검토의견 1부.   끝.

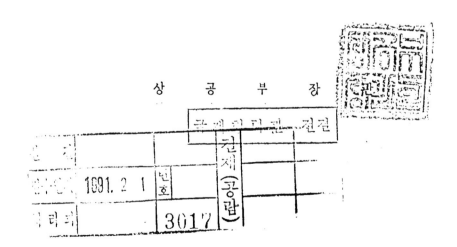

상 공 부 장

1991. 2. 1   3017

0048

UR/Safeguards GATT 사무국 협정안 (90.12.6) 검토

===

1. 새로운 협정안 주요내용

  o 선별적용 관련 조항을 없애는 대신,

   - 수량규제시 특정 수출국이 전체 피해에 미친 정도를 고려하여, 시정 점유율의
     5% point 감축, 수출량의 30% 감축중 적은 범위내에서 cut-back 가능
   - 회색조치는 3-4년 이내에 철폐하되, 예외적으로 특정 품목에 대해서는
     8년까지 시한을 연장할 수 있는 예외적 상황 설정
   - 개도국 우대조치로 시장 점유율 1% 이하인 개도국 상품에 대한 SG 조치
     발동 금지와 개도국이 SG 조치를 발동할 경우 최대 10년간 발동 및
     동일 품목에 대한 재발동 가능시점을 2년의 최저 기간은 유지하되,
     과거 SG 조치 기간의 절반이 경과된 후로 완화

2. 검토의견

  가. 기본입장

   o 수량규제시 쿼타 감축 (cut-back)은 반대 (평균 수출 물량은 보장)

    - SG 조치는 공정 수출에 대한 규제이므로 쿼타 감축은 과도한 규제
    - 명목적으로 MFN 원칙이 유지되나 우리나라등 수출 구조상 시장 점유율이
      상대적으로 높은 국가에는 사실상 실질적인 선별적용 효과 발생

   o 기타 협정 요소는 융통성 있게 대처, 협상 타결 유도

    - 선별적용 및 cut-back이 철회될시 회색조치 철폐기간 (최대 8년 이내),
      보상. 보복 면제기간 (최대한 최초 발동기간), 총 SG 조치기간 (최대
      10년), 재발동 금지 기간의 예외, 개도국 우대조치 등에 대해서는
      융통성 있게 대처

0049

나. 협상전략 : cut-back에 대한 적극적인 반대 주장은 자제

　　o EC의 선별적용 철회를 환영하면서 여타 협상 요소에서 융통성 있는
　　　대안을 제시, 우리나라도 협상 타결에 기여할 것임을 표명

　　o cut-back에 관해서는 대부분의 국가 특히 개도국의 강한 반대로 인해
　　　합의 가능성이 없으므로 브랏셀 회의에서의 농산물 협상 대응전략을
　　　경험삼아 소극적으로 대응

다. 주요 협상 요소별 입장

　　o EC (관세동맹)의 지위 : 2항 주석

　　　- 우리나라로서는 역외국가에 대한 차별 방지를 위해 EC를 단일 주체로 인정해온
　　　　기존입장을 유지하되, 협상 타결의 장애 요소가 되지 않도록 GATT 전체
　　　　차원의 문제로 명시한 사무국안에 대해 특별히 반대할 필요는 없음

　　o 예외적인 선별적용 관련 조항 : 5항

　　　- 우리나라의 기본 입장과 같이 선별적용이 허용되는 예외적인 상황을
　　　　제거하고 MFN 원칙하에 SG 조치를 발동하는 내용이므로 지지

　　o SG 발동시의 규제조치 (쿼타 감축) : 8항 , 9항

　　　- 쿼타 감축안은 선별적용 철회 조건으로 제시된 것이나, 발동대상
　　　　선정시에 MFN 원칙이 지켜지더라도 규제조치시에 시장 점유율 1%
　　　　미만 상품 수출국을 제외하고 수출국별 쿼타량을 수입국의 자의적
　　　　판단에 따라 조정, 감축할 경우에는 사후에 정당성 입증 의무만을
　　　　지면서 사실상 선별적용 효과를 발생시키게 되어 효과면에서는
　　　　선별 적용보다 강한 규제 결과가 됨

　　　- 따라서, 수출구조상 선진수입국과의 경쟁이 불가피하고 SG 조치 규제
　　　　대상이 될 가능성이 높은 우리나라로서는 동 조치 허용은 MFN 원칙이라는
　　　　명분하에 제한된 조건하에 선별적용을 허용하는 것 보다 강한 규제
　　　　효과가 발생되는 불이익이 예견되므로 반대

　　　　. 또한, 쿼타 감축은 과거 3년간의 평균 수입물량을 보장하고 이를 국별로
　　　　　할당시 수출국과의 합의가 없을 경우에는 과거 3년간의 평균
　　　　　점유율을 적용하여 쿼타를 배분하도록 하고 있는 GATT 규정
　　　　　(13조 2항 (b))과 어긋나게 됨

　　　- 관세, 비관세, 구조조정 지원조치등 조치형태의 발동국 선택은 현실적으로
　　　　별다른 변동이 없으므로 수용 가능

0050

o 개도국 우대 (예외) : 19항, 20항

  - 개도국 우대조치 이므로 반대할 명분은 없으나, 이들 국가의 제외시
    상대적으로 우리나라에 대한 불이익이 발생뇌므로 기존의 소극적
    반대 입장을 유지

    . 개도국의 SG 조치 발동에 대한 2년의 발동기간 연장 및 재발동
      금지기간 단축은 지지 가능하나, 1% 이하의 시장 점유율 국가의
      제외는 지지 곤란

o 특정 회색조치의 철폐시한 연장 : 23항

  - 우리나라는 MFN 준수시 회색조치 철폐시한에 대한 융통성을 표명한 바
    있으므로 3-4년의 철폐원칙과 예외적인 8년 시한을 수용함

    . 단, 확고한 철폐원칙과 예외적 상황 설정시 수출국과의 협의가
      전제 되어야 함을 주장하여 철폐시한 까지의 규제하 수출 물량의
      증대등 양자협상 입장을 강화시키는 효과를 기대할 수 있도록 함

0051

발 신 전 보

분류번호	보존기간

번   호 : WGV-O158   910131 1612   AO 종별 : _____

수   신 : 주   제네바   대사. 총영사

발   신 : 장 관 (통기)

제   목 : UR/세이프 가드 협상

암호화

대 : GVW-0178

대호 SG 새로운 협정안의 주요 쟁점에 대한 아국 입장을 아래 회시 하니,
이를 기초로 2.1 비공식 협의에서 적의 대처 바람.

1. 기본 입장

  ㅇ 수량규제시 쿼타 감축(cut-back)은 반대 (평균 수출 물량은 보장)

    - SG 조치는 공정 수출에 대한 규제이므로 쿼타 감축은 과도한 규제

    - 명목적으로 MFN원칙이 유지되나 우리나라등 수출 구조상 시장점유율이
      상대적으로 높은 국가에는 사실상 실질적인 선별적용 효과 발생

  ㅇ 기타 협정 요소는 융통성 있게 대처, 협상 타결 유도

    - 선별적용 및 cut-back 이 철회될시 회색조치 철폐기간 (최대 8년 이내),
      보상. 보복 면제기간 (최대한 최초 발동기간), 총 SG 조치기간 (최대
      10년), 재발동 금지 기간의 예외, 개도국 우대조치등에 대해서는
      융통성 있게 대처

// 계 속 ...

보안통제

앙고재	91년 1월 31일	통기과	기안자성명 조영준		과장	심의관	국장 전결		차관	장관

외신과통제

0052

2. 협상전략 : cut-back에 ~~대한 적극적인~~ 반대 ~~주장은~~ 자제 <u>하리 선두배의 3,3,3,3인 반대는</u>

- o EC의 선별적용 철회를 환영하면서 여타 협상 요소에서 융통성 있는
   대안을 제시, 우리나라도 협상 타결에 기여할 것임을 표명
- ~~o cut-back에 관해서는 대부분의 국가 특히 개도국의 강한 반대로 인해~~
   ~~합의 가능성이 없으므로 브랏셀 회의에서의 농산물 협상 대응 전략을~~
   ~~경험삼아 소극적으로 대응~~

3. 주요 협상 요소별 입장

- o EC (관세동맹)의 지위 : 2항 주석
  - 우리나라로서는 역외국가에 대한 차별 방지를 위해 EC를 단일 주체로
    인정해온 기존입장을 유지하되, 협상 타결의 장애 요소가 되지 않도록
    GATT 전체 차원의 문제로 명시한 사무국안에 대해 특별히 반대할
    필요는 없음.

- o 예외적인 선별적용 관련 조항 : 5항
  - 우리나라 ~~의~~의 기본입장과 같이 선별적용이 허용되는 예외적인 상황을
    제거하고 MFN 원칙하에 SG조치를 발동하는 내용이므로 지지

- o SG 발동시의 규제조치(쿼타 감축) : 8항, 9항
  - 쿼타 감축안은 선별적용 철회 조건으로 제시된 것이나, 발동대상
    선정시에 MFN 원칙이 지켜지더라도 규제조치시에 시장 점유율 1% 미만
    상품 수출국을 제외하고 수출국별 쿼타량을 수입국의 자의적 판단에
    따라 조정, 감축할 경우에는 사후에 정당성 입증 의무만을 지면서
    사실상 선별적인 효과를 발생시키게 되어 효과면에서는 선별 적용보다
    강한 규제 결과가 됨.
  - 따라서, 수출구조상 선진수입국과의 경쟁이 불가피하고 SG 조치 규제
    대상이 될 가능성이 높은 우리나라로서는 동 조치 허용은 MFN 원칙
    이라는 명분하에 제한된 조건하에 선별적용을 허용하는 것 보다 강한
    규제 효과가 발생되는 불이익이 예견되므로 반대

0053

. 또한, 쿼타 감축은 과거 3년간의 평균 수입물량을 보장하고 이를

국별로 할당시 수출국과의 합의가 없을 경우에는 과거 3년간의

평균 점유율을 적용하여 쿼타를 배분하도록 하고 있는 GATT 규정

(13조 2항 (b))과 어긋나게 됨.

- 관세, 비관세, 구조조정 지원조치등 조치형태의 발동국 선택은 현실적

으로 별다른 변동이 없으므로 수용 가능

o 개도국 우대 (예외) : 19항, 20항

- 개도국 우대조치 이므로 반대할 명분은 없으나, 이들 국가의 제외시

상대적으로 우리나라에 대한 불이익이 발생되므로 기존의 소극적

반대 입장을 유지

. 개도국의 SG 조치 발동에 대한 2년의 발동기간 연장 및 재발동

금지기간 단축은 지지 가능하나, 1% 이하의 시장 점유율 국가의

제외는 지지 곤란

o 특정 회색조치의 철폐 시한 연장 : 23항

- 우리나라는 MFN 준수시 회색조치 철폐시한에 대한 융통성을 표명한

바 있으므로 3-4년의 철폐원칙과 예외적인 8년 시한을 수용함.

. 단, 확고한 철폐원칙과 예외적 상황 설정시 수출국과의 협의가

전제 되어야 함을 주장하여 철폐시한 까지의 규제하 수출 물량의

증대등 양자협상 입장을 강화시키는 효과를 기대할 수 있도록 함.

끝.

(통상국장 김삼훈)

0054

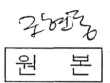

외 무 부

종 별 :

번 호 : GVW-0178

일 시 : 91 0128 1430

수 신 : 장관(봉기/상공부)

발 신 : 주 제네바대대사대리

제 목 : UR/ 세이프가드 협상

연: 제네(경) 20644-1298(90.12.14)

UR/ 세이프가드 협상과 관련한 비공식 협의가 2.1. 홍콩대표부에서 개최될 예정인바, 연호 새로운 협정안에 포함된 주요 쟁점 (OUT-BACK등)에 대한 본부 의견회시 바람.

끝.

(대사대리 박영우-국장)

주제협력과박처영 사무관
(미주통상과 거래협과사무관 :주w 256호)

통상국   2차보   상공부

PAGE 1

91.01.29   06:27 DA

외신 1과 통제관

0055

외 무 부

종   별 :

번   호 : GVW-0233   일   시 : 91 0204 1800

수   신 : 장관(통기), 경기원, 재무부, 농림수산부, 상공부)

발   신 : 주 제네바대사대리

제   목 : UR/세이프가드 협상

연:GVW-0178

대: WGV-0158

2.1. 홍콩대표부 CHOI 부대표가 주최한 오찬시 대호 세이프가드 협정안에 대해 개괄적인 의견교환을 하였는바, 주요 내용 아래 보고함.

(아국, 태국, 싱가폴, 말레시아, 놀웨이, 인도, 스위스 참석)

1. 대부분의 참석자들은 동 협정안이 브랏셀 각료회의 이전에 제출된 세이프 가드 협정안보다 많은 쟁점에 대한 괄호를 줄였다는 점에서 이를 환영하고 우선 협상의 기초가 될 수 있다고 연기면서도 본 협정안이 실질적으로 선별 적용을 전제하고 있다는 것이 가장 큰 문제점이라고 지적함.

2. 특히 수량규제 쿼타감축(CUT-BACK)은 시장점유 신장율이 고하에 관계없이 모든 대소 수출국에 적용된다는 점에 비추어 참석국들이 모두 이를 수용 할 수 없다는 입장을 분명히 하였으며 홍콩, 싱가폴등은 선별적용을 인정한 SG 협정을 수락하는 것보다는 차라리 SG 협정이 없는 현상 유지가 오히려 바람직 하다는 입장을 밝힘.(브랏셀에서 비공식 회의를 통해 동 협정안을 작성시 EC 측은 일반적인 선별조치 포기를 위해서는 선별적인 쿼타 감축이 필요불가결하다고 강조했다 함,)

3. 기타 SG 조치의 기간, 회색조치 기한의 철폐기한, 보복면제등이 괄호로 되어 있지 않으나 이는 전혀 합의된 것이 아니라는 점이 지적되었고, 태국은 SG 협정안이 농산물에도 적용되는 것으로 일반적으로 이해하나 현 협정안이 공산품 교역 개념에 입각하여 초안되어 있어 문제가 있다고 지적하였음.

4. 오찬사관은 협상 타결을 위해 가능한 모든 노력을 경주코져 한다는 것이 아국의 기본입장이나 , 상기 선별적용 문제는 여타 국가와 마찬가지로 받아들이기 어렵다고 밝히고, MFN 에 기초한 SG 협정을 채택할 수 있다면 여타 분야에서 최대한 융통성을

통상국 농수부	장관 상공부	차관	1차보	2차보	청와대	안기부	경기원	재무부

일반문서로. 재분류(1991 . 6 . 30.)

91.02.05   04:55
외신 2과 통제관 CF

0056

발휘 할수 있을 것이라고 하였음. 또한 선별적용을 수용하기보다 차라리 협정을
채택하지 않는 것이 바람직하다고 하는 문제에 관한 결정은 협상의 최종단계에서나
결정 가능한 문제로 남겨두는 것이 협상 전략상 타당할 것임을 지적한바, 참석자들도
이에 동감을 표시함.

（대사대리 박영우-국장）

예고:91.6.30 까지

외   무   부

종   별 :

번   호 : GVW-0339   일   시 : 91 0221 1900

수   신 : 장 관(통기, 경기원, 재무부, 농림수산부, 상공부)(사본:박수길 대사)

발   신 : 주 제네바 대사대리

제   목 : UR/규범제정 관련 주요국 비공식 협의

연:GVW-0337

2.21(목) 16:00 DUNKEL 사무총장 주제로 개최된 규범 제정분야 주요국 비공식협의 결과 아래보고함.(박공사, 오참사관 참석)

1. 표제협의는 DUNKEL 사무총장이 규범제정 협상재개를 위한 차기회의의 일자, 향후 협상과제등에 관한 STATEMENT (별첨)를 청취하고 산회함.

2. 규범제정 협상 차기회의는 3.14(목) (필요시 3.15까지 연장) 개최예정이며, 아래 협상 분야를 포함예정인바, 각 분야별 협상과제에 관한 사무총장의 언급 내용은 아래임.

가. 보조금 및 상계관세
- 협상의 기초에 관한 협의, 우선 기술적인작업 (예: 개도국 우대 문제) 진행

나. 반덤핑
- 우선 기술적인 작업을 진행하며, 협상의 기초에 관해서도 협의

다. 세이프가드
- 세이프가드 협상 현황 및 향후 협상 추진방안에 관해 협의 (주로 정치적인 결정만 남아있음)

라. 선적권 검사
- 브랏셀 회의에서의 협상진전 사항 확인

마. 원산지 규정
- 브랏셀 회의에서의 협상진전 사항 확인

바. 기술장벽
- 브랏셀 회의 협상 진전 사항 확인

사. 수입허가 절차

통상국	2차보	경기원	재무부	농수부	상공부	우우극(대사)

-. 추가 기술적 작업 불요

아. 관세평가

- 추가 기술적 작업 불요

자. 정부조달

- 추가기술적 작업 불요

차. 갓트 조문

- 갓트 조문 협상 방향협의: 가능한 대로 35조 및24조 협의

첨부: 규정제정분야 STATEMENT 1 부. 끝

(GVW(F)-73)

(대사대리 박영우-국장)

PAGE 2

0053

GVW (제)-0073 /022//

GVW -33P 편1

RULE MAKING

Thursday, 21 February 1991, p.m.

Note for Chairman

1.   In his closing remarks at the Brussels Ministerial Meeting,
Minister Gros Espiell requested me to pursue intensive consultations with
the specific objective of achieving agreements in all the areas of the
negotiating programme in which differences remain outstanding. These
consultations will, he said, be based on document MTN.TNC/W/35/Rev.1, dated
3 December 1990, including the cover page which refers to the Surveillance
Body and the communications which various participants sent to Brussels.
He added that I would also take into account the considerable amount of
work carried out at the Brussels meeting, although it did not commit any
delegation.

2.   We are dealing with a number of negotiating areas in this meeting, in
particular: subsidies and countervailing duties, anti-dumping, safeguards,
preshipment inspection, rules of origin, technical barriers to trade,
import licensing procedures, customs valuation, government procurement and
a number of specific GATT Articles. I intend to take these up one by
one. Issues in some of these areas are closely related to the main
political problems facing the negotiations and in such cases political and
technical questions overlap.

Subsidies and countervailing duties

3.   Pages 83 to 134 of MTN.TNC/W/35/Rev.1 contain a text on subsidies and
countervailing duties and a commentary on that text which refers
specifically to a number of communications from delegations. The issues
that remain to be dealt with in this area are set out in that document.

6-1

0060

4.   I suggest that when work is restarted in this area, at a further
meeting of the type that we are having today, to be held on Thursday,
14 March and Friday, 15 March if necessary, participants should be invited
to comment on the basis for their discussions and negotiations in this
area, and on the way in which we should proceed. I would note that the
commentary on page 83 of W/35/Rev.1 states that, while the text in that
document requires a number of drafting changes, these can be done once
major political problems have been resolved. Until major political
decisions are taken, I suggest that we should focus on technical work. One
example of an area on which technical work might be done is in the area of
special and differential treatment for developing countries (Article 27 and
Annex VIII of the draft on pages 118, 119, 133 and 134 of W/35/Rev.1).

Anti-dumping

5.   You will recall that MTN.TNC/W/35/Rev.1 does not contain a text on
anti-dumping and this is therefore one area in which we do not have a basis
for negotiations. The commentary on page 43 of that document merely listed
out some (but not all) of the points on which basic differences continue to
exist and stated that political decisions were needed to overcome these
basic differences.

6.   As in our discussions on other areas, I would suggest that technical
work should be restarted on anti-dumping and that participants first be
given the opportunity of commenting on the basis of our discussions and
negotiations in this area and on the way in which they should be tackled.

7.   You will also, however, wish to identify those specific issues in this
area which can usefully be discussed in the near future. In doing so, I
expect that you will be taking up work carried out in Brussels.

6-2

0061

Safeguards

8. MTN.TNC/W/35/Rev.1 contains a detailed text on safeguards, which you will find on pages 183 to 192 of that document. The commentary on that text sets out the main points in that text that remained to be settled.

9. When participants meet again, they should be given an opportunity of commenting on where they stand now in the safeguards negotiations and where they should go from here, taking due account of work done in Brussels, as appropriate.

10. They will also consider whether there is any technical work we might usefully start on in this area. My own assessment of the situation is that negotiations are now faced with a number of major issues requiring substantive decisions and that, in this area, it is therefore unlikely that you will identify areas on which technical work is required or would be useful at the present stage.

Preshipment Inspection

11. The text on preshipment inspection is reproduced on pages 31 to 42 of MTN.TNC/W/35/Rev.1. The commentary on page 30 of the document drew attention to the main decision that needed to be taken at the Brussels Meeting.

·12. Substantial work appears to have been done in Brussels on this point.

13. At our next meeting the group should determine how far the progress made in Brussels should be confirmed. The legal form of the text will have to be examined but I suggest that this should be done, in this and in other areas, only at a later stage when discussions and negotiations on the Final Act are further advanced. Consultations have been going on between the International Chamber of Commerce and the International Federation of

6-)

0062

Inspection Agencies on whom we would be relying for the implementation of an important part of an agreement. In this area I suggest that a way be found of keeping them informed of any developments in the Uruguay Round which would affect their plans and that participants respond to the suggestions that ICC and IFIA have already made in this regard.

Rules of Origin

14. The text on rules of origin is reproduced on pages 13 to 29 of MTN.TNC/W/35/Rev.1. The commentary on page 12 of the document drew attention to the issues on which an overall compromise needed to be found.

15. Here again, considerable work seems to have been done in Brussels. At its next meeting this group should determine how far the progress made in Brussels should be confirmed.

16. The document recalls that the legal form of the text will have to be examined but I suggest that this be done, in this and other areas, only at a later stage when discussions and negotiations on the Final Act are further advanced.

Technical barriers to trade

17. Pages 45 to 69 of W/35/Rev.1 contain the draft text of a new agreement on technical barriers to trade. The commentary on page 44 of W/35/Rev.1 drew attention to the questions which remained to be settled with respect to this text.

18. In Brussels substantial progress was made on the new text for Article 1.5 concerning the relationship of the Agreement to the Decision on Sanitary and Phytosanitary regulations and on the text on Consultation and Dispute Settlement Procedures (Article 14 and Annex 2). This remains dependent, however, on an agreement on the issue relating to the second level obligations (i.e. obligations and provinces, states and municipalities).

0063

19. I would therefore suggest that we should first focus on the second level obligation issue. Further discussions may also be necessary on the proposal by one delegation for clarification of Article 2.2 (provisions relating to unnecessary obstacles to trade).

Import licensing procedures

20. Pages 73 to 82 of W/35/Rev.1 contain the text of a new draft agreement on import licensing procedures which was agreed on an _ad referendum_ basis prior to the Brussels Meeting. I understand that one delegation maintains a reservation on this text made prior to the Brussels Meeting and reflected on page 72 of W/35/Rev.1, pending agreement that a GATT Working Party be established to develop rules in the area of export licensing procedures in the post-Uruguay Round period.

21. Since the text was agreed on an _ad referendum_ basis prior to the Brussels Meeting, subject to this one reservation, it would appear that no further technical work may be needed in this area unless the request for the establishment of a Working Party on export restrictions raises technical questions which can be clarified at the present stage.

Customs valuation

22. Pages 135 to 137 of W/35/Rev.1 contain the texts of two draft recommendations from the CONTRACTING PARTIES to the Committee on Customs Valuation, and of an accompanying understanding which were accepted on an _ad referendum_ basis prior to the Brussels Meeting. It would, therefore appear that no further technical work is needed in the framework of the Round with respect to these texts.

Government procurement

23. Page 138 of W/35/Rev.1 contains the text of an agreement on accession to the Government Procurement Code. This text, which was the result of

6-5

0064

consultations held prior to the Brussels Meeting, was accepted on an
ad referendum basis in Brussels.

24.   However, delegations should, of course, be given an opportunity for
offering comments on this text which takes the form of a recommendation
from the CONTRACTING PARTIES to the Committee on Government Procurement.
However, it seems to me that further technical work is unlikely to be
required in this area.

GATT Articles

25.   The state of the work on GATT Articles is precisely as set out in
MTN.TNC/W/35/Rev.1.   That document described, for each of the Articles
which had been the subject of work in the Negotiating Group, the status of
the draft agreement, where such a draft existed, and in the case of the
balance of payments provisions the position reached in the discussions.   It
will be remembered that agreement had been reached ad referendum on
Articles II:1(b), XVII and XXVIII;   certain participants had maintained
reservations on the draft decisions on Articles XXIV and XXXV;   and it was
understood that final decisions on Article XXV:5 and the Protocol of
Provisional Application could only be taken in the light of results in
other areas of the negotiations.   On the Balance of Payments provisions it
had not been decided whether or not to engage in negotiations.

26.   Delegations will be given an opportunity to express their views on the
way in which we should work in the GATT Articles area.   My suggestion is
that we start by discussing Article XXXV and maybe Article XXIV.

6-6

0065

외 무 부

종 별 :

번 호 : GVW-0558   일 시 : 91 0325 1930

수 신 : 장 관(봉기, 경기원, 재무부, 농림수산부, 상공부)

발 신 : 주제네바대사

제 목 : UR/ 규범제정 비공식 회의

　　3.25(월) 15:00-17:00 간 던켈 사무총장 주재로표제회의가 개최되었는바 주요 협의 내용 아래보고함.(본직, 오참사관, 엄재무관, 강상무관참석)

　　1. 보조금.상계관세

　　- 의장은 동분야에서도 기술적 사항과 실질적문제의 구분이 어려우나 정치적 결정을 요하는 사항과 관련, 어떤 선택을 할 것인지를 예단하지 말고 기술적 사항으로 논의될 분야를 논의할 것을 요청함.

　　- 멕시코는 협정(안) 제 2조 제 14조(E)와 관련, 국내 가격 정책수행을 위한 특정물품2중 가격제도 운영 및 정부물품 공급제도 등은 보조금 규율대상에서 제외되어야 한다는 종전의주장을 반복하고 기술적 사항으로 논의되어야 한다고하였음.

　　- 인도는 협정(안) 제 14조 및 개도국 우대관련, 기준 수출보조금 수준을 계산하기 위한 논의도 기술적 사항이라고 주장하였는바 파키스탄은 ANNEX 8중 특히 주석 2에 대하여 불합리하다는 이견을 달았으며, 미국은 인도가 주장하는 내용은 매우정치적결정을 필요로 하는 사항과 직결되는 것이라고 반대의견을 표시하였으며 EC 도 이에동조하였음.

　　- 의장은 논의 대상 기술적 사항으로 멕시코가주장하는 국내적용문제, 헝가리가주장하는 전환경제 체제 국가문제를 포함토록 하는 한편인도가 주장하는 보조금 계산 문제는 대상에는포함하되 토의는 차후 적절한 때까지 갖지 않도록하겠다 하였음.

　　2. 반덤핑

　　- 의장은 반덤핑 분야에서 기술적 토의가 불필요한것으로 생각한다고 하고 브랏셀회의에서작성된 초안(TRANCHE 1 과 2)을 각국에 배포할 것이라고 하였으며 이에 각국이 동의함.

통상국　　2차보　　　　　　청와대　　경기원　　재무부　　농수부　　상공부

PAGE 1

3. 세이프가드
- 의장은 기술적인 차원에서의 토의가 불필요하다고 하였으며 각국이 이에 동의함.

4. 선적전 검사
- 의장은 선적전 검사 협정 초안 제4조(재심절차)의 시행과 관련한 ICC 와 IFIA의 의견이 각국에 배포되었음을 상기시키고 추후 이문제를 토론키로 함.

5. 기술장벽 협정
- 의장은 다음번 회의에서는 우선 (1) 제 2조2항(불필요한 무역에 대한 장벽)의명료화 (2)자발적 표준에 대해 미국이 제시하는 문제에 대해 토론키로 하고 추후 지방정부 의무 문제와 농산물검역 규정과 기술장벽 협정과의 관계를 논의키로 하여 합의됨.

6. 수입허가 절차 협정
- 인도는 UR 이 연기되었음을 고려하여 동협정에 수출허가 절차를 포함시키는 문제가 UR에서 논의되어야 한다고 하고 수출허가 절차의 차이에 대한 기술적 토론을 할 것을 주장함.
- EC, 브라질,이집트등이 기술적 토론에 대해 찬성하였으며 뉴질랜드,미국,카나다 등은 이에 반대함.
- 이에따라 의장은 주요국 협의를 거쳐 동 문제를 다음번 회의에서 토론하겠다고제의함.

7. 관세평가협정 및 정부조달협정
- 의장은 상기 협정에 대해서는 브랏셀 회의이전에 잠정 합의가 있었으므로 기술적 작업 필요성이 없다고 언급함.

8. 갓트조문
- 의장은 24조(관세 동맹 및 자유무역지대)를기술적 차원에서 다룰 수 있을지 여부를 문의한바, EC 가 24조 문제는 UR 협상의 결과(GLOBAL PACKAGE) 를 본 후 논의할 것을 제의함.
- 미국은 BOP 문제를 기술적 차원에서 다룰것을 희망한다고 하였으나 이에 동조하는 국가가없었음.끝.

(대사 박수길-국장)

당부 검토 의견

'91.5.8. 무역위원회가 피해 긍정 판정을 내린 바 있으나, 수입 조제 팝콘 옥수수와 국제 팝콘 옥수수의 HS 품목 분류번호 상이, 국내 팝콘 옥수수 생산량의 년도별 불규칙성에 따른 국내 평균 생산량 설정의 난점, 시장점유율 하락이 있으나 국내 팝콘 옥수수의 절대 판매량 증대 사실 등으로 GATT 세이프가드 조치 발동요건 충족에 미흡한 것으로 판단되고, 동 품목 수입 전량이 미국에서 수입되고 있는 점을 고려, 국경조치 채택은 통상마찰 방치 차원에서도 바람직하지 않음.

다만, 불가피한 경우 동 품목이 미양허 품목임을 감안 관세율 인상에 한하여 국경조치 가능하다고 봄. 끝.

0068

RESTRICTED

MTN.GNG/RM/W/3

6 June 1991

Special Distribution

Group of Negotiations on Goods (GATT)
Negotiating Group on Rule Making and
Trade-Related Investment Measures

SAFEGUARDS

Note by the Secretariat

The draft text of an agreement on safeguards drawn up prior to the
Ministerial Meeting of the TNC held in Brussels from 3 to 7 December 1990,
is contained on pages 183 to 192 of MTN.TNC/W/35/Rev.1. As explained in
the commentary to that text, reproduced on page 182 of the document, an
overall compromise remained to be found on a number of issues reflected by
square brackets in the text of the draft agreement.

Consultations held in Brussels have led to a compromise on some of
these issues. The revised text, attached hereto, was circulated to
participants in the Green Room meeting chaired by Minister Crosbie of
Canada, but was not discussed.

Outstanding issues contained in the latest draft text are reflected by
square brackets.

GATT SECRETARIAT
UR-91-0048

0069

AGREEMENT ON SAFEGUARDS

The attached text is drawn up on the understanding that no paragraph is agreed unless all paragraphs in it are agreed and on the assumption that there is a satisfactory outcome in other areas of the negotiations.

0070

AGREEMENT ON SAFEGUARDS

PREAMBLE

The CONTRCTING PARTIES:

Having in mind the overall objective of the contracting parties to improve and strengthen the international trading system based on the General Agreement on Tariffs and Trade;

Recognizing the need to clarify and reinforce the disciplines of the General Agreement, and specifically those of its Article XIX (Emergency Action on Imports of Particular Products), to re-establish multilateral control over safeguards and eliminate measures that escape such control;

Recognizing the importance of structural adjustment and the need to enhance rather than limit competition in international markets; and

Recognizing further that, for these purposes, a comprehensive agreement, applicable to all contracting parties and based on the basic principles of the General Agreement, is called for;

Hereby agree as follows:

0071

I

GENERAL

1.   This agreement establishes rules for the application of safeguard measures which shall be understood to mean those measures provided for in Article XIX of the General Agreement.

II

CONDITIONS

2.   A contracting party[1] may apply a safeguard measure to a product only if the importing contracting party has determined, pursuant to the provisions set out below, that such product is being imported into its territory in such increased quantities, absolute or relative to domestic production, and under such conditions as to cause or threaten to cause serious injury to the domestic industry that produces like or directly competitive products.

3.   (a)   A contracting party may apply a safeguard measure only following an investigation by the competent authorities of the importing contracting party pursuant to procedures previously established and made public in consonance with Article X of the General Agreement. This investigation shall include reasonable public notice to all interested parties and public hearings or other appropriate means in which importers, exporters and other interested parties could present evidence and their views, including the opportunity to respond to the presentations of other parties and to submit their views, inter alia, as to whether or not the application of a safeguard measure would be in the public interest. The competent authorities shall publish a report setting forth their findings and reasoned conclusions reached on all pertinent issues of fact and law.

---

[1]A customs union may apply a safeguard measure as a single unit or on behalf of a member state. When a customs union applies a safeguard measure as a single unit, all the requirements for the determination of serious injury or threat thereof under this agreement shall be based on the conditions existing in the customs union as a whole. When a safeguard measure is applied on behalf of a member state, all the requirements for the determination of serious injury or threat thereof shall be based on the conditions existing in that member state and the measure shall be limited to that member state. Nothing in this agreement prejudges the interpretation of the relationship between Article XIX and Article XXIV:8 of the General Agreement.

0072

(b) Any information which is by nature confidential or which is provided on a confidential basis shall, upon cause being shown, be treated as such by the competent authorities. Such information shall not be disclosed without permission of the party submitting it. Parties providing confidential information may be requested to furnish non-confidential summaries thereof and, if such parties indicate that such information cannot be summarized, the reasons why a summary cannot be provided. However, if the competent authorities find that a request for confidentiality is not warranted and if the party concerned is either unwilling to make the information public or to authorize its disclosure in generalized or summary form, the authorities would be free to disregard such information unless it can be demonstrated to their satisfaction from appropriate sources that the information is correct.

4. In critical circumstances where delay would cause damage which it would be difficult to repair, a provisional safeguard measure may be taken pursuant to a preliminary determination that there is clear evidence that increased imports have caused or are threatening to cause serious injury. The duration of the provisional measure shall not exceed 200 days, during which period the pertinent requirements of this Section and Section VII shall be met. Such measures should take the form of tariff increases to be promptly refunded if the subsequent investigation referred to in paragraph 7 below does not determine that increased imports have caused or threatened to cause serious injury to a domestic industry. The duration of any such provisional measure shall count towards the initial period and any extension referred to in paragraphs 10, 11 and 12 below.

5. Safeguard measures shall be applied to a product being imported irrespective of its source.

6. For the purposes of this agreement:

(a) serious injury shall be understood to mean a significant overall impairment in the position of a domestic industry;

(b) in determining injury, a domestic industry shall be understood to mean the producers as a whole of the like or directly competitive products operating within the territory of a contracting party, or those whose collective output of the like or directly competitive products constitutes a major proportion [, i.e. normally 50 per cent or more but in no case less than 33 per cent,] of the total domestic production of those products; and

0073

(c) threat of serious injury shall be understood to mean serious injury that is clearly imminent, in accordance with the provisions of paragraph 7 below. A determination of the existence of a threat of serious injury shall be based on facts and not merely on allegation, conjecture or remote possibility.

7. (a) In the investigation to determine whether increased imports have caused or are threatening to cause serious injury to a domestic industry under the terms of this agreement, the competent authorities shall evaluate all relevant factors of an objective and quantifiable nature having a bearing on the situation of that industry, in particular, the rate and amount of the increase in imports of the product concerned in absolute and relative terms, the share of the domestic market taken by increased imports, changes in the level of sales, production, productivity, capacity utilization, profits and losses, and employment.

(b) The determination referred to in sub-paragraph 7(a) shall not be made unless this investigation demonstrates, on the basis of objective evidence, the existence of the causal link between increased imports of the product concerned and serious injury or threat thereof. When factors other than increased imports are causing injury to the domestic industry at the same time, such injury shall not be attributed to increased imports.

(c) The competent authorities shall publish promptly, in accordance with the provisions of paragraph 3 above, a detailed analysis of the case under investigation as well as a demonstration of the relevance of the factors examined.

8. Safeguard measures shall be applied only to the extent as may be necessary to prevent or remedy serious injury and to facilitate adjustment. Contracting parties should choose measures most suitable for the achievement of these objectives.

9. [No quantitative restriction shall reduce the quantity of imports below the level of a recent representative period which shall normally be the average of imports in the last three representative years for which statistics are available.] [In cases in which a quota is allocated among supplying countries, and in the absence of agreement with the suppliers concerned, the importing contracting party may allot quota shares proportionately to the quantities supplied during the previous representative period, subject to the possibility of taking into account clear evidence on the extent each supplier has contributed to the assessed global injury, provided that any modification in individual quota allotments necessary to remedy injury may not exceed five percentage points or 30 per cent of the proportion supplied during the representative period, whichever is the smaller. No such modification shall be applied to contracting parties whose market share of the product concerned does not exceed one per cent. Whenever any such modification occurs, the importing contracting party shall provide justification as to the reasons for it.]

0074

10.   Safeguard measures shall be applied only for a period of time as may be necessary to prevent or remedy serious injury and to facilitate adjustment.   It shall not exceed four years, unless this is extended under paragraph 11 below.

11.   The period mentioned in paragraph 10 above may be extended provided that the competent authorities of the importing contracting party have determined, in conformity with the procedures set out in this Section, that: the safeguard measure continues to be necessary to prevent or remedy serious injury;   that there is evidence that the industry is adjusting; and that the pertinent provisions of Sections III and VII below are observed.

12.   The total period of a safeguard measure including the period of application of any provisional measure, the period of initial application, and any extension thereof shall not exceed eight years.

13.   In order to facilitate adjustment, if the expected duration of a safeguard measure as notified under the provisions of paragraph 25 is over one year, it shall be progressively liberalized at regular intervals during the period of application.   If the duration of the measure exceeds three years, the contracting party applying such a measure shall review the situation not later than the mid-term of the measure and, if appropriate, withdraw it or increase the pace of liberalization.   A measure extended under paragraph 10 above shall not be more restrictive than it was at the end of the initial period, and should continue to be liberalized.

14.   No safeguard measure shall be applied again to the import of a product which has been subject to such a measure, taken after the date of entry into force of this agreement, for a period of time equal to that during which such measure had been previously applied, provided that the period of non-application is at least two years.

15.   Notwithstanding the provisions of paragraph 14 above, a safeguard measure with a duration of 180 days or less may be applied again to the import of a product if:

   (a)   at least one year has elapsed since the date of introduction of a safeguard measure on the import of that product;   and

   (b)   such a safeguard measure has not been applied on the same product more than twice in the five-year period immediately preceding the date of introduction of the measure.

0075

III

LEVEL OF CONCESSIONS AND OTHER OBLIGATIONS

16. A contracting party proposing to apply a safeguard measure or seeking an extension shall endeavour to maintain a substantially equivalent level of concessions and other obligations to that existing between it and the exporting contracting parties which would be affected by such a measure under the General Agreement, in accordance with the provisions of paragraph 27 below. To achieve this objective, the contracting parties concerned may agree on any means of trade compensation for the adverse effects of the measure on their trade.

17. If no agreement is reached [adequate] within 30 days in the consultations under paragraph 27 below, then the affected exporting contracting parties are free, not later than 90 days after the measure is applied, to suspend, upon the expiration of 30 days from the day on which written notice of such suspension is received by the CONTRACTING PARTIES, the application of substantially equivalent concessions or other obligations under the General Agreement, to the trade of the contracting party applying the safeguard measure, the suspension of which the CONTRACTING PARTIES do not disapprove.

18. The right of suspension referred to in paragraph 17 above shall not be exercised if the duration of the measure does not exceed three years, provided such a measure conforms to this agreement.

IV

DEVELOPING COUNTRIES

[19. Safeguard measures shall not be applied against a product originating in a less-developed contracting party whose market share in the product concerned does not exceed one per cent.]

20. Less-developed and least-developed contracting parties shall have the right to extend the period of application of a safeguard measure for a period of up to two years beyond the maximum period provided for in paragraph 12 above. Notwithstanding the provisions of paragraph 14 above, less-developed and least-developed contracting parties shall apply a [may] safeguard measure again to the import of a product which has been subject to such a measure, taken after the date of entry into force of this agreement, for a period of time equal to half that during which such a measure has been previously applied, provided that the period of non-application is at least two years.

V

EXISTING ARTICLE XIX MEASURES

21. Contracting parties shall terminate all existing safeguard measures taken pursuant to Article XIX of the General Agreement not later than eight years after the date on which they were first applied or [five] [six] years after the date of entry into force of this agreement, whichever comes later.

VI

PROHIBITION AND ELIMINATION OF CERTAIN MEASURES

22. No trade-restrictive measure shall be sought or taken by a contracting party unless it conforms with the provisions of Article XIX as interpreted by the provisions of this agreement, or is consistent with other provisions of the General Agreement, or protocols and agreements or arrangements concluded within the framework of the General Agreement. These include actions taken by a single contracting party as well as actions under agreements, arrangements and understandings entered into by two or more contracting parties. Any such measure in effect at the time of entry into force of this agreement shall either be brought into conformity with the provisions of Article XIX and this agreement or phased out in accordance with paragraph 23 below.

23. The provisions of paragraph 22 above shall be carried out according to timetables to be presented to the Safeguards Committee by the contracting parties concerned not later than 180 days after the date of entry into force of this agreement. These timetables shall provide for all measures referred to in paragraph 22 above to be phased out or brought into conformity with this agreement within a period not exceeding [three] [four] years, [subject to exceptions up to a maximum of eight years, set out in Annex 1,] after the date of entry into force of this agreement.

24. Contracting parties shall not encourage nor support the adoption or maintenance by public and private enterprises of non-governmental measures equivalent to those referred to in paragraph 22 above.

VII

NOTIFICATION AND CONSULTATION

25. A contracting party shall immediately notify the CONTRACTING PARTIES upon:

   (a) initiating an investigatory process relating to serious injury or threat thereof and the reasons for it;

0077

    (b) making a finding of serious injury or threat thereof caused by
         increased imports; and

    (c) taking a decision to apply or extend a safeguard measure.

26. In making the notifications referred to in sub-paragraphs 25(b)
and (c) above, the contracting party proposing to apply or extend a
safeguard measure shall provide the CONTRACTING PARTIES with all pertinent
information, which shall include evidence of serious injury or threat
thereof caused by increased imports, precise description of the product
involved and the proposed measure, proposed date of introduction, expected
duration and timetable for progressive liberalization. In the case of an
extension of a measure, evidence that the industry concerned is adjusting
shall also be provided. The CONTRACTING PARTIES or the Safeguards
Committee may request such additional information as they may consider
necessary from the contracting party proposing to apply or extend the
measure.

27. A contracting party proposing to apply or extend a safeguard measure
shall provide adequate opportunity for prior consultations with those
contracting parties having a substantial interest as exporters of the
product concerned, with a view to, _inter alia_, reviewing the information
provided under paragraph 26 above, exchanging views on the measure and
reaching an understanding on ways to achieve the objective set out in
paragraph 16 above.

28. A contracting party shall make a notification before taking a
provisional safeguard measure referred to in paragraph 4 above.
Consultations shall be initiated immediately after the measure is taken.

29. The results of the consultations referred to in this Section, as well
as the results of mid-term reviews referred to in paragraph 13, any form of
compensation referred to in paragraph 16, and proposed suspensions of
concessions and other obligations referred to in paragraph 17, shall be
notified immediately to the CONTRACTING PARTIES by the contracting parties
concerned.

30. Contracting parties shall notify promptly the CONTRACTING PARTIES of
their laws, regulations and administrative procedures relating to safeguard
measures as well as any modifications made to them.

31. Contracting parties maintaining measures described in paragraphs 21
and 22 above which exist at the date on which this agreement enters into
force shall notify such measures to the CONTRACTING PARTIES, not later than
60 days after the entry into force of this agreement.

32.   Any contracting party may notify the CONTRACTING PARTIES of all laws, regulations, administrative procedures and any measure or action dealt with in this agreement that has not been notified by other contracting parties that are required by this agreement to make such notifications.

33.   Any contracting party may notify the CONTRACTING PARTIES of any non-governmental measures referred to in paragraph 24 above.

34.   All notifications to the CONTRACTING PARTIES referred to in this agreement shall normally be made through the Safeguards Committee.

35.   The provisions on notification in this agreement shall not require any contracting party to disclose confidential information which would impede law enforcement or otherwise be contrary to the public interest or would prejudice the legitimate commercial interests of particular enterprises, public or private.

VIII

SURVEILLANCE

36.   There shall be a Safeguards Committee under the authority of the CONTRACTING PARTIES, which shall be open to the participation of any contracting party indicating its wish to serve on it.   The Committee will have the following functions:

  (a)   to monitor, and report annually to the CONTRACTING PARTIES on, the general implementation of this agreement and make recommendations towards its improvement;

  (b)   to find, upon request of an affected contracting party, whether or not the procedural requirements of this agreement have been complied with in connection with a safeguard measure, and report its findings to the CONTRACTING PARTIES;

  (c)   to assist contracting parties, if they so request, in their consultations under the provisions of this agreement;

  (d)   to examine measures covered by paragraphs 21 and 22, monitor the phase-out of such measures and report as appropriate to the CONTRACTING PARTIES;

  (e)   to review, at the request of the contracting party taking a safeguard action, whether proposals to suspend concessions or other obligations are "substantially equivalent", and report as appropriate to the CONTRACTING PARTIES;

0079

(f) to receive and review all notifications provided for in this
     agreement and report as appropriate to the CONTRACTING PARTIES;
     and

(g) to perform any other function connected with this agreement that
     the CONTRACTING PARTIES may determine.

37. To assist the Committee in carrying out its surveillance function, the
secretariat shall prepare annually a factual report on the operation of the
agreement based on notifications and other reliable information available
to it.

IX

DISPUTE SETTLEMENT

38. Contracting parties which consider that their rights under this
agreement are being nullified or impaired have recourse to the dispute
settlement provisions of the General Agreement.

0080

(<u>ANNEX 1</u>)

(<u>EXCEPTIONS REFERRED TO IN PARAGRAPH 23</u>)

0081

무 역 위 원 회

조 이 28003-83   504-4817   1991. 6.25

수 신   외무부(통상국장)

제 목   "팝콘옥수수" 생산업피해 구제방안 검토를 위한 회의개최

    1. 우리 무역위원회는 '90.11.16 농업협동조합중앙회에서 대외
무역법 제32조 규정에 의거 신청한 "조제팝콘옥수수 수입으로 인한 팝콘
옥수수생산업 피해조사 신청건"에 대하여 그간 조사를 실시하여 '91. 5.
8일 제50차 무역위원회에서 "피해긍정 판정"을 한바 있으며, 이에 따라
동법 제34조의 규정에 의거 산업피해 구제조치 방안을 검토중에 있습니다.

    2. 이와 관련하여 별첨계획과 같이 "팝콘옥수수" 생산업 피해구제
방안검토를 위한 관계부처 회의를 갖고자 하오니 참석하여 주시기 바랍니다.

    첨 부: "팝콘옥수수" 생산업 피해구제방안 검토를 위한 관계부처 회의개최
          계획 1부.   끝.

0082

"팝콘옥수수" 생산업피해 구제방안 검토를 위한 관계부처 회의개최 계획

1. 일   시 : '91. 6.27 (목) 15:00

2. 장   소 : 정부 제2청사 3동 106-1호 (무역위원회 "심결정")

3. 주   재 : 무역조사실장

4. 참석대상

   - 경제기획원 : 산업1과장

   - 외무부   : 통상기구과장

   - 재무부   : 산업관세과장

   - 보건사회부 : 식품유통과장

   - 농림수산부 : 양정과장, 농산과장, 통상협력담당관

   - 상공부   : 국제협력담당관, 통상협력담당관, 무역정책과장,

5. 안   건

   ① 검토가능한 산업피해 구제조치 방안

     o 산업구조 조정지원

       - 생산자의 자구노력, 경쟁력향상 대책, 유통구조 개선등

     o 수입수량제한

     o 관세율의 조정

     o 국내외 가격차액 보상

     o 국산품 우선구매 지원

     o 각 방안의 복합시행

   ② 각 구제조치 방안별 구제효과, 국민경제 및 국제통상면에 미치는 영향 검토

   ③ 기타 : 규제절차등

* 회의자료는 당일 배포

0083

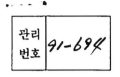

외　무　부

종　별 :

번　호 : GVW-2099　　　　　　　　　일　시 : 91 1023 1100

수　신 : 장관(통기,경기원,재무부,상공부)

발　신 : 주　제네바　대사

제　목 : UR/분야별 협상 대책(규범제정 분야-세이프가드)

연: GVW-2083

일반문서로 재분류(1091.12.31.

1. 주요 쟁점 사항

가. 예외적 선별 적용 및 쿼타 감축(CUT-BACK)

0 쟁점의 내용(9 항)

- 브랏셀회의 비공식 협의시 EC 가 종전의 선별적용(SELECTIVITY)철회 조건으로 제시

- 세이프가드 발동시 과거 대표적 기간의 수출 물량에 따라 쿼타를 배정(시장 점유율 1% 미만의 수출국은 제외)하되

- 전체 산업피해(GLOBAL INJURY)에 대한 개별 수출자의 기여도를 감안 수입국이 특정 수출자로 부터의 수입물량을 감량(CUT-BACK)가능

0 주요국 입장

- EC: 선별 적용 포기 위해서는 선별적 CUT-BACK 은 필수적

- 미국, 카나다: 수용 가능

- 대다수 국가: 시장점유 신장율 고하에 관계없이 대소 수출국에 모두 적용된다는 점에 비추어 수용할수 없다는 입장

- 홍콩, 싱가폴: 사실상의 선별 적용을 인정하는 내용이므로 수용불가(SG 협정 없는 현상 유지가 오히려 바람직하다는 입장 표명)

나. 회색조치 철폐 시한

0 현 초안 내용(23 항)

- 협정 발효후 (3), (4) (ANEXX I 에 열거된 경우 예외적으로 최대 8 년)내, 기존 회색조치 철폐

다. 보상, 보복의 면제 기간

통상국	장관	차관	1차보	2차보	외정실	분석관	청와대	안기부
경기원	재무부	상공부						

PAGE 1　　　　　　　　　　　　　　　　　91.10.23　20:47

외신 2과　통제관 FM

0084

O 현 초안 내용(18 항)

- 협정과 일치되게 발동되는 3 년 이내의 SG 에 대해서는 보복 면제

O 주요국 입장

- 미국: 4 년

- EC: 5 년

라. 최초 및 최대 발동기간

- 최초 4 년, 최대 8 년

마. 개도국 우대

O 현 초안 내용(19,20 항)

- 시장점유율부하였음% 미만의 개도국 상품에 대해서는 불적용 (19 항)

- 개도국 발동 SG 에 대한 2 년간의 발동 기간 연장 및 발동 금지 기간 단축(20 항)

2. 최근의 협상 동향 및 전망

- 브랏셀 회의후 주요국의 입장 변화 없음.

- 선별적용 문제는 UR 최종단계에서 타결될 전망

3. 우리의 관심사항

- 선별적용 도입이나 쿼타 감축에 반대

- 기타 협상 요소는 융봉성있게 대처

4. 관심사항 반영 방안

북기사항없음. 끝

(대사 박수길-국장)

예고:91.12.31. 까지

외 무 부

종 별 :

번 호 : GVW-2176   일 시 : 91 1029 1830

수 신 : 장관(통기, 경기원, 재무부, 상공부)

발 신 : 주 제네바 대사

제 목 : UR/세이프 가드

10.29 오전으로 예정된 세이프가드 비공식 협의를 앞두고 일본대표부 ASAKAI 공사 주최로 10.28 동대표부에서 12개 주요국(아국, 일본, 호주, 브라질, 카나다, 홍콩, 인도, 말련, 뉴질랜드, 놀웨이, 싱가폴, 스위스) 실무 오찬 협의가 개최되어 QUOTA MODULATION 문제, 국내 산업의 JAJOR PROPORTION에 대한 양적 규정문제, 국경조치 한정 또는 보조금, 구조 조정 조치의 인정 여부, 상대적 수량 증가인정 여부, 지역 협정등에 관하여 의견 교환이 있었는바, 동 결과를 아래 보고함.

1. QUOTA MODULATION

0 아국, 홍콩, 싱가폴, 인도, 말련, 브라질, 일본등이 QM 은 사실상의 선별 조치이며, 경우에 따라서 더욱 위험한 요소를 내포하고 있으므로 수락할수 없으며, 동 처리를 위해서는 여타 요소에서 신축적 자세를 취할수도 있다는 의견을 개진

- 특히 홍콩은 QM 이 인정되는 협정을 받아들이기 보다는 차라리 협정을 체결치않는 것이 바람직하다는 강경 입장

- 단, 싱가폴은 보상, 보복의 면제를 대가로 지불하는 것에는 검토를 요한다는 신중론 피력

- 또한 홍콩, 싱가폴, 인도, 말련등은 현 TEXT 5항이 달리 해석될수도 있으므로 MFN 을 확실히 보장할수 있도록 문안 강화 필요성을 지적

0 반면 카나다, 놀웨이, 호주는 현 문안이 상당한 문제점이 있어 받아들일수 없는 것은 사실이나, 협상 타결을 위해서는 구체적으로 규정된 예외적상황의 경우에 한하며, 엄격한 규율(DISCIPLINE)하에서의 적용등 추가 검토의 가능성을 배제하지 않는것이 바람직 하다는 의견을 개진

2. 국내 산업의 MAJOR PROPORTION 에 대한 양적 규정

0 아국, 홍콩, 싱가폴, 놀웨이, 인도등이 양적정의 설정에 반대입장을 피력

통상국   2차보   경기원   재무부   상공부

91.10.30   10:11 DQ

외신 1과 통제관

0086

- 홍콩, 인도는 GATT 19 조상 당연히 해당 산업전체로 해석됨에도 불구하고 MAJOR PROPORTION개념 도입을 인정한 것 자체가 상당한 양보이므로 50 프로도 부족하다고보며, 따라서 차라리 양적 정의를 않는 것이 유리하다는 의견(인도는 6항 B 전체를삭제하는 것이 가장 바람직하다는 의견 추가)

0 반면 카나다는 반덤핑의 예를 들면서 양적 규정설정이 유용할 수도 있다는 의견을 개진(이에대해 싱가폴이 AD 와 SG 의 차이점을 들어 반론 제기)하였으며, 호주도 기본적으로는 규정치 않는 것이 바람직하나 협상 타결을 위해 절충할 필요성도 있음을 언급함.

0 한편, 브라질은 50 프로안이 가장 바람직하며 양적규정을 않는 방안을 차선책으로 수락 가능하다는 의견 피력

3. 국경조치 한정 또는 국내조치 인정 여부

0 뉴질랜드가 국경조치 한정을 선호하면서 8항이 대상조치 선정의 자유를 규정한데 대해 문제점을 지적(싱가폴도 8항 문제점 지적)

0 스위스는 엄격한 기준하의 일정한 보조금 인정 필요성을 주장하였고, 브라질도 광범위한 보조행위의 용인을 바라는 EC 와는 입장이 다르다는 점을 전제한후 일정한 한도의 국내 구조조정 조치 인정은 필요하다는 의견을 밝혔으며, 인도 또한 MFN 의확실한 보장등 장점도 없지 않으므로 경우에 따라 구조조정 조치가 국경조치 보다바람직할수도 있다는 의견을 개진

4. 지역 협정 문제

0 아국, 뉴질랜드가 지역 협정은 단일 주체로서만 SG 조치를 발동해야 한다는 입장 피력

0 인도는 FOOTNOTE 1 에 문제점은 있으나 해결책을 제시할수 있는 입장은 아니라고 함.

5. 상대적 수량 증가 인정문제

0 홍콩, 싱가폴, 말련, 인도가 상대적 수량 증가를 인정해서는 안된다는 의견을피력

6. 기타

0 BRAZIL 은 개도국 조항이 QUOTA MODULATION 과 밀접히 연결돼 있음을 언급하면서, 동 조항을 제안한 이집트가 최근 진정한 MFN 이 확실히 보장될 경우 이를 철회할 용의가 있음을 피력한것으로 안다고 언급

PAGE 2

0087

O 싱가폴, 호주가 잠정 SG 인정 기간 200 일은 너무 장기간이라는 의견 피력. 끝
(대사 박수길-국장)

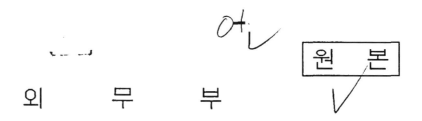

외　무　부

원　본

종　별 :

번　호 : GVW-2191　　　　　　　　　일　시 : 91 1030 1730

수　신 : 장 관(봉기,상공부)

발　신 : 주 제네바 대사

제　목 : UR/세이프가드 비공식 협의

　　1. 표제 회의가 10.29 오전 MARCIEL 의장 주재로 개최되어 REVISED TEXT (MTN/GNG/RM/2 3, 91.6.6)에 대한 1차 조문별 검토를 가졌으나 쟁점 사항에 대한 뚜렷한 의견 접근을 보이지 않음으로서 의장은 금주중 비공식 협의를 다시 소집하기로 함.(이성주참사관, 김영학 사무관 참석)

　　2. 조문별로 각국이 표명한 입장은 아래와 같음.

　　가. 제 2항(절대적 또는 상대적 증가)

　　0 홍콩이 SG 는 정당무역에 대한 조치이며, GATT19조에도 명시적 언급이 없다는점을 내세워 'RELATIVE,의 삭제를 주장하고, 아국, 멕시코, 싱가포, 인도, 알젠틴등이 동조

　　0 미국이 GATT 19 조는 절대적 증가는 물론 상대적 증가의 개념도 포함하고 있다 하면서 삭제에 반대입장(EC, 놀웨이 동조)을 표명함으로써 멕시코가 'ABSOLUTE' 및 'RELATIVE'를 모두 삭제하자고 주장(상기 'RELATIVE' 삭제주장국 대부분이 동조)

　　나. 제 3항 주석 1 (관세동맹)

　　0 뉴질랜드가 FOOTNOTE 1 의 제 3문장의 삭제를 주장한데 대해, EC가 본그룹이 결정할 사항이 아니라면서 반대

　　다. 제 4항(잠정 SG)

　　0 호주, 싱가폴이 90로 단축을 요구, 미국, EC가 불가입장 표명

　　라. 제 5항(MFN)

　　0 홍콩, 싱가폴, 브라질등이 MFN 보장을 확실히 하는 방향으로 표면 강화를 주장한데 대해, EC가 강력히 (현 초안은 최대한의 양보선) 반대

　　마. 제 6항 B (국내 산업의 MAJOR PROPORTION)

　　0 홍콩이 괄호 내용의 완전 삭제를 주장하고 아국, 인도, 싱가폴, 뉴질랜드, 카나

통상국　　2차보　　상공부

PAGE 1　　　　　　　　　　　　　　　　　　　　91.10.31　　09:17 WH

외신 1과　통제관

0089

다들이 동조

  - 인도, 싱가폴은 차라리 6항 B 전체의 삭제가 최선이며, 불연이면 괄호 내용만삭제하자는 입장

  0 스위스는 상당히 높은 수치로 명시하는 것이 가장 바람직하나, 받아들여지기 어렵다고 보기 때문에 삭제하는 것이 좋다는 입장 표명

  0 상기에 대해 미국, EC 가 반대입장 표명

  - 특히 EC 는 지역산업 관련 EC 의 관심을 반영시켜줄 경우 삭제 용의가 있으며,6항 B전체를 삭제하는 문제는 입장을 유보(OPEN)하겠다는 반응

  사. 제 7항 B (인과관계)

  0 스위스가 피해의 결정은 수입 증가 사실만으로도 충분하다고 하면서 수입증가가 국내 산업의 경쟁력 결여 때문이 아니라는 증거를 제시해야한다는 내용의 문안으로7 항 B 의 마지막문장을 대체할것을 주장했으나, 미국, 놀웨이, 카나다, EC 등 다수국이 반대

  아. 제 8항 (SG 조치의 수준 및 형태)

  0 미국은 국경조치 한정, 관세조치 선호 입장에 변함이 없으며, 현문안이 보조금 지급등에 악용소지가 있다 하면서 W/25/REV 3(90.10) 문안으로되 돌아가기를 희망(멕시코, 뉴질랜드, 싱가폴, 홍콩, 카나다 등이 동조)

  0 EC 는 국경 조치에 한정하는 것은 국가권한에 대한 지나친 제한이 되므로 수락할수없다는 입장이었으며, 스위스도 모든 형태의 보조행위 허용을 바라는 것은 아니나 국내 조치에 대한 최소한의 OPTION 은 주어야 한다는 입장

  0 싱가폴은 ' MOST SUITABLE' 표현이 OMA 등 회색조치로 악용될 소지가 있으므로 이를 명료화해야 한다고 주장(일본도 현 문안이 불분명하다는 의견)

  자. 제 9항(QUOTA MODULATION)

  0 첫번째 BRACKET 에 대해서는 대부분의 국가가 일부 보완 필요성외에는 큰 문제가 없다는 의견

  0 두번째 BRACKET 에 대해서는 아국, 홍콩, 싱가폴, 스위스, 인도, 파키스탄 등이 QUOTALMODULATION 은 사실상의 SELECTIVITY 이므로 절대로 받아들일수 없다는 점을강조(의장이 'PROVIDEDTHAT THERE IS NO OPPOSITION FROM THE C. P' 라는 단서를 추가하면 어떻겠느냐는 의견을 제시한바, 상기국가 모두가 반대)

  - 아국은 동 개념 자체에 문제가 있기 때문에DRAFTING 차원에서 해결될 문제가 아니며, GATT13조 2(B) 와의 합치성 여부에 의문이 있다는의견 피력

- 홍콩은 GATT 13 조상 QUOTA ALLOTMENT 가의무적(MANDATORY)인것이 아니라 하면서 EC가 GLOBAL QUOTA 만 설정하지 않고 이를 MODULATE하려는 이유를 납득치 못하겠다고 언급

0 캐나다는 MFN 의 지지가 자국의 기본 입장이라 하면서 QM 이 MFN 과 어떻게 조화를 이루는지, QM 시행에 관한 세부 절차가 결여되 있다는점을 문제로 지적

0 EC 는 상기 홍콩 및 아국의 언급에 대해 GATT 13 조는 상당히 복잡한 조문을 QM 이 의문적인 것은 아니지만 금지된 것도 아니며, 단순한 산술적 조정은 극히 불공평하다고 보기때문에 MODULATION 에 대한 기준이 필요하다고 주장하고 이문제 역시 EC로 서는 더이상 양보할수 없다고 언급.

차. 제 10, 12항(최초 및 최대 발동기간)

0 아국, 홍콩, 싱가폴, 호주, 인도등이 가급적단 기간을 선호(단, SELECTIVITY 철폐와 연계신축성 시사)

카. 제 18항(보상 보복의 면제)

0 홍콩, 싱가폴이 괄호는 없으나, SELECTIVITY 와 연계되어 있음을 상기

타. 제 19항(개도국 우대)

0 의장의 괄호 제거에 대해 참가국의 동의를 구했으나 미국이 19항 전체를 삭제할 것을 주장.

0 이에 대해 멕시코, 파키스탄이 반대

파. 제 21항(기존 SG 조치)

0 미국이 5년 내 철폐, EC 가 6년 철폐 주장.

하. 제 22항(회색 조치 철폐)

0 미국이 현 문안상의 TRADE-RESTRICTIVE MEASURES 가 SG 목적이 아닌 무역제한조치의 포함등 지나치게 광범위하며, 또한 GATT 에 명시적으로 허용된 조치만 허용함으로써 묵시적으로 허용된 (명시적으로 금지 되지 않은) 조치는 금지 되는등 현 문안의문 제점을 지적하고 별첨 수정문안을 제시

0 상기에 대해 EC, 홍콩, 카나다, 호주, 싱가폴, 놀웨이등이 검토 용의를 표명하였으며, 일본, 놀웨이는 미국안이 현 문안의 SUBSTANCE 를 변경할 가능성도 있다는우려를 표명

0 미국이 재검토 한후 다시 수정문안을 제기 하기로 함.

거. 제 23항 (회색조치 철폐시한)

PAGE 3

0091

o 의장이 철폐기간으로 4년을 인정해주는 대신 EC 에 대해 예외 8년을 포기하도록 권유

너. 제 38항(분쟁해결)

o 분쟁해결분야 결과를 참작, 문안을 수정키로 합의. 끝 첨부: 제 22항 관련 미국 수정안 (GVW(F)-461)

(대사 박수길-국장)

Gvw3) - 461 11030 1800

Gvw - 21P 1 된것

29/10/91 US proposal

22.   No Contracting Party shall avoid recourse to the procedures
of this Article by requesting another Contracting Party to adopt
measures that are <u>otherwise</u> inconsistent with the provisions of
the General Agreement.   Nor shall the requested Party adopt such
measures.   Measures, for these purposes, shall include those
taken under any agreement, arrangement, or understanding reached
between the Parties or with other Parties.   Any such measure
being applied at the time of the entry into force of this
agreement shall either be brought immediately into conformity
with this provision or be phased out in accordance with paragraph
23.

independently (. ।乃)

0093

외 무 부

종 별 :

번 호 : GVW-2206   일 시 : 91 1031 1730

수 신 : 장 관(통기,경기원,상공부,재무부)

발 신 : 주 제네바대사

제 목 : UR 세이프가드 비공식 협의

연: GVW-2176

1. 표제 협의가 연호에 이어 10.30 오후 MARCIEL의장 주재하에 속개되어, 제 22항(회색조치의 철폐)관련 미국의 2차 수정안 및 알젠틴 수정안을 검토한 바, 동 결과아래 보고함.(이성주참사관 참석)

가. 미국은 자국의 제 2차 수정안(별첨 1)을 제시하고제안 설명을 통해 회색조치의 완벽한 정의가 어렵기 때문에 서술 부분(첫 3개 PARAGRAPH)이 필요했으며, 자국의 의도는 3.25.TEXT상의무역제한 조치의 범위가 너무 광범위하다고 보기때문에 ~~SG~~ ~~위원회가 관장할 무역 제한조치의 범위가 너무 광범위하다고 보기때문에~~ SG위원회가 관장할 무역 제한조치의 범위를 가급적 축소하는데 있다고함.

나. 알젠틴도 자국 수정안(별첨 2) 설명을 통해, 3.25. TEXT문안 수락 용의가 있었으나 미국이 이를 축소하려 하기 때문에 가급적 대상 범위를 넓혀 모든 무역제한조치를 포함하고자 하는 것이 동제안의 취지라고 언급함.

다. 일부국가로 부터 미국제안 서술부의 필요성, 서술부문 제 2문장과 SUB-PARA(A)간의 모순,(A) 항 'WHERE' 이하 관련 국가간 협정이 있으면 GATT와 합치한다는 의미로 해석될 가능성등에 대한 질문이 있는 이외에는 양제안은 검토해 충분한 시간이 필요하다는 중론에 따라 구체 토의는 없었음.

라. 스위스도 인과관계(7.B항) 관련 연호내용을 서면 수정 형식으로 제출하였음.,마. 한편 EC 는 현단계에서 상기 22조 수정안에 대해서 언급할 입장이 아니라고 한후 협상 교착을 풀어나가기 위해 노력중이며 이는 EC 에게는 대단히 고통스러운 과정인바, 이에 상응하는 대가가 있어야 할 것이라고 언급함

바. 의장은 현재까지 미결 쟁점을 일일이 열거(총13개) 한후 현재까지의 결과를 10.31.개최 예정인 규범 제정 공식회의에 보고하겠다고 하였으며, 또한 참가국간

통상국   2차보   경기원   재무부   상공부

PAGE 1   91.11.01   09:40 WH

외신 1과 통제관

0094

개별적인 접촉을 통해 이견을 좁히려는 노력을 강화해 줄것을 촉구하였음

　　사.　참고로　회의　종료후　개별적으로　접촉한　사무국관계관은　금번　비공식
협의기간중에도 전혀 진전이 없음에 대해 깊은 우려를 표명하였음.

　　2. 상기 회색조치 범위관련 본부의견 회시바람.

　　첨부:1. 미국의 수정안

　　2. 알젠틴 수정안

　　3. 스위스 수정안

　　(GVW(F)-0466).끝

　　(대사 박수길-국장)

22.   The CONTRACTING PARTIES recognize that Contracting Parties
have had recourse to certain trade-restrictive measures outside the
procedures of this Article.   Such measures have in some cases been
taken pursuant to an agreement, arrangement, or understanding
between or among Contracting Parties and in other cases have been
taken at the request of another Party.

The CONTRACTING PARTIES further recognize that it is presently
uncertain whether such measures are inconsistent with the General
Agreement.

In order to resolve this question and to ensure that Parties use
the procedures available to them under this Article, as interpreted
by this Agreement, in relevant cases:

a)   No Contracting Party shall take any measure restricting trade
with another Contracting Party pursuant to an agreement,
arrangement, or understanding with that Party, or at the request
of such other Party, where the measure would not be consistent with
the General Agreement in the absence of such agreement,
arrangement, understanding, or request.

b)   Nor shall any Contracting Party request another Contracting
Party to take such a measure.

c)   Any such measure being applied at the time of entry into force
of this agreement shall either be immediately brought into
conformity with this provision or be phased out in accordance with
paragraph 23.

0096

3-1

(별첨 2.)

30/10/31
체결세미나스

ARGENTINE PROPOSAL

PROHIBITION AND ELIMINATION OF CERTAIN MEASURES

22.-   No trade-restrictive measure shall be sought or taken
by a contracting party unless it conforms with the provisions
of Article XIX as interpreted by the provisions of this
agreement, or is specifically provided for in the General
Agreement, or protocols and agreements or arrangements
concluded within the framework of the General Agreement.
These include action taken by a single contracting party as
well as actions under agreements, arrangements and
understandings entered into by two or more contracting
parties. Any such measure in effect at the time of entry into
force of this agreement shall either be brought into
conformity with the provisions of Article XIX and this
agreement or phased out in accordance with paragraph 23
below.

0097

3-2

(別첨 3)

7 b...... At the same time, evidence shall be given that the increase of import is not due to the lack of competitiveness of the domestic industry in the importing country or to other foreseeable factors.

October 30, 1991

3~3

0098

외 무 부

종 별 :

번 호 : GVW-2434　　　　　　　　　　일 시 : 91 1125 1700

수 신 : 장 관(통기, 경기원, 상공부)

발 신 : 주 제네바대사

제 목 : UR/쎄이프가드 비공식 협의

연: GVW-2206

　　11.19 및 22 양일간 MACIEL 의장 주재하에 개최된 표제 비공식협의에서는 주로 금지 대상무역 제한 조치의 범위(91.6.6 사무국 TEXT MTN. GNG/RM/W/3 제 22항) 문제가 논의된 바, 동결과등을 아래 보고함. (이성주 참사관 참석)

　　1. 11.19 회의시 의장은 10.30 논의결과를 기초로 별첨 1 자신의 초안을 제시한바 이와 관련 아래의견이 표출됨.

　　- 홍콩, 카나다는 체약국이 동 초안 2번째 문장이 상정하는 조치(예: 반덤핑 조치 등)를 취하면서 과연 19조 상황을 이유로 내세우겠느냐 하면서 'TO REMEDY SITUATIONS ADDRESSED BY ART XIX'의 문제점을 지적하고, 인도도 이에 동조, 두번째문장에 많은 문제점이 있다는 의견 피력

　　- 호주, 인도등으로부터 첫째 문장의 'ANY SAFEGUARDMEASURES'를 'ANY TRADE RESTRICTIVE MEASURES'로 바꾸자는 의견이 있었으나, 미국은 반대

　　- 알젠틴은 금지대상 무역 제한 조치의 가장 확실한 판단 기준은 합치성(CONSISTENCY)일수밖에 없으며, 따라서 합치 여부를 둘러싼 상후분쟁 소지를 제거하기 위해서는 자국의 제안대로 'SPECIFICALLY PROVIDED FOR'가 최선의 방책임을 다시 강조

　　- 의장 초안이 갓트 19조 상황만을 다루고 있다는 점에서 자국의 의견이 상당히반영된 것으로 보는 미국은 아직도 범위가 광범위 하다는 점 및2번째 문장에 대해 구체적 논의 용의가 있다는점을 지적한 외에는 적극적인 의견 개진을 하지않음.

　　- 기타 호주, 뉴질랜드는 금지 대상조치가 가급적 광범위 해야 한다는 일반적 의견을 피력하였고, 브라질은 2번째 문장관련 여타 GATT 규정 및 협정에 일치하는 조치는 허용된다는 점이 불분명하다는 문제점을 지적.

통상국　　2차보　　경기원　　상공부

PAGE 1　　　　　　　　　　　　　　　　　91.11.26　　09:39 WH

외신 1과 통제관

0099

3. 11.22 회의시 의장은 새로이 자신의 수정초안(별첨 2)을 제시한바, 이에 대한 각국의 언급사항은 아래와 같음.

- 미국, EC 는 아직도 범위가 광범위하다고 보나 계속 토의 용의가 있음을 피력

- 놀웨이, 호주, 브라질등은 광범위한 범위를 선호 한다는 일반적 의견 반복

- 인도는 의장 초안의 FORMULATION 을 변경, 2번째 문장에서는 ~~KZE~~ 갓트 규정 및협정에 의해 최급되는 조치는 SG 협정의 범위 밖이라고(FFALL OUTSIDE THE PERVIEW OF SG AGREELIMENT) 규정하여 이를 일단 제외하고, 3번째 문장에 가서 여타의회색 조치를 다루는 방식으로 문안을 재구성하자는 의견을 제시한 바, 싱가폴이 이를 지지

4. 의장은 상기 양일간의 토의 결과를 종합, 금지대상 조치는 가급적 광범위해야한다는 것이 대체적인 의견이었으나, 어느정도 광범위해야 하는지의 여부가 문제라고 하면서, 인도가 제의한 방향에 따라 초안을 재작성해 보겠다고 함.

5. 한편, 11.19 협의시 스위스가 10.30 제시한 7항(B)관련 연호 수정안에 관한 협의도 있었는 바, 브라질, 파키스탄이 입증 책임은 가능한한 수입국이 많이 부담해야한 다는 차원에서 지지입장을, 인도도 수입증가와 피해 발생과의 인과관계를 강화하는 의미라면 지지 가능하다는 입장을 각각 표명한 반면, 다수국은 동 개념이 이미 7항(A) 또는 (B) 에 포함되어 있고 스위스 초안이 의도하는 바가 불분명하다고 하면서입장 표명을 유보

6. 기타, 91.6.6 초안 관련 의장은 아래와 같은 경미한 정정이 있을 것임을 언급함.

- 3항 B 의 6째줄 'ANY'를 'OR' 로 변경
- 20항 5째줄 'SHALL'을 'MAY'로 변경
- 16항 7째줄 'ANY MEANS' 를 'ANY ADEQUATE MEANS'로 변경

끝

첨부: 1. 91.11.19 자 의장초안
2. 91.11.22 자 의장초안)(GVW(F)-533)
(대사 박수길-국장)

18.11.1991

VI

22. A contracting party shall not take or seek any safeguard measures
unless such measures conform with the provisions of Article XIX of the
General Agreement to be applied in accordance with this agreement.   Nor
shall a contracting party seek or take measures under any other specific
provision of the General Agreement or protocols, agreements or arrangements
concluded within the framework of the General Agreement to remedy
situations addressed by Article XIX.   Neither shall a contracting party in
seeking to remedy such situations enter into agreements, arrangements or
understandings with another contracting party that would result in measures
inconsistent with the provisions of Article XIX.   Any such measures in
effect at the time of entry into force of this agreement shall either be
brought into conformity with the provisions of Article XIX as applied in
accordance with this agreement or phased out in accordance with
paragraph 23 below.[1]

---

[1]For the purpose of this agreement such measures shall include those
taken by a single contracting party to safeguard its own domestic industry
or the domestic industry of another contracting party, as well as similar
actions by two or more contracting parties, including voluntary restraint
agreement, voluntary export restraint agreement or other measures having a
similar effect.

SG/PARA22

533-2-1

0101

N4B2.
22/14/91

91. 11.22 외통양

PROHIBITION AND ELIMINATION OF CERTAIN MEASURES

A contracting party shall not take or seek any emergency action on imports
of particular products in the circumstances set forth in paragraph 1(a) of
Article XIX unless such action conforms with the provisions of Article XIX
of the General Agreement to be applied in accordance with this agreement.

Measures sought or taken by a contracting party so as to afford protection
to its domestic industry from imported products, which are not covered by
Article XIX and this agreement, shall be in conformity with other pertinent
provisions of the General Agreement, or protocols and agreements or
arrangements concluded within the framework of the General Agreement.

These include unilateral actions as well as actions under agreements,
arrangements and understandings entered into by two or more contracting
parties, such as voluntary export restraint agreements, orderly marketing
arrangements, price undertakings or other measures having a similar nature.

Such measures in effect at the time of entry into force of this agreement
shall be brought into conformity with the provisions of Article XIX and
this agreement, or with other pertinent provisions of the General
Agreement, protocols and agreements or arrangements concluded within the
framework of the General Agreement, or be phased out in accordance with
paragraph 23 below.

§33-2-2

0102

대 한 민 국
외 무 부

91 -   1991. 11. 21.

아래 문건을 수신자에게 전달하여 주시기 바랍니다.

제 목 : UR/세이프가드 협상(회벽조치) 관련 검토의견

수 신 : 상공부 국제협력과 (김 영민)
        (FAX NO : 503-9496, 503-3142)

발 신 : 외무부 통상기구과

(총 4 매)

0103

UR/세이프가드 협상(회색조치) 관련 검토 의견

미국이 제2차 세이프가드 협정안(91.6.62자) 제22조(회색조치)와 관련, 수정안을 제출한 것과 관련(GVW-2206) 이에 대한 검토 의견은 아래와 같음.

1. 미국의 수정안 제출 의도

가. Safeguards 협정안 22조에 따르면 무역제한 조치를 취할 수 있는 조치를
- 갓트 19조 및 Safeguards 협정에 일치하는 조치(세이프가드) 및
- 갓트협정상의 여타 조항이나, 갓트협정에 의거하여 체결된 의정서,
  협정 또는 협약에 근거한 조치
  로 규정함으로써 갓트협정이나 갓트협정에 근거하여 체결된 의정서,
  협정, 협약에 근거한 무역제한 조치만이 합법적으로 취해질 수 있으며,
  따라서 모든 회색조치의 발동 및 유지를 금지하고 있음.
  (이는 명시적으로 회색조치를 갓트에 불일치하는 조치로 규정하는 것은
  아니나 실질적으로 모든 회색조치의 발동·유지를 금지함으로써 Safeguards
  협정상 회색조치를 불법화시키는 효과를 가짐)

나. 이에 반해, 미측 수정안은 갓트협정에 근거하거나 갓트협정에 의거하여
  체결된 의정서, 협정 또는 협약에 근거한 조치에 대해서는 언급함이 없이,
  회색조치(measures taken pursuant to an agreement, arrangement or
  understanding between or among Contrading Parties or at the request
  of another Party)의 갓트 합치성 여부가 불확실하다고 체약국단이
  인정하도록 함(둘째 para.)과 동시에 회색조치를 Safeguards 협정상의
  금지 대상 조치의 범위에서 제외 시킴(4번째 para.)으로써 Safeguards
  협정하에서도 회색조치를 계속 유지할 수 있는 근거 마련을 시도하고 있는
  것으로 분석됨.

1

0104

o 이러한 미측의 의도는 수정안 4번째 para 단서조항인 "where the measure would not be consistent with the General Agreement in the absence of such agreement, arrangement, understanding or request"에 드러나 있음.

o 4번째 para.는 의도적으로 그 해석을 어렵게 하도록 drafting 되어 있는바, 이를 직역하면 "체약국은(근거가 되는) agreement, arrangement, understanding 혹은 request가 존재치 않을 경우 갓트 협정에 합치하지 않는 무역 제한조치를 취해서는 안된다"임

   - 이를 분석해 보면,

      1) 회색조치는 그 근거가 되는 agreement, arrangement, understanding 혹은 request에 의해 취해지게 마련인데도 불구하고, 그러한 agreement, arrangement, understanding 혹은 request가 없는 경우 갓트에 합치하지 않는 조치는 동 areement, arrangement, understanding 혹은 request에 의거하여 취할 수 없다고 규정함으로써 그 자체로서 논리적 모순이며

      2) 굳이 동 para에 논리적 의미를 부여한다면 "회색조치의 근거가 되는 agreement, arrangement, understanding 혹은 request가 철폐되거나 시효가 만료되어 종료 되었음에도 불구하고 이에 근거하여 취해졌던 회색조치를 계속해서 취할 수 없다"는 해석은 가능할 것임.

      3) 가장 중요한 것은 미국이 수정안 둘째 para에서 제안한 바와 같이 회색조치의 근거가 되는 agreement, arrangement, understanding 혹은 request의 갓트 위반 여부가 불분명하다고 체약국단이 인정하는 경우, 동 agreement, arrangement, understanding 혹은 request가 갓트에 불일치하는 것은 아니라는 주장이 가능(이에 대해 효과적인 반론 제기가 불가능)하므로 4번째 para, 특히 where 이하 단서조항의 해석과 관련, 회색조치의 근거가 되는 agreement, arrangement, understanding 혹은 request가 존재하는한(효력을 갖는한) 이에 근거한 회색조치를 발동 또는 유지할 수 있다는 논리가 가능케 됨.

2

0105

o 결국 미측은 회색조치의 갓트 합치성 여부를 불분명하게 하고 이를
체약국단이 인정토록 함으로써, 관련 agreement, arrangement,
understanding 혹은 request가 존재하는 경우 이에 근거한 회색조치가
갓트협정에 위반하는 조치가 아니라는 해석을 가능케 함으로써 회색
조치의 발동내지 유지에 제한을 받지 않도록 하려는 의도이며, 따라서
미측의 수정안은 제2차 Safeguards 협정 22조의 취지(회색조치 철폐)에
정면으로 배치되는 제안임.

2. 기타 minor point로서, 의장안 22조는 회색조치의 유형으로서 actions taken by
a single contracting party, 즉 동 actions의 근거가 되는 법적문서(agreement,
arrangement 혹은 understanding)가 존재치 않는 조치를 열거하고 있는데 반해
미측 수정안에는 이에 대한 명시적인 표현이 없음. 단, measures taken at the
request of another party(미측 수정안 첫번째 para 말미)가 이에 해당한다는
해석이 가능함.

3. 미측 수정안에 대한 검토 의견
    상기 분석대로 미측은 회색조치의 근거가 되는 agreement, arrangement,
    understanding, request의 갓트 합치 여부가 불분명하다는 점을 공인토록 함으로써
    이에 근거한 회색조치의 발동 및 유지를 가능케 하려는 의도로 분석되며, 이러한
    미측의 의도는 모든 회색조치를 Safeguards 협정을 통해 불법화하여 3-4년내에
    모두 철폐시키려는 협상 목표에 정면으로 위배되므로, 제2차 Safeguards 협정안
    고수가 바람직함.   끝.

3

외　무　부

종　별 :

번　호 : GVW-2459　　　　　　　　　일　시 : 91 1127 1030

수　신 : 장 관(봉기, 경기원,재무부,상공부)

발　신 : 주 제네바 대사

제　목 : UR/세이프가드 비공식 협의

연: GVW-2434

1. 11.26 표제 비공식 협의(MACIEL 의장주재)에서는 11.22 협의시 인도가 제시한방향에따라 MACIEL 의장이 사무국과 협조 재작성,제시한 22항에 관한 새로운 문안(별첨)을 일부문안 수정 및 재배열을 거쳐 WORKING TEXT 로잠정적으로 합의함.(이성주참사관 참석)

2. 이에 따라 MACIEL 의장은 상기 조항을 포함한 새로운 WORKING PAPER 를 11.28(목) 11:00 개최예정인 규범제정분야 공식회의에 제출키로하였음.

3. 상세 토의 내용은 아래와 같음.

- 의장 제시문안 (A)항은 당연한 (OBVIOUS)내용의 언급에 불과하긴 하지만, 22항전체문맥(CONTEXT)상 유지가 필요하다는 점에 모든참가국이 의견 일치

- (C) 항의 INDICATIVE LIST 에 대해서는 멕시코, 알젠틴을 제외한 대다수 국가가 유용성을 인정

- 한편 (B) 항을 보조금 CODE 각주 38 및 반덤핑 코드 각주 16과 같은 형식으로각주화하자는의견이 호주, 카나다로 부터 제시되고 미국이 호의적반응을 보였으나,인 도, 싱가폴등이 전혀 CONTEXT가 다르다는 점등을 이유로 반대입장 표명..-논의의촛 점은 (C)항 'OTHER MEASURES OF ASIMILAR NATURE'에 모아졌는바, 홍콩은 'OREFFECT'을 추가할것을, 일본은 'OTHER MEASURESWHICH RESTRICT EXPORTS AND IMPORTSSO AS TO AFFORDPROTECTION TO DOMESTIC INDUSTRY OF IMPORTING COUNTRY FROMIMPORTED PRODUCTS'로의 수정을 제의함.

- 상기 양제의에 대해 미국은 모두 반대입장을 표명하고, 특히 일본 제안에 대해서는 최근수주간의 논의를 다시 원점으로 돌리는 것이라평가(미국은 구체적으로 어떠한 조치가 금지 대상이되는지 불명확한 상태로 금지 약속을 하기어렵다는 점을

통상국 상공부	장관	차관	1차보	2차보	청와대	안기부	경기원	재무부

PAGE 1

강조)

 - 의장은 일본제의가 수입측면을 강조한점 및자신의 문안 (C) 항 'THAT ARE NO
CONSISTENT.,.,.'이하의 문단으로 2중 수식(DOUBLE QUALIFIER)됨을 지적하면서
미국의우려는 지나치다고언급하고 ' OR ANY OTHER MEASURES OF SIMILAR
NATUREDESIGNED TOAFFORD .., UNLESS THEY ARE CONSISTENT .. '로WORKING TEXT 를
작성하겠다는 뜻을표명 (이에대해 미국의 반대의사 표시 없었음)

 - 또한 홍콩은 22항 전체의 논리상 (C) 항을 서두에 FURTHUR MORE 등의 접속사를
붙여서 (A)항 바로뒤에 연결시킬것을 제의한바 이에 대해다수국이 동조

 - 한편 EC 는 22항 전체를 괄호처리 할것을주장했으나, 대부분의 국가가 반대(특히
홍콩이강경) 함으로써 의장이 공식회의 제출시 구두또는 INTRODUCTORY COVER 등을
통해 이의 제기가있었다는 점을 밝히는 선에서 절충

 - 기타 호주가 농산물, 섬유 협상등에서 새로이 정립될 잠정적 합의(TRANSITIONAL
ARRANGEMENTS)사항에 관한 규정 마련 필요성을 제기하였으나,인도가 반대 (B
항에의하여 COVER 될 뿐아니라 잠정적 성격의 SG 와 항구적 성격의SG 의 명백한 구분
필요) 하였고 또한 호주 및홍콩이 (B) 항, (C) 항의 GATT 규정 및 여타협정등과의
일치성(CONSINTENCY) 판단 주체가 불명하다는 문제를, 인도는 (C)항이 GATT 및여타
협정등과 일치하는 VER.OMA 가 있을수있다는 해석이 가능할 수도 있다는
문제점을제기하였으나 이에 대한 특별한 관심 표명이나토의는 없었음.

 첨부: 22항 관련 91.11.26 의장문안. 끝

 (GVW(F)-544)

 (대사 박수길-국장)

1VW(下)-0544 -26 /030

"GVW-245 P 첨부"

26.11.91

PROHIBITION AND ELIMINATION OF CERTAIN MEASURES

22. (a) A contracting party shall not take or seek any emergency action
         on imports of particular products in the circumstances set forth
         in paragraph 1(a) of Article XIX unless such action conforms with
         the provisions of Article XIX of the General Agreement applied
         in accordance with this agreement.

    (b) Measures sought or taken by a contracting party so as to afford
         protection to its domestic industry from imported products which
         are covered by other provisions of the General Agreement, or
         protocols and agreements or arrangements concluded within the
         framework of the General Agreement, and are in conformity with
         these provisions and instruments, are not included in the scope
         of this agreement.

    (c) A contracting party shall not seek, take or maintain any
         voluntary export restraints, orderly marketing arrangements,
         price undertakings or other measures of a similar nature on the
         export or the import side that are not consistent with the
         General Agreement, or protocols and agreements or arrangements
         concluded within the framework of the General Agreement. These
         include actions taken by a single contracting party as well as
         actions under agreements, arrangements and understandings entered
         into by two or more contracting parties. Any such measure in
         effect at the time of entry into force of this agreement shall be
         brought into conformity with this provision or phased out, in
         accordance with paragraph 23 below.

1-1

0109

외 무 부

종 별 :

번 호 : GVW-2519

일 시 : 91 1129 1930

수 신 : 장 관(봉기, 경기원, 재무부, 상공부)

발 신 : 주 제네바대사

제 목 : UR/세이프가드

연: GVW-2434

연호 11.26 비공식 협의 결과에 따라 11.28규범제정 분야 공식회의시 배포된 세이프가드분야WORKING TEXT를 별첨 송부함.

(GVW(F)-0561). 끝

(대사 박수길-국장)

통상국   2차보   경기원   재무부   상공부

PAGE 1

91.11.30   09:34 WH

외신 1과 통제관

0110

DRAFT AGREEMENT ON SAFEGUARDS

PREAMBLE

The CONTRACTING PARTIES:

Having in mind the overall objective of the contracting parties to improve and strengthen the international trading system based on the General Agreement on Tariffs and Trade;

Recognizing the need to clarify and reinforce the disciplines of the General Agreement, and specifically those of its Article XIX (Emergency Action on Imports of Particular Products), to re-establish multilateral control over safeguards and eliminate measures that escape such control;

Recognizing the importance of structural adjustment and the need to enhance rather than limit competition in international markets; and

Recognizing further that, for these purposes, a comprehensive agreement, applicable to all contracting parties and based on the basic principles of the General Agreement, is called for;

Hereby agree as follows:

- 2 -

I

GENERAL

1. This agreement establishes rules for the application of safeguard measures which shall be understood to mean those measures provided for in Article XIX of the General Agreement.

II

CONDITIONS

2. A contracting party[1] may apply a safeguard measure to a product only if the importing contracting party has determined, pursuant to the provisions set out below, that such product is being imported into its territory in such increased quantities, absolute or relative to domestic production, and under such conditions as to cause or threaten to cause serious injury to the domestic industry that produces like or directly competitive products.

3. (a) A contracting party may apply a safeguard measure only following an investigation by the competent authorities of the importing contracting party pursuant to procedures previously established and made public in consonance with Article X of the General Agreement. This investigation shall include reasonable public notice to all interested parties and public hearings or other appropriate means in which importers, exporters and other interested parties could present evidence and their views, including the opportunity to respond to the presentations of other parties and to submit their views, inter alia, as to whether or not the application of a safeguard measure would be in the public interest. The competent authorities shall publish a report setting forth their findings and reasoned conclusions reached on all pertinent issues of fact and law.

---

[1] A customs union may apply a safeguard measure as a single unit or on behalf of a member state. When a customs union applies a safeguard measure as a single unit, all the requirements for the determination of serious injury or threat thereof under this agreement shall be based on the conditions existing in the customs union as a whole. When a safeguard measure is applied on behalf of a member state, all the requirements for the determination of serious injury or threat thereof shall be based on the conditions existing in that member state and the measure shall be limited to that member state. Nothing in this agreement prejudges the interpretation of the relationship between Article XIX and Article XXIV:8 of the General Agreement.

0112

RM/SGA *561-10-2*

- 3 -

(b) Any information which is by nature confidential or which is provided on a confidential basis shall, upon cause being shown, be treated as such by the competent authorities. Such information shall not be disclosed without permission of the party submitting it. Parties providing confidential information may be requested to furnish non-confidential summaries thereof or, if such parties indicate that such information cannot be summarized, the reasons why a summary cannot be provided. However, if the competent authorities find that a request for confidentiality is not warranted and if the party concerned is either unwilling to make the information public or to authorize its disclosure in generalized or summary form, the authorities would be free to disregard such information unless it can be demonstrated to their satisfaction from appropriate sources that the information is correct.

4.   In critical circumstances where delay would cause damage which it would be difficult to repair, a provisional safeguard measure may be taken pursuant to a preliminary determination that there is clear evidence that increased imports have caused or are threatening to cause serious injury. The duration of the provisional measure shall not exceed 200 days, during which period the pertinent requirements of this Section and Section VII shall be met. Such measures should take the form of tariff increases to be promptly refunded if the subsequent investigation referred to in paragraph 7 below does not determine that increased imports have caused or threatened to cause serious injury to a domestic industry. The duration of any such provisional measure shall count towards the initial period and any extension referred to in paragraphs 10, 11 and 12 below.

5.   Safeguard measures shall be applied to a product being imported irrespective of its source.

6.   For the purposes of this agreement:

(a) serious injury shall be understood to mean a significant overall impairment in the position of a domestic industry;

(b) in determining injury, a domestic industry shall be understood to mean the producers as a whole of the like or directly competitive products operating within the territory of a contracting party, or those whose collective output of the like or directly competitive products constitutes a major proportion [, i.e. normally 50 per cent or more but in no case less than 33 per cent,] of the total domestic production of those products; and

- 4 -

(c) threat of serious injury shall be understood to mean serious injury that is clearly imminent, in accordance with the provisions of paragraph 7 below. A determination of the existence of a threat of serious injury shall be based on facts and not merely on allegation, conjecture or remote possibility.

7. (a) In the investigation to determine whether increased imports have caused or are threatening to cause serious injury to a domestic industry under the terms of this agreement, the competent authorities shall evaluate all relevant factors of an objective and quantifiable nature having a bearing on the situation of that industry, in particular, the rate and amount of the increase in imports of the product concerned in absolute and relative terms, the share of the domestic market taken by increased imports, changes in the level of sales, production, productivity, capacity utilization, profits and losses, and employment.

(b) The determination referred to in sub-paragraph 7(a) shall not be made unless this investigation demonstrates, on the basis of objective evidence, the existence of the causal link between increased imports of the product concerned and serious injury or threat thereof. When factors other than increased imports are causing injury to the domestic industry at the same time, such injury shall not be attributed to increased imports.

(c) The competent authorities shall publish promptly, in accordance with the provisions of paragraph 3 above, a detailed analysis of the case under investigation as well as a demonstration of the relevance of the factors examined.

8. Safeguard measures shall be applied only to the extent as may be necessary to prevent or remedy serious injury and to facilitate adjustment. Contracting parties should choose measures most suitable for the achievement of these objectives.

9. [No quantitative restriction shall reduce the quantity of imports below the level of a recent representative period which shall normally be the average of imports in the last three representative years for which statistics are available.] [In cases in which a quota is allocated among supplying countries, and in the absence of agreement with the suppliers concerned, the importing contracting party may allot quota shares proportionately to the quantities supplied during the previous representative period, subject to the possibility of taking into account clear evidence on the extent each supplier has contributed to the assessed global injury, provided that any modification in individual quota allotments necessary to remedy injury may not exceed five percentage points or 30 per cent of the proportion supplied during the representative period, whichever is the smaller. No such modification shall be applied to contracting parties whose market share of the product concerned does not exceed one per cent. Whenever any such modification occurs, the importing contracting party shall provide justification as to the reasons for it.]

RM/SGA   561-10-∅   0114

- 5 -

10.   Safeguard measures shall be applied only for a period of time as may be necessary to prevent or remedy serious injury and to facilitate adjustment. It shall not exceed four years, unless this is extended under paragraph 11 below.

11.   The period mentioned in paragraph 10 above may be extended provided that the competent authorities of the importing contracting party have determined, in conformity with the procedures set out in this Section, that: the safeguard measure continues to be necessary to prevent or remedy serious injury; that there is evidence that the industry is adjusting; and that the pertinent provisions of Sections III and VII below are observed.

12.   The total period of a safeguard measure including the period of application of any provisional measure, the period of initial application, and any extension thereof shall not exceed eight years.

13.   In order to facilitate adjustment, if the expected duration of a safeguard measure as notified under the provisions of paragraph 25 is over one year, it shall be progressively liberalized at regular intervals during the period of application. If the duration of the measure exceeds three years, the contracting party applying such a measure shall review the situation not later than the mid-term of the measure and, if appropriate, withdraw it or increase the pace of liberalization. A measure extended under paragraph 10 above shall not be more restrictive than it was at the end of the initial period, and should continue to be liberalized.

14.   No safeguard measure shall be applied again to the import of a product which has been subject to such a measure, taken after the date of entry into force of this agreement, for a period of time equal to that during which such measure had been previously applied, provided that the period of non-application is at least two years.

15.   Notwithstanding the provisions of paragraph 14 above, a safeguard measure with a duration of 180 days or less may be applied again to the import of a product if:

   (a)   at least one year has elapsed since the date of introduction of a safeguard measure on the import of that product; and

   (b)   such a safeguard measure has not been applied on the same product more than twice in the five-year period immediately preceding the date of introduction of the measure.

0115

RM/SGA

- 6 -

III

LEVEL OF CONCESSIONS AND OTHER OBLIGATIONS

16. A contracting party proposing to apply a safeguard measure or seeking an extension shall endeavour to maintain a substantially equivalent level of concessions and other obligations to that existing between it and the exporting contracting parties which would be affected by such a measure under the General Agreement, in accordance with the provisions of paragraph 27 below. To achieve this objective, the contracting parties concerned may agree on any adequate means of trade compensation for the adverse effects of the measure on their trade.

17. If no agreement is reached within 30 days in the consultations under paragraph 27 below, then the affected exporting contracting parties are free, not later than 90 days after the measure is applied, to suspend, upon the expiration of 30 days from the day on which written notice of such suspension is received by the CONTRACTING PARTIES, the application of substantially equivalent concessions or other obligations under the General Agreement, to the trade of the contracting party applying the safeguard measure, the suspension of which the CONTRACTING PARTIES do not disapprove.

18. The right of suspension referred to in paragraph 17 above shall not be exercised if the duration of the measure does not exceed three years, provided such a measure conforms to this agreement.

IV

DEVELOPING COUNTRIES

[19. Safeguard measures shall not be applied against a product originating in a less-developed contracting party whose market share in the product concerned does not exceed one per cent.]

20. Less-developed and least-developed contracting parties shall have the right to extend the period of application of a safeguard measure for a period of up to two years beyond the maximum period provided for in paragraph 12 above. Notwithstanding the provisions of paragraph 14 above, less-developed and least-developed contracting parties may apply a safeguard measure again to the import of a product which has been subject to such a measure, taken after the date of entry into force of this agreement, for a period of time equal to half that during which such a measure has been previously applied, provided that the period of non-application is at least two years.

RM/SGA

0116

- 7 -

V

EXISTING ARTICLE XIX MEASURES

21. Contracting parties shall terminate all existing safeguard measures taken pursuant to Article XIX of the General Agreement not later than eight years after the date on which they were first applied or [five] [six] years after the date of entry into force of this agreement, whichever comes later.

VI

PROHIBITION AND ELIMINATION OF CERTAIN MEASURES

22. (a) A contracting party shall not take or seek any emergency action on imports of particular products in the circumstances set forth in paragraph 1(a) of Article XIX unless such action conforms with the provisions of Article XIX of the General Agreement applied in accordance with this agreement.

(b) Furthermore, a contracting party shall not seek, take or maintain any voluntary export restraints, orderly marketing arrangements, price undertakings or any other measures of a similar nature on the export or the import side designed to afford protection to domestic industry, not consistent with the General Agreement, or protocols and agreements or arrangements concluded within the framework of the General Agreement. These include actions taken by a single contracting party as well as actions under agreements, arrangements and understandings entered into by two or more contracting parties. Any such measure in effect at the time of entry into force of this agreement shall be brought into conformity with this provision or phased out, in accordance with paragraph 23 below.

(c) Measures sought or taken by a contracting party so as to afford protection to its domestic industry from imported products which are covered by other provisions of the General Agreement, or protocols and agreements or arrangements concluded within the framework of the General Agreement, and are in conformity with these provisions and instruments, are not included in the scope of this agreement.

23. The provisions of paragraph 22 above shall be carried out according to timetables to be presented to the Safeguards Committee by the contracting parties concerned not later than 180 days after the date of entry into force of this agreement. These timetables shall provide for all measures referred to in paragraph 22 above to be phased out or brought into conformity with this agreement within a period not exceeding [three] [four] years, [subject to exceptions up to a maximum of eight years, set out in Annex 1.] after the date of entry into force of this agreement.

RM/SGA

0117

maintenance by public and private enterprises of non-governmental measures
equivalent to those ref⸻d to in paragraph 22 above.

VII

NOTIFICATION AND CONSULTATION

25. A contracting party shall immediately notify the CONTRACTING PARTIES
upon:

> (a) initiating an investigatory process relating to serious injury or
> threat thereof and the reasons for it;
>
> (b) making a finding of serious injury or threat thereof caused by
> increased imports; and
>
> (c) taking a decision to apply or extend a safeguard measure.

26. In making the notifications referred to in sub-paragraphs 25(b)
and (c) above, the contracting party proposing to apply or extend a
safeguard measure shall provide the CONTRACTING PARTIES with all pertinent
information, which shall include evidence of serious injury or threat
thereof caused by increased imports, precise description of the product
involved and the proposed measure, proposed date of introduction, expected
duration and timetable for progressive liberalization. In the case of an
extension of a measure, evidence that the industry concerned is adjusting
shall also be provided. The CONTRACTING PARTIES or the Safeguards
Committee may request such additional information as they may consider
necessary from the contracting party proposing to apply or extend the
measure.

27. A contracting party proposing to apply or extend a safeguard measure
shall provide adequate opportunity for prior consultations with those
contracting parties having a substantial interest as exporters of the
product concerned, with a view to, inter alia, reviewing the information
provided under paragraph 26 above, exchanging views on the measure and
reaching an understanding on ways to achieve the objective set out in
paragraph 16 above.

28. A contracting party shall make a notification before taking a
provisional safeguard measure referred to in paragraph 4 above.
Consultations shall be initiated immediately after the measure is taken.

29. The results of the consultations referred to in this Section, as well
as the results of mid-term reviews referred to in paragraph 13, any form of
compensation referred to in paragraph 16, and proposed suspensions of
concessions and other obligations referred to in paragraph 17, shall be
notified immediately to the CONTRACTING PARTIES by the contracting parties
concerned.

RM/SGA

561-10-8

0118

- 9 -

30. Contracting parties shall notify promptly the CONTRACTING PARTIES of their laws, regulations and administrative procedures relating to safeguard measures as well as any modifications made to them.

31. Contracting parties maintaining measures described in paragraphs 21 and 22 above which exist at the date on which this agreement enters into force shall notify such measures to the CONTRACTING PARTIES, not later than 60 days after the entry into force of this agreement.

32. Any contracting party may notify the CONTRACTING PARTIES of all laws, regulations, administrative procedures and any measure or action dealt with in this agreement that has not been notified by other contracting parties that are required by this agreement to make such notifications.

33. Any contracting party may notify the CONTRACTING PARTIES of any non-governmental measures referred to in paragraph 24 above.

34. All notifications to the CONTRACTING PARTIES referred to in this agreement shall normally be made through the Safeguards Committee.

35. The provisions on notification in this agreement shall not require any contracting party to disclose confidential information which would impede law enforcement or otherwise be contrary to the public interest or would prejudice the legitimate commercial interests of particular enterprises, public or private.

VIII

SURVEILLANCE

36. There shall be a Safeguards Committee under the authority of the CONTRACTING PARTIES, which shall be open to the participation of any contracting party indicating its wish to serve on it. The Committee will have the following functions:

(a) to monitor, and report annually to the CONTRACTING PARTIES on, the general implementation of this agreement and make recommendations towards its improvement;

(b) to find, upon request of an affected contracting party, whether or not the procedural requirements of this agreement have been complied with in connection with a safeguard measure, and report its findings to the CONTRACTING PARTIES;

(c) to assist contracting parties, if they so request, in their consultations under the provisions of this agreement;

(d) to examine measures covered by paragraphs 21 and 22, monitor the phase-out of such measures and report as appropriate to the CONTRACTING PARTIES;

RM/SGA

0119

- 10 -

(e) to review, at the request of the contracting party taking a safeguard action, whether proposals to suspend concessions or other obligations are "substantially equivalent", and report as appropriate to the CONTRACTING PARTIES;

(f) to receive and review all notifications provided for in this agreement and report as appropriate to the CONTRACTING PARTIES; and

(g) to perform any other function connected with this agreement that the CONTRACTING PARTIES may determine.

37. To assist the Committee in carrying out its surveillance function, the secretariat shall prepare annually a factual report on the operation of the agreement based on notifications and other reliable information available to it.

IX

DISPUTE SETTLEMENT

38. Consultations and the settlement of disputes with respect to any matter affecting the operation of this instrument shall be subject to the rules and procedures of Articles XXII and XXIII of the General Agreement, and the dispute settlement rules and procedures as adopted by the CONTRACTING PARTIES.

RM/SGA

0120

외 무 부

종 별 :

번 호 : GVW-2631   일 시 : 91 1214 1830

수 신 : 장 관(통기, 경기원, 재무부, 상공부)

발 신 : 주 제네바 대사

제 목 : UR/세이프가드 비공식 회의

연: GVW-2434

1. 12.13(금) 표제회의가 MACIEL 의장 주재로 개최되어 11.28 자 의장 초안을 수정한 별첨 의장 초안을 중심으로 협의가 진행되었는바, 새로운 의장 초안은 11.28 자 의장 초안상의 괄호들을 전부 정리한 초안으로서 지금까지 논란이 되어온 9 항(QUOTA MODULATION)의 괄호도 동시에 삭제함으로써 사실상 QM 을 수용하고 있음에 따라 아국, 홍콩, 싱가폴, 일본, 파키스탄, 스위스, 알젠틴, 멕시코, 인도, 브라질등은 동 협상 분야의 대다수 참가국들이 공봉되게 QM 을 반대하고 있음에도 불구하고 1-2 개국의 입장이 의장 초안상에 반영된점에 강한 이의를제기하고, 현 의장 초안에서 수출국들이 QM 을 제외한 회색조치등 여타분야에서 많은 양보를 한 만큼 수입국측에서도 QM 을 양보하는 것이 협상의 균형에 맞는다고 주장한 반면, 이씨는 자신은 균형된 협정 문안을 원할뿐 이라는 반응을 보였고 미국은 동문제에 대한 양측의 여하한 타결도 수락할 용의가 있음을 시사하였음.(김서기관 참석)

2. 상기 QM 이외에 금번 회의에 제기된 사항은 아래와 같음.

가. 23 항 말미의 ANNEX 1 내용에 대한 구체적인 협의가 지금까지 없었으며, 현 의장 초안 내용대로 ANNEX 1 이 공란으로 TNC 에 보고될수 없을 것이라는 의견이 제시됨에 따라 의장은 ANNEX 1 에 예외적인 회색조치의 명기를 희망하는 국가는 12.15(일) 정오까지 동 내용을 자신에게 통보할 것을 요청함.

나. 22 항(B) 의 회색조치 내용 명기와 관련, 동 내용을 보다 자세히 예시적으로 명기하자는 의견 제기

다. 7 페이지 주 1 의 내용이 QM 과 관련이 있어 보이는 만큼 삭제 희망

라. 9 항 첫째 문장 UNLESS 이하가 자의적으로 해석될 가능성이 있을 것이라는 의견 제시

통상국   2차보   경기원   재무부   상공부

3. 의장은 12.15(일) 15:00 비공식 회의를 개최하여 금일 거론된 문제들을 다시 협의키로 함.

첨부: 12.13 자 의장초안 1 부. 끝

(GVW(F)-619)

(대사 박수길-국장)

예고 91.12.31. 까지

주 제 네 바 대 표 부

번 호 : GVW(F) - 61P   년월일 : 11.2.14   시간 : 18:00

수 신 : 장 관 (통기, 경기원, 재무부, 상공부)

발 신 : 주 제 네 바 대 사

제 목 : " 첨부 "

총   매 (표지포합)

보 안 봄 제	

외신과 통 제	

61P—12—1

0123

13 December 1991

DRAFT AGREEMENT ON SAFEGUARDS

PREAMBLE

The CONTRACTING PARTIES:

Having in mind the overall objective of the contracting parties to improve and strengthen the international trading system based on the General Agreement on Tariffs and Trade;

Recognizing the need to clarify and reinforce the disciplines of the General Agreement, and specifically those of its Article XIX (Emergency Action on Imports of Particular Products), to re-establish multilateral control over safeguards and eliminate measures that escape such control;

Recognizing the importance of structural adjustment and the need to enhance rather than limit competition in international markets; and

Recognizing further that, for these purposes, a comprehensive agreement, applicable to all contracting parties and based on the basic principles of the General Agreement, is called for;

Hereby agree as follows:

RM/SGA1

0124

- 2 -

I

GENERAL

1.   This agreement establishes rules for the application of safeguard measures which shall be understood to mean those measures provided for in Article XIX of the General Agreement.

II

CONDITIONS

2.   A contracting party[1] may apply a safeguard measure to a product only if the importing contracting party has determined, pursuant to the provisions set out below, that such product is being imported into its territory in such increased quantities, absolute or relative to domestic production, and under such conditions as to cause or threaten to cause serious injury to the domestic industry that produces like or directly competitive products.

3.   (a)   A contracting party may apply a safeguard measure only following an investigation by the competent authorities of the importing contracting party pursuant to procedures previously established and made public in consonance with Article X of the General Agreement. This investigation shall include reasonable public notice to all interested parties and public hearings or other appropriate means in which importers, exporters and other interested parties could present evidence and their views, including the opportunity to respond to the presentations of other parties and to submit their views, <u>inter alia</u>, as to whether or not the application of a safeguard measure would be in the public interest. The competent authorities shall publish a report setting forth their findings and reasoned conclusions reached on all pertinent issues of fact and law.

_____

[1]A customs union may apply a safeguard measure as a single unit or on behalf of a member state. When a customs union applies a safeguard measure as a single unit, all the requirements for the determination of serious injury or threat thereof under this agreement shall be based on the conditions existing in the customs union as a whole. When a safeguard measure is applied on behalf of a member state, all the requirements for the determination of serious injury or threat thereof shall be based on the conditions existing in that member state and the measure shall be limited to that member state. Nothing in this agreement prejudges the interpretation of the relationship between Article XIX and Article XXIV:8 of the General Agreement.

0125

RM/SGA1

- 3 -

(b) Any information which is by nature confidential or which is
     provided on a confidential basis shall, upon cause being shown,
     be treated as such by the competent authorities. Such
     information shall not be disclosed without permission of the
     party submitting it. Parties providing confidential information
     may be requested to furnish non-confidential summaries thereof
     or, if such parties indicate that such information cannot be
     summarized, the reasons why a summary cannot be provided.
     However, if the competent authorities find that a request for
     confidentiality is not warranted and if the party concerned is
     either unwilling to make the information public or to authorize
     its disclosure in generalized or summary form, the authorities
     would be free to disregard such information unless it can be
     demonstrated to their satisfaction from appropriate sources that
     the information is correct.

4.   In critical circumstances where delay would cause damage which it
would be difficult to repair, a provisional safeguard measure may be taken
pursuant to a preliminary determination that there is clear evidence that
increased imports have caused or are threatening to cause serious injury.
The duration of the provisional measure shall not exceed 200 days, during
which period the pertinent requirements of this Section and Section VII
shall be met. Such measures should take the form of tariff increases to be
promptly refunded if the subsequent investigation referred to in
paragraph 7 below does not determine that increased imports have caused or
threatened to cause serious injury to a domestic industry. The duration of
any such provisional measure shall count towards the initial period and any
extension referred to in paragraphs 10, 11 and 12 below.

5.   Safeguard measures shall be applied to a product being imported
irrespective of its source.

6.   For the purposes of this agreement:

(a) serious injury shall be understood to mean a significant overall
     impairment in the position of a domestic industry;

(b) in determining injury, a domestic industry shall be understood to
     mean the producers as a whole of the like or directly competitive
     products operating within the territory of a contracting party,
     or those whose collective output of the like or directly
     competitive products constitutes a major proportion of the total
     domestic production of those products; and

0126

RM/SGA1

- 4 -

(c) threat of serious injury shall be understood to mean serious injury that is clearly imminent, in accordance with the provisions of paragraph 7 below. A determination of the existence of a threat of serious injury shall be based on facts and not merely on allegation, conjecture or remote possibility.

7. (a) In the investigation to determine whether increased imports have caused or are threatening to cause serious injury to a domestic industry under the terms of this agreement, the competent authorities shall evaluate all relevant factors of an objective and quantifiable nature having a bearing on the situation of that industry, in particular, the rate and amount of the increase in imports of the product concerned in absolute and relative terms, the share of the domestic market taken by increased imports, changes in the level of sales, production, productivity, capacity utilization, profits and losses, and employment.

(b) The determination referred to in sub-paragraph 7(a) shall not be made unless this investigation demonstrates, on the basis of objective evidence, the existence of the causal link between increased imports of the product concerned and serious injury or threat thereof. When factors other than increased imports are causing injury to the domestic industry at the same time, such injury shall not be attributed to increased imports.

(c) The competent authorities shall publish promptly, in accordance with the provisions of paragraph 3 above, a detailed analysis of the case under investigation as well as a demonstration of the relevance of the factors examined.

8. Safeguard measures shall be applied only to the extent as may be necessary to prevent or remedy serious injury and to facilitate adjustment. Contracting parties should choose measures most suitable for the achievement of these objectives.

9. No quantitative restriction shall reduce the quantity of imports below the level of a recent period which shall be the average of imports in the last three representative years for which statistics are available, unless clear justification is given that a different level is necessary to remedy serious injury. In cases in which a quota is allocated among supplying countries, and in the absence of agreement with the suppliers concerned, the importing contracting party may allot quota shares proportionately to the quantities supplied during the previous representative period, subject to the possibility of taking into account clear evidence on the extent each supplier has contributed to the assessed global injury, provided that any modification in individual quota allotments necessary to remedy injury may not exceed five percentage points or 30 per cent of the proportion supplied during the representative period, whichever is the smaller, and provided the CONTRACTING PARTIES do not disapprove. No such modification shall be applied to contracting parties whose market share of the product concerned does not exceed one per cent. Whenever any such modification occurs, the importing contracting party shall provide justification as to the reasons for it.

- 5 -

10.   Safeguard measures shall be applied only for a period of time as may be necessary to prevent or remedy serious injury and to facilitate adjustment.   It shall not exceed four years, unless this is extended under paragraph 11 below.

11.   The period mentioned in paragraph 10 above may be extended provided that the competent authorities of the importing contracting party have determined, in conformity with the procedures set out in this Section, that: the safeguard measure continues to be necessary to prevent or remedy serious injury;   that there is evidence that the industry is adjusting; and that the pertinent provisions of Sections III and VII below are observed.

12.   The total period of a safeguard measure including the period of application of any provisional measure, the period of initial application, and any extension thereof shall not exceed eight years.

13.   In order to facilitate adjustment, if the expected duration of a safeguard measure as notified under the provisions of paragraph 23 is over one year, it shall be progressively liberalized at regular intervals during the period of application.   If the duration of the measure exceeds three years, the contracting party applying such a measure shall review the situation not later than the mid-term of the measure and, if appropriate, withdraw it or increase the pace of liberalization.   A measure extended under paragraph 10 above shall not be more restrictive than it was at the end of the initial period, and should continue to be liberalized.

14.   No safeguard measure shall be applied again to the import of a product which has been subject to such a measure, taken after the date of entry into force of this agreement, for a period of time equal to that during which such measure had been previously applied, provided that the period of non-application is at least two years.

15.   Notwithstanding the provisions of paragraph 14 above, a safeguard measure with a duration of 180 days or less may be applied again to the import of a product if:

   (a)   at least one year has elapsed since the date of introduction of a safeguard measure on the import of that product;   and

   (b)   such a safeguard measure has not been applied on the same product more than twice in the five-year period immediately preceding the date of introduction of the measure.

0128

RM/SGA1

67P-12-6

- 6 -

III

LEVEL OF CONCESSIONS AND OTHER OBLIGATIONS

16. A contracting party proposing to apply a safeguard measure or seeking an extension shall endeavour to maintain a substantially equivalent level of concessions and other obligations to that existing between it and the exporting contracting parties which would be affected by such a measure under the General Agreement, in accordance with the provisions of paragraph 27 below. To achieve this objective, the contracting parties concerned may agree on any adequate means of trade compensation for the adverse effects of the measure on their trade.

17. If no agreement is reached within 30 days in the consultations under paragraph 27 below, then the affected exporting contracting parties are free, not later than 90 days after the measure is applied, to suspend, upon the expiration of 30 days from the day on which written notice of such suspension is received by the CONTRACTING PARTIES, the application of substantially equivalent concessions or other obligations under the General Agreement, to the trade of the contracting party applying the safeguard measure, the suspension of which the CONTRACTING PARTIES do not disapprove.

18. The right of suspension referred to in paragraph 17 above shall not be exercised for the first three years that a safeguard measure is in effect, provided that serious injury is caused or threatened to be caused by an absolute increase in imports and that such a measure conforms to the provisions of this agreement.

IV

DEVELOPING COUNTRIES

19. For any product originating in a less-developed contracting party, safeguard measures need not be applied as long as the contracting party's market share in the product concerned does not exceed one per cent.

20. A less-developed contracting party shall have the right to extend the period of application of a safeguard measure for a period of up to two years beyond the maximum period provided for in paragraph 12 above. Notwithstanding the provisions of paragraph 14 above, a less-developed contracting party may apply a safeguard measure again to the import of a product which has been subject to such a measure, taken after the date of entry into force of this agreement, for a period of time equal to half that during which such a measure has been previously applied, provided that the period of non-application is at least two years.

- 7 -

V

EXISTING ARTICLE XIX MEASURES

21. Contracting parties shall terminate all existing safeguard measures taken pursuant to Article XIX of the General Agreement not later than eight years after the date on which they were first applied or five years after the date of entry into force of this agreement, whichever comes later.

VI

PROHIBITION AND ELIMINATION OF CERTAIN MEASURES

22. (a) A contracting party shall not take or seek any emergency action on imports of particular products as set forth in Article XIX unless such action conforms with the provisions of Article XIX of the General Agreement applied in accordance with this agreement.

    (b) Furthermore, a contracting party shall not seek, take or maintain any voluntary export restraints, orderly marketing arrangements[1] or any other similar measures on the export or the import side. These include actions taken by a single contracting party as well as actions under agreements, arrangements and understandings entered into by two or more contracting parties. Any such measure in effect at the time of entry into force of this agreement shall be brought into conformity with this provision or phased out, in accordance with paragraph 23 below.

    (c) Measures sought, taken or maintained by a contracting party pursuant to other provisions of the General Agreement, or protocols and agreements or arrangements concluded within the framework of the General Agreement are not included in the scope of this agreement.

23. The provisions of paragraph 22 above shall be carried out according to timetables to be presented to the Safeguards Committee by the contracting parties concerned not later than 180 days after the date of entry into force of this agreement. These timetables shall provide for all measures referred to in paragraph 22 above to be phased out or brought into conformity with this agreement within a period not exceeding four years, subject to exceptions up to a maximum of eight years, set out in Annex 1, after the date of entry into force of this agreement.

----

[1]An import quota applied as a safeguard measure in conformity with the provisions of this agreement may, by mutual agreement, be administered by the exporting contracting party.

RM/SGA1

0130

61P-12-8

- 8 -

24. Contracting parties shall not encourage nor support the adoption or maintenance by public and private enterprises of non-governmental measures equivalent to those referred to in paragraph 22 above.

VII

NOTIFICATION AND CONSULTATION

25. A contracting party shall immediately notify the CONTRACTING PARTIES upon:

(a) initiating an investigatory process relating to serious injury or threat thereof and the reasons for it;

(b) making a finding of serious injury or threat thereof caused by increased imports; and

(c) taking a decision to apply or extend a safeguard measure.

26. In making the notifications referred to in sub-paragraphs 25(b) and (c) above, the contracting party proposing to apply or extend a safeguard measure shall provide the CONTRACTING PARTIES with all pertinent information, which shall include evidence of serious injury or threat thereof caused by increased imports, precise description of the product involved and the proposed measure, proposed date of introduction, expected duration and timetable for progressive liberalization. In the case of an extension of a measure, evidence that the industry concerned is adjusting shall also be provided. The CONTRACTING PARTIES or the Safeguards Committee may request such additional information as they may consider necessary from the contracting party proposing to apply or extend the measure.

27. A contracting party proposing to apply or extend a safeguard measure shall provide adequate opportunity for prior consultations with those contracting parties having a substantial interest as exporters of the product concerned, with a view to, inter alia, reviewing the information provided under paragraph 26 above, exchanging views on the measure and reaching an understanding on ways to achieve the objective set out in paragraph 16 above.

28. A contracting party shall make a notification before taking a provisional safeguard measure referred to in paragraph 4 above. Consultations shall be initiated immediately after the measure is taken.

29. The results of the consultations referred to in this Section, as well as the results of mid-term reviews referred to in paragraph 13, any form of compensation referred to in paragraph 16, and proposed suspensions of concessions and other obligations referred to in paragraph 17, shall be notified immediately to the CONTRACTING PARTIES by the contracting parties concerned.

RM/SGA1

0131

- 9 -

30. Contracting parties shall notify promptly the CONTRACTING PARTIES of their laws, regulations and administrative procedures relating to safeguard measures as well as any modifications made to them.

31. Contracting parties maintaining measures described in paragraphs 21 and 22 above which exist at the date on which this agreement enters into force shall notify such measures to the CONTRACTING PARTIES, not later than 60 days after the entry into force of this agreement.

32. Any contracting party may notify the CONTRACTING PARTIES of all laws, regulations, administrative procedures and any measure or action dealt with in this agreement that has not been notified by other contracting parties that are required by this agreement to make such notifications.

33. Any contracting party may notify the CONTRACTING PARTIES of any non-governmental measures referred to in paragraph 24 above.

34. All notifications to the CONTRACTING PARTIES referred to in this agreement shall normally be made through the Safeguards Committee.

35. The provisions on notification in this agreement shall not require any contracting party to disclose confidential information which would impede law enforcement or otherwise be contrary to the public interest or would prejudice the legitimate commercial interests of particular enterprises, public or private.

VIII

SURVEILLANCE

36. There shall be a Safeguards Committee under the authority of the CONTRACTING PARTIES, which shall be open to the participation of any contracting party indicating its wish to serve on it. The Committee will have the following functions:

   (a) to monitor, and report annually to the CONTRACTING PARTIES on, the general implementation of this agreement and make recommendations towards its improvement;

   (b) to find, upon request of an affected contracting party, whether or not the procedural requirements of this agreement have been complied with in connection with a safeguard measure, and report its findings to the CONTRACTING PARTIES;

   (c) to assist contracting parties, if they so request, in their consultations under the provisions of this agreement;

   (d) to examine measures covered by paragraphs 21 and 22, monitor the phase-out of such measures and report as appropriate to the CONTRACTING PARTIES;

RM/SGA1   0132

61P-12-10

- 10 -

(e) to review, at the request of the contracting party taking a safeguard action, whether proposals to suspend concessions or other obligations are "substantially equivalent", and report as appropriate to the CONTRACTING PARTIES;

(f) to receive and review all notifications provided for in this agreement and report as appropriate to the CONTRACTING PARTIES; and

(g) to perform any other function connected with this agreement that the CONTRACTING PARTIES may determine.

37. To assist the Committee in carrying out its surveillance function, the secretariat shall prepare annually a factual report on the operation of the agreement based on notifications and other reliable information available to it.

IX

DISPUTE SETTLEMENT

38. The provisions of Articles XXII and XXIII of the General Agreement, and the Understanding on Rules and Procedures Governing the Settlement of Disputes under Articles XXII and XXIII of the General Agreement on Tariffs and Trade as adopted by the CONTRACTING PARTIES shall apply to consultations and the settlement of disputes under this instrument.

- 11 -

(ANNEX 1)

(EXCEPTIONS REFERRED TO IN PARAGRAPH 23)

외 무 부

종 별 : 지급

번 호 : GVW-2680

일 시 : 91 1216 2100

수 신 : 장관(봉기,경기원,재무부,농림수산부,상공부,특허청)

발 신 : 주 제네바대사

제 목 : UR/세이프가드 협상 비공식회의

연: GVW-2631

1. 12.15(일) 표제회의가 MACIEL 의장 주재로 개최되어 12.13. 자 의장 초안을 조금 수정한 별첨 의장 초안을 중심으로 협의가 진행되었는바,(김봉주서기관 참석) 가장 논란이 되고 있는 9 항의 QUOTA MODULATION 과 관련, 아국, 홍콩,파키스탄, 싱가폴, 뉴질랜드, 카나다, 알젠틴, 호주, 스웨덴(북구대표), 스위스, 인도, 이집트, 멕시코, 말련, 브라질, 일본등이 12.15 자 의장 초안에서도 동 조항이 삭제되지 않고 있는데 강한 불만을 표시하고 동 조항의 삭제를 강력 요구한 반면, 미국은 동 조항을 두고 현재협상 분위기가 타협의 여지가 없이 전부를 얻느냐 혹은 전부를 잃느냐(ALL OR NOTHING)의 분위기로 가고 있다고 불만을 표시하였으며, EC 는 자신은 1 개 협상 참가국이기는 하나, 12 개 체약국으로구성되어 있기 때문에 다른 협상 참가국과는 다른 성격을 갖고 있는 만큼, 모든 협상 참가국의 반대에도 불구하고 1 개 참가국의 요구에 의장이 따르고 있다는 표현은 적절치 못하다고 언급하고 현재 분위기는 협상을 하려는 태도가 아니라고 불만을 토로함.

2. 이에 의장은 QM 관련 부분을 의장 초안에 그대로 유지하고 대신에 QM 조항의 적용 여부는 체약국단의 결정에 따른다는 내용을 추가하여 TNC 의장에게 제출할 것을 주장하였으나 QM 을 반대하는 국가들은 동 의견에 강력 반대함으로써 동 문제에 대한 결론에 도달치 못하였음.

3. 여타 금번 회의에서 협의된 사항은 아래와 같음.

가. 연호 2 항 가, ANNEX 1 에 예외적인 회색조치 명기 문제와 관련, 미국이 별첨 23 항 수정안을 통하여 각 수입국들이 2 개의 예외를 갖도록 하자고 제안한데 대하여 참가국들은 만일 모든 참가국들이 2 개씩 예외를 가질 경우 엄청난 혼란을 초래할 것이라는 의견을 제시함으로써 미국 자신도 더 검토하겠다는 태도를 보임.

통상국 차관 2차보 분석관 정와대 경기원 재무부 농수부 상공부
특허청

PAGE 1

91.12.17   17:27

외신 2과 통제관 BW

0135

나. 9 항의 첫번째 문장을 8 항으로 합칠 것을 의장이 제안하였으나 합의에도달하지 못하였고, UNLESS 이하를 삭제할 것을 검토하였으나 합의에 미도달

4. MACIEL 의장은 금번회의를 끝으로 지금까지 토의된 내용을 검토 종합한 의장안을 12.20 TNC 의장에게 제출할 예정임을 밝혔으며, 이에따라 아국, 홍콩, 스위스 협상 참가자들은 현재까지협상진행 상황에 비추어 9 항 QM 이 의장안에서삭제될 가능성이 크지 않다고 판단, QM 반대국에의한 공동 DEMARCHE 의 필요성에 합의함.

첨부: 1. 12.15. 자 의장초안 1 부

2. 미국의 23 항 수정안 1 부.

(GVW(F)-0632)끝

(대사 박수길-국장)

예고:92.6.30 까지

주 제 네 바 대 표 부

번 호 : GVF(F) - *632*　　　년월일 : *11216*　　　시간 : *2100*

수 신 : 장　　　판 (*통기, 경기원, 2내무부, 농림수산부, 상공부, 특허청*)

발 신 : 주 제네바대사

제 목 : *첨부*

총 *13* 매 (표지포함)

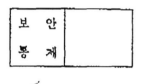

15 December 1991

<u>DRAFT AGREEMENT ON SAFEGUARDS</u>

PREAMBLE

The CONTRACTING PARTIES:

Having in mind the overall objective of the contracting parties to improve and strengthen the international trading system based on the General Agreement on Tariffs and Trade;

Recognizing the need to clarify and reinforce the disciplines of the General Agreement, and specifically those of its Article XIX (Emergency Action on Imports of Particular Products), to re-establish multilateral control over safeguards and eliminate measures that escape such control;

Recognizing the importance of structural adjustment and the need to enhance rather than limit competition in international markets; and

Recognizing further that, for these purposes, a comprehensive agreement, applicable to all contracting parties and based on the basic principles of the General Agreement, is called for;

Hereby agree as follows:

RM/SGA1

632-13-2

0138

I

GENERAL

1. This agreement establishes rules for the application of safeguard measures which shall be understood to mean those measures provided for in Article XIX of the General Agreement.

II

CONDITIONS

2. A contracting party[1] may apply a safeguard measure to a product only if the importing contracting party has determined, pursuant to the provisions set out below, that such product is being imported into its territory in such increased quantities, absolute or relative to domestic production, and under such conditions as to cause or threaten to cause serious injury to the domestic industry that produces like or directly competitive products.

3. (a) A contracting party may apply a safeguard measure only following an investigation by the competent authorities of the importing contracting party pursuant to procedures previously established and made public in consonance with Article X of the General Agreement. This investigation shall include reasonable public notice to all interested parties and public hearings or other appropriate means in which importers, exporters and other interested parties could present evidence and their views, including the opportunity to respond to the presentations of other parties and to submit their views, inter alia, as to whether or not the application of a safeguard measure would be in the public interest. The competent authorities shall publish a report setting forth their findings and reasoned conclusions reached on all pertinent issues of fact and law.

---

[1] A customs union may apply a safeguard measure as a single unit or on behalf of a member state. When a customs union applies a safeguard measure as a single unit, all the requirements for the determination of serious injury or threat thereof under this agreement shall be based on the conditions existing in the customs union as a whole. When a safeguard measure is applied on behalf of a member state, all the requirements for the determination of serious injury or threat thereof shall be based on the conditions existing in that member state and the measure shall be limited to that member state. Nothing in this agreement prejudges the interpretation of the relationship between Article XIX and Article XXIV:8 of the General Agreement.

(b) Any information which is by nature confidential or which is provided on a confidential basis shall, upon cause being shown, be treated as such by the competent authorities. Such information shall not be disclosed without permission of the party submitting it. Parties providing confidential information may be requested to furnish non-confidential summaries thereof or, if such parties indicate that such information cannot be summarized, the reasons why a summary cannot be provided. However, if the competent authorities find that a request for confidentiality is not warranted and if the party concerned is either unwilling to make the information public or to authorize its disclosure in generalized or summary form, the authorities would be free to disregard such information unless it can be demonstrated to their satisfaction from appropriate sources that the information is correct.

4. In critical circumstances where delay would cause damage which it would be difficult to repair, a provisional safeguard measure may be taken pursuant to a preliminary determination that there is clear evidence that increased imports have caused or are threatening to cause serious injury. The duration of the provisional measure shall not exceed 200 days, during which period the pertinent requirements of this Section and Section VII shall be met. Such measures should take the form of tariff increases to be promptly refunded if the subsequent investigation referred to in paragraph 7 below does not determine that increased imports have caused or threatened to cause serious injury to a domestic industry. The duration of any such provisional measure shall count towards the initial period and any extension referred to in paragraphs 10, 11 and 12 below.

5. Safeguard measures shall be applied to a product being imported irrespective of its source.

6. For the purposes of this agreement:

(a) serious injury shall be understood to mean a significant overall impairment in the position of a domestic industry;

(b) in determining injury, a domestic industry shall be understood to mean the producers as a whole of the like or directly competitive products operating within the territory of a contracting party, or those whose collective output of the like or directly competitive products constitutes a major proportion of the total domestic production of those products; and

- 4 -

(c) threat of serious injury shall be understood to mean serious injury that is clearly imminent, in accordance with the provisions of paragraph 7 below. A determination of the existence of a threat of serious injury shall be based on facts and not merely on allegation, conjecture or remote possibility.

7. (a) In the investigation to determine whether increased imports have caused or are threatening to cause serious injury to a domestic industry under the terms of this agreement, the competent authorities shall evaluate all relevant factors of an objective and quantifiable nature having a bearing on the situation of that industry, in particular, the rate and amount of the increase in imports of the product concerned in absolute and relative terms, the share of the domestic market taken by increased imports, changes in the level of sales, production, productivity, capacity utilization, profits and losses, and employment.

(b) The determination referred to in sub-paragraph 7(a) shall not be made unless this investigation demonstrates, on the basis of objective evidence, the existence of the causal link between increased imports of the product concerned and serious injury or threat thereof. When factors other than increased imports are causing injury to the domestic industry at the same time, such injury shall not be attributed to increased imports.

(c) The competent authorities shall publish promptly, in accordance with the provisions of paragraph 3 above, a detailed analysis of the case under investigation as well as a demonstration of the relevance of the factors examined.

8. Safeguard measures shall be applied only to the extent as may be necessary to prevent or remedy serious injury and to facilitate adjustment. Contracting parties should choose measures most suitable for the achievement of these objectives.

9. No quantitative restriction shall reduce the quantity of imports below the level of a recent period which shall be the average of imports in the last three representative years for which statistics are available, (unless clear justification is given that a different level is necessary to prevent or remedy serious injury.) In cases in which a quota is allocated among supplying countries, and in the absence of agreement with the suppliers concerned, the importing contracting party may allot quota shares proportionately to the quantities supplied during the previous representative period, subject to the possibility of taking into account clear evidence on the extent each supplier has contributed to the assessed global injury, provided that any modification in individual quota allotments necessary to remedy injury may not exceed five percentage points or 30 per cent of the proportion supplied during the representative period, whichever is the smaller, and provided the CONTRACTING PARTIES do not disapprove. No such modification shall be applied to contracting parties whose market share of the product concerned does not exceed one per cent. Whenever any such modification occurs, the importing contracting party shall provide justification as to the reasons for it.

RM/SGA1

10. Safeguard measures shall be applied only for a period of time as may be necessary to prevent or remedy serious injury and to facilitate adjustment. It shall not exceed four years, unless this is extended under paragraph 11 below.

11. The period mentioned in paragraph 10 above may be extended provided that the competent authorities of the importing contracting party have determined, in conformity with the procedures set out in this Section, that: the safeguard measure continues to be necessary to prevent or remedy serious injury; that there is evidence that the industry is adjusting; and that the pertinent provisions of Sections III and VII below are observed.

12. The total period of a safeguard measure including the period of application of any provisional measure, the period of initial application, and any extension thereof shall not exceed eight years.

13. In order to facilitate adjustment, if the expected duration of a safeguard measure as notified under the provisions of paragraph 25 is over one year, it shall be progressively liberalized at regular intervals during the period of application. If the duration of the measure exceeds three years, the contracting party applying such a measure shall review the situation not later than the mid-term of the measure and, if appropriate, withdraw it or increase the pace of liberalization. A measure extended under paragraph 11 above shall not be more restrictive than it was at the end of the initial period, and should continue to be liberalized.

14. No safeguard measure shall be applied again to the import of a product which has been subject to such a measure, taken after the date of entry into force of this agreement, for a period of time equal to that during which such measure had been previously applied, provided that the period of non-application is at least two years.

15. Notwithstanding the provisions of paragraph 14 above, a safeguard measure with a duration of 180 days or less may be applied again to the import of a product if:

  (a) at least one year has elapsed since the date of introduction of a safeguard measure on the import of that product; and

  (b) such a safeguard measure has not been applied on the same product more than twice in the five-year period immediately preceding the date of introduction of the measure.

- 6 -

III

LEVEL OF CONCESSIONS AND OTHER OBLIGATIONS

16. A contracting party proposing to apply a safeguard measure or seeking an extension shall endeavour to maintain a substantially equivalent level of concessions and other obligations to that existing between it and the exporting contracting parties which would be affected by such a measure under the General Agreement, in accordance with the provisions of paragraph 27 below. To achieve this objective, the contracting parties concerned may agree on any adequate means of trade compensation for the adverse effects of the measure on their trade.

17. If no agreement is reached within 30 days in the consultations under paragraph 27 below, then the affected exporting contracting parties are free, not later than 90 days after the measure is applied, to suspend, upon the expiration of 30 days from the day on which written notice of such suspension is received by the CONTRACTING PARTIES, the application of substantially equivalent concessions or other obligations under the General Agreement, to the trade of the contracting party applying the safeguard measure, the suspension of which the CONTRACTING PARTIES do not disapprove.

18. The right of suspension referred to in paragraph 17 above shall not be exercised for the first three years that a safeguard measure is in effect, provided that the safeguard measure has been taken as a result of an absolute increase in imports and that such a measure conforms to the provisions of this agreement.

IV

DEVELOPING COUNTRIES

19. For any product originating in developing contracting parties, safeguard measures need not be applied as long as the developing contracting party's market share in the product concerned does not exceed one per cent. If a safeguard measure is not applied to any particular product from such a contracting party, the measure shall not be applied to all such contracting parties.

20. A developing-contracting party shall have the right to extend the period of application of a safeguard measure for a period of up to two years beyond the maximum period provided for in paragraph 12 above. Notwithstanding the provisions of paragraph 14 above, a developing contracting party shall have the right to apply a safeguard measure again to the import of a product which has been subject to such a measure, taken after the date of entry into force of this agreement, for a period of time equal to half that during which such a measure has been previously applied, provided that the period of non-application is at least two years.

RM/SGA1

632 -13 -0

0143

- 7 -

V

EXISTING ARTICLE XIX MEASURES

21. Contracting parties shall terminate all existing safeguard measures taken pursuant to Article XIX of the General Agreement not later than eight years after the date on which they were first applied or five years after the date of entry into force of this agreement, whichever comes later.

VI

PROHIBITION AND ELIMINATION OF CERTAIN MEASURES

22. (a) A contracting party shall not take or seek any emergency action on imports of particular products as set forth in Article XIX unless such action conforms with the provisions of Article XIX of the General Agreement applied in accordance with this agreement.

(b) Furthermore, a contracting party shall not seek, take or maintain any voluntary export restraints, orderly marketing arrangements or any other similar measures on the export or the import side.[1][2] These include actions taken by a single contracting party as well as actions under agreements, arrangements and understandings entered into by two or more contracting parties. Any such measure in effect at the time of entry into force of this agreement shall be brought into conformity with this provision or phased out, in accordance with paragraph 23 below.

(c) Measures sought, taken or maintained by a contracting party pursuant to other provisions of the General Agreement, or protocols and agreements or arrangements concluded within the framework of the General Agreement are not included in the scope of this agreement.

23. The provisions of paragraph 22 above shall be carried out according to timetables to be presented to the Safeguards Committee by the contracting parties concerned not later than 180 days after the date of entry into force of this agreement. These timetables shall provide for all measures referred to in paragraph 22 above to be phased out or brought into conformity with this agreement within a period not exceeding four years, subject to exceptions up to a maximum of seven years, set out in Annex 1, after the date of entry into force of this agreement.

---

[1] An import quota applied as a safeguard measure in conformity with the relevant provisions of the General Agreement may, by mutual agreement, be administered by the exporting contracting party.

[2] Examples of similar measures include export moderation, export-price or import-price monitoring system, export or import surveillance, compulsory import cartels and discretionary export or import licensing scheme.

RM/SGA1

632-13 -8

0144

- 8 -

24. Contracting parties shall not encourage nor support the adoption or maintenance by public and private enterprises of non-governmental measures equivalent to those referred to in paragraph 22 above.

VII

NOTIFICATION AND CONSULTATION

25. A contracting party shall immediately notify the CONTRACTING PARTIES upon:

    (a) initiating an investigatory process relating to serious injury or threat thereof and the reasons for it;

    (b) making a finding of serious injury or threat thereof caused by increased imports; and

    (c) taking a decision to apply or extend a safeguard measure.

26. In making the notifications referred to in sub-paragraphs 25(b) and (c) above, the contracting party proposing to apply or extend a safeguard measure shall provide the CONTRACTING PARTIES with all pertinent information, which shall include evidence of serious injury or threat thereof caused by increased imports, precise description of the product involved and the proposed measure, proposed date of introduction, expected duration and timetable for progressive liberalization. In the case of an extension of a measure, evidence that the industry concerned is adjusting shall also be provided. The CONTRACTING PARTIES or the Safeguards Committee may request such additional information as they may consider necessary from the contracting party proposing to apply or extend the measure.

27. A contracting party proposing to apply or extend a safeguard measure shall provide adequate opportunity for prior consultations with those contracting parties having a substantial interest as exporters of the product concerned, with a view to, inter alia, reviewing the information provided under paragraph 26 above, exchanging views on the measure and reaching an understanding on ways to achieve the objective set out in paragraph 16 above.

28. A contracting party shall make a notification before taking a provisional safeguard measure referred to in paragraph 4 above. Consultations shall be initiated immediately after the measure is taken.

29. The results of the consultations referred to in this Section, as well as the results of mid-term reviews referred to in paragraph 13, any form of compensation referred to in paragraph 16, and proposed suspensions of concessions and other obligations referred to in paragraph 17, shall be notified immediately to the CONTRACTING PARTIES by the contracting parties concerned.

RM/SGA1

632-13 -⊗

0145

- 9 -

30. Contracting parties shall notify promptly the CONTRACTING PARTIES of their laws, regulations and administrative procedures relating to safeguard measures as well as any modifications made to them.

31. Contracting parties maintaining measures described in paragraphs 21 and 22 above which exist at the date on which this agreement enters into force shall notify such measures to the CONTRACTING PARTIES, not later than 60 days after the entry into force of this agreement.

32. Any contracting party may notify the CONTRACTING PARTIES of all laws, regulations, administrative_procedures and any measure or action dealt with in this agreement that has not been notified by other contracting parties that are required by this agreement to make such notifications.

33. Any contracting party may notify the CONTRACTING PARTIES of any non-governmental measures referred to in paragraph 24 above.

34. All notifications to the CONTRACTING PARTIES referred to in this agreement shall normally be made through the Safeguards Committee.

35. The provisions on notification in this agreement shall not require any contracting party to disclose confidential information which would impede law enforcement or otherwise be contrary to the public interest or would prejudice the legitimate commercial interests of particular enterprises, public or private.

VIII

SURVEILLANCE

36. There shall be a Safeguards Committee under the authority of the CONTRACTING PARTIES, which shall be open to the participation of any contracting party indicating its wish to serve on it. The Committee will have the following functions:

    (a) to monitor, and report annually to the CONTRACTING PARTIES on, the general implementation of this agreement and make recommendations towards its improvement;

    (b) to find, upon request of an affected contracting party, whether or not the procedural requirements of this agreement have been complied with in connection with a safeguard measure, and report its findings to the CONTRACTING PARTIES;

    (c) to assist contracting parties, if they so request, in their consultations under the provisions of this agreement;

    (d) to examine measures covered by paragraphs 21 and 22, monitor the phase-out of such measures and report as appropriate to the CONTRACTING PARTIES;

- 10 -

(e) to review, at the request of the contracting party taking a
     safeguard action, whether proposals to suspend concessions or
     other obligations are "substantially equivalent", and report as
     appropriate to the CONTRACTING PARTIES;

(f) to receive and review all notifications provided for in this
     agreement and report as appropriate to the CONTRACTING PARTIES;
     and

(g) to perform any other function connected with this agreement that
     the CONTRACTING PARTIES may determine.

37.   To assist the Committee in carrying out its surveillance function, the
secretariat shall prepare annually a factual report on the operation of the
agreement based on notifications and other reliable information available
to it.

IX

DISPUTE SETTLEMENT

38.   The provisions of Articles XXII and XXIII of the General Agreement,
and the Understanding on Rules and Procedures Governing the Settlement of
Disputes under Articles XXII and XXIII of the General Agreement on Tariffs
and Trade as adopted by the CONTRACTING PARTIES shall apply to
consultations and the settlement of disputes arising under this instrument.

- 11 -

ANNEX

EXCEPTIONS REFERRED TO IN PARAGRAPH 23

632-1)-12

0148

23.   The provisions of paragraph 22 above shall be carried out according to timetables to be presented to the Safeguards Committee by the contracting parties concerned not later than 180 days after the date of entry into force of this agreement.   These timetables shall provide for all measures referred to in paragraph 22 above to be phased out or brought into conformity with this agreement within a period not exceeding four years, subject to no more than two exceptions per importing participant, up to a maximum of seven years after the date of entry into force of this agreement.   Any such exceptions must be mutually agreed by the parties directly concerned and identified before the entry into force of this agreement.

12/15/91

672-13-13

0149

외 무 부

종 별 :

번 호 : GVW-2681 일 시 : 91 1216 2130

수 신 : 장관(봉기,경기원,재무부,농림수산부,상공부,특허청)

발 신 : 주 제네바 대사

제 목 : UR/세이프가드 협상 이해 일치국 공동 DEMARCHE

연 : GVW-2680

1. 연호 협상 참가자들간 공동 DEMARCHE 에 대한 합의에 따라 12.16(월) 오전 아국, 스위스, 브라질, 싱가폴, 홍콩등 5 개국 대표(아국은 김삼훈 대사, 홍콩은 CHANG 무역청장, WONG 대표 및 여타국 대사 참석)들이 MACIEL 의장을 면담함 (김봉주 서기관 동석)

가. 5 명의 대표들은 한결같이 QM 의 삭제를 강력히 주장, 아래 입장을 개진함.

첫째 QM 은 갓트의 근간인 MFN 원칙에 위배되는 원칙의 문제임.

둘째, 회색조치의 철폐 내지 개선은 UR 협상의 근본 취지이며, 회색조치와 QM 을 연계시키는 것은 부당함.

셋째, 절대다수 국가가 반대하는 내용을 협상결과에 반영하는 것은 이들로 하여금 협상결과를 수락할수 없게 만드는 커다란 위험성을 가지고 있음.

나. 이에 동의장은 금일 DEMARCHE 의 뜻을 충분히 이해하며 원칙의 문제라는 점에 동의한다고 전제하고 그러나 자신의 과거 동경 라운드시 협상 경험 및 금번 협상 경과에 비추어 볼때 9 항의 QM 은 22 항의 회색 조치와 관련 연계되어있는만큼 자신으로서도 어려운 입장이라는 반응을 보이면서 9 항과 22 항 동시삭제에 대한 의견을 문의함.

2. 이에 아국, 스위스, 싱가폴, 홍콩대사들은 MACIEL 의장 면담후 갓트 로비에서 별도 회합을 갖고 사안의 중요성에 비추어 보다 강력한 공동 대책 수입 필요성에 인식을 같이하고 지난 11.26 RULE MAKING 분야에서의 획기적인 개선 필요성에 공동서명한 30 개국을 비롯한 관심국 대사 공동명의의 QM 반대서한을 작성, 명 12.17(화) MACIEL 의장에게 전달하고 이를 대외 공표키로 함.

3. 이에 따라 아국, 홍콩, 스위스 협상 실무자간 (아국은 김봉주 서기관 참석)

통상국 안기부	장관 경기원	차관 재무부	1차보 농수부	2차보 상공부	경제국 특허청	외정실	분석관	정와대

91.12.17 07:22

외신 2과 통제관 BD

0150

별첨 문안을 작성, QM 을 반대하는 여타 국가 대사들에게 동 공동 DEMARCHE 에의 참여를 요청하고 있으며, 참여국이 결정되는 대로 명 12.17(화) MACIEL 의장에게 QM 반대국의 공동 입장을 전달할 예정인바, 결과 추보하겠음.

4. 관찰 및 건의

가. 상기에 비추어 12.20 TNC 의장에게 제출될 의장문안에는 QM 이 삭제되지 않고 제출될 가능성이 크다고 보여짐.

나. 이경우 QM 반대국들이 강한 반대에 비추어 92.1.13 이후에도 동문제에 대한 협의가 계속될 가능성도 배제할수 없는 만큼 상기 의장의 9 항 QM 부분과 22항을 동시에 삭제하는 방안에 대한 아국입장 검토 회시 바람.

첨부: 상기서한 1 부. 끝

(GVW(F)-633)

(대사 박수길-국장)

예고 91.12.31. 까지

주 제 네 바 대 표 부

번 호 : GVW(F) - 0633   년월일 : 11-16   시간 : 2/30

수 신 : 장   관 (총기, 경가원, 재무부, 농림수산부, 상공부, 특허청)

발 신 : 주 제네바대사

제 목 : 첨부

총 3 매(표지포함)

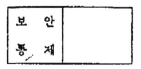

633 - 3 - 1   0152

URGENT

BY FAX

From: The Permanent Mission of Switzerland
          (Ambassador P.L. Girard)

          The Permanent Mission of Korea
          (Ambassador S.G. Park)

          The Hong Kong Economic and Trade Office
          (Joseph W.P. Wong, Permanent Representative)

To: The Permanent delegations of:
          Argentina, Austria, Brazil, Canada, Chile,
          Colombia, Czechoslovakia, Egypt, El Salvador,
          Finland, Iceland, India, Indonesia, Japan,
          Malaysia, Mexico, Morocco, Nicaragua, Nigeria,
          Norway, Pakistan, Peru, Philippines, Poland,
          Singapore, Sweden, Thailand, Uruguay and
          Venezuela.

16.12.91
- -

Safeguards

Following is a draft letter to the chairman of
the N.G. on Rule-making and TRIMs concerning the proposal
on Quota Modulation in the latest Chairman's paper on an
Agreement on Safeguards dated the 15th December.
Assuming that your delegation is willing to sign this
letter, please let us know before 17.00h today, 16th
December when we can get the signature of the head of
your delegation between 8.00 - 10.00h tomorrow 17th
December.

- ends -

633-3-2

0153

Mr. Chairman,

Referring to the communication in MTN.GNG/RM/W/8 of 26 November 1991, the following countries/participants in the negotiations express deep concern about the inclusion of the quota modulation proposal in para 9 of the Chairman's paper on an Agreement on Safeguards dated 15 December 1991.

Recalling the importance we attach to "an unambiguous non-discriminatory safeguard mechanism", these countries/participants strongly urge that the proposal on quota modulation be deleted from the text which you will submit to the Chairman of the TNC.

Yours sincerely,

633-3-3

0154

원 본

외 무 부

종 별 :

번 호 : GVW-2693

일 시 : 91 1217 2030

수 신 : 장 관(봉기, 경기원, 재무부, 농림수산부, 상공부, 특허청)

발 신 : 주 제네바 대사

제 목 : UR/세이프가드 협상 이해 일치국 공동 DEMARCHE

연: GVW-2681

1. 연호 QUOTA MODULATION 에 반대하는 20 개국 대사들이 공동 서명한 별첨서한을
12.17(화) MACIEL 의장에게 전달하였음. (던켈 총장에게는 사본 전달)

2. 상기관련 금일 저녁 EC 가 강한 반발을 보인것으로 알려짐.

첨부: 상기서한 1 부

(GVW(F)-0640). 끝

(대사 박수길-국장)

예고:92.6.30 까지

검 토 필 (1991. 12. 31.) 김

통상국	장관	차관	1차보	2차보	외정실	분석관	청와대	안기부
경기원	재무부	농수부	상공부	특허청				

주 제 네 바 대 표 부

번 호 : GVW(F) - 0640   년월일 : 11/2/7   시간 : 2030

수 신 : 장   관 (통기.경기원,재우부,농림수산부,상공부, 특허청).

발 신 : 주 제네바대사

제 목 : 첨 부

총 4 매 (표지포함)

보 안 통 제	

회신과 통 제	

640-4-1

Geneva, December 17 1991

H.E. Mr. George Maciel
Ambassador
Chairman of the Negotiating Group on Rule
Making and TRIMs
GATT, Centre William Rappard

1200 Geneva

Mr. Chairman

The following countries/participants in the negotiations:

Argentina, Brazil, Chile, Colombia, El Salvador, Hong Kong, Korea, India, Indonesia, Japan, Malaysia, Mexico, Nigeria, Pakistan, Philippines, Singapore, Switzerland, Thailand, Uruguay and Venezuela

Referring to the communication in MTN.GNG/RM/W/8 of 26 November 1991, express deep concern about the inclusion of the quota modulation proposal in paragraph 9 of the Chairman's draft paper on an Agreement on Safeguards dated 15 december 1991.

Recalling the importance we attach to "an unambiguous non-discriminatory safeguard mechanism" for a strengthened multilateral system, these countries/participants strongly urge that the proposal on quota modulation be deleted from the text which you will submit to the Chairman of the TNC.

enclosure: List of signatures

cc: Mr. Arthur Dunkel, Chairman of the Trade Negotiations Committee

640-4-2

0157

List of signatures

Delegation		Representative
HONG KONG		J. Wong, Permanent Representative to GAT:
SWITZERLAND		W. Rossier, Ambassador
El Salvador		L. Saurel (Mrs.), Ambassador
Chile		P. Leiva, Ambassador
México		J. Seade, Ambassador
Colombia		F. Jaramillo, Ambassado:
Argentina		N. Stancanelli, Minister-Counsellor
MALAYSIA		S. Manickam, Minister
THAILAND		T. Bunnag, Ambassador
SINGAPORE		C.M. See, Ambassador
INDONESIA		H.S. Kartadjoemena, Ambassador
URUGUAY		J.A. Lacarte, Ambassador
PHILIPPINES		J.A. Buencamino for Ambassador Escaler
INDIAN		B.K. Zutshi, Ambassador
BRASIL		C. Amorim, Ambassador
Korea		B.G. Park, Ambassador
PAKISTAN		A. Kamal, Ambassador

0158

List of signatures

Delegation	Representative	
VENEZUELA		J.F. Misle, Minister-Counsellor
NIGERIA		A. Rimdap, Minister
JAPAN		K. Asakai, Minister

640 - 4 - 4

외 무 부

종   별 :

번   호 : GVW-2718   일   시 : 91 1219 0130

수   신 : 장관(봉기, 경기원, 재무부, 농림수산부, 상공부, 특허청)

발   신 : 주 제네바 대사

제   목 : UR/세이프가드 비공식협의

1.   12.18(수)   표제협의가   MACIEL   의장
주재로개최되어(김삼훈대사, 최혁심의관, 김봉주서기관참석)   12.18자   별첨   의장
초안(9항 QUOTA MODULATION전체 삭제)을 중심으로 협의하였는바, EC는동 삭제에 강한
불만을   제기하고   아국, 홍콩, 싱가폴에   대해서는   UR   협상   결과   이행시
반덤핑, 보조금, 상계관세 및 세이프가드협상 분야에서의 개도국 특별 우대 혜택을
부여치않겠다고   발언하였음.   이에 아국, 홍콩, 싱가폴은   강한   이의를   제기하였으며
캐나다, 우루과이, 스위스도 QM 조항은 삭제되어야한 다는 입장을 제시함.

2. 아국은 UR협상 초기부터 일관된 태도로 협상의 성공을 위하여 모든 협조를
아끼지않았으며, 갓트가 기본원칙에 따라 시행되기를 원하는 만큼 한체약국이
특정국가들을 명시적으로 언급하여 차별적 대우를 하겠다는 발언에 유감과 놀라움을
금치못하겠으며, 세이프가드 협상에서 개도국 우대 문제를 거론하는것은 이해하기
어려운 만큼 UR 협상 결과가 갓트의 원칙에따라 모든 체약국에 적용되고 QM조항도
갓트 원칙에따라 계속 삭제된체로 남아야 한다고 언급하였으며, 홍콩, 싱가폴등도
아국과 동일한 취지로 EC만의 요청으로 QM조항이 재삽입되거나, EC가 일방적인
조치를통하여 대개도국 우대를 선별적으로 적용 배제할수 없다는 강한 반발을 보임.

3. EC가 9항과 19항에 대한 별첨 수정안을 제출하였으나 이를 지지하는 국가는 없
었으며, 의장은 타결방안의 하나로 기존 9항 내용중 쿼타삭감 상한을 시장점유율 5퍼
센트에서 3퍼센트로, 그리고 수출량 30 퍼센트에서 15 퍼센트 감축하는안을 제시하였
으나 아무런지지를 얻지 못함.

4. 이에 의장은 QM 이 갓트 원칙을 벗어난 내용이라는 점과 EC안을 지지하는 나라
가없음을 언급하고, 20:00 협상그룹 의장단 그린룸회의시까지 소그룹이 의견을 집약,
새로운   안을가져오기   바란다고   하고   회의를   종결함. (동   회의종료후

통상국	장관	1사보	2차보	외정실	분석관	정와대	안기부	경기원
재무부	농수부	상공부	특허청					

외신 1과 통제관

0160

EC,미국,북구,호주,뉴질랜드등이 별도 회동하는 것으로 파악됨)

5. 상기와같이 EC의 QM안을 지지하는 나라가없고 아국포함 절대 다수국이 강하게반대하고있음에 비추어, 12:20 에 제출될 최종협정안에 QM 조항이 삭제될 것으로 보는 견해가 유력하나, UR협상 타결의 관건을 쥐고있는 EC가 강하게 반발하고 있음에 비추어 금일 회의종료직전 의장이 제시한 상기 3항 타협안이 반영될 가능성도 배제하수 없을 것으로 봄.

첨부: 1. 12.18 자 의장 초안 1부

2. EC 수정안 1부

(GVW(F)-0653).끝

(대사 박수길-국장)

주 제 네 바 대 표 부

번 호 : GVW(F) - *0653*   년월일 : *11219*   시간 : *0130*

수 신 : 장   관 *(동기 , 껑가원, 재무부, 농림수산부, 상곡부, 특허청)*

발 신 : 주 제네바대사

제 목 : *GVW-2718 첨부*

총 *14*매(표지포함)

보 안 통 제	

외신과 통 제	

653 - 14 - 1

0162

18 December 1991

DRAFT AGREEMENT ON SAFEGUARDS

PREAMBLE

The CONTRACTING PARTIES:

　　Having in mind the overall objective of the contracting parties to improve and strengthen the international trading system based on the General Agreement on Tariffs and Trade;

　　Recognizing the need to clarify and reinforce the disciplines of the General Agreement, and specifically those of its Article XIX (Emergency Action on Imports of Particular Products), to re-establish multilateral control over safeguards and eliminate measures that escape such control;

　　Recognizing the importance of structural adjustment and the need to enhance rather than limit competition in international markets; and

　　Recognizing further that, for these purposes, a comprehensive agreement, applicable to all contracting parties and based on the basic principles of the General Agreement, is called for;

　　Hereby agree as follows:

RM/SGAD

0163

653-14-2

- 2 -

I

GENERAL

1.   This agreement establishes rules for the application of safeguard measures which shall be understood to mean those measures provided for in Article XIX of the General Agreement.

II

CONDITIONS

2.   A contracting party[1] may apply a safeguard measure to a product only if the importing contracting party has determined, pursuant to the provisions set out below, that such product is being imported into its territory in such increased quantities, absolute or relative to domestic production, and under such conditions as to cause or threaten to cause serious injury to the domestic industry that produces like or directly competitive products.

3.   (a)   A contracting party may apply a safeguard measure only following an investigation by the competent authorities of the importing contracting party pursuant to procedures previously established and made public in consonance with Article X of the General Agreement. This investigation shall include reasonable public notice to all interested parties and public hearings or other appropriate means in which importers, exporters and other interested parties could present evidence and their views, including the opportunity to respond to the presentations of other parties and to submit their views, _inter alia_, as to whether or not the application of a safeguard measure would be in the public interest. The competent authorities shall publish a report setting forth their findings and reasoned conclusions reached on all pertinent issues of fact and law.

---

[1]A customs union may apply a safeguard measure as a single unit or on behalf of a member state. When a customs union applies a safeguard measure as a single unit, all the requirements for the determination of serious injury or threat thereof under this agreement shall be based on the conditions existing in the customs union as a whole. When a safeguard measure is applied on behalf of a member state, all the requirements for the determination of serious injury or threat thereof shall be based on the conditions existing in that member state and the measure shall be limited to that member state. Nothing in this agreement prejudges the interpretation of the relationship between Article XIX and Article XXIV:8 of the General Agreement.

RM/SGAD

0164

_652-14-3_

- 3 -

(b) Any information which is by nature confidential or which is
     provided on a confidential basis shall, upon cause being shown,
     be treated as such by the competent authorities. Such
     information shall not be disclosed without permission of the
     party submitting it. Parties providing confidential information
     may be requested to furnish non-confidential summaries thereof
     or, if such parties indicate that such information cannot be
     summarized, the reasons why a summary cannot be provided.
     However, if the competent authorities find that a request for
     confidentiality is not warranted and if the party concerned is
     either unwilling to make the information public or to authorize
     its disclosure in generalized or summary form, the authorities
     would be free to disregard such information unless it can be
     demonstrated to their satisfaction from appropriate sources that
     the information is correct.

4.   In critical circumstances where delay would cause damage which it
would be difficult to repair, a provisional safeguard measure may be taken
pursuant to a preliminary determination that there is clear evidence that
increased imports have caused or are threatening to cause serious injury.
The duration of the provisional measure shall not exceed 200 days, during
which period the pertinent requirements of this Section and Section VII
shall be met. Such measures should take the form of tariff increases to be
promptly refunded if the subsequent investigation referred to in
paragraph 7 below does not determine that increased imports have caused or
threatened to cause serious injury to a domestic industry. The duration of
any such provisional measure shall count towards the initial period and any
extension referred to in paragraphs 10, 11 and 12 below.

5.   Safeguard measures shall be applied to a product being imported
irrespective of its source.

6.   For the purposes of this agreement:

     (a) serious injury shall be understood to mean a significant overall
          impairment in the position of a domestic industry;

     (b) in determining injury, a domestic industry shall be understood to
          mean the producers as a whole of the like or directly competitive
          products operating within the territory of a contracting party,
          or those whose collective output of the like or directly
          competitive products constitutes a major proportion of the total
          domestic production of those products; and

     (c) threat of serious injury shall be understood to mean serious
          injury that is clearly imminent, in accordance with the
          provisions of paragraph 7 below. A determination of the
          existence of a threat of serious injury shall be based on facts
          and not merely on allegation, conjecture or remote possibility.

- 4 -

7. (a) In the investigation to determine whether increased imports have
         caused or are threatening to cause serious injury to a domestic
         industry under the terms of this agreement, the competent
         authorities shall evaluate all relevant factors of an objective
         and quantifiable nature having a bearing on the situation of that
         industry, in particular, the rate and amount of the increase in
         imports of the product concerned in absolute and relative terms,
         the share of the domestic market taken by increased imports,
         changes in the level of sales, production, productivity, capacity
         utilization, profits and losses, and employment.

    (b) The determination referred to in sub-paragraph 7(a) shall not be
         made unless this investigation demonstrates, on the basis of
         objective evidence, the existence of the causal link between
         increased imports of the product concerned and serious injury or
         threat thereof. When factors other than increased imports are
         causing injury to the domestic industry at the same time, such
         injury shall not be attributed to increased imports.

    (c) The competent authorities shall publish promptly, in accordance
         with the provisions of paragraph 3 above, a detailed analysis of
         the case under investigation as well as a demonstration of the
         relevance of the factors examined.

8. Safeguard measures shall be applied only to the extent as may be
necessary to prevent or remedy serious injury and to facilitate adjustment.
If a quantitative restriction is used, such a measure shall not reduce the
quantity of imports below the level of a recent period which shall be the
average of imports in the last three representative years for which
statistics are available, unless clear justification is provided that a
different level is necessary to prevent or remedy serious injury.
Contracting parties should choose measures most suitable for the
achievement of these objectives.

9.

RM/SGAD

653-18-5

0166

- 5 -

10. Safeguard measures shall be applied only for a period of time as may be necessary to prevent or remedy serious injury and to facilitate adjustment. It shall not exceed four years, unless this is extended under paragraph 11 below.

11. The period mentioned in paragraph 10 above may be extended provided that the competent authorities of the importing contracting party have determined, in conformity with the procedures set out in this Section, that: the safeguard measure continues to be necessary to prevent or remedy serious injury; that there is evidence that the industry is adjusting; and that the pertinent provisions of Sections III and VII below are observed.

12. The total period of a safeguard measure including the period of application of any provisional measure, the period of initial application, and any extension thereof shall not exceed eight years.

13. In order to facilitate adjustment, if the expected duration of a safeguard measure as notified under the provisions of paragraph 25 is over one year, it shall be progressively liberalized at regular intervals during the period of application. If the duration of the measure exceeds three years, the contracting party applying such a measure shall review the situation not later than the mid-term of the measure and, if appropriate, withdraw it or increase the pace of liberalization. A measure extended under paragraph 11 above shall not be more restrictive than it was at the end of the initial period, and should continue to be liberalized.

14. No safeguard measure shall be applied again to the import of a product which has been subject to such a measure, taken after the date of entry into force of this agreement, for a period of time equal to that during which such measure had been previously applied, provided that the period of non-application is at least two years.

15. Notwithstanding the provisions of paragraph 14 above, a safeguard measure with a duration of 180 days or less may be applied again to the import of a product if:

   (a) at least one year has elapsed since the date of introduction of a safeguard measure on the import of that product; and

   (b) such a safeguard measure has not been applied on the same product more than twice in the five-year period immediately preceding the date of introduction of the measure.

RM/SGAD

653-14-6

0167

- 6 -

III

LEVEL OF CONCESSIONS AND OTHER OBLIGATIONS

16. A contracting party proposing to apply a safeguard measure or seeking
an extension shall endeavour to maintain a substantially equivalent level
of concessions and other obligations to that existing between it and the
exporting contracting parties which would be affected by such a measure
under the General Agreement, in accordance with the provisions of
paragraph 27 below. To achieve this objective, the contracting parties
concerned may agree on any adequate means of trade compensation for the
adverse effects of the measure on their trade.

17. If no agreement is reached within 30 days in the consultations under
paragraph 27 below, then the affected exporting contracting parties are
free, not later than 90 days after the measure is applied, to suspend, upon
the expiration of 30 days from the day on which written notice of such
suspension is received by the CONTRACTING PARTIES, the application of
substantially equivalent concessions or other obligations under the General
Agreement, to the trade of the contracting party applying the safeguard
measure, the suspension of which the CONTRACTING PARTIES do not disapprove.

18. The right of suspension referred to in paragraph 17 above shall not be
exercised for the first three years that a safeguard measure is in effect,
provided that the safeguard measure has been taken as a result of an
absolute increase in imports and that such a measure conforms to the
provisions of this agreement.

IV

DEVELOPING COUNTRIES

19. For any product originating in developing contracting parties,
safeguard measures need not be applied as long as the developing
contracting party's market share in the product concerned does not exceed
one per cent. If a safeguard measure is not applied to any product from
such a contracting party, the measure shall not be applied to all such
contracting parties.

20. A developing contracting party shall have the right to extend the
period of application of a safeguard measure for a period of up to two
years beyond the maximum period provided for in paragraph 12 above.
Notwithstanding the provisions of paragraph 14 above, a developing
contracting party shall have the right to apply a safeguard measure again
to the import of a product which has been subject to such a measure, taken
after the date of entry into force of this agreement, for a period of time
equal to half that during which such a measure has been previously applied,
provided that the period of non-application is at least two years.

RM/SGAD

653-14-7

0168

- 7 -

V

EXISTING ARTICLE XIX MEASURES

21. Contracting parties shall terminate all existing safeguard measures taken pursuant to Article XIX of the General Agreement not later than eight years after the date on which they were first applied or five years after the date of entry into force of this agreement, whichever comes later.

VI

PROHIBITION AND ELIMINATION OF CERTAIN MEASURES

22. (a) A contracting party shall not take or seek any emergency action on imports of particular products as set forth in Article XIX unless such action conforms with the provisions of Article XIX of the General Agreement applied in accordance with this agreement.

     (b) Furthermore, a contracting party shall not seek, take or maintain any voluntary export restraints, orderly marketing arrangements, or any other similar measures on the export or the import side.[1,2] These include actions taken by a single contracting party as well as actions under agreements, arrangements and understandings entered into by two or more contracting parties. Any such measure in effect at the time of entry into force of this agreement shall be brought into conformity with this provision or phased out, in accordance with paragraph 23 below.

     (c) Measures sought, taken or maintained by a contracting party pursuant to other provisions of the General Agreement, or protocols and agreements or arrangements concluded within the framework of the General Agreement are not included in the scope of this agreement.

23. The phasing out of existing measures referred to in paragraph 22 above shall be carried out according to timetables to be presented to the Safeguards Committee by the contracting parties concerned not later than 180 days after the date of entry into force of this agreement. These timetables shall provide for all measures referred to in paragraph 22 above to be phased out or brought into conformity with this agreement within a period not exceeding four years after the date of entry into force of this

---

[1] An import quota applied as a safeguard measure in conformity with the relevant provisions of the General Agreement may, by mutual agreement, be administered by the exporting contracting party.

[2] Examples of similar measures include export moderation, export-price or import-price monitoring systems, export or import surveillance, compulsory import cartels and discretionary export or import licensing schemes, any of which afford protection.

RM/SGAD

653-1F-8

0169

- 8 -

agreement, subject to not more than one specific measure per importing
contracting party[1], the duration of which shall not extend beyond
December 31, 1999. Any such exception must be mutually agreed between the
parties directly concerned and notified to the Safeguard Committee for its
review and acceptance within 90 days of the coming into force of this
agreement. The Annex indicates a measure which has been agreed as falling
under this exception.

24. Contracting parties shall not encourage nor support the adoption or
maintenance by public and private enterprises of non-governmental measures
equivalent to those referred to in paragraph 22 above.

                                   VII

NOTIFICATION AND CONSULTATION

25. A contracting party shall immediately notify the CONTRACTING PARTIES
upon:

      (a) initiating an investigatory process relating to serious injury or
           threat thereof and the reasons for it;

      (b) making a finding of serious injury or threat thereof caused by
           increased imports; and

      (c) taking a decision to apply or extend a safeguard measure.

26. In making the notifications referred to in sub-paragraphs 25(b)
and (c) above, the contracting party proposing to apply or extend a
safeguard measure shall provide the CONTRACTING PARTIES with all pertinent
information, which shall include evidence of serious injury or threat
thereof caused by increased imports, precise description of the product
involved and the proposed measure, proposed date of introduction, expected
duration and timetable for progressive liberalization. In the case of an
extension of a measure, evidence that the industry concerned is adjusting
shall also be provided. The CONTRACTING PARTIES or the Safeguards
Committee may request such additional information as they may consider
necessary from the contracting party proposing to apply or extend the
measure.

27. A contracting party proposing to apply or extend a safeguard measure
shall provide adequate opportunity for prior consultations with those
contracting parties having a substantial interest as exporters of the
product concerned, with a view to, inter alia, reviewing the information
provided under paragraph 26 above, exchanging views on the measure and
reaching an understanding on ways to achieve the objective set out in
paragraph 16 above.

_____
[1] The only such exception to which the European Community is entitled is
indicated in the Annex.

RM/SGAD

                        657-14-ρ   0170

- 9 -

28. A contracting party shall make a notification before taking a provisional safeguard measure referred to in paragraph 4 above. Consultations shall be initiated immediately after the measure is taken.

29. The results of the consultations referred to in this Section, as well as the results of mid-term reviews referred to in paragraph 19, any form of compensation referred to in paragraph 16, and proposed suspensions of concessions and other obligations referred to in paragraph 17, shall be notified immediately to the CONTRACTING PARTIES by the contracting parties concerned.

30. Contracting parties shall notify promptly the CONTRACTING PARTIES of their laws, regulations and administrative procedures relating to safeguard measures as well as any modifications made to them.

31. Contracting parties maintaining measures described in paragraphs 21 and 22 above which exist at the date on which this agreement enters into force shall notify such measures to the CONTRACTING PARTIES, not later than 60 days after the entry into force of this agreement.

32. Any contracting party may notify the CONTRACTING PARTIES of all laws, regulations, administrative procedures and any measure or action dealt with in this agreement that has not been notified by other contracting parties that are required by this agreement to make such notifications.

33. Any contracting party may notify the CONTRACTING PARTIES of any non-governmental measures referred to in paragraph 24 above.

34. All notifications to the CONTRACTING PARTIES referred to in this agreement shall normally be made through the Safeguards Committee.

35. The provisions on notification in this agreement shall not require any contracting party to disclose confidential information which would impede law enforcement or otherwise be contrary to the public interest or would prejudice the legitimate commercial interests of particular enterprises, public or private.

VIII

SURVEILLANCE

36. There shall be a Safeguards Committee under the authority of the CONTRACTING PARTIES, which shall be open to the participation of any contracting party indicating its wish to serve on it. The Committee will have the following functions:

   (a) to monitor, and report annually to the CONTRACTING PARTIES on, the general implementation of this agreement and make recommendations towards its improvement;

RM/SGAD

653-14-10

0171

- 10 -

(b) to find, upon request of an affected contracting party, whether or not the procedural requirements of this agreement have been complied with in connection with a safeguard measure, and report its findings to the CONTRACTING PARTIES;

(c) to assist contracting parties, if they so request, in their consultations under the provisions of this agreement;

(d) to examine measures covered by paragraphs 21 and 22, monitor the phase-out of such measures and report as appropriate to the CONTRACTING PARTIES;

(e) to review, at the request of the contracting party taking a safeguard action, whether proposals to suspend concessions or other obligations are "substantially equivalent", and report as appropriate to the CONTRACTING PARTIES;

(f) to receive and review all notifications provided for in this agreement and report as appropriate to the CONTRACTING PARTIES; and

(g) to perform any other function connected with this agreement that the CONTRACTING PARTIES may determine.

37. To assist the Committee in carrying out its surveillance function, the secretariat shall prepare annually a factual report on the operation of the agreement based on notifications and other reliable information available to it.

IX

DISPUTE SETTLEMENT

38. The provisions of Articles XXII and XXIII of the General Agreement, and the Understanding on Rules and Procedures Governing the Settlement of Disputes under Articles XXII and XXIII of the General Agreement on Tariffs and Trade as adopted by the CONTRACTING PARTIES shall apply to consultations and the settlement of disputes arising under this instrument.

RM/SGAD

653-14-11

0172

- 11 -

ANNEX

EXCEPTION REFERRED TO IN PARAGRAPH 23

Parties concerned	Product	Termination
EC / Japan	Passenger cars, off road vehicles, light commercial vehicles, light trucks (up to 5 tonnes), and the same vehicles in wholly knocked-down form (CKD sets).	31 December, 1999.

RM/SGAD

0173

— Six years after the entry into force of this agreement, the
Safeguards Committee shall carry out a review of the operation of
the provisions of paragraph 9 of this agreement. This review shall
in particular examine any trade difficulties which may have arisen
from the application of Paragraph 9 including the possibility of
considering modifications of this provision.

— When applicable, notifications shall also include a clear and
detailed justification of the criteria used by the importing
contracting party to establish the level of a quantitative
restriction, or to allocate quota shares, on a basis other than the
prior representative period.

653-14-13

0174

Safeguard measures (shall) (should) not be applied against a product originating in a less developed contracting party whose share of imports in the product concerned does not exceed 3 per cent, provided that, in the case of several less developed contracting party suppliers, their collective share of imports does not exceed 8 per cent.

653-18-14

0175

관리 번호	91-851

외 무 부

종 별 : 지급

번 호 : GVW-2719 　　　　　일 시 : 91 1219 0130

수 신 : 장 관(봉기,구일,경기원,재무부,농림수산부,상공부)

발 신 : 주 제네바 대사　　　　사본: 주 EC 대사-직송필

제 목 : UR/세이프가드 협상

검 토 필 (1991.12.31.) 긴

연: GVW-2718

표제 협상진전과 관련 금 12.18(수) 23:00 현재 파악한 내용을 아래 보고함.

1. QUATA MODULATION 조항 문제

가. 금일 오후 MACIEL 의장 주재 회의 종료후 EC 가 주도하는 소그룹은 이시간 현재 회의를 계속중이며, 9 항 QM 발동 조건과 기준을 강화하는 내용의 새조항을 DRAFT 중이며, 삭감수치는 당초안에 제시되어 있던 5 퍼센트, 30 퍼센트 보다 낮은 수준인 것으로 파악되고 있음.

나. 동 회의에는 EC, 미, 북구, 호주, 뉴질랜드, 인도가 참여중이며, 알젠틴, 브라질, 칠레는 도중에 QM 반대 의사를 분명히 하고 퇴장한 것으로 파악됨.

다. EC 는 동 QM 조항 설정이 한국, 싱가폴, 홍콩등 주종 수출에만 불리하고 후발저개발국에는 상대적으로 유리한 내용이라는 요지로 개도국을 분리.격파하는 전략을 구사하는 한편, 일부 개도국에게는 여타 분야(섬유, TRIPS 등)에서 대가 보장을 약속한 것 같다는 정보도 있음.

라. 연호 보고와 같이 결국 EC 의 강력한 반대로 결국 수정된 QM 내용이 포함될 가능성이 있는 것으로 판단되고 있음.

2. EC 의 한국, 싱가폴, 홍콩에 대한 개도국 대우 적용 배제문제

가. 금일 오전 회의시 EC 가 한국, 싱가폴, 홍콩에 대하여는 세이프가드, 반덤핑, 보조금상계관세 분야에서 개도국에 대한 특혜대우 조항을 적용하지 않겠다고 선언한 이후(아국을 비롯 3 개국 공히 도저히 이해할 수 없고 근거없는 부당한 주장이라는 반박 즉각 제시), EC 는 동 요지를 규범제정분야 TEXT 에 FOOT NOTE 로 하여 포함시켜 줄것을 MACIEL 의장에게 요청함.

나. 이에 3 개국 대사는 공동으로 오후 회의 종료후 MACIEL 의장을 접촉, 사실

통상국	장관	차관	1차보	2차보	구주국	경제국	외정실	분석관
정와대	안기부	경기원	재무부	농수부	상공부			

PAGE 1

91.12.19　09:54

외신 2과 통제관 BS

0176

여부를 확인하고 그 부당성을 지적, 도저히 수락할 수 없다는 입장을 밝힌바, 동의장도 원칙에 위배되는 것으로 TEXT 에 포함시키지 않겠다고 약속하였으며, 그후 MACIEL 의장이 EC 의 TRAN 대사에게 전화 EC 요청을 갓트 차원에서 공식으로 조치를 취할수 없다는 입장을 통보한 것으로 확인됨.

다. TRAN 대사는 EC 입장을 갓트 문서로 회람시킬 것을 요청하는 방안등 필요한 조치를 취하겠다는 의사를 견지하였다고 하는 바, 이시간 현재 홍콩, 싱가폴 대사등을 갓트 복도에서 접촉, 협의한바, EC 의 금일 발언은 본부의 승인없이 TRAN 대사가 단독으로 결정, 취한 행동으로 EC 본부의 승인이 없는한 문서화조치등 추가 조치는 없을 것으로 보고 있음.

(만약 EC 가 문서로 회람시키는 경우 3 개국이 공동으로 동 반박문서를 즉각 회람시키기로 일단 합의)

라. 한편 홍콩 대표와 싱가폴 대사에 의하면, TRAN 대사의 금일 언동은 본부의 승인도 없이 개도국을 DIVIDE AND RULE 하여 목전의 목적을 달성키 위해 행한 이례적이고 부당한 것으로서 본국정부에 보고, EC 측에 대해 정치적 수준에서의 항의등을 건의 적절한 조치를 취하게 될것이라고 함을 참고로 보고함.끝.

(대사 박수길-차관)

예고:92.12.30 까지

외 무 부

종 별 : 지 급

번 호 : GVW-2720   일 시 : 91 1219 0150

수 신 : 장 관(통기, 경기원, 재무부, 농림수산부, 상공부, 특허청)

발 신 : 주 제네바 대사

제 목 : UR/세이프 가드 협상

　　　　연: GVW-2718

　　　1. 12.19(목) 01:00 의장초안 9항에 대한 EC 주도새로운 제안을 입수 별첨 송부함.

　　　2. 동 제안은 기본적으로 당초 EC안에 비해 큰변경이 없이 일부요건과 숫자만이 바뀐것으로 금오전 이를 수락할수 없다는 아국입장을 통보코겨하는바 별도 지침있으면 회시바람.

　　　첨부: 상기초안1부(2매)

　　　(GVW(F)-0654).끝

　　　(대사 박수길-국장).

통상국　　2차보　　경기원　　재무부　　농수부　　상공부　　특허청

91.12.19　　09:58 WG

외신 1과 통제관

0178

주 제 네 바 대 표 부

번 호 : GVR(F) - *0654*   년월일 : *11218*   시간 : *0150*

수 신 : 장   관 (총기, 경기원, 재무부, 농림수산부, 상공부, 특허청)

발 신 : 주 제네바대사

제 목 : *GVW-2720 첨부*

총 *3* 매(표지포함)

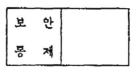

보 안	
통 제	

외신과	
통 제	

654 - 3-1

0179

23:40

18.12.91

9(a) In cases in which a quota is allocated among supplying countries, the contracting party applying the restrictions may seek agreement with respect to the allocation of shares in the quota with all other contracting parties having a substantial interest in supplying the product concerned. In cases in which this method is not reasonably practicable, the contracting party concerned shall allot to contracting parties having a substantial interest in supplying the product shares based upon the proportions, supplied by such contracting parties during a previous representative period, of the total quantity or value of imports of the product, due account being taken of any special factors which may have affected or may be affecting the trade in product.

9(b) The contracting party applying such a measure may depart from the above provisions if it demonstrates to the Safeguards Committee that imports from countries to be affected by the measures have increased at least 1.5 times the rate of the general increase in the imports of the product in question. However such a departure shall not exceed 4.5 percentage points or 25% of the proportion supplied in the representative period referred to in Article XIII.2d of the General Agreement, whichever is the smaller. No reduction under this provision is permitted if the import share for the product concerned for that country does not exceed 5%. Any modification of quota shares under this provision shall be applied on an equitable basis to all suppliers which meet the criteria established under this paragraph. Any available quantities resulting from a reduction of the quota shares of certain suppliers shall be in part reserved to the benefit of new suppliers and partly allocated to those suppliers whose quota share has not been reduced. The contracting party applying the measures so adjusted shall justify to the Safeguards Committee the reasons for it. The duration of any such measure shall not be extended beyond the initial period under paragraph 10 below, unless the quotas are allocated in accordance with the provisions of paragraph 1(a). The provisions of paragraph 18 below shall not apply to the measure. Any suspension under Article 17 shall be limited to the difference between the quantity allotted under this paragraph and the one which would have resulted from the application of paragraph 9a'

A:DP
diskette SG

654-3-2

0180

18.12.91

Addition to paragraph 36

Every four years after the entry into force of this agreement, the Safeguards Committee shall carry out a comprehensive review of the provisions of paragraph 9 of this agreement. This review shall examine any trade difficulties which could arise including possible modifications of this provision.

Addition to paragraph 26

When applicable, notifications shall also include a clear and detailed justification of the criteria used by the importing contracting party to establish the level of a quantitative restriction, or to allocate quota status, on a basis other than the representative period mentioned in paragraph 8 and 9.

Paragraph 19

Safeguard measures shall not be applied against a product originating in a less developed contracting party whose share of imports in the product concerned does not exceed 3 per cent, provided that, in the case of several less developed contracting party suppliers, their collective share of imports does not exceed 9 per cent'

A:DP
diskette SG

$654-3-3$

0181

발 신 전 보

분류번호	보존기간

번 호 : WGV-1863   911219 2253   FN   종별: **긴급**

수 신 : 주   제네바   대사. 총영사/

발 신 : 장 관   (통 기)

제 목 : UR/세이프가드 협상

대 : GVW-2720

대호 관련 귀관 건의대로 조치바람.   끝.   (통상국장   김 용 규)

보안통제	Ⅿ

앙고재	91년12월19일	기안자성명		과장	국장	차관	장관
					전결		

외신과통제

0182

정 리 보 존 문 서 목 록

기록물종류	일반공문서철	등록번호	2019040165	등록일자	2019-04-23
분류번호	764.51	국가코드		보존기간	영구
명 칭	UR(우루과이라운드) / GATT(관세및무역에관한일반협정) 조문 협상 그룹 회의, 1991				
생 산 과	통상기구과	생산년도	1991~1991	담당그룹	
내 용 목 차					

0001

23710

기 안 용 지

분류기호 문서번호	통기 20644-	(전화: 720 - 2188)	시 행 상 특별취급	
보존기간	영구. 준영구 10. 5. 3. 1.	장 관		
수 신 처 보존기간				
시행일자	1991. 5.22.			

보조기관	국 장	전 결	협조기관		문 서 통 제 [인] DL 5.23 동 지 과
	심의관	刻			
	과 장	れ			
기안책임자	송 봉 헌				발 송 인

경 유 수 신 참 조	상공부장관 국제협력관	발 신 명 의	[접수인] 반수 1991. 5. 23

제 목	UR/갓트조문 협상 현황 자료

대 : 국협 28140-197 (91.5.14)

대호, UR/갓트조문 협상 진행상황 및 아국 입장에 관한

자료를 별첨 송부합니다.

첨 부 : 상기 자료 1부.   끝.

0002

UR/갓트조문 협상 진행상황 및 아국 입장

1. 진전상황

가. 주요협상 경과

○ '88.12. 중간평가를 통하여 아래 사항에 합의

- 갓트 조문의 명료화 및 개선에 협상력 집중

- 본 협상 그룹내 쟁점과 타협상 그룹의 쟁점간에 관련성 고려

- 명확한 협상 쟁점 설정

○ '90.10.19 (10.9. TNC 비공식 회의에서 설정된 협상 시한)까지 모든 조문에 대한 그룹 차원의 협상은 일단 종료

- 합의문 : MTN.TNC/W/35/Rev.1 참조

○ '90.11.2. TNC 수석대표 비공식 협의에서 2조1(b)항, 17조, 28조는 잠정합의가 이루어진 분야로, 24조, 25조 5항, 35조 및 잠정적용 의정서는 합의된 협상 기초가 있는 분야로 분류 되었으며, 다만 BOP 조항만이 합의된 협상 기초조차 없는 분야로 분류

○ 91.2.21 갓트 조문 협상 관련 Dunkel 사무총장 statement 요지

- 잠정 합의 : 2조1항(b), 17조, 28조

- 몇몇 참가국의 합의 유보 : 24조, 35조

- 여타분야 협상 결과 고려 최종 결정 : 25조 5항, 잠정 적용 의정서

- 협상 여부 미합의 : 18조 B

1

0003

나. 합의사항

    ㅇ 잠정합의를 도출하여 향후 각료들의 확인 절차만을 남긴 조문

      - 2조 1(b)항 : 관세 양허표상의 기타 과세 및 부과금 *JuN*

      - 17조 : 국영무역 기업 */ AuG 1510*

      - 28조 : 관세 양허 재협상 절차

    ㅇ 향후 철폐시한만 결정되면 타결될 조문

      - 25조 5항 : 웨이버

      - 잠정 적용 의정서 및 가입 의정서상의 조부조항

    ㅇ 일부 참가국들(인도, 브라질, 멕시코등)의 초안 내용의 법적의미에
대한 검토 완료시까지 유보한 조문

      - 35조 : 갓트 협정 부적용

다. 미합의사항

    ㅇ 24조 : 관세동맹 및 지역 협정

    ㅇ 18조 B : BOP 조항

2. 미결쟁점 및 아국 입장

가. 쟁점별 주요국 입장

    ㅇ 24조(관세 동맹 및 지역 협정)

      - 관세동맹 및 지역 협정의 결성 및 확대에 따른 보상지불 문제
(24조 6항)

        . 의장 초안 : 추가 보상 필요시, 다른 품목의 공동 관세인하로 보상

        . EC : 추가 보상 필요시, 타회원국의 다른 품목에 관한 관세
인하분까지 고려대상에 포함

2

0004

. 미국 : 반대

. 아국 : 의장 초안과 동일 입장

- 지방정부 또는 기관의 조치 및 행위에 대한 연방 또는 중앙정부의
  갓트상 책임 문제

  . 의장 초안 : 지방정부의 조치 및 행위는 중앙정부의 책임

  . EC : 연방 또는 중앙정부의 책임으로 함으로써 분쟁해결 절차
          명료화

  . 미국, 캐나다, 인도등 : 중앙정부가 갓트 규정의 준수를 위한
                          합리적인 조치를 취하는 것은 헌법상
                          허용된 한도내에서만 가능

  . 아국 : 의장 초안과 동일 입장

- 24조 관련 분쟁시 특별구제 절차

  . 의장 초안 : 갓트 분쟁해결 절차 원용 가능

  . EC, 캐나다, 오지리 : 24조 관련 분쟁도 갓트 분쟁해결 절차
                        원용 가능

  . 아국 및 일본 : 역외국의 특별한 권익 보호를 위하여 동 조항
                  관련 분쟁이 당사국간 협의로 타결되지 않을
                  경우, 위원회나 체약국단에 회부하여 권고로 해결

ㅇ 18조 B (BOP 조항)

- 동 조문에 대한 협상을 실시할 것인지에 대한 선진.개도국간
  합의 부재

ㅇ 조부조항, 웨이버

- X년이후 철폐에 합의 하였으나, X년에 대한 구체적 논의는 아직
  진행되지 않고 있음.

나. 쟁점별 아국 입장

  ㅇ 반영 필요분야

    - 24조 관련 분쟁시 특별구제 절차

      . 위원회나 체약국단에 회부하여 권고로 해결

    - 관세 동맹 및 지역협정의 결성과 확대에 따른 보상 지불 문제

      . 추가 보상 필요시, 다른 품목의 관세인하로 보상

  ㅇ 양보 가능분야

    - 지방정부 또는 기관의 조치 및 행위에 대한 연방 또는 중앙정부의
      갓트상 책임 문제

      . 지방정부의 조치 및 행위는 중앙정부의 책임이라는 것이 우리
        입장이나, 강한 주장은 불필요(의장 초안에 이미 반영)

  ㅇ 구체적인 입장 표명 불필요 분야

    - BOP 조항

다. 협상 전략

  ㅇ 관세동맹 및 지역협정 결성시 보상지불 문제는 미국의 입장을 지원하면서,
    일본과 함께 24조 관세 분쟁시 특별구제절차 마련에 주력

  ㅇ 지방정부 또는 기관의 조치 및 행위를 연방 또는 중앙정부의 책임으로
    하는 것이 바람직하나, 상기 반영 필요 분야에서의 미국등과의 협조
    관계를 고려하여 강한 주장은 자제

  ㅇ BOP 조항은 선진.개도국의 첨예한 의견 대립을 보이는 미묘한 문제이고
    아국은 이미 BOP 졸업이 합의된만큼 구체적 입장 표명 자제

    - BOP 조항 개정 가능성은 거의 없으며, 다만 선진국들이 섬유협상과
      연계하는 카드로 사용

    - BOP조항 개정 찬성시 개도국들이 우리에게 강력히 반발할 것이므로
      적극 찬성 의사표명 자제

4

0006

○ 24조 12항 적극 활용

　　- 과거 관세위주의 GATT 규율에서는 중앙정부의 의무수행으로 조약의
　　　효과적 집행이 가능했으나 보조금, 무역관련 투자, 서비스등 UR에서의
　　　논의사항들은 지방정부의 의무수행이 조약내용의 효과적인 이행에 긴요

　　- 지방정부의 의무강화에 반대하는 나라 대부분(미국, 카나다, 호주)이
　　　농산물 수출국으로서 농산물 협상과 연결한 협상 카드로 이용 가능

4.　향후 협상 전망

○ 24조의 현 의장 초안은 양허 재협상 절차 및 용어의 해석을 명료화 함으로써
　일본, 호주, 뉴질랜드, 아국등 협정 비가입국의 입장을 적절히 반영하고
　있으며, EC등 협정 가입국들의 반대도 크지 않음에 비추어 향후 큰 논란없이
　채택될 전망

○ 또한 상금 미합의사항인 관세 동맹 및 지역협정 결성에 따른 보상문제,
　지방정부의 조치에 대한 중앙정부의 책임문제, 24조 관련 분쟁시 특별구제
　절차 설정 문제도 현 의장안의 내용이 다수국들의 주장에 따르고 있음에
　비추어 현 문안대로 채택될 가능성이 큼

○ BOP 조항에 대해서는 치열한 의견 대립이 전망되는바, 이는 UR 협상 전체
　Package의 한 주요쟁점으로 부각될 전망.　　　　　　　끝.

0007

5

갓트 17조(국영무역) 개요 및 검토 의견

1991. 5.23.
통상기구과

1. 현행 규정 및 UR 협상에서의 잠정 합의 요지

현행 규정 요지	UR 협상 잠정 합의 요지
○ 일반 의무 　- 수출·입에 수반되는 구매 또는 　　판매에 있어서 무차별 원칙 준수 　- 상업적 고려에 의한 거래 　- 타체약국 기업에 대한 경쟁적 참여 　　기회 부여 　- 관세 또는 과징금의 인하등에 관해 　　관심 표명 국가와 협의 ○ 통보 의무 　- 해당품목을 체약국단에 통보 ○ 정보제공 의무 　- 비양허 품목의 경우 다체약국의 　　요청에 의거 해당품목의 수입 및 　　판매가격간의 차액(import mark-up)에 　　대한 정보제공 　- 양허품목의 경우 양허표에 정해진 　　보호를 초과해 독점권 운영 불가 　　(갓트 2조 4항) ○ 수량제한등 수입제한적 원용 금지 　- 갓트 11조, 12조, 18조등에 의한 　　수량제한 금지 의무는 국영무역에도 　　적용됨 (갓트 부속 규정)	○ 통보 의무 및 감시 기능 강화 　- 통보 대상기업 : marketing board를 　　포함한 정부 또는 비정부 기업 　- 대상기업 통보시 체약국단을 　　대신한 작업반이 해당기업의 　　운용 현황, 국제무역에의 영향 　　등을 평가할 수 있도록 최대한의 　　명료성 확보에 유의 　- 통보기업 누락시 타체약국은 　　작업반에 의한 검토를 위해 　　역통보 가능 　- 작업반은 통보 및 역통보 내용 　　검토 　- 체약국단은 작업반의 검토 내용에 　　따라 통보내용의 적정성, 추가 　　정보 필요성과 관련한 권고 가능

1

0008

2. 농산물에 대한 갓트 17조 원용 현황

가. 원용 국가

o 일본, 호주, 오지리, 놀웨이, 스위스, 남아공등 일부 국가

- 주로 비축등 수급조절, 가격안정이 원용 목적

- 농산물에 대한 주요국별 국영무역 내용 갓트 통보 현황 : 별첨

나. 일본의 원용 사례 및 갓트 패널 결과 (88.2)

1) 대상품목 (63년, 86년 갓트 통보)

o 소맥, 대맥, 쌀, 생사, 쇠고기, 버터등 유제품

- 생사의 경우 잠사.사탕 사업단이 수입 독점권을 보유하고 있으나 수입자유화된 품목

- 쇠고기의 경우 91.4.1부터 수입자유화 조치 및 축산진흥사업단의 쇠고기 수입 업무 수행 불허 조치

2) 갓트 패널 결과 (88.2)

o 경 위

- 미국의 제소에 따라 일본의 12개 농산물 수입규제 관련 갓트 패널 설치 (86.10)

. 탈지분유등 유제품, 가공치즈, 잡두, 전분, 낙화생, 우유 조제품, 설탕 조제품, 과즙, 파인애플 조제품, 과일 쥬스, 토마토 케찹, 기타 식량조제품

- 87.2. 갓트이사회에서 패널 보고서 채택

o 패널 보고서 결론

- 갓트 11조 1항(수량제한의 일반적 금지)에 의거한 수량제한 금지 의무는 수입 할당이나 국영무역에 의한 수입제한에도 적용됨.

2

0009

- 따라서, 11조 2항 C에 의한 수입제한이 일부 인정되는 잡두,
  낙화생을 제외한 여타 10개품목에 대한 수입제한은 갓트 위배
  . 여타 10개품목중에는 일본이 국영무역을 이유로 수입규제
  해온 탈지분유등 유제품이 포함

3. 아국 관련사항

가. 현 황

○ 국영무역을 공식화하여 갓트에 통보한 바 없음.

○ 거래형태에 비추어 사실상 국영무역이 실시되고 있는 것으로 간주되는
  품목
  - 쌀, 파종용 종자, 식물성 맥즙, 조제 식료품, 연초, 제조연초
    (88.7. BOP 협의 대책 자료)
  - 쇠고기, 인삼류등

나. 관계부처의 고려사항 (경제기획원)

○ UR 협상 결과에 대비한 향후 검토 과제로서 상정한 것이며, 세부계획
  상금 미정

○ 쇠고기, 엽연초등 현재 사실상 국영무역이 행해지고 있는 품목에 대해
  통고, 상업적 고려등 갓트상의 의무 이행을 통한 명료성 제고 도모

○ 극히 일부품목에 대하여 갓트 규정에 일치하는 범위내에서 국내 수급
  조절 가능성 모색

3

0010

4. 검토 의견

○ 국영무역을 이유로한 수입제한 조치는 갓트 위배

  - 갓트 규정에 위배되지 않는 국내법규에 따라 수입 독점권 설정등
    국영무역을 실시하는 것은 일반적 예외로 인정되나, 동 수입 독점권을
    갖고 있는 기업의 조치가 수량제한의 일반적 금지등 어타 갓트 규정을
    위배하여서는 안됨 (상기 일본관련 패널 결론 및 갓트 부속규정)

○ UR 갓트 조문 협상에서의 잠정 합의사항에 비추어 국영무역 원용 가능성
  점차 축소

○ 아국이 향후 농산물 수입과 관련하여 갓트 17조등 제반규정에 맞게 국영무역을
  실시코자 할 경우 하기 요건 충족 필요

  - 수입제한 조치 자체의 갓트상 근거는 17조이외의 어타규정(예 : 11조 2항
    C등)에 합치되어야 하고,
  - 해당품목에 대한 수입 독점권을 특정기업에 줄 경우에도 구매, 판매에
    있어서 무차별 원칙등 제반 갓트의 원칙과 규정을 준수하여야 하며,
  - 동 기업의 운용 현황, 무역에의 영향등 상세 정보를 갓트에 통보하여야 하고,
  - 이해 당사국 요청에 의한 협의에 응해야 하는등 갓트의 제반 규정을
    준수해야 함.

○ 또한, 국영무역에 의한 수입 독점의 경우, 수입물량 및 국내 판매가격등이
  시장경쟁 원리와 수요.공급의 원칙에 입각하지 않고 어느정도 자의적으로
  정해질 수 밖에 없으므로 실질적 무역 효과면에서는 수입제한의 성격을
  배제할 수 없기 때문에 이해 관계국의 갓트 제소등 분쟁의 소지가 큼

○ 따라서, 국영무역을 통한 수입제한 의도 유무를 불문하고 자유화된 농산물에
  대한 국영무역 실시 여부는 신중히 검토되어야 함.

첨 부 : 농산물에 대한 주요국별 국영무역 내용 갓트 통보 현황.   끝.

4

0011

(첨 부)

농산물에 대한 주요국별 국영무역 내용 갓트 통보 현황

국 가 명	국영무역 품목	국영무역 사유
놀 웨 이	밀, 보리, 호밀, 귀리, 사료	- 식량비축 - 식량안보
호　　주	사과, 배, 복숭아 통조림, 밀, 살구 통조림, 꿀, 유제품, 쇠고기, 양고기, 소, 양, 염소, 설탕등	- 관련 농산물 유통, 수출 업무 지원 및 관리 - 관련 농산물 경쟁력 제고등
페　　루	쌀, 기초식량등	- 적정수준의 유통, 공급, 가격 확보
스 위 스	버터	- 적정수준의 가격, 공급, 유통 확보
남 아 공	바나나, 유제품, 건조과일, 육류, 감자, 사료곡물등	- 가격, 유통안정등
핀 랜 드	밀, 보리, 호밀, 귀리, 사료용 옥수수	- 비축 및 가격안정
오 지 리	연초, 소금	

0012

1. 갓트 조문

    가. 목 표

        ㅇ 현재 GATT 조문, 규정 및 규율을 재검토하여 필요시 협상 수행

    나. 협상 현황

        ㅇ '90.11.2. TNC 수석대표 비공식 협의

            - 2조1(b)항, 17조, 28조는 잠정합의가 이루어진 분야로 분류

            - 24조, 25조 5항, 35조 및 잠정 적용 의정서는 합의된 협상 기초가
              있는 분야로 분류

            - BOP 조항만 합의된 협상 기초조차 없는 분야로 분류

        ㅇ '91.2.21. 갓트 조문 협상 관련 Dunkel Statement 요지

            - 잠정 합의 : 2조 1항(b), 17조, 28조

            - 몇몇 참가국 합의 유보 : 24조, 35조

            - 여타분야 협상 결과 고려 최종 결정 : 25조 5항, 잠정 적용 의정서

            - 협상 여부 미합의 : 18조 B

    다. 합의사항

        ㅇ 잠정 합의를 도출하여 향후 각료들의 확인 절차만을 남긴 조문

            - 2조1(b)항 : 관세 양허표상의 기타 및 부과금

            - 17조 : 국영무역 기업

            - 28조 : 관세 양허 재협상 절차

        ㅇ 향후 철폐시한만 결정되면 타결될 조문

            - 25조 5항 : Waiver

            - 잠정 적용 의정서 및 가입 의정서상의 조부조항

1

o 일부 참가국들(인도, 브라질, 멕시코등) 초안 내용의 법적 의미에
  대한 검토 완료시까지 유보한 조문
  - 35조 : 갓트 협정 부적용

라. 미합의사항
  o 24조 : 관세동맹 및 지역 협정
  o 18조 B : BOP 조항

마. 주요쟁점 및 아국 입장

  o 24조 (관세동맹 및 지역협정)
    - 관세동맹 및 지역협정의 결정 및 확대에 따른 보상지불 문제(24조 6항)
      . 의장 초안 : 추가 보상 필요시, 다른 품목의 공동 관세인하로 보상
      . E C : 추가 보상 필요시, 타회원국의 다른품목에 관한 관세
        인하분까지 고려 대상 포함
      . 미 국 : 반 대
      . 아 국 : 의장 초안과 동일
    - 지방정부 또는 기관의 조치 및 행위는 중앙정부의 갓트상 책임 문제
      . 의장 초안 : 지방정부의 조치 및 행위는 중앙정부의 책임
      . E C : 연방 또는 중앙정부의 책임으로 함으로써 분쟁해결 절차
        명료화
      . 미국, 카나다, 인도등 : 중앙정부가 갓트 규정의 준수를 위한
        합리적인 조치를 취하는 것은 헌법상 허용된 한도내에서만 가능
      . 아 국 : 의장 초안과 동일 입장
    - 24조 관련 분쟁시 특별 구제 절차
      . 의장 초안 : 갓트 분쟁해결 절차 원용 가능
      . EC, 카나다, 오지리 : 24조 관련 분쟁도 갓트 분쟁해결 절차
        원용 가능

2

0014

. 아국 및 일본 : 역외국의 특별한 권익 보호를 위하여 동 조항
  관련 분쟁이 당사국간 협의로 타결되지 않을 경우, 위원회나
  체약국단에 회부하여 권고로 해결

o 18조 B (BOP 조항)

 - 동 조문에 대한 협상을 실시할 것인지에 대한 선진.개도국간
   합의 부재

o 조부조항, Waiver

 - X년후 철폐에 합의 하였으나 X년에 대한 구체적 논의는 아직
   진행되지 않고 있음.

마. 향후 협상 전망

o 24조 현 의장 초안 : 일본, 호주, 뉴질랜드, 아국등 협정 비가입국의
  입장을 적절히 반영하고 있으며 EC등 협정 가입국들의 반대도 크지
  않음에 비추어 향후 큰논란 없이 채택될 전망

o 24조 관련 타 쟁점도 현 의장의 내용이 다수국들의 주장에 따르고
  있음에 비추어 현 문안대로 채택될 가능성이 큼.

o BOP 조항 : 치열한 의견 대립이 전망되는 바, 이는 UR 협상 전체
  Package의 한 주요쟁점으로 부각될 전망.

갓트 기능

1991. 6.14.
통상기구과

(목   적)

ㅇ 체약국의 무역정책 및 관행에 대한 감시기능 강화

ㅇ 각료의 참여를 통한 갓트의 효율성 및 의사 결정 기능 개선

ㅇ 국제통화, 금융기구와 갓트의 연계 강화

1. 추진 상황

가. 주요 협상 결과

1) 88.12. 중간평가

ㅇ 국별 무역정책 검토 제도 문제 합의

ㅇ 각료급 참여 확대 문제 합의

ㅇ 국제통화 및 금융기구와의 관계 강화 방안에 대하여는 계속
검토키로 합의

2) 90.10.26. (10.9. TNC 비공식 회의에서 설정한 시한)

ㅇ 그룹차원의 협상 종료 및 브랏셀 각료회의에 제출할 각료의
결정 초안 채택

3) 90.11.2. TNC

ㅇ TNC 수석대표 비공식 협의에서 합의된 협상 기초가 있는 분야로
분류됨.

4) 90.12. Brussel 각료회의시 갓트 기능에 대하여 협의 없었음.

1

0016

2. 합의된 사항

가. 감시 기능 강화

1) 국별 무역정책검토(TPRM)
   o 89.4. 중간평가시 합의되어 조기 시행중인 TPRM의 존재 재확인
   o 장기 검토 일정을 91.6.까지 결정
   o 92.10에 TPRM 운용 재평가 검토

2) 국제무역 환경 검토
   o 89.4. 중간 평가시 합의되어 조기 시행중인 특별이사회에서의 연례
     국제무역환경 검토 제도를 계속키로 재확인

3) Domestic transparency
   o 각국의 무역정책 결정과 관련한 명료성 (예 : 공청회 개최, 독립
     연구기관을 통한 손익분석등)을 제고한다는 권고적인 성격의
     결정문 합의

4) 통고 제도 개선
   o 통고 의무의 강화 (1979년 양해사항 재확인 및 통고 대상 사항
     목록 합의)
   o 중앙통고 기탁소 설치
     - 제반 갓트 규정에 의거한 통고사항 취합, 각국의 통고의무 준수
       여부 주의 환기
   o 기존 통고 의무 및 절차를 재검토하여 단순화, 체계화하기 위한
     작업반을 UR 협상 종료 직후에 설치

나. 기구적 측면의 갓트 강화
   o 89.4. 중간평가시 2년 1회의 갓트 각료급 총회 개최에 합의

2

0017

3. 미합의 쟁점

가. 기구적 측면의 갓트 강화

1) 소규모 각료회의 설치 문제
   ㅇ 미국, 호주외에 대체로 반대 의견이며, 정치적으로 결정되어야
     할 문제로 인식
     - 인도등 강경론자들은 각료회의 회부에도 반대한 바 있음.
   ㅇ 최근 미국은 갓트 관리 이사회(Management Board) 설치를 제의한 바,
     이는 주요 정책 결정 기관으로서 IMF의 Interim Committee와 동등한
     지위에서 협력하며, 18개국으로 구성(4대국은 상설회원, 무역
     고순으로 16위 국가까지는 격년제 참가, 여타 국가는 순번대로
     1년씩 교대)

2) MTO/WTO 설치 문제
   ㅇ EC(공식 제안), 캐나다(비공식 제기)는 다음 사항을 포함하는
     신기구 설치 협정 체결을 제안
     - 회원국 규정 및 기구적 조직
     - UR 협상 결과의 이행, 특히 모든 협정에 통용되는 분쟁해결
       절차 이행을 위한 법적 근거
     - 사무총장 및 사무국
     - 예산 규정
     - 기타 기구의 법적인 지위, 특권과 면제, 기타 기구와의 관계등
       행정 규정
   ㅇ 각국 입장
     - 미국이 소극적이었으며, 개도국들은 Cross-sectoral retaliation에
       우려 소극적 입장
     - 개도국은 UN, UNCTAD 등에서 ITO 설치 거론

3

0018

나. 통화, 금융, 무역정책간의 일관성 (coherence)

1) IMF, IBRD, GATT의 정치적 합동 각료선언

○ 당초 EC는 3기구 담당 각료들간의 합동 각료 선언을 채택하여,
일관성 문제에 대한 정치적 결의를 보여야 한다고 주장

○ 이러한 EC의 제의에 대해, 개도국이 동조 하였으나 미국을 위시
여타 선진국은 반대의사 여타 선진국은 반대 의사 표명

- 미국은 각국 정부의 자체적 책임, 개도국의 무역자화 필요성
등을 강조하는 각료선언만 제안

○ 이에따라 일단 갓트의 일방적인 각료선언을 각료회의 결정의
형태로 초안 하였으나 실질문제(환율, 금리, 개도국의 교역조건,
개도국에 대한 금융지원)에 대한 언급문제와 관련 다수 미합의사항
(   ) 존재

2) 사무국간 실용적 협력

○ 중소 선진국들이 강력히 추진하는 3개기구 사무국간 인전교류,
연규협력, 감시기능 관련 협력등 사무국간 협력 강화 차원의
실용적 접근 방식

○ EC가 상기 합동 각료선언과 연계하여 반대함에 따라 합의되지
못하고, 일단 갓트 사무총장으로 하여금 실용적 협력 방안을
포함하여 가능한 일관성 강화 방안을 연구하여 91.12.31.까지
보고토록 요청 내용만 합의

4. 아국 입장

가. 감시 기능 강화
- 과도한 예산 증대, 기구 확장없는한 찬성
- TPRM 설치 목적상 필요한 수준 이상으로 무역 외적 사항에 대해
감시 기능을 확대하는데는 소극적 입장

4

0019

나. 소규모 각료회의

  - 아국의 참여 확보가 최우선의 관심사항

다. 갓트 관리이사회

  - 의사 결정기관이 아니고 자문적인 성격을 띤 협의기구로 하는것이 바람직

라. MTO/WTO

  - 원칙적으로 찬성이나 UR 종료후에 논의하는 것이 바람직

마. Coherence 문제

  - 중.소 선진국들이 제안한 실용적 접근방안이 현실적으로 바람직하나
    아국에 특별한 이해관계 없는 사항이므로 개도국 입장을 고려,
    입장 표명 자제

5. 협상 전망

  ㅇ MTO/WTO 설치 문제는 UR이후 구체적인 논의 가능성

  ㅇ 소규모 각료회의 설치 및 갓트관리이사회 구성 문제는 참여범위 설정에
    어려움으로 타결 난망

  ㅇ 각기구간 MANDATE 차이 및 각기구의 독자적인 결의 절차에 비추어 실질
    협력은 대단히 어려운 작업으로 사료됨.   끝.

5

GATT 조문

1. 협상 배경 및 목표

가. 배 경

○ 기존의 GATT 협정문을 GATT 설립이후 급변한 국제무역 및 경제환경에 맞게 개선 보강할 필요에 따라 UR 협상의 의제로 채택

나. 목 표

○ 현존 GATT 조문, 규정 및 규율을 재검토하며 필요시 협상 수행

2. 진전상황

가. 주요협상 경과

○ '88.12 중간평가를 통하여 아래 사항에 합의

  - GATT 조문의 명료화 및 개선에 협상력 집중
  - 본 협상그룹내 쟁점과 타협상 그룹 쟁점간에 관련성 고려
  - 명확한 협상쟁점 설정

○ '90.11.2 TNC 수석대표 비공식 협의에서 2조1(B)항, 17조, 28조는 잠정합의가 이루어진 분야로, 24조, 25조 5항, 35조 및 잠정적용 의정서는 합의된 협상기초가 있는 분야로 분류 되었으며, 다만 BOP 조항만이 합의된 협상기초조차 없는 분야로 분류됨

○ 91.3.26. 주요국 수석대표급 비공식 협의에서 규범제정 (Rule making) 협상 그룹의 일부로 재구성됨.

0021

나. 합의사항

○ 잠정합의를 도출한 조문

- 2조 1(B)항 : 관세 양허표상의 기타 과세 및 부과금

- 17조 : 국영무역기업

- 28조 : 관세 양허재협상 절차

○ 철폐시한만 결정되면 타결될 조문

- 25조 5항 : 웨이버

- 잠정적용 의정서 및 가입 의정서상의 조부 조항

○ 일부 참가국들이 초안내용의 법적의미에 대한 검토 완료시까지 유보한 조문

- 35조 : GATT 협정 부적용

다. 미합의사항

○ 24조 : 관세동맹 및 지역협정

○ 18조 B : BOP 조항

3. 쟁점별 주요국 입장

가. 24조(관세동맹 및 지역협정)

○ 관세동맹 및 지역협정의 결성 및 확대에 따른 보상 지불문제(24조 6항)

- E C : 추가보상 필요시, 타회원국의 다른 품목에 대한 관세인하분까지 고려대상에 포함

- 미국등 : 추가보상 필요시, 다른 품목의 공동 관세인하로 보상

0022

o 지방정부 또는 기관의 조치 및 행위에 대한 연방 또는 중상정부의
 GATT상 책임문제
   - E C : 연방 또는 중앙정부의 책임으로 함으로써 분쟁해결절차 명료화
   - 미국, 카나다, 인도등 : 중앙정부가 GATT 규정의 준수를 위한
     합리적인 조치를 취하는 것은 헌법상 허용된 한도내에서만 가능

나. 18조 B (BOP 조항)
 o 동 조문에 대한 협상을 실시한 것인지에 대한 선진.개도국간 합의 부재

다. 조부 조항, 웨이버
 o X년이후 철폐에 합의
 o 철폐에 관한 구체적 사항은 타협상그룹(특히 농산물)의 협상결과를
   감안하여 결정

4. 쟁점별 아국 입장

가. 24조

 o 24조 관련 세이프가드 조치의 선별적용 반대 및 분쟁시 GATT 분쟁해결
   절차 원용 근거 확보

 o 관세동맹 및 지역협정의 결성과 확대에 따른 보상 지불문제
   - 추가보상 필요시, 다른 품목의 관세인하로 보상

 o 지방정부 또는 기관의 조치 및 행위에 대한 연방 또는 중앙정부의
   GATT상 책임문제
   - 지방정부의 조치 및 행위는 중앙정부의 책임

나. BOP 조항
 o 구체적인 입장 표명 불필요.   끝.

'0023

UR/갓트조문 협상 대책

1. 협상 동향 및 예상 합의 수준

가. 협상 동향

ㅇ 현재 미합의로 남아있는 주요쟁점

- 관세동맹 및 자유무역의 결성, 확대에 따른 특정품목 양허 변경시의 보상 지급 문제 명료화 (24조 6항)

- 지방정부 및 기관의 조치에 대한 연방, 중앙정부의 갓트상 책임 강화 문제 (24조 12항)

- BOP 조항의 개정을 위한 협상 여부 (18조 B)

나. 예상 합의 수준

ㅇ 24조

- 상금 미합의 사항인 관세동맹 및 지역협정에 따른 보상문제, 지방 정부의 조치에 대한 중앙정부의 책임문제, 24조 관련 분쟁시 특별 구제 절차 설정문제도 현 의장안의 내용이 다수국들의 주장에 따르고 있음에 비추어 현 문안대로 채택될 가능성이 큼.

ㅇ BOP 조항

- 협상 실시 자체를 반대하는 개도국의 완강한 태도로 협상 최종 단계에서 정치적 타결될 전망

0024

2. 협상 대책 및 대응 논리

가. 전체 협상과 연계, 입장 반영이 필요한 사항

1) BOP 조항

○ 대 책

- 선.개도국간 치열한 의견 대립이 전망되는 바, 이는 UR 협상 전체 Package 의한 주요쟁점으로 부각될 전망임.
- 아국은 이미 BOP 졸업이 합의된만큼 구체적 입장 표명은 자제

○ 대응 논리

- 아국은 BOP 조항의 원용을 중단 하였으므로 동 조항의 원용절차 개선을 위한 개정에 반대치 않음.
- 그러나, BOP 조항은 선.개도국간의 정치적인 협상으로서 특별한 이해관계가 없는 제3자가 협상의 일방을 지지하기는 어려움. 특히, 아국은 개도국 그룹의 일원으로서 BOP 조항 개정 찬성시 개도국들이 아국에게 강력히 반발할 것이므로 적극 찬성의 표명 자제

나. 협상 대세 수용 분야

○ 24조

- 의장 초안은 아국등 협정 비가입국의 입장을 적절히 반영하고 있으며 EC등 협정 가입국들의 반대도 크지 않음에 비추어 큰 논란없이 채택될 전망임.   끝.

0025

33318

기 안 용 지

분류기호 문서번호	통기 20644-	(전화 : 720 - 2188)	시 행 상 특별취급	
보존기간	영구 · 준영구 10. 5. 3. 1.	장	관	
수 신 처 보존기간				
시행일자	1991. 7. 15			

보 조 기 관	국 장	전 결	협 조 기 관	문 서 통 제
	심의관			(인) 1991. 7. 15
	과 장			
기안책임자		송 봉 헌		발 송 인

경 유 수 신 참 조	상공부장관 국제협력관	발 명 의	(인) 1991. 7. 15 외부무

제 목	UR/규범제정 및 투자분야 자료

대 : 국협 28140-268(91.7.9)

1. 대호 당부소관 협상분야(BOP)에 대한 자료를 별첨 송부

합니다.   관련 갓트조문

2. 금번 협상에는 당부에서 직원을 파견치 않고, 그간 UR/갓트

조문 협상에 참여해온 주 제네바 대표부 관계관을 참석케 할 예정임을

첨언합니다.   0026

- 2 -
첨 부 : 상기 자료 1부.　　　　　끝.
0027

BOP 조항 협상현황 및 아국 입장

1. 협상 현황

   o BOP 조항의 개선, 강화와 동 조항에 근거한 기존 수입제한 조치의 점진적
     철폐를 주장하는 미, EC등 선진국과 협상 자체를 반대하는 인도, 브라질등
     개도국의 첨예한 의견 대립으로 협상에 돌입 할 것인지에 대한 기본 합의 부재

2. 협상 전망

   o 선·개도국간 의견 대립이 계속될 것으로 예상되며, UR 협상 전체 package의
     하나로 부각될 전망

3. 아국 입장

   o 아국의 BOP 졸업에 비추어 동 조항 개선이 바람직하나 개도국들과의 기존
     협조 관계를 고려, 관망자세 견지

0028

상 공 부

국 협 28140- 281   (2396)   1991. 7. 19

수 신 외무부장관

제 목 UR/규범제정분야 회의 참석

    '91. 7. 22 (월) ~ 7. 26 (금)긴 스위스 제네바에서 개최되는
UR 규범제정분야 회의에 참가하기 위하여 다음과 같이 출장코자 하오니
정부대표 임명등 필요한 조치를 하여 주시기 바랍니다.

               " 다   음 "

    1. 출장개요

직 위	성 명	출 장 기 간	비 고
국제협력관실 행정 사무관	김 영 민	'91. 7. 20 (토) ~ 7. 28 (일)	UR 규범제정분야 회의 참가

    2. 예산근거 : 상공부 예산

점 부 : 아국 입장 1부.

         상 공 부 장

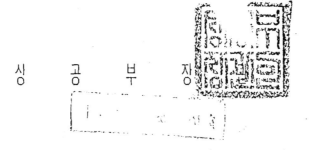

                                                    0029

UR/규범제정 및 투자분야협상 (7.22~26)에 대한 입장

1. 전반적인 입장

o 규범제정 분야는 장기적인 관점에서 우리의 이익에 직결되는 중요한 협상 분야임

- 특히, 반덤핑 협정 개정을 통해 기존 규범을 강화함으로써 공정한 무역질서를
확립하고, 긴급수입제한조치의 명료화를 통해 선진국의 수입규제 대응해
나갈 수 있도록 아국이 적극적인 입장을 취하고 있는 분야이며,

- 보조금/상계관세 협상은 동 협상 결과에 따라 우리나라 산업정책의 전반적인
방향을 수정해야 할 중요한 분야임

o 현재 규범 제정 분야에서의 대부분 쟁점은 기술적인 문제가 아닌 정치적인 절충을
요하는 사항이므로 농산물 협상에서 돌파구를 찾아 UR 전체 협상의 분위기
전환이 없는 한 각국의 기존 입장만 되풀이 할 것으로 보이며,

- 금번 7월회의에서도 각국이 기존 입장의 타협을 기대할 수 없을 것으로
전망되며 각 분야별로 정치적 타결을 요하는 쟁점만 확인할 것으로 예상됨

o 기본적으로 금번 협상에서는 기존의 입장을 유지하고, 선진국과 개도국간의
중도적 입장에서 협상의 성공적인 타결을 위해서 노력하고 있다는 입장을 밝힘

- 한국은 UR협상이 성공적으로 타결되어 갓트를 중심으로 한 세계자유무역체제가
강화되어야 한다고 믿고, 그동안 협상타결을 위해 노력해 왔고, 앞으로도
노력할 것임을 강조

- 규범제정분야는 실질적으로 다자간 무역체제 확립을 위한 가장 중요한 분야로서
아직까지 협상의 기초가 마련되지 않은 분야는 각국이 자국의 기대수준을
낮춤으로써 협상 타결에 기여토록 노력할 필요성을 강조하고,
수출국과 수입국, 선진국과 개도국간의 이익이 균형있게 반영된 협상text
마련 필요성 언급

o 농산물 협상에서 돌파구가 마련될 경우 규범제정 분야는 주요국간 정치적 타협을
통해 급속도로 진행될 가능성이 있으므로 이에 대비하여 각 분야별로 밀히
반영하여야 할 정치적 쟁점 및 우선순위 재점검

0030

2. 반덤핑 협정

o 반덤핑 조치의 남용 방지를 위해 현행 협정을 강화하고 명료성을 확보하자는
  아국의 기존 입장 유지

  - 덤핑, 피해 판정 기준의 공정성 및 객관성 확보
  - 조사 개시 요건등 조사 절차의 강화
  - 소멸 시효의 설정

o 선진 수입국 (미국, EC)이 주장하는 우회덤핑 방지 조항 도입을 최대한 저지토록 함

  - 다만, 순수한 우회덤핑 (수출국내 단순조립)의 경우는 규제 인정 가능하나
    남용 방지를 위해 그 기준 설정을 엄격히 해야함

o 주요 항목별 입장 (별첨)

3. 보조금. 상계관세 협상

o 금번 회의시 UR/보조금.상계관세협상에 관한 각국의 기본입장 및 현재의 협상
  상황에 대한 개괄적 평가가 있을 경우

  - 이번 회의가 브랏셀 각료회의후 재개되는 성격임을 감안하어 아국은 본 협상의
    성공적인 타결을 위해 노력하고 있음을 홍보
  - 현재 협상의 기초가 되는 브랏셀 각료회의 의장 보고서는 그간의 쟁점사항을
    종합화한 점에서 긍정적으로 평가하나, 아직 개선의 여지가 많음을 언급
  - 주요국의 입장 및 협상 동향을 면밀히 파악하여 향후 아국의 최종안 수립에
    참고토록 준비

o 세부 쟁점별 공식. 비공식 협의가 진행될 경우 첨부한 쟁점별 아국 입장에
  의거, 적의 대처

0031

4. TRIMs 협상

o 투자제한조치 협상 타결시 아국기업의 해외투자 환경개선을 기대할 수 있는 반면 외국인 투자를 추가로 개방하여야 하는 부담이 거의 없으므로 아국으로서는 협상이 타결되는 것이 유리

o 협상결과에 선진국 및 일부개도국만 참여하고 다수 개도국이 불참하는 경우에도 아국으로서는 참여가 불가피한 바 이 경우 ①아국의 대개도국 투자환경 개선을 기대할 수 없고 ② 선진국에 비하여 상대적으로 제한조치가 많은 아국이 개선 요청을 많이 받을 것으로 예상할 때 아국으로서는 다수 개도국이 참여하는 것이 유리함

- 그러나 선.개도국간 입장차이가 현격하므로 이에 대한 노력 필요

o 주요 항목별 입장 (별첨)

5. BOP 조항

o BOP 조항은 선진. 개도국간의 첨예한 의견 대립을 보이는 미묘한 문제이고 아국은 이미 BOP 조항을 졸업한만큼 구체적인 입장 표명 자제

- BOP 조항 개정 가능성은 거의 없으며, 다만 선진국들이 섬유 협상등 여타 협상 분야와 연계 카드로 사용

- BOP 조항 개정 찬성시 개도국들이 우리에게 강력히 반발할 것이므로 찬성 의사 표명 자제 (별첨 BOP 논의 현황)

0032

UR 규범제정 및 투자분야 협상 회의 참가자료

('91. 7. 22 ~ 7. 26)

91. 7

상 공 부
국 제 협 력 관 실

0033

I. 회의개요

o '91년 4월 UR 협상 그룹이 7개로 통합된 이후에 MTN 협정, GATT조문, 보조금
 상계관세 협정, 세이프가드, 원산지 규정, 선적전 검사 및 무역관련 투자
 협상 분야가 규범제정 및 투자분야 그룹에서 논의되고 있음

   - 규범제정 및 투자분야 의장 : Marciel (브라질 전 제네바 주재대사)

o 지난해 말 개최된 브라셀 각료회의에서도 규범제정 분야가 통합되어 협상이 진행
 된 바 있으며, 최근 공식.비공식 회의가 6월에 제네바에서 개최됨

   - 지난 6월 회의에서 규범제정 분야의 협상진행방안에 대하여 논의하여 아래와
    같이 결정함
    . 규범제정 분야 소관 11개 분야중 반덤핑, 보조금/상계관세, 세이프가드,
     국제수지(BOP), 무역관련 투자조치 등 5개 분야를 우선적으로 다루어야 할
     중요분야로 선정함 (5개 분야에 대한 우선 순위는 없음)

o 금번 공식/비공식 회의는 반덤핑, 보조금/상계관세, 무역관련투자조치, BOP조항에
 대하여 91.7.22 - 26간 제네바에서 개최될 예정

   - 7. 22 : 전체 공식회의,   7. 23 : 반덤핑,   7. 24 : 보조금/상계관세,
    7. 25 : 무역관련 투자조치(TRIMs),   7. 26 : BOP, 전체 공식회의 순으로
    진행될 예정

   - 금번회의에서는 협상진전상황 평가 및 의제별 주요쟁점 확인 정도에 그칠
    전망임

0034

라. 무역관련 투자제한조치 (TRIMs)

1) 진전상황

   o 주요협상 경위

   - UR/TRIMs 협상은 서비스. 지적소유권과 함께 GATT 협상의 새로운 분야
     (new issue)로써 외국인 투자에 대한 각종 규제와 제한을 철폐함으로써
     국제간 투자를 촉진하고 세계무역 증진을 도모하기 위하여 UR 협상에 포함,
     '87.4월부터 협상을 개최한 이후, '90년말까지 20여 차례의 실무자간
     협상과 수차례의 Green Room 회의를 가졌음

   - 그러나, 기본적으로 자국기업의 해외투자를 촉진. 보호하여야 할 입장에
     있는 선진국이 투자대상국 (Host Country)의 투자제한조치 (TRIMs)를
     규제하여야 한다고 주장하는 반면, 해외투자 실적이 거의 없고 자국
     산업을 보호해야 할 입장에 있는 개도국이 투자제한 조치에 대한 규제를
     반대하고 있는등 주요 쟁점에 대하여 선진국과 개도국간에 입장 차이가
     현격함

   - 지난해 브랏셀 각료 회의에서도 선진국과 개도국간의 입장 조정에 실패

2) 미결쟁점 및 아국 입장

   가) 협상의 범위

   o 선진국 입장

   - TRIMs은 신규투자뿐 아니라 기존 외국인 투자기업의 전반적인 영업
     활동과 관련하여 부과되는 제한 조치를 폭넓게 포함하여야 함

   - 보조금등 특혜부여의 조건으로 부과되는 조치도 규제대상이 되어야 함

0035

o 개도국 입장

- TRIMs은 신규투자와 관련 부과되는 경우만 포함

- 보조금등 특혜부여와 관련 부과되는 조치는 보조금. 상계관세협상
  그룹에서 논의할 사항임

o 아국입장

- 투자제한조치중 내.외국 기업에 동등하게 부과하는 경우에는 TRIMs
  범위내에서 제외 되어야 함

- 아국은 조세감면등 혜택을 부여하면서 투자제한조치를 부과하는 사례가
  없는 반면, 개도국은 부과 사례가 많음. 따라서, 아국의 해외
  투자 측면을 고려할때 이를 TRIMs에 포함 규제 대상이 되어야 함

나) 규제의 방법

o 선진국 입장

- 국산부품사용 조건등과 같이 GATT 제 3조, 제 11조에 위반되는
  TRIMs은 금지 대상이 되도록 규정하여야 함

- 수출이행 조건도 무역왜곡 효과가 심각하므로 금지 대상이 되어야 함

o 개도국 입장

- 어떤 경우도 TRIMs을 일반적인 금지 대상으로 할 수는 없으며,
  Case by Case로 검토후 무역왜곡 효과를 치유토록 하여야 함

- 수출이행 조건은 GATT의무 위반이 아니므로 규제 대상이 됨수 없음

o 아국입장

- 무역왜곡효과가 직접적이고 심각한 TRIMs은 금지대상으로 하되
  개도국에 대한 예외 범위를 확대

- 수출이행 조건도 TRIMs으로 규제대상이 되어야 하나, 개도국의
  국제수지 개선등의 목적상 불가피한 경우 예외 인정

0036

다) 개도국에 대한 배려

   o 선진국 입장

    - 개도국에 대한 배려는 GATT 제 18조 (개도국에 대한 예외)의 규정에
      따라 잠정적이고 제한적이어야 함

   o 개도국 입장

    - 개도국의 경제개발 필요성등을 고려, 개도국이 필요시 TRIMs을 운용할
      수 있도록 전반적인 예외를 인정하여야 함

   o 아국입장

    - 개도국에 대하여는 GATT 제 18조에서 규정하고 있는 범위 이상으로
      TRIMs 의무에 대한 예외 인정

라) 제한적 사업관행 (Restrictive Business Practice)

   o 선진국 입장
    - 제한적 사업관행은 '86.9월 Punta del Este 각료선언에 의한 협상범위
      에 포함되지 않음

   o 개도국 입장

    - 다국적 기업등이 제한적 사업관행으로 무역을 심각하게 왜곡하는 사례가
      많으므로 본 협상에 포함 하어야 함

   o 아국입장

    - 다국적 기업의 제한적 사업관행도 본 협상 범위에 포함하어야 함

0037

3) 협상 전망

o 선진국과 개도국간의 입장 차이가 현격하여 TRIMs 협상 자체로는 타결 되기가
  어려우나 농산물등 주요 분야에서 정치적인 타협이 이뤄져 UR 협상이
  전반적으로 타결되는 방향으로 합의가 되면 TRIMs 협상도 정치적 결단에
  의해 타결된 수 있을 것임

o 그러나 최빈 개도국의 경우에는 UR 협상타결 이후에도 TRIMs 협정에
  참여하지 않는 경우도 예상할 수 있음

4) 협상 대응 방향

o 투자제한조치 (TRIMs) 협상 타결시 아국기업의 해외투자 환경 개선을 기대할 수
  있는 반면, 외국인 투자를 추가로 개방하여야 하는 부담은 거의 없으므로
  아국으로서는 협상이 타결되는 것이 유리함

o 다만, 협상 결과에 선진국 및 일부 개도국만 참여하고 다수 개도국이 불참할
  경우에도 아국으로서는 참여가 불가피한 바, 이 경우 ① 아국의 대개도국
  투자환경 개선을 기대할 수 없고 ② 선진국에 비하여 상대적으로 제한조치가
  많은 아국이 개선 요청을 많이 받을 것 등을 예상할 때 아국으로서는 다수
  개도국이 참여하는 것이 유리하므로 이에 대한 노력 필요

0038

라. BOP 조항

1) BOP 조항 개선 입장

가) 논의이유

　　o 갓트 12 ·조 및 18조 B에 의한 갓트 일반원칙에 대한 에외는 무역체제의
　　　중요 요소이며, 갓트 규정의 다른 쟁점처럼 다루어져야 함

　　o BOP 조항에 근거한 조치 특히, 무역 왜곡 조치에 대하여는 효율적인 규율
　　　이 없으며, 갓트 의무에 대한 영구적인 에외가 되고 있고, 동 조항 적용
　　　국가나 상대국가에 붑필요한 비용을 야기하여, 다자간 체제의 약점 및
　　　붑협화음의 원인이 됨

나) EC, 카나다, 미국의 제안 요지(1979년 선언음 대체할 BOP 목적의 무역조치에
　　관한 새로운 선언안)

　　o 선진국의 BOP 목적을 이유로 한 무역제한조치 금지 공약의 강화

　　o 12조나 18조 B에 근거한 무역조치는 BOP 문제의 정도에 비례해야 하며
　　　보호의 목적이 아니라 국내 구조조정정책이 효과가 있기까지의 일시적인
　　　조치로써 사용해야 함

　　o 무역조치는 명료해야 하고, 무차별적이고, 제시될 철폐 및 점진적 완화
　　　계획에 따른 기간의 제한이 있어야 함(선진국은 개도국보다 짧은 기간 허용)

　　　* EC : 제한조치 철폐를 위한 일반적으로 적용가능한 고정된 철폐 계획이
　　　　　아닌 "합리적인" 철폐기간 계획이 제시 요구

0039

o 수량제한 조치보다 가격에 기초한 조치가 바람직

  - 수량제한 조치가 불가피한 경우에도 가격에 기초한 조치보다 빨리 철폐
    되거나 가격에 기초한 조치로 대체

o BOP 위원회에서의 협의는 제한 조치의 적용 또는 강화후 4개월 이내에 시작

  - full consultation은 2년마다 개최
  - 개도국이 제시한 철폐 계획에 따른 때에는 simplified 절차를 적용할
    수 없음

o BOP 위원회는 검토중인 조치의 갓트와의 일관성 및 적절한 수정에 관하여
  이사회에 권고하여야 함

o BOP 위원회는 협의중인 체약국의 수출 이익의 증대를 위하여 체약국단이
  취할 수 있는 조치를 제안할 수 있음

    * 카나다, 미국 : BOP 위원회 협의에서의 IMF의 역할을 좀더 분명히
                   정의해야 함. 동 위원회가 당해조치의 GATT 적합 여부
                   문제에 관한 권고에 합의할 수 없을 경우, 영향을 받은
                   체약국은 갓트 분쟁해결절차로 동 문제를 해결할 수 있음

    * E C : 특정산업의 설립을 촉진하기 위한 18조 C항에 대하여 동조에 의하여
           취해진 조치로 영향을 받은 체약국의 보복 가능성을 제한하면서
           거치 관세 인상을 용이하게 함으로써 동 조항의 원용을 쉽게 할 것을
           제안

다) 지지국가

  o 대부분의 선진국이 지지.   단, 몇몇 선진국의 12조를 강화하는 것은 협의
    간 가능하나, 현 단계에서 12조를 사용하지 않겠다는 약속은 곤란하다느
    의견 제시

0040

2) BOP 조항 논의의 반대 입장 (이집트, 페루등 개도국)

    o 1979년 "BOP 목적의 무역 조치에 관한 선언"이 채택된 이후 동 문제가
      취급되어야 하는지에 의문

    o 많은 개도국의 외적인 경제환경이 대외 부채 증가, 자본유입, 교역조건의
      악화, 환율 및 이자율 불안정등 여러면에서 악화되고 있음

    o 만약 18조 B항상의 무역 조치에 관한 협상이 있어야 한다면 그 목적이
      보다 엄격한 조건을 부과하는것이 아니라 동 조항의 사용에 보다 융통성을
      부여 하는데 두어야 함

    o 기존의 규정과 BOP 위원회의 관련 절차는 잘 운용되고 있고, 그 운용상의
      문제점은 UR 협상과 관련해서가 아니라 동 위원회에서 다루어져야 함

※ 18조 B항의 flexibility

    o 18조 B항에 의한 개도국에 허가된 융통성은 갓트 체제하의 권리, 의무의
      균형의 필수적인 요소이며, 동 규정이 정상적인 갓트 규정의 예외로
      간주 되어서는 안됨

    o 동 조항은 개도국의 국제 수지상의 문제점이 구조적이고 영속적이라는
      점을 인정하여 체약국단에 의하여 합의 되었으며, 체약국단에 의하여
      허락된 융통성은 국가 개발 계획의 효과적인 관리를 위하여 필요한 조건임
      무역제한 조치가 오랫동안 유지되어도 좋다는 것은 국제수지 문제의
      구조적인 성격을 반영하고 주요 수출 시장에 대한 개도국의 접근이
      불충분하다는 사실을 반영함

      - 단순화된 협의 절차는 상황과 정책이 상대적으로 안정된 국가와의 빈번한
        전체 협의에서 오는 위원회와 당해국가의 부담을 완화하기 위하여 도입
        되어야 함
      - 위원회에서의 consensus에 도달하는 어려움은 실질 내용에 서로 다른 견해가
        있는 것이며, 이것이 동 절차가 취약하다는 증거로 간주되어선 안됨

0041

3) 지금까지의 논의에서 의견이 일치된 점

가) 18조 B의 필요성

   o 12조 및 18조 B의 내용 자체는 번화되어서는 안됨

   o BOP상의 어려운 시기에 무역조치를 사용하는 권한이 배제되어서는 안됨

   o 장기간의 BOP상의 어려움은 국내정책, 거시경제정책 및 무역관련 조치에
     의한 국내문제와 무역장벽 제거 및 채무, 금융 이동에 관한 국제문제로
     취급될 필요성은 인정

나) 18조 B에 의한 무역제한 조치의 문제점 인식

   o 제한적 무역조치는 어떤 상황에서는 피합수는 없지만 일반적으로 BOP 균형을
     유지, 회복하기 위해서는 비효과적인 수단임을 인정

   o 동 조치는 특정산업이나 분야를 보호할 목적으로 사용되어서는 안됨을 인정

   o 동조치 사용시 체약국은 무역에 가장 적게 영향을 미치는 조치를 우선
     하여야 함을 인정

   o 개도국의 경우 각국의 개발, 금융, 무역상황이 고려되어야 함을 인정

4) 협상 전망

   o BOP 조항은 UR 협상 결과의 선.개도국간 균형여부등 UR 전체 협상 차원에서
     다루어질 전망임

5) 우리나라 입장

   o BOP 조항은 선진.개도국간의 첨예한 의견 대립을 보이는 미묘한 문제이고
     아국은 이미 BOP 조항을 졸업한 만큼 구체적인 입장 표명 자제

     - BOP 조항 개정 가능성은 거의 없으며, 다만 선진국들이 섬유협상등 어타
       협상분야와 연계카드로 사용

     - BOP 조항 개정 한정시 개도국들이 우리에게 강력히 반발할 것이므로 찬성
       의사 표명 자제

0042

兩者協議關聯 資料準備 및 推進日程

1. 協調事項

가. 代表團構成: 9.10까지 確定

나. 對策資料作成

① 綜合對策分野

- 別冊 對策資料案을 중심으로 작성하여 代表團 全員이 活用

- 資料提出: 9.10까지
  ○ UR協商 全般에 대한 評價: 補完
  ○ 分野別 對應方案: 部處別 作成

② 分野別 細部對策 資料準備

- 協商分野別 擔當部處 作成

- EPB에 提出(9.12까지) 總括對策資料와 合本活用

다. 分野別 UR對策 實務會議 開催日程

- 8. 30: 市場接近
- 9. 3: TRIPs
- 9. 6: 農産物,   市場接近
- 9. 9주간 : 서비스, 여타분야, 最終對策會議

0043

2. 推進日程

- 9.23 兩者協議前提

區 分	豫想日程
① 我國의 協商代表團 構成	9. 10
② 對策資料의 作成	
- 綜合對策分野 資料提出	9. 10
○ 總括部門 英文資料는 經濟企劃院과 外務部에서 協調하여 作成	
○ 分野別 資料中 對應方案部門은 關係部處에서 Talking Point 形式으로 作成	
- 分野別 細部對策 資料提出	9. 12
③ 分野別 爭點事項에 대한 我側立場調整 會議	
○ 市場接近	8. 30
○ TRIPs	9. 3
○ 農産物	9. 6
○ 市場接近	9. 6
○ 規範分野	9. 9 주간
○ 纖維	"
○ 서비스	"
○ 制度分野 및 最終議定書	"
④ 最終對策 會議	"
⑤ 綜合資料 주제네바 송부	9. 18
⑥ 豫想質問 및 答辯資料作成	9.10~21

0044

이.오 上 갓트림, 세이라운)

상 공 부

국 협 28140-337   (503-9446)   1991. 9. 2.

수 신 수신처 참조

제 목 UR/한.미 양자협의 규범분야 대책자료 작성

　　　　1. UR/한.미 양자협의 대비하여 8월30일(금)에 개최된 UR대책 실무회의 결과,
각 분야별로 종합대책 대응방안과 세부 대책자료를 작성하여 UR대책 실무회의에 상정
키로 하였으며, 규범분야에 대한 UR 실무대책 회의는 9월9일 주간에 개최키로 하였습니다.

　　　　2. 이와 관련하여 귀부의 담당 의제별 한.미 양자협의 대비 종합대책 대응
방안과 세부대책 자료를 별첨 양식을 참고로 9월 6일까지 당부로 제출하여 주시기 바랍니다.

첨　　부 : 자료 작성 양식 1부.　　　　끝.

상 공 부 장

수신처 : 재무부 장관(관세협력과장, 투자진흥과장), 외무부 장관(통상기구과장)

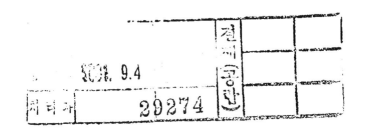

〈별 첨〉　　　　　　　자료 작성 양식
　　　　　　　　　　================

1. 종합대책 분야 작성 양식

　　○ 기본 방향

　　　- 우리의 기존 입장 견지가 불가피한 분야에 대해서는 보다
　　　　논리적이고 설득력이 있는 자료를 작성하여 진지하게 설명

　　　- 우리 경제에 별다른 영향이 없는 분야에 대해서는 협상의
　　　　대세를 검토하여 미측입장을 수용하는 방향으로 검토함으로써
　　　　실리확보

　　○ 작성 양식(3~4page로 간략히 작성)

　　　- 주요 쟁점 및 협상동향 평가
　　　- 미측 예상 제기 사항
　　　- 아국의 기존입장
　　　- 대응 방안 (Talking Point 형식으로 작성)

2. 세부 대책자료 작성 양식

　　○ 협상 진전 상황
　　○ 주요국 동향
　　○ 하반기 협상 전망
　　○ 주요 쟁점 사항
　　○ 아국입장

　　　- 기본 입장
　　　- 세부 쟁점별 기존입장
　　　- 입장 재정립 가능분야

0046

44984

기 안 용 지

분류기호 서번호	통기 20644-	기 안 용 지 (전화 : 720 - 2188)	시 행 상 특별취급	
보존기간	영구. 준영구 10. 5. 3. 1.	장　　　관		
수 신 처 보존기간				
시행일자	1991. 9.10.			

보조 기관	국 장	전 결	협 조 기 관		문 서 통 제
	심의관				검토 1991.9.11
	과 장				
기안책임자		이 찬 범			발　　송　인 발 송 1991 9 11 외무부

경 유 수 신 참 조	상공부장관 국제협력관	발 신 명 의	

제 목	UR/한.미 양자협의 갓트 조문 대책 자료

대 ： 국협 28140-337

　UR/한.미 양자협의 관련, 당부 소관인 UR/갓트조문 분야 대책

자료를 별첨과 같이 송부하니 업무에 참고하시기 바랍니다.

　첨 부 : 1. 갓트조문 협상 종합 대책자료.

　　　　　2. 갓트조문 협상 세부 대책자료.　　　　　끝. 0047

GATT 조문 협상 종합대책 자료

1991. 9.

외 무 부 통 상 국

0048

1. 주요쟁점 및 협상 동향 평가

    1) 협상 쟁점

        ○ 관세동맹 및 자유무역 협정의 결성, 화대에 따른 특정 품목 양허 변경시의
          보상 지급 문제 명료화 (24조 6항)

        ○ 지방정부 및 기관의 조치에 대한 연방, 중앙정부의 갓트상 책임 강화
          문제 (24조 12항)

        ○ BOP 조항의 개정을 위한 협상 여부 (18조 B)

    2) 전   망

        ○ 24조에 대한 협상 계속

            - 상금 미합의 사항인 관세 동맹 및 지역협정에 따른 보상문제, 지방
              정부의 조치에 대한 중앙정부의 책임문제, 24조 관련 분쟁시 특별구제
              절차 설정 문제도 현 의장안의 내용이 다수국들의 주장에 따르고
              있음에 비추어 현 문안대로 채택될 가능성이 큼.

        ○ BOP 조항에 대해서는 동 조항에 대한 협상 실시 자체를 반대하는 개도국의
          완강한 태도로 협상 최종 단계에서 정치적 타결될 전망

2. 미측 예상 제기사항

    ○ BOP 조항 개정에 대한 아국 협조 요청이 예상됨.

3. 아국 기존 입장

    1) 24조

        ○ 관세동맹 및 지역협정의 결성과 화대에 따른 역외국에 대한 보상 지불
          의무 강화 지지

            - 추가 보상 필요시, 다른 품목의 관세인하로 보상

        ○ 지방정부 또는 기관의 조치 및 행위에 대한 연방 또는 중앙정부의
          GATT상 책임 강화 지지

            - 지방정부의 조치 및 행위는 중앙정부의 책임

1

2) BOP 조항

　　o BOP 조항은 선진.개도국의 첨예한 의견 대립을 보이는 미묘한 문제이고
　　　아국은 이미 BOP 졸업이 합의된 만큼 구체적 입장 표명 자제

　　　- BOP 조항 개정 가능성은 거의 없으며, 다만 미국 및 타 선진국들이
　　　　섬유협상과 연계하는 카드로 사용

　　　- BOP 조항 개정 찬성시 개도국들이 우리에게 강력히 반발할 것이므로
　　　　적극 찬성 의사 표명은 자제

4.　대응 방안

　　o 우리나라는 BOP 조항의 원용을 중단 하였으므로 동 조항의 원용 절차 개선을
　　　위한 개정에 반대치는 않음.

　　o 그러나, BOP 조항 협상은 선.개도국간의 정치적 협상으로서 특별한 이해관계가
　　　없는 제3자가 협상의 일방을 지지하기 어려움. 특히 한국은 개도국 그룹의
　　　일원으로서 BOP 조항 개정 협상을 적극 지원하기 어려움.　　　　　　　끝.

2

0050

1991. 9. 10.

외 무 부 통 상 국

0051

1. 협상 진전상황

   가. 주요협상 경과

      ○ '88.12 중간평가를 통하여 아래 사항에 합의

         - GATT 조문의 명료화 및 개선에 협상력 집중

         - 본 협상그룹내 쟁점과 타협상 그룹 쟁점간에 관련성 고려

         - 명확한 협상쟁점 설정

      ○ '90.11.2. TNC 수석대표 비공식 협의에서 2조1(B)항, 17조, 28조는
        잠정합의가 이루어진 분야로, 24조, 25조 5항, 35조 및 잠정 적용
        의정서는 합의된 협상 기초가 있는 분야로 분류 되었으며, 다만
        BOP 조항만이 합의된 협상 기초조차 없는 분야로 분류됨.

      ○ 91.3.26. 주요국 수석대표급 비공식 협의에서 규범제정(Rule making)
        협상 그룹의 일부로 재구성됨.

      ○ 91.7.30. TNC앞 협상그룹 의장 보고서는 BOP 조항만을 우선 협상 과제로
        지적하고 나머지 쟁점은 기술적 사항으로서 추후 협의키로 제의함.

   나. 합의사항

      ○ 잠정합의를 도출한 조문
         - 2조1(B)항 : 관세 양허표상의 기타 과세 및 부과금
         - 17조 : 국영무역기업
         - 28조 : 관세 양허 재협상 절차

      ○ 철폐시한만 결정되면 타결될 조문
         - 25조 5항 : 웨이버
         - 잠정 적용 의정서 및 가입 의정서상의 조부 조항

      ○ 일부 참가국들이 초안 내용의 법적 의미에 대한 검토 완료시까지
        유보한 조문
         - 35조 : GATT 협정 부적용

1

0052

다. 미합의사항

    ㅇ 24조 : 관세동맹 및 지역협정

    ㅇ 18조 B : BOP 조항

2. 주요 쟁점사항 및 주요국 동향

가. 24조 (관세동맹 및 지역협정)

    ㅇ 관세동맹 및 지역협정의 결성 및 확대에 따른 관세 조정에 대한 보상
      지불문제 (24조 6항)

      - E C : 타회원국의 동일 품목 관세인하로 부족할 경우 타회원국의
          다른 품목에 대한 관세인하분도 고려대상에 포함

      - 미국등 : 타회원국의 동일 품목 관세인하로 부족할 경우 다른 품목의
          공동 관세인하로 보상

    ㅇ 지방정부 또는 기관의 조치 및 행위에 대한 중앙정부의 GATT상 책임문제
      (24조 12항)

      - E C : 중앙정부의 책임으로 함으로써 분쟁해결 절차 명료화

      - 미국, 카나다, 인도등 : 중앙정부가 GATT 규정의 준수를 위한
          합리적인 조치를 취하는 것은 헌법상 허용된 한도내에서만 가능

나. BOP 조항

1) 선진국(미국, 카나다, EC) 제안 요지

    ㅇ 선진국의 BOP 목적을 이유로 한 무역 제한조치 금지 공약의 강화

    ㅇ 12조나 18조 B에 근거한 무역조치는 BOP 문제의 정도에 비례해야
      하며 일시적인 조치로서 사용

    ㅇ 무역조치는 명료, 무차별적이어야 하며, 일정한 기간내 철폐 및
      점진적 완화를 약속해야 함 (선진국은 개도국보다 짧은기간내 철폐)

    ㅇ 수량제한 조치보다 가격에 기초한 조치가 바람직

o BOP 위원회에서의 협의는 제한조치의 적용·또는 강화후 4개월
  이내에 시작

o BOP 위원회는 협의중인 체약국의 수출 이익의 증대를 위하여
  체약국단이 취할 수 있는 조치를 제안

  - BOP 위원회 협의에서의 IMF의 역할을 좀 더 분명히 정의

  - 동 위원회가 당해 조치의 GATT 적합 여부 문제에 관한 권고에
    합의할 수 없을 경우, 영향을 받은 체약국은 갓트 분쟁해결 절차
    원용 가능

2) 개도국 입장

o 많은 개도국의 외적인 경제환경이 대외 부채 증가, 자본 유입, 교역
  조건의 악화, 환율 및 이자율 불안정등 여러면에서 악화되고 있음.

o 만약 BOP 조항이 협상의 대상이 된다면 그 목적은 보다 엄격한
  조건을 부과하는 것이 아니라 동 조항의 사용에 보다 융통성을
  부여하는데 두어야 함.

o 기존의 규정과 BOP 위원회의 관련 절차는 잘 운용되고 있고,
  그 운용상의 문제점은 UR 협상과 관련해서가 아니라 동 위원회에서
  다루어져야 함.

3) 지금까지의 협상 동향

가) 18조 B의 필요성은 공감

  o 12조 및 18조 B의 내용 자체는 변화되어서는 안됨.

  o BOP상의 어려운 시기에 무역조치를 사용하는 권한이 배제되어서는
    안됨.

  o 장기간의 BOP상의 어려움은 국내정책, 거시경제정책 및 무역관련
    조치에 의한 국내문제로서 뿐만 아니라 무역장벽 제거 및 채무,
    금융 이동에 관한 국제문제로서도 취급될 필요성은 인정

나) 18조 B에 의한 무역제한 조치의 문제점 인식

  o 제한적 무역조치는 어떤 상황에서는 피할수는 없지만 일반적으로
    BOP 균형을 유지, 회복하기 위해서는 비효과적인 수단임을 인정

3

0054

　　　　　ㅇ 동 조치는 특정산업이나 분야를 보호할 목적으로 사용되어서는
　　　　　　 안됨을 인정

　　　　　ㅇ 동 조치 사용시 체약국은 무역에 가장 적게 영향을 미치는
　　　　　　 조치를 우선하여야 함을 인정

　　　　　ㅇ 개도국의 경우 각국의 개발, 금융, 무역상황이 고려되어야 함을
　　　　　　 인정

　　다. 조부 조항, 웨이버

　　　　ㅇ X년이후 철폐에 합의

　　　　ㅇ 철폐에 관한 구체적 사항은 타협상그룹(특히 농산물)의 협상 결과를
　　　　　 감안하여 결정

4. 아국 입장

가. 기본 입장

　　　1) 24조

　　　　ㅇ 관세동맹 및 자유무역 협정으로 인한 역외국가에 대한 불이익 최소화

　　　2) BOP 조항

　　　　ㅇ BOP 조항 개정에 불반대하나 개도국의 강한 입장을 고려 입장 표명
　　　　　 유보

나. 세부 쟁점별 기존 입장

　　　1) 24조

　　　　ㅇ 관세동맹 및 지역협정의 결성과 확대에 따른 보상 지불
　　　　　- 타회원국의 동일품목의 관세 인하로 보상이 충분치 못할 경우,
　　　　　　 다른 품목에 대한 공동 관세인하로 보상

ㅇ 지방정부의 기관의 조치에 대한 중앙정부의 책임

  - 지방정부의 행위는 중앙정부의 책임

2) BOP조항

  ㅇ 구체적 입장 표명 불요

3) 조부조항, 웨이버

  ㅇ 협상 결과에 따름

다. 입장 재정립 가능 분야 : 기존 입장에 따름.   끝.

5

외 무 부

종 별 :

번 호 : GVW-2100

일 시 : 91 1023 1100

수 신 : 장관(통기,경기원,재무부,상공부)

발 신 : 주 제네바 대사

제 목 : UR/분야별 협상 대책(규범제정 분야- 갓트 조문)

연: GVW-2083

1. 분야별 쟁점

0 24 조

- 관세동맹 및 자유무역 협정의 결정, 확대에 따른 특정 품목 양허 변경시의 보상 지급 문제 명료화(24 조 6 항)

- 지방정부 및 기관의 조치에 대한 연방. 중앙정부의 갓트상 책임 강화 문제(24 조 12 항)

0 BOP 조항

- 동 조항 원용 조건을 강화하려는 선진국과 동 조항에 대한 협의 자체 조차도 반대하는 개도국이 대립

2. 최근의 협상 동향 및 전망

특별한 변화 없음.

3. 우리관심분야(우선 순위별)

0 24 조 6 항

- 역외국에 대한 보상지불의 강화 지지

0 24 조 12 항

- 지방 정부조치에 대한 연방정부의 갓트상 책임 강화 지지

0 BOP 조항

- 선진.개도국의 대립을 감안, 중립적 입장 견지

4. 관심사항 반영 방안

특기사항 없음. 끝

(대사 박수길-국장)

통상국 안기부	장관 경기원	차관 재무부	1차보 상공부	2차보	경제국	외정실	분석관	정와대

예고 91.12.31. 까지

외 무 부

종 별 : 지 급

번 호 : GVW-2162   일 시 : 91 1028 1800

수 신 : 장관(통기, 경기원, 재무부, 농림수산부, 상공부)

발 신 : 주제네바대사

제 목 : UR/갓트조문-BOP

1. BOP 관련 비공식 협의가 10.26(토) 개최되어, 의장 초안이 배포된바, 관련사항아래 보고함.(동초안 FAX 송부)

가. 회의경과

0 의장은 그간 자신이 각국 대표와 광범위한 접촉을 해 왔으며, 그룹간에도 많은접촉이있었다고 하고, 동 접촉 과정에서 감지된 상호(선진국,개도국간) 간 유연성을바탕으로 의장초안을 작성하였다고 언급함.

0 또한 의장은 동 초안을 검토할 시간적 여유를 가진후 내주중(10.28-11.2중)회의를 소집, 코멘트를 듣자고 하고 회의를 종료함

나. 의장 초안의 배경과 주요국 1차 반응

0 동 초안 관련 각국 대표와 접촉해본바, 이는 주로 EC 와 개도국간 접촉의 산물로서, 기존 EC측 제안을 중심으로, 표현을 완화하고 예외를 반영한 것이라고 하였음.

- BOP 조항 발동시 가능한한 조속히 제한 철폐시간 계획 공표

0 사정에 따라 동 시간 계획 변경 가능

0 공표하지 않을 경우 사유(JUSTIFICATION) 제시

- 가격조치(PRICE-BASED MEASURES)가 국제수지의 급속한 악화를 막을수 있는한,수량제한 도입회비 추구

- 동일산품에 대하여 1개 제한조치 이상 취하지않는 것으로 양해

- 제한은 부명하게(IN A TRANSPARENT MANNER) 시행

- 기본적 수요를 충족시키는 필수 산품의 경우 또는 수출을 위해 필요한 물품의경우, 전반적으로 적용되는 부과금 적용에서 제외 가능

- 제한 조치 관련 주요 변화(SIGNIFICANT CHAUGES)는 사전 또는 발표후 30일 이내

통상국   2차보   분석관   정와대   안기부   경기원   재무부   농수부   상공부

체약국단에 통보

0 EC,카나다는 동 초안 그대로 수용 가능하다 하며 칠레도 지지 가능하다는 반응이었음.

0 브라질, 인도등은 EC측과 사전 접촉이있었던 것으로 보이나, 본 초안에 대한반응표명을 자제하였음.

2. 상기 초안 관련 차기 협의시 아측이 취할 입장을 하시바람.

첨부: 상기 초안 1부(FAX)

(GVW(F)-0455).끝

(대사 박수길-국장)

GVW(F)-0455　11-28 1800

DRAFT　"GVW-2162 첨부," 25 October 1991

Balance of Payments Provisions

[Preamble]

...

Contracting parties confirm their commitment to publicly announce, as soon as possible, time-schedules for the removal of restrictive import measures taken for balance of payments purposes. It is understood that such time-schedules may be modified as appropriate [in consultation with the Committee] to take into account changes in the balance of payments situation. Wherever a time-schedule is not publicly announced, justification shall be provided as to the reasons therefor.

Contracting parties confirm their commitment to give preference to those measures which have the least disruptive effect on trade. Such measures (hereafter referred to as "price-based measures") shall be understood to include import surcharges, import deposit requirements or other equivalent trade measures with an impact on the price of imported goods. It is understood that, notwithstanding the provisions of Article II, price-based measures taken for balance of payments purposes may be applied in excess of the duties inscribed in the schedule of a contracting party. Furthermore, the amount by which the price-based measure exceeds the bound duty shall be clearly and separately indicated. Contracting parties shall seek to avoid the imposition of new quantitative restrictions for balance of payments purposes unless, because of a critical BOP situation, price-based measures cannot arrest a sharp deterioration in the external payments position. In those cases in which a contracting party applies quantitative restrictions, justification shall be provided as to the reasons why price-based measures are not an adequate instrument to deal with the balance of payments situation. A contracting party maintaining quantitative restrictions shall indicate in successive consultations the progress made in significantly reducing the incidence and restrictive effect of such measures. It is understood that not more than one type of restrictive import measures taken for balance of payments reasons may be applied on the same product.

0061

30295

F-1

- 2 -

Contracting parties confirm that restrictive import measures taken for balance of payments reasons may only be applied to control the level of imports and may not exceed what is necessary to address the balance of payments situation. In order to minimise any incidental protective effects, restrictions shall be administered in a transparent manner. The authorities of the importing contracting party shall provide adequate justification as to the criteria used to determine which products are subject to restriction. As provided in Articles XII:3 and XVII:B:10, parties may, in the case of certain essential products, exclude or limit the application of surcharges applied across the board or other measures applied for balance of payments reasons. The term essential products shall be understood to mean products which meet basic consumption needs or which contribute to a party's effort to improve its balance of payments situation, such as inputs needed for export production. In the administration of quantitative restrictions, discretionary licensing shall be used only when unavoidable and be progressively phased out. Appropriate justification shall be provided as to the criteria used to determine allowable import quantities or values.

Procedures for BOP consultations

The GATT Committee on Balance of Payments Restrictions (hereafter referred to as "Committee") shall carry out consultations in order to review all restrictive import measures taken for balance of payments purposes. The membership of the Committee is open to all contracting parties indicating their wish to serve in it. The Committee shall follow the procedures for consultations on balance of payments restrictions approved by the Council on 28 April 1970 and set out in BISD, Eighteenth Supplement, pages 48-53 (hereafter referred to as "Full consultation Procedures"), subject to the provisions set out below. Consultations shall be carried out in accordance with the "Plan of Discussions" set out in Annex 1 to this Declaration.

Contracting parties applying new restrictions or raising the general level of its existing restrictions by a substantial intensification of the measures shall enter into consultations with the Committee within four

0062

BOPSS   t-2

- 3 -

months of the adoption of such measures. The contracting party adopting
such measures may request that a consultation be held under
Article XII:(4)(a) or Article XVIII:12(a). If no such request has been
made, the Chairman of the Committee shall invite a contracting party to
hold such consultation. Factors that may be examined in the consultation
would include, inter alia, the introduction of new types of restrictive
measures for balance of payment purposes, an increase in the level or
product coverage of restrictions.

All restrictions applied for balance of payments purposes shall be
subject to periodic review in the Committee under paragraph 4(b) of
Article XII or under paragraph 12(b) of Article XVIII, subject to the
possibility of altering the periodicity of consultations in agreement with
the consulting contracting party or pursuant to any specific review
procedure that may be recommended by the Council.

Consultations may be held under simplified procedures in the case of
least developed contracting parties or in the case of less developed
contracting parties which are pursuing liberalisation efforts in conformity
with the schedule presented to the Committee in previous consultations.
Simplified consultations may also be held when the TPRM review of a less
developed contracting party is scheduled for the same calendar year as the
date fixed for the consultations. In such cases the decision as to whether
a Full Consultation should be held will be made on the basis of the factors
enumerated in paragraph 8 of the 1979 Declaration. Except in the case of
least developed contracting parties, no more than two successive
consultations may be held under simplified procedures.

Notification and Documentation

Contracting parties shall notify to the CONTRACTING PARTIES the
introduction or any changes in the application of restrictive import
measures taken for balance of payments purposes. Significant changes shall
be notified to the CONTRACTING PARTIES prior to or not later than 30 days
after their announcement. A consolidated notification, including all

0063

BOPGS

- 4 -

changes in laws, regulations, policy statement or public notices, shall be
made available to the GATT secretariat on a yearly basis for examination by
contracting parties. Notifications shall include full information, as far
as possible at the tariff line level, on the type of measures applied, the
criteria used for their administration, product coverage and trade flows
affected.

At the request of any contracting party, notifications may be reviewed
by the Committee. Such reviews would be limited to the clarification of
specific issues raised by a notification or to examine whether a
consultation under Article XII(4)(a) or Article XVIII:12(a) is required.
Contracting parties which have reasons to believe that a restrictive import
measure applied by another contracting party was taken for balance of
payments reasons may bring the matter to the attention of the Committee.
The Chairman of the Committee shall request information on the measure and
make it available to all contracting parties. Without prejudice to the
right of any member of the Committee to seek appropriate clarifications in
the course of consultations, questions may be submitted in advance for
consideration by the consulting contracting party.

The consulting contracting party shall prepare a Basic Document for
the Consultations which, in addition to any other information considered to
be relevant, should include: (a) an overview of the balance of payments
situations and prospects, including a consideration of the internal and
external factors having a bearing on the balance of payments situation and
the domestic policy measures taken in order to restore equilibrium on a
sound and lasting basis; (b) a full description of the restrictions
applied for balance of payments reasons, legal basis and steps taken to
reduce incidental protective effects; (c) measures taken since the last
consultation to liberalise import restrictions, in the light of the
conclusions of the Committee; plan for the elimination and progressive
relaxation of remaining restrictions. References may be made, when
relevant, to the information provided in other GATT notifications or
reports. Under Simplified Consultations, the consulting contracting party
shall submit a written statement containing essential information on the
elements covered by the Basic Document.

0064

BOPS5

- 5 -

The GATT secretariat shall, with a view to facilitating the consultations in the Committee, prepare a factual background paper dealing with the different aspects of the plan for consultations. In the case of less developed contracting parties, the secretariat document will include relevant background and analytical material on the incidence of the external trading environment on the balance of payments situation and prospects of the consulting country. The technical assistance services of the GATT secretariat shall, at the request of a less developed contracting party, assist in preparing the documentation for the consultations.

Conclusions of BOP consultations

The Committee shall report on its consultations to the Council. In the case of full consultations, the report should indicate the Committee's conclusions on the different elements of the plan for consultations, as well as the facts and reasons on which they are based. The Committee shall endeavour to include in its conclusions proposals for Council recommendations aimed at promoting the implementation of Articles XII, XVIII:B and this Declaration. Whenever the Council has made specific recommendations, the rights and obligations of contracting parties shall be assessed in the light of such recommendations. In those cases in which a time-schedule has been presented for the removal of restrictive measures taken for balance of payments reasons, the Council may recommend that, in adhering to such a time-schedule, a contracting party shall be deemed to be in compliance with its GATT obligations. In the absence of specific recommendations, the conclusions should record the different views expressed in the Committee. In the case of simplified consultations, the report shall include a summary of the main elements discussed in the Committee and a decision on whether Full Consultations are required.

0065

30255

5 - 5

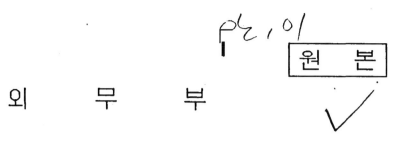

외 무 부

종 별 :

번 호 : GVW-2183　　　　　　　　　일 시 : 91 1029 2030

수 신 : 장 관(통기, 경기원, 재무부, 농림수산부, 상공부)

발 신 : 주 제네바대사

제 목 : UR/갓트조문(BOP 제외)

　　　연: GVW-2162

　　　표제 갓트조문 관련 비공식 협의가 10.29(화)RAMSAUER 의장 사회로 개최된 바, 토의 경과를 아래 보고함(위성락 서기관 참석)

　　　1. 의장은 조문관련 주요 난제가 별도로 협의되고 있으므로(MACIEL 의장 사회하에 진행되고 있는 연호 BOP 협의를 지칭) 그동안 여타 조문에 대한 협의를 마무리지어 UR 최정 협상안 마련에 대비키 위해 회의를 소집하였음을 밝히고, 브랏셀 초안(MTN.TNC/W/35/REV.1)중 시간의 경과에 따라 부적절하게 된 표현의 수정을 다음과 같이 제의하여 동의를 득함

　　　0 2조 1항 B(기타 과세 및 부과금 관련)

　　　- 2번째 문단 2번째줄 말미의 '(1990)'을 삭제

　　　0 17조(국영무역 관련)

　　　- 5번째 문단 끝에서 2번째줄 'IT SHALL MEETBEFORE THE END OF 1991 AND THEREAFTER AT LEAST ONCE A YEAR'를 ' IT SHALL MEET WITHIN ONE YEAR OF THE ENTRY INTOFORCE OF THIS DECISION 으로 수정'.

　　　2. 한편 의장은 BOP 조항이외 여타 조문은 상기수 정이 반영된 브랏셀 초안데로최종 협상안에 포함될 것임을 확인한 바, 미국, 호주가 25조부분에 대하여는 여타 분야 협상 결과에 따라 수락여부를 정한다는 입장을 재천명한 이외, 별이의 없이 토의가 종료되었음. 끝

　　　(대사 박수길-국장)

통상국　　2차보　　경기원　　재무부　　농수부　　상공부

PAGE 1　　　　　　　　　　　　　　　　　　　91.10.30　　10:28 WH

　　　　　　　　　　　　　　　　　　　　　　　외신 1과 통제관

　　　　　　　　　　　　　　　　　　　　　　　　　　　　0066

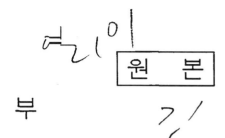

외 무 부

종 별 :

번 호 : GVW-2232   일 시 : 91 1101 1930

수 신 : 장 관(봉기,경기원,재무부,농수부,상공부)

발 신 : 주 제네바대사

제 목 : UR/갓트 조문-BOP

대: WGV-1491

연: GVW-2162

1. 대호 BOP 비공식 협의가 금 10.31. 개최된바, 토의 결과를 아래 보고함.

(우성락 서기관 참석)

가. MACIEL의장은 연호 초안이 각 그룹의 주장을 어느정도 반영한 것으로 본다고하면서, 각국의 입장 개진을 요청하고, 자신으로서 동 초안을 TNC에 제출할 근거로삼을 의도는 없으며, 토의의 기초로 삼고자 할뿐임을 부연함.

나. 이에 대한 개도국의 언급 동향

0 필리핀

- 동 초안을 의장 초안이라기 보다 NON-PAPER 라고하면서, 충분한 협의 과정없이이러한 문서가 나온데 대해 강한의념(MISGIVING)을 표하지 않을수 없다고 함.

- 또한 내용 측면에서도 동 초안이 EC주장을 기준으로 한 인상이며, 위원회의 공표 일정수정권한, 이사회가 특정 권고를 할 경우 이에따라 해당국의 권리, 의무가평가된다(ASSESSED)는 표현의 모호성, 협의절차관련 부분등을 볼때 BOP 조항 사용을억제하는 데만 주안점을 두었다고 비판함.

0 브라질, 인도, 이집트, 유고, 알젠틴, 페루

- 모두 구체적인 언급은 추후로 미루면서, 본초안에는 BOP 조항을 이용하는 측에어려움을 주는 내용이 있어, BOP 조항의 본질을 해치지 않고 개선하는 방향(권리와의무간 균형강조)으로 더 협의해야 한다는 입장이었으며, 전반적 거부입장은 표하지않음.

- 특히 인도는 본 초안과 79년 BOP 선언과의 관계에 의문을 (과거 EC초안은 79 선언을 대체하는 선언임을 명백히 하였으나 금번초안에는 전문이 생략되어 있어

통상국   2차보   경기원   재무부   농수부   상공부

PAGE 1   91.11.02   09:03 WH

외신 1과 통제관

0067

이점이 불명한점을 지칭) 제기함.

- 알젠틴은 먼저 절차적 측면과 본질적 측면간의 구분을 명확히 해야 한다고 강조함.

- 한편 페루는 여타국 보다 좀더 비판적인 태도를 취하면서, 본 초안에 대한 수정안을 놓고 토의하여야 한다고 함.

0 콜럼비아, 우루과이, 헝가리

- 초안이 유용한 문건이라고 하고 토의의 기초로 하는데 동의한다고 함.

- 그러나, 우루과이는 권리,의무간 균형에도 언급함.

0 칠레

- 동 초안에 적극적인 지지를 표명(특히 명확하고 명료한 적용 가능성을 증대시키는점, 철폐일정을 정하고, 가격 조치를 선호하는 점등 지적)하고, 수량제한은 심각한 상황에서만 사용되어야 하므로 초안중 '수량제한 회피를 추구한다'는 (SHALL SEEK TO AVOID)부분을 'SHALL AVOID'로 바꿀 것을 제안함.

- 또한 전반적 제한 적용시 예외가 되는 ESSENTIAL PRODUCT를 보다 분명히 한점을 평가함.

다. EC, 미국, 캐나다, 일본, 스웨덴(노르딕 국가대표), 스위스 등 선진국들의 언급 동향

0 공히 동 초안이 균형있는 내용으로서 의미있는 타협을 위한 기초가 된다고 하고, UR 막바지단계에서 이의 본격 토의 필요성을 강조함.

0 특히 미국은 동 초안이 BOP 조항적용에 있어 DISCIPLINE 을 강화 하면서, 동시에 이의발동을 제약하지 않는 원칙에 충실하다고 평가함.

0 한편 일본은 BOP 가 빠질 경우 UR 협상이 붕괴하리라고 하는등 BOP 문제에 강한 입장을 표명함.

2.금일 회의 진행 상황과 각국 접촉결과에 따른 당관 관찰은 아래와 같음.

0 현재 BOP 조항을 협상의 대상으로 한다는데대하여는 선,개도국간 공감대가 이룩된 단계까지 진전되었으나, 일부 개도국은 상금 절차적 개선이상은 수락하기 어렵다는 입장임.

0 상기 초안은 EC 와 일부 개도국간 협의의 산물이나 의장의 개입정도가 적어 의장 자신의 안이라고 하기는 어려운 측면이 있으며, (비율빈,알젠틴은 이를 NON-PAPER라고 지칭), 의장도 이점과 일부 개도국의 반발을 의식, 동 초안을 TNC에 넘길 근거로 하지

않겠다고 조심스럽게 접근하는 것으로 보임.

　0 브라질, 인도등 EC와 접촉이 있었던 것으로 보이는 국가들은 강경한 입장을 취하지 않고 협의해 나가면서,수정하려는 태도였으며, 사전 협의과정에 참여치 못한 것으로 보이는 국가가 강하게 반발하는 양상이었으나, 개도국내에도입장이 서로 달라,향 후 본격적 논의가 예상됨.끝

　(대사 박수길-국장)

외 무 부

종 별 :

번 호 : GVW-2183   일 시 : 91 1029 2030

수 신 : 장 관(통기, 경기원, 재무부, 농림수산부, 상공부)

발 신 : 주 제네바대사

제 목 : UR/갓트조문(BOP 제외)

연: GVW-2162

표제 갓트조문 관련 비공식 협의가 10.29(화)RAMSAUER 의장 사회로 개최된 바, 토의 경과를 아래 보고함(위성락 서기관 참석)

1. 의장은 조문관련 주요 난제가 별도로 협의되고 있으므로(MACIEL 의장 사회하에 진행되고 있는 연호 BOP 협의를 지칭) 그동안 여타 조문에 대한 협의를 마무리지어 UR 최정 협상안 마련에 대비키 위해 회의를 소집하였음을 밝히고, 브랏셀 초안(MTN.TNC/W/35/REV.1)중 시간의 경과에 따라 부적절하게 된 표현의 수정을 다음과 같이 제의하여 동의를 득함

O 2조 1항 B(기타 과세 및 부과금 관련)

- 2번째 문단 2번째줄 말미의 '(1990)'을 삭제

O 17조(국영무역 관련)

- 5번째 문단 끝에서 2번째줄 'IT SHALL MEETBEFORE THE END OF 1991 AND THEREAFTER AT LEAST ONCE A YEAR'를 ' IT SHALL MEET WITHIN ONE YEAR OF THE ENTRY INTOFORCE OF THIS DECISION 으로 수정'.

2. 한편 의장은 BOP 조항이외 여타 조문은 상기수 정이 반영된 브랏셀 초안대로최종 협상안에 포함될 것임을 확인한 바, 미국, 호주가 25조부분에 대하여는 여타 분야 협상 결과에 따라 수락여부를 정한다는 입장을 재천명한 이외, 별이의 없이 토의가 종료되었음. 끝

(대사 박수길-국장)

통상국   2차보   경기원   재무부   농수부   상공부

PAGE 1   91.10.30   10:28 WH

외신 1과 통제관

0070

발 신 전 보

번   호 : WGV-1495   911030 1445 FN   종별 : _____

수   신 : 주   제네바   대사. 총영사

발   신 : 장   관 (통 기)

제   목 : UR/갖트 조문(BOP)

대 : GVW-2162

1. 18조 B항은 선.개도국간 첨예한 의견 대립으로 동 조항을 협상 대상으로 할
   것인지의 여부 자체에 대해서도 상금 합의가 이루어지지 않은 분야로서,
   대호 의장 초안은 동 조항의 명료화와 개선을 추구한다는 협상 목표에 충실하는
   일방, 18조 B항의 원용절차를 엄격하게 개정하는데 대한 개도국들의 우려를
   최소화하려는 방향으로 작성된 것으로 평가됨.

2. 동 의장안중에서 개도국들이 특히 문제삼을 소지가 있는 부분으로서 1)국제수지
   목적의 수입제한 조치 발동시 철폐일정의 가급적 조속 공표 공약 2)수입제한
   대상품목 선정기준 관련 정당한 근거 제시 의무 3) 수량제한 조치 발동의 엄격한
   제한 4)국제수지위원회 보고서 결론부분에 가급적 이사회 권고 문안이 포함되도록
   한것등을 들수 있을 것이며, 현재로서는 동 의장안의 수락 가능성이 불투명한
   것으로 분석됨.

3. 동 의장안에 대한 아국 입장
   18조 B항 원용을 이미 중단한 아국으로서는 동 조항의 원용을 엄격하게 하는
   방향으로 개정하는데에 반대할 이유가 없으나, 여타 개도국과의 관계를 고려,
   의장안에 대한 찬성의사 표명을 자제하고 협상 대세를 관망함이 바람직함.
   끝.   (통상국장   김 용 규)

보 안 통 제	

앙고재	91년 10월 3일	기안자 성명		과 장	국 장	차 관	장 관

외신과통제

0071

이 안

외 무 부

종   별 :

번   호 : GVW-2629   일   시 : 91 1214 1800

수   신 : 장관(통일,경기원,재무부,농림수산부,상공부,특허청)

발   신 : 주 제네바 대사

제   목 : UR/갓트 조문-BOP

　　1.12.13(금) 표제 협상이 MACIEL 의장 주재로 개최되어 10.25 자 의장 초안을 다소 수정한 별첨의장안을 중심으로 협의가 진행되었는바, 동의장안 내용을 수정을 요구하고 개도국들과 현의장안에 대한 지나친 수정은 선진.개도국간 BOP 조항에 대한 합의의 기초를 심각하게 훼손시킬 위험이 있음을 들어 지나친 수정에 반대하는 선진국들의 입장이 대립하였음.

　　(김서기관 참석)

　　2. 개도국들은 새로 제시된 의장안이 대체로 협상의 기초로 수용 가능하다는 입장을 보이면서도 당초 의장안을 별첨과 같이 수정할 것을 요구함. 미국, EC, 스웨덴, 스 위스등 선진국들은 개도국들의 지나친 수정 요구에 당혹감을 금치못하겠다고 언급하고, GATT 관련 규정과 1979년 선언을 실질적으로 변경시키지 않은 현의장안에 대한 수정은 지나친 요구라는 입장을 보임.

　　3. 특히 미국은 BOP 조항의 개선은 과거부터 협의되어온 문제로서 현 의장안의 지나친 수정은 선진.개도국간의 합의 가능여지(MIDDLE GROUND)를 없애는 것이라고 반박하고 지난 5년간의 UR노력이 공정적인 (POSITIVE) 방향으로 종결되기를 희망한다고 언급하면서 BOP 조치에대한 IMF 의 의견 제시 및 동 조치에 대한 갓트분쟁해결 절차의 원용을 가능케하는 별첨수정안을 제시함(개도국 반대입장 표명)

　　4. 의장은 금일 협의된 내용을 검토한 새로운수정안을 12.20 TNC 의장에게 제출키로 함.

　　첨부: 1. 12.13 자 의장 초안(수정 부분은 개도국들의 수정 요청 내용)

　　　　 2. 미국의 수정제안

　　(GVW(F)-617)

　　(대사 박수길-국장)

통상국	차관	2차보	안기부	경기원	재무부	농수부	상공부	특허청

주 제 네 바 대 표 부

번 호 : GVW(F) - 617   년월일 : 1214   시간 : 1800

수 신 : 장　판 (총기, 경기원, 재무부, 농법축산부, 상광부, 특허청)

발 신 : 주 제네바대사

제 목 : GVW-262과 관영

총 8 매(표지포함)

보　안	
봉　제	

외신과	
봉　제	

617-8-1

Balance-of-Payments Provisions of the
General Agreement on Tariffs and Trade

Reaffirming
Recognising the provisions of Articles XII, XVIII:B of the General
Agreement and of the 1979 Declaration on Trade Measures taken for
Balance-of-Payments Purposes (hereafter referred to as the
"1979 Declaration"). and in order to clarify the procedure thereon

Decide as follows:

The following provisions are not intended to
modify the relevant provisions of the
General Agreement or the 1979 Declaration

Application of Measures

Contracting parties confirm their commitment to publicly announce, as
soon as possible, time-schedules for the removal of restrictive import
measures taken for balance-of-payments purposes. It is understood that
such time-schedules may be modified as appropriate [in consultation with
the Committee] to take into account changes in the balance-of-payments
situation. Wherever a time-schedule is not publicly announced,
justification shall be provided as to the reasons therefor.

Contracting parties confirm their commitment to give preference to
those measures which have the least disruptive effect on trade. Such
measures (hereafter referred to as "price-based measures") shall be
understood to include import surcharges, import deposit requirements or
other equivalent trade measures with an impact on the price of imported
goods. It is understood that, notwithstanding the provisions of
Article II, price-based measures taken for balance-of-payments purposes may
be applied in excess of the duties inscribed in the schedule of a
contracting party. Furthermore, the amount by which the price-based
measure exceeds the bound duty shall be clearly and separately indicated
under the notification procedures of this Decision.

BOPS5

617-8-2

0074

321 P06   WOI   '91-12-15 03:00

Contracting parties shall seek to avoid the imposition of new quantitative restrictions for balance-of-payments purposes unless, because of a critical BOP situation, price-based measures cannot arrest a sharp deterioration in the external payments position. In those cases in which a contracting party applies quantitative restrictions, justification (Explanation) shall be provided as to the reasons why price-based measures are not an adequate instrument to deal with the balance-of-payments situation. A contracting party maintaining quantitative restrictions shall indicate in successive consultations the progress made in significantly reducing the incidence and restrictive effect of such measures. It is understood that not more than one type of restrictive import measure taken for balance-of-payments reasons may be applied on the same product.

Contracting parties confirm that restrictive import measures taken for balance-of-payments reasons may only be applied to control the general level of imports and may not exceed what is necessary to address the balance-of-payments situation. In order to minimise any incidental protective effects, restrictions shall be administered in a transparent manner. The authorities of the importing contracting party shall provide adequate justification as to the criteria used to determine which products are subject to restriction. As provided in Articles XII:3 and XVIII:B:10, parties may, in the case of certain essential products, exclude or limit the application of surcharges applied across the board or other measures applied for balance-of-payments reasons. The term essential products shall be understood to mean products which meet basic consumption needs or which contribute to the contracting party's effort to improve its balance-of-payments situation, such as input needed for export production. In the administration of quantitative restrictions, discretionary licensing shall be used only when unavoidable and be progressively phased out. Appropriate justification shall be provided as to the criteria used to determine allowable import quantities or values.

BOP65

617-8-3

321 P07   WOI

'91-12-15 03:01

0075

Procedures for Balance-of-Payments consultations

The GATT Committee on Balance of Payments Restrictions (hereafter referred to as "Committee") shall carry out consultations in order to review all restrictive import measures taken for balance-of-payments purposes. The membership of the Committee is open to all contracting parties indicating their wish to serve in it. The Committee shall follow the procedures for consultations on balance-of-payments restrictions approved by the Council on 28 April 1970 and set out in BISD, Eighteenth Supplement, pages 48-53 (hereafter referred to as "Full consultation Procedures"), subject to the provisions set out below.

A contracting party applying new restrictions or raising the general level of its existing restrictions by a substantial intensification of the measures shall enter into consultations with the Committee within _four_ _one year_ _months_ of the adoption of such measures. The contracting party adopting such measures may request that a consultation be held under Article XII:(4)(a) or Article XVIII:12(a) as appropriate. If no such request has been made, the Chairman of the Committee shall invite the contracting party to hold such consultation. Factors that may be examined in the consultation would include, _inter alia_, the introduction of new types of restrictive measures for balance-of-payments purposes, or an increase in the level or product coverage of restrictions.

All restrictions applied for balance-of-payments purposes shall be subject to periodic review in the Committee under paragraph 4(b) of Article XII or under paragraph 12(b) of Article XVIII, [subject to the possibility of altering the periodicity of consultations] in agreement with the consulting contracting party or pursuant to any specific review procedure that may be recommended by the Council.

Consultations may be held under simplified procedures in the case of least-developed contracting parties or in the case of less-developed contracting parties which are pursuing liberalisation efforts in conformity with the schedule presented to the Committee in previous consultations. ~~Simplified~~ consultations _should_ ~~may also~~ be ~~held when~~ _waivered_ _if_ the TPRM review of a less-developed contracting party is scheduled for the same calendar year as the

BOP65

611-8-4

0076

321 P

date fixed for the consultations. In such cases the decision as to whether
a full consultation should be held will be made on the basis of the factors
enumerated in paragraph 8 of the 1979 Declaration. Except in the case of
least-developed contracting parties, no more than two successive
consultations may be held under simplified procedures.

Notification and Documentation

Contracting party shall notify to the CONTRACTING PARTIES the
introduction or any changes in the application of restrictive import
measures taken for balance-of-payments purposes. Significant changes shall
be notified to the CONTRACTING PARTIES prior to or not later than 30 days
after their announcement. A consolidated notification, including all
changes in laws, regulations, policy statements or public notices, shall be
made available to the GATT secretariat on a yearly basis for examination by
contracting parties. Notifications shall include full information, as far
as possible, at the tariff line level, on the type of measures applied, the
criteria used for their administration, product coverage and trade flows
affected.

At the request of any contracting party, notifications may be reviewed
by the Committee. Such reviews would be limited to the clarification of
specific issues raised by a notification or examinination of whether a
consultation under Article XII(4)(a) or Article XVIII:12(a) is required.
Contracting parties which have reasons to believe that a restrictive import
measure applied by another contracting party was taken for
balance-of-payments reasons may bring the matter to the attention of the
Committee. The Chairman of the Committee shall request information on the
measure and make it available to all contracting parties. Without
prejudice to the right of any member of the Committee to seek appropriate
clarifications in the course of consultations, questions may be submitted
in advance for consideration by the consulting contracting party.

The consulting contracting party shall prepare a Basic Document for
the consultations which, in addition to any other information considered to

BOPS5

617-8-5

0077

321 P09   WOI   '91-12-15 03:02

be relevant, should include: (a) an overview of the balance-of-payments situation and prospects, including a consideration of the internal and external factors having a bearing on the balance-of-payments situation and the domestic policy measures taken in order to restore equilibrium on a sound and lasting basis; (b) a full description of the restrictions applied for balance-of-payments reasons, their legal basis and steps taken to reduce incidental protective effects; (c) measures taken since the last consultation to liberalise import restrictions, in the light of the conclusions of the Committee; (d) plan for the elimination and progressive relaxation of remaining restrictions. References may be made, when relevant, to the information provided in other GATT notifications or reports. Under Simplified Consultations, the consulting contracting party shall submit a written statement containing essential information on the elements covered by the Basic Document.

The GATT secretariat shall, with a view to facilitating the consultations in the Committee, prepare a factual background paper dealing with the different aspects of the plan for consultations. In the case of less developed contracting parties, the secretariat document will include relevant background and analytical material on the incidence of the external trading environment on the balance-of-payments situation and prospects of the consulting country. The technical assistance services of the GATT secretariat shall, at the request of a less developed contracting party, assist in preparing the documentation for the consultations.

Conclusions of Balance-of-Payments consultations

The Committee shall report on its consultations to the Council. In the case of full consultations, the report should indicate the Committee's conclusions on the different elements of the plan for consultations, as well as the facts and reasons on which they are based. The Committee shall endeavour to include in its conclusions proposals for Council recommendations aimed at promoting the implementation of Articles XII, XVIII:B, the 1979 Declaration and this Decision. In those cases in which a time-schedule has been presented for the removal of restrictive measures

BOPS5

0078

- 6 -

taken for balance-of-payments reasons, the Council may recommend that, in adhering to such a time-schedule, a contracting party shall be deemed to be in compliance with its GATT obligations. Whenever the Council has made specific recommendations, the rights and obligations of contracting parties shall be assessed in the light of such recommendations. In the absence of specific proposals for Council recommendations, the Committee's conclusions should record the different views expressed in the Committee. In the case of simplified consultations, the report shall include a summary of the main elements discussed in the Committee and a decision on whether Full Consultations are required.

0079

BOPS5

IMPROVING THE BOPS TEXT (UNITED STATES)

First page

Add before last sentence: Restrictive import measures taken for BOP purposes shall not be taken for the purpose of protecting a particular industry or sector. (Language taken from 1979 Declaration, 5th preambular point).

Notification and Documentation

Add a point (e) to the first sentence: (e) the IMF shall provide such material to help the Committee understand the activities or the information contained in the Basic Documentation for Consultations and shall continue to provide its assessment of the BOP situation including information on matters covered by the Basic Document for Consultations. The IMF shall give its view on the effectiveness of Balance-of-Payments adjustment measures.

Dispute Settlement

The dispute settlement provisions of the General Agreement may be invoked with respect to any matters arising from the application of restrictive import measures for balance-of-payment purposes. This includes cases where the Committee has been unable to agree on specific recommendations.

617-8-8

BOPS13

외 무 부

종 별 :

번 호 : GVW-2705   일 시 : 91 1218 1500

수 신 : 장관(봉기,경기원,재무부,농림수산부,상공부,특허청)

발 신 : 주 제네바 대사

제 목 : UR/갓트 조문 협의

연: GVW-2664

1. 12.17(화) 표제협의가 MACIEL 의장 주재로 개최되었는바, 동 회의는 미국이 당초 갓트가입시 원용한 잠정가입의정서(PPA)를 철폐할 수 없다는 서한을 규범제정 의장에게제출하므로 개최되었음(미국이 PPA 를 원용한 부분은 <u>연안해운</u>에 운항하는 선박은 미국내보조선박만 사용해야 한다는 것임)

(최혁심의관, 김봉주서기관 참석)

2. 미국 대표는 MTN.GNG/NG7/22 에 명기된대로 잠정적용 의정서에 관한 결정안(DRAFTDECISION)잠정 합의시, 일부 체약국들은 동결정안의 수락이 다른 분야의 협상결과와 연계되어 있음을 분명히 한바있다고 전제하고,자국은 시장접근, 농산물분야등 현협상결과에비추어 상기 결정안을 12.20 최종협상아네포함시키는데 반대한다는 입장을 표명함. 이에 EC등이 강한 반발을 보였으며, 아국이 타협안을 제시하였으나 미국은 대안이 없다(NOALTERNATIVE)는 입장을 되풀이 함에 따라 <u>의장은 동 문제에 대한 합의가 없었다는 결론을 내리고 회의 종결함.</u>

3. 상기 회의시 EC는 동 분야의 양보를 얻기위하여 자신들은 <u>갓트 24조에서 많은</u> 양보를했음을 밝히고, 선박구매 문제하나로 지난 40여년간 갓트의 DEGROGATION 을받아온 동조항철폐를 지지하는 것은 도저히 수용 묵살할 수 없을것이라는 강한 반응을 보였으며, 브라질, 카나다,알젠틴이 BIG PACKAGE 를 주장해 미국입자의 후퇴가 UR 협상 전체에 매우 부정적인 영향을 미칠 것임을 우려함.

4. 아국은 미국의 어려움은 이해하나 12.20 제시될 협상 결과를 본후에 동 문제를 재검토한다는 내용의 주(FOOTNOTE)를 달아서 12.20 최종협정안에 포함시키자는 내용의 제안을하였음. EC는 이에 대해 아국제안이 검토할 가치가 있다는 반응을 보였으나 미국은 기존입장을 되풀이 함.

통상국   2차보   외정실   분석관   청와대   안기부   경기원   재무부   농수부
상공부   특허청

PAGE 1   91.12.19   08:11 BX

외신 1과 통제관

5. 상기와 같이 미국이 PPA 에 근거한 수입제한조치의 철폐에 대한 잠정합의안의전면 철폐를 강하게 요청한것은 , 일응 미국내 조선 및 해운업계의 강한 로비에 따른 것으로보이는바, 현단계에서 이러한 입장을 가지고나오게된 정확한 저의는 분명치않음.끝

(대사 박수길-국장)

정 리 보 존 문 서 목 록

기록물종류	일반공문서철	등록번호	2017050022	등록일자	2017-05-12
분류번호	764.51	국가코드		보존기간	영구
명 칭	UR(우루과이라운드) / Standstill & Rollback 감시기구 회의, 1990-91				
생 산 과	통상기구과	생산년도	1990~1991	담당그룹	다자통상
내용목차	1. 1990년도 2. 1991년도				

0001

1.   1990 년도

0001-1

주 제 네 바 대 표 부

OUTGOING:

CLASSFICATION

번 호 : GVW(F)- 0041

일 시 : 002/5 1630

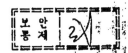

소 신 : 장 관 (복기,경기원,재무부,상공부).

발 신 : 주 제네바 대사

제 목 : UR/감시기구

90. 3. 14 개최되는 표제회의 의제를 별첨 송부함.

첨 부 : GATT/AIR/2929 1부. 끝.

(대사 이상욱 - 국장)

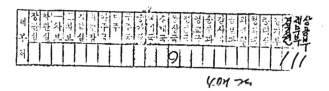

(총 2매)

2-1

0002

GATT/AIR/2929   14 FEBRUARY 1989

SUBJECT: URUGUAY ROUND - SURVEILLANCE BODY

1.   THE SURVEILLANCE BODY WILL HOLD ITS NEXT MEETING AT 10 A.M. ON
WEDNESDAY, 14 MARCH 1990, IN THE CENTRE WILLIAM RAPPARD.

2.   PROPOSED AGENDA:

    (A)   STANDSTILL

        (I)   EXAMINATION OF STANDSTILL NOTIFICATIONS
              (MTN.SB/SN/SERIES) SUBMITTED IN ACCORDANCE WITH THE
              AGREED PROCEDURES (MTN.TNC/W/10/REV.1).

              UNDER THESE PROCEDURES, NOTIFICATIONS ON STANDSTILL
              RECEIVED BY THE SECRETARIAT BY MONDAY, 19 FEBRUARY CAN BE
              EXAMINED AT THE PRESENT MEETING.

        (II) CONSIDERATION OF ANY STATEMENTS BY PARTICIPANTS
              CONCERNING OTHER ASPECTS OF THE STANDSTILL COMMITMENT.

    (B)   ROLLBACK

          CONSIDERATION OF STATEMENTS CONCERNING THE ROLLBACK
          COMMITMENT, IN THE LIGHT OF THE AGREED PROCEDURES
          (MTN.TNC/W/10/REV.1).

    (C)   OTHER BUSINESS, INCLUDING FUTURE WORK AND THE DATE OF THE NEXT
          MEETING.

3.   NOTES ON THE PREVIOUS MEETINGS ARE CONTAINED IN MTN.SB/1-11.

4.   GOVERNMENTS PARTICIPATING IN THE MULTILATERAL TRADE NEGOTIATIONS,
WHICH WISH TO BE REPRESENTED AT THIS MEETING, ARE INVITED TO INFORM ME OF
THE NAMES OF THEIR REPRESENTATIVES AS SOON AS POSSIBLE.

                                        A. DUNKEL

90-0188

2-2

0003

END

종 별 :

번 호 : GVW-0419   일 시 : 90 0314 1830

수 신 : 장 관 (봉기,경기원,재무부,농림수산부,상공부)

발 신 : 주 제네바 대사대리 (사본: 이상옥대사)

제 목 : UR/ 감시기구

3.14. MATHUR 의장 사회로 개최된 표제 협상그룹회의 요지를 아래 보고함 (홍서기관 참석)

1. STANDSTILL 통고 검토

0 알젠틴은 이씨의 고급 옥수수에 대한 보조금지불 행위 (SB/SN/20/REV.1) 에 대해 SS공약위배 및 UR 농산물 협상 분야의 89.4.TNC 결정 14항 (보조금 동결) 위배라고 지적하였으며, 호주, 미국, 우루과이, 브라질등이 지지함. 이씨는 동 보조행위는 갓트규정에 합치하는 생산보조이므로 SS 공약위배가 될수 없으며, 농산물 협상결정 위배여부는 감시기구의 영역이 아니라고 함

0 호주는 스웨덴의 양고기 수입부과금 인하조치 (SB/2/9) 를 환영하나, 아직도 UR 협상 개시시점보다 부과금이 높은 수준이라는데 우려를 표시함

2. STANDSTILL 공약 관련 검토 (조기 경보적 사안포함)

0 이씨는 입안중인 미국의 90 농업법에 언급, 동법에 의거 광범위한 품목에 대한 생산비 보조지원 (DEFICIENCY PAYMENT) 이 예상되며, 이경우 SS 공약 위배 및 UR 협상 지위 강화가 우려된다고 언급함.

0 미국은 동 법안이 85 농업법의 연장이므로 SS공약위배가 아니며, UR 협상의 맥락에서 농업개혁을 목표로 한것은 아니므로 UR협상과는 무관하다고 하고, UR 협상의 결과를 보아 기본적인 개혁을 추진할 것이나 이는 다자간의 농업개혁 노력을 전제로 한다고 언급함.

0 호주는 미국이 수출장려계획 (EEP) 에 의거 소련에 대한 육류 수출에 상여금지급이 가능한 점에 주목한다고 함.

0 미구은 이씨가 검토중인 제 4기술기준 (FOURTH CRITERION) 이 유전공항에 의해 생산된 농산품의 수입을 '사회.경제적' 고려에 의해 규제하는 방안을 포함하고 있는데

통상국   2차보   구주국   구주국   청와대   경기원   재무부   농수부   상공부

국기국

PAGE 1

주목하고, 동기준이 SS 공약에 위배되고, 농산물 위생검역협상에 영향을 미칠수도 있다고 언급함.

0 미국은 이씨가 92 구주 단일시장 이후 대일본 수입자율 규제를 이씨 회원국 전역에 확대하고 특히 제 3국에서 생산된 일본 자동차도 일본산과 같이 취급하려는 동향에 대해 우려를 표시함

3. ROLLBACK 공약 관련 검토

0 루마니아는 스웨덴 루마니아산 상품에 대한 차별적 수입제한 조치 (RBC/21) 가 RB 공약에 의해 철폐되어야 한다고 주장함.

0 이씨의 자발적 OFFER (RBC/19/REV.1) 에 대해 항가리, 폴란드가 환영을 표시한 반면, 일본은 이씨가 상금 차별적 수입규제 조치를 유지하고 있는데 우려를 표시함

0 미국, 칠레는 최근 알젠틴의 자발적 관세인하조치 (SB/RBN/3) 를 환영함

4. 감시기구의 향후 협상방향

0 뉴질랜드는 RB 공약의 이행강화를 위한 자국제안 (SB/W/8) 이 회색조치의 처리문제, 패널에 의해 불법 판정된 사안의 처리등 정치적으로 어려운 사안을 포함하고 있으나 최종 각료회의시 모든 문제를 한꺼번에 처리할수는 없으므로 동제안을 적절한 시기에 협의키를 희망한바, 이씨는 동 협의를 마지막 단계로 미룰것을 희망함.

0 의장은 89.12. TNC 에서도 감시기구가 SS/RB 공약이행 상황을 계속 검토보고토록 위임받았으므로, 90.4.9. TNC 회의에 89.10. 이후 감시기구회의록과 SS/RB 공약행상황 요약문을 제출할 것이라함.

0 의장은 감시기구의 활동도 90.7. TNC회의시까지는 구체적 실적을 남겨야 할것이나 실적이 극히 부진하므로, 각국은 현안중인 RB협의를 조기에 종결하고, 앞으로자발적인 RB조치 (패널권고 이행등도 포함)도 가급적 많이 감시기구에 봉보해 줄것을 촉구함.

0 90.7 TNC 회의에 제출될 SS/RB 공약이행현황 검토보고서 작성을 위해 각국은90.5월말까지 이행현황을 사무국에 봉보키로 함.

5. 차기회의는 7.5 (목) 개최 예정인바, 의장은 푼타선언에 비추어 회색조치등 갓트위배 사항의 철폐 또는 갓트 합법화 문제가 감시기구의 소간사항이라고 생각되며, 최근 관심도도 높아지고 있으므로 차기회의에서는 이문제를 협의하기를 희망함. 이에대해 뉴질랜드는 갓트패널에서 불법판정된 사항의 처리문제도 아울러 협의 바란다고 함. 끝.

PAGE 2

276 우루과이라운드 제도 및 기타 분야 협상 2

0005

주 제 네 바 대 표 부

OUTGOING:

CLASSIFICATION

번 호 : GVW(F)- 0169

일 시 : 00807 1000

수 신 : 장 관 (롱기,경기원,재부부,상공부)

발 신 : 주 제네바 대사

제 목 : UR/감시기구

'90. 7. 5. 개최되는 UR/감시기구 회의 의재를 별첨 송부함.

첨 부 : GATT/AIR/3012. 1부. 끝.

(대사 이상옥 - 국장)

(총 매)

(대사 이상옥 - 국장)

(총 2 매)

0006

2~1

SUBJECT: URUGUAY ROUND - SURVEILLANCE BODY

1.   THE SURVEILLANCE BODY WILL HOLD ITS NEXT MEETING AT 10 A.M. ON
THURSDAY, 5 JULY 1990, IN THE CENTRE WILLIAM RAPPARD.

2.   PROPOSED AGENDA:

   (A)   STANDSTILL

      (I)   EXAMINATION OF STANDSTILL NOTIFICATIONS
            (MTN.SB/SN/SERIES) SUBMITTED IN ACCORDANCE WITH THE
            AGREED PROCEDURES (MTN.TNC/W/10/REV.1).

            UNDER THESE PROCEDURES, NOTIFICATIONS ON STANDSTILL
            RECEIVED BY THE SECRETARIAT BY MONDAY, 11 JUNE CAN BE
            EXAMINED AT THE PRESENT MEETING.

      (II) CONSIDERATION OF ANY STATEMENTS BY PARTICIPANTS
            CONCERNING OTHER ASPECTS OF THE STANDSTILL COMMITMENT.

   (B)   ROLLBACK

         CONSIDERATION OF STATEMENTS CONCERNING THE ROLLBACK COMMITMENT,
         IN THE LIGHT OF THE AGREED PROCEDURES (MTN.TNC/W/10/REV.1), AND
         THE DECISION ON PROGRESS REPORTS ON ROLLBACK AT THE LAST
         SURVEILLANCE BODY MEETING (MTN.SB/12).

   (C)   OTHER BUSINESS, INCLUDING FUTURE WORK AND THE DATE OF THE NEXT
         MEETING.

3.   NOTES ON THE PREVIOUS MEETINGS ARE CONTAINED IN MTN.SB/1-12.

4.   GOVERNMENTS PARTICIPATING IN THE MULTILATERAL TRADE NEGOTIATIONS,
WHICH WISH TO BE REPRESENTED AT THIS MEETING, ARE INVITED TO INFORM ME OF
THE NAMES OF THEIR REPRESENTATIVES AS SOON AS POSSIBLE.

                                             A. DUNKEL

90-0760

0007

2-2

외 무 부

종 별 :

번 호 : GVW-1238   일 시 : 90 0705 1900

수 신 : 장 관(통기), 경기원, 재무부, 농림수산부, 상공부) 사본: 주미대사 (중계요)

발 신 : 주 제네바 대사

제 목 : UR/감시기구 회의

표제회의가 7.5(목) MATHUR의장 사회로 개최된 바 요지 아래 보고함.

(홍서기관, 민서기관 참석)

1. STANDSTILL 통고 검토

0 신규 통고 없음.

0 호주는 지난 회의에 이어 스웨덴의 양고기 수입부과금 인하조치에도 불구 아직도 부과금이 높은수준에 있음을 지적함.

0 이씨는 미국의 CUSTOM USER FEE 패널 권고 이행현황에 대해 관심을 표시함.

2. STANDSTILL 공약관련 검토 (조기 경보적 사안)

0 호주는 미국의 수출장려계획 (EEP) 에 의거 대소련 육류 수출에 대해 보조금 지급이 가능하다는점에 대해 우려를 표시함.

0 호주는 이씨가 검토중인 낙농품 쿼타 조정이 보조를 증액하여 국제 낙농품 가격 인하를 초래할수 있다는 우려를 표시함.

0 미국은 아국의 사치품 과소비자제 조치의 수입제한적 차별적 성격에 대해 우려를 표명하고 대통령의 정부 개입 금지 및 수입 자유화의 계속 지시를 평가하여 행정부가 적절한 조치를 취할것을 촉구한다고 언급함.

0 이씨는 미국의 새로운 섬유 법안 (CAUCUS BILL)보호주의적 성격이 강한데도 불구 미국의회에서 지지폭이 넓어지고 있는데 우려를 표시함.

3. ROLLBACK 현황 검토

0 루마니아는 스웨덴의 루마니아산 상품에 대한 차별적 수입조치 (RBC/21) 의 철폐 문제를 다시거론함.

0 미국은 일본의 ROLLBACK 현황통보 (RBC/22)에 감사하고 일본의 지속적인 ROLLBACK 조치를 희망함.

통상국   2차보   경기원   재무부   농수부   상공부

PAGE 1   공람   90.07.06   09:24 WG

외신 1과 통제관

0008

0 핀란드는 90.6.6.자로 바나나, 채소등 일부 농산물에 대한 수입 허가제도를 철폐하였으며 이를 곧 정식으로 통보하겠다고 함.

4. 7월 TNC 앞 보고서 검토

0 의장은 7월 TNC 에의 제출을 위해 자신이 작성한 SS/RB 이행 현황에 관한 요약 보고서 초안을 배포하고, 이에대한 각국의 의견이 있을경우 이를 반영하여 TNC 에 제출하겠다함.(보고서 초안 파편 송부)

0 동 초안에 대해 전반적인 지지표시가 있었는바, 일부 수정 또는 추가 요청 사항은 아래임.

- 이씨는 자국의 추가 ROLLBACK 조치 (RBC/19/REV.1)가 동구 및 일본에 대한 무차별적 조치임을 명시할 것을 희망함.

- 호주는 각국이 취한 조치의 성격에 대한 분석을 추가 할 것을 제의하였으나, 의장은 그 경우 보고서 분량이 과도하게 늘어남을 들어 반대함.

0 모로코, 콜롬비아는 자국의 자유화 계획 내용을 금년 가을에 통보 하겠다고 함.

5. 차기회의

- 10.30(화) 에 개최키로 함.끝.

(대사 이상옥-국장)

PAGE 2

0009

주 제 네 바 대 표 부

제네(경) 20644-6ρ7   1990. 7. 5

수 신 : 장   관

참 조 : 통상국장

제 목 : UR/감시기구

    연 : GVW-1238

    연호, 감시기구가 TNC에 제출할 보고서 초안을 별첨 송부합니다.

첨 부 : 상기 보고서 1부. 끝.

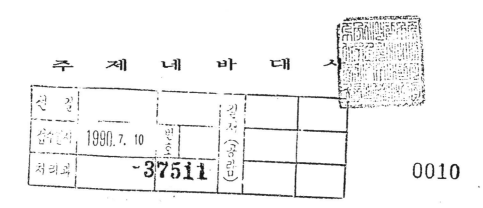

주 제 네 바 대 사

연 길			감		
접수일자	1990. 7. 10		차		
처리과	-37511		(공 람)		

0010

1573

Uruguay Round
Surveillance Body

        The Chairman of the Surveillance Body proposes to take up for
consideration, in the meeting of the Surveillance Body on 5 July 1990, the
attached draft summary of the current situation on implementation of the
standstill and rollback commitments. The intention is that a sumary should
be presented to the TNC meeting in July 1990.

0011

29 ~~July~~ June 1990

DRAFT

CHAIRMAN'S SUMMARY OF THE CURRENT SITUATION ON IMPLEMENTATION
OF THE STANDSTILL AND ROLLBACK COMMITMENTS

1.   The Punta del Este Ministerial Declaration contains the following
commitments on standstill and rollback:

"Standstill

(i)   not to take any trade restrictive or distorting measure
       inconsistent with the provisions of the General Agreement or
       the instruments negotiated within the framework of GATT or
       under its auspices;

(ii)   not to take any trade restrictive or distorting measure in the
       legitimate exercise of its GATT rights, that would go beyond
       that which is necessary to remedy specific situations, as
       provided for in the General Agreement and the Instruments
       referred to in (i) above;

(iii) not to take any trade measures in such a manner as to improve
       its negotiating positions."

"Rollback

(i)   that all trade restrictive or distorting measures inconsistent
       with the provisions of the General Agreement or Instruments
       negotiated within the framework of GATT or under its auspices,
       shall be phased out or brought into conformity within an agreed
       time-frame not later than by the date of the formal completion
       of the negotiations, taking into account multilateral
       agreements, undertakings and understandings, including
       strengthened rules and disciplines, reached in pursuance of the
       Objectives of the Negotiations;

(ii)   there shall be progressive implementation of this commitment on
       an equitable basis in consultations among participants
       concerned, including all affected participants. This
       commitment shall take account of the concerns expressed by any

0012

participant about measures directly affecting its trade
interests;

(iii) there shall be no GATT concessions requested for the
elimination of these measures."

2.   The aim of this note is to provide the TNC with a full summary of the
implementation of the standstill and rollback commitments, and to outline
arrangements accepted in the Surveillance Body for further work on
rollback.

3.   The Surveillance Body has held twelve meetings. Detailed reports are
contained in MTN.SB/1-13. The latest list of notifications and
communications on standstill and rollback is contained in MTN.SB/W/3/Rev.8.

4.   A consolidated text of the Ministerial commitments on standstill and
rollback, and of the procedures agreed by the TNC and by the Surveillance
Body, is contained in document MTN.TNC/W/10/Rev.1.

(a)   Standstill

5.   Since the standstill commitment took effect on 20 September 1986, a
total of 25 notifications, by 11 participants against 8 participants, have
been made as of 27 June 1990. All notifications but one were made during
the period October 1986 to November 1988. There were no notifications in
1989. During the first six months of 1990, there was one notification.

6.   Sixteen notifications cited violation of paragraph (i) of the
standstill commitment. Two notifications cited violations of both
paragraphs (i) and (ii). Eleven notifications referred to paragraph (iii)
of the commitment, three to paragraphs (i) and (iii), and one to paragraphs
(ii) and (iii). There was one notification which did not specify
particular paragraphs.

7.   To date, only one standstill notification has been withdrawn, in
1988.

8.   Four measures referred to in six notifications under standstill have
been subject to Article XXIII:2 Panel proceedings. Four of these measures
were found by the Panels to be inconsistent with the General Agreement.
The Council has adopted these Panel reports. The fourth measure is
currently under examination by a Panel.

9.   In the Surveillance Body's "early warning" discussions on proposed
legislation and other actions affecting trade, [32] cases have been subject
to discussions, some being repeatedly discussed. Ten cases were brought up
in 1987, eight in 1988, ten in 1989, and [four, to date,] in 1990.

(b)   Rollback

10.   Twenty rollback requests, by eight participants addressed to seven
participants, have been made as of 27 June 1990. All requests but one were

made during the period June 1987 to October 1988. There were no new requests in 1989. During the first six months of 1990, there was one request.

11. Twenty-one consultations were held on fifteen of these requests. There have been no consultations on the remaining five requests. The Surveillance Body had agreed on a target of 30 days for beginning the process of consultations following receipt of requests. In many cases, this target has not been met. The frequency of consultations has greatly diminished (five consultations in 1987, thirteen in 1988, three in 1989 and no consultations in 1990).

12. There have been two notifications on rollback actions which are partly related to the rollback requests: one by Japan on the termination of import allocation systems on eight categories of agricultural products (MTN.SB/RBN/1), and the other by the European Communities on the elimination of a range of quantitative restrictions (RBC/19/Rev.1).

13. The above-mentioned notification by the European Communities also contained some autonomous rollback measures. Three other participants (Argentina, Canada and Australia) have notified autonomous trade liberalisation measures (MTN.SB/RBN/3, MTN.SB/W/6 and 7).

14. The notifications by Japan and Canada included the liberalisation of some measures which had been the subject of Panel reports. The United States also made a rollback notification on legislation to amend the Superfund tax in pursuance of Panel recommendations (MTN.SB/RBN/2). The tax was subject to standstill notifications from other participants.

(c) **Proposals for the implementation of rollback commitment following the Mid-Term review**

15. Following the Mid-Term Review, proposals were put forward by Australia (MTN.SB/W/7) and New Zealand (MTN.SB/W/8) for ways to ensure the fulfilment of the rollback commitment. Australia proposed that the TNC agree on the full implementation of all outstanding Panel reports adopted by the CONTRACTING PARTIES. New Zealand proposed that the Surveillance Body should agree on the following ways in which the rollback commitment might be evaluated:

(i) through the implementation of individual offers to roll back measures;

(ii) through the implementation of any multilateral agreements, undertakings and understandings reached in the course of the multilateral negotiations which established that certain types of measures, the present GATT status of which was not necessarily agreed, would henceforth be inconsistent with GATT provisions,

(iii) through the phasing-out of measures ruled inconsistent with the GATT by Panel reports adopted by the CONTRACTING PARTIES.

0014

16.   The Surveillance Body has discussed these proposals on a number of occasions. However, to date, there has been no consensus to adopt these proposals.

(d)   <u>Provision of further information to the TNC</u>

17.   The Surveillance Body has considered what information should be provided which would be relevant to the fulfilment of the above standstill and rollback commitments. The Surveillance Body considers that it should endeavour to provide the fullest possible information to the TNC on actions taken in respect of the commitments entered into at Punta del Este, together with an account of the present situation. Accordingly, it proposes that:

(i)   full reports should be submitted by participants which have made rollback requests and those addressed by such requests, either jointly or separately, concerning consultations, if any, which have been held and their outcome. The objective would be to give an indication of rollback action actually taken or still under discussion and the status of all pending requests;

(ii)   other rollback measures taken by participants autonomously since the inception of the commitment, which have not yet been notified, should be communicated to the Surveillance Body;

(iii) participants would also be invited to communicate any other measures which they propose to roll back before the completion of the Uruguay Round.

It is understood that such communications would be without prejudice to the question of consistency with the General Agreement of the measures listed.

18.   It is proposed that, in order to permit the compilation of as detailed a list as possible of all measures taken in response to requests or otherwise communicated, all such communications should be received by the Secretariat not later than 28 September.

19.   The question has been raised whether the Secretariat could provide a list of "measures inconsistent with the GATT" which remain in force. In this connection, the Secretariat might be requested to examine whether it could supply, for the October meeting of the Surveillance Body, a list of measures which have been found by the CONTRACTING PARTIES, following Panel findings, to be inconsistent with the General Agreement, and any information available regarding actions taken in response to such findings.

20.   Until now, there has been no discussion of an agreed time-frame for the phasing out, or bringing into conformity, of restrictions. In this connection, it is to be noted that the rollback commitment requires that the measures mentioned should be phased out or brought into conformity "within an agreed time-frame not later than by the date of the formal completion of the negotiations, taking into account multilateral

agreements, undertakings and understandings, including strengthened rules
and disciplines, reached in pursuance of the Objectives of the
Negotiations". The point has been made that agreement on a time-frame need
not necessarily imply that all such measures should be phased out or
brought into conformity before the end of the Uruguay Round. It has also
been pointed out that the full details of multilateral agreements,
undertakings and understandings reached, including strengthened rules and
disciplines, may emerge only towards the end of the Uruguay Round.

21. The TNC might wish to make an evaluation of the situation in the
light of the elements presented above.

0016

		기 안 용 지		시 행 상	
분류기호 문서번호	통기20644-	(전화 :)		특별취급	
보존기간	영구·준영구. 10.5.3.1.		장 관		
수 신 처 보존기간					
시행일자	1990.8 .22.				
보 조 기 관	국 장	전결	협 조 기 관	제1차관보	문 서 통 제
	과 장				
기안책임자	조 현 동				발 송 인
경 유 수 신 참 조		수신처 참조	발 신 명 의		
제 목		RB 공약 이행실적 GATT 통보			

40472

1. 우루과이라운드 SS/RB 감시기구 의장은 지난 90.7월

TNC 회의시 제출한 보고서를 통해 GATT 규정 합치 여부에 관계없이

각국이 UR 개시 이후 시행한 RB 실적 및 UR 종료시까지의 RB 계획을

90.10.12. 한 제출토록 제의 한바 있습니다.

2. 아국은 지난 86.9. UR 협상 개시 이래 공산품, 농산품

열대산품등 각분야에서 수입자유화, 관세인하등 GATT 규정 합치 여부에

관계없이 RB성격의 자발적 조치들을 시행하여 왔는바, 이를 종합, UR

협상에의 기여 실적으로 GATT에 제출함이 바람직할것으로 판단됩니다. / 계속 /

1505-25(2-1) 일(1)갑
85. 9. 9. 승인   "내가아낀 종이 한장 늘어나는 나라살림"

190㎜×268㎜ 인쇄용지 2급 60g/㎡
가 40-41 1990. 3. 30

0017

3. 이를위해, 귀부 소관 사항중 상기 RB 실적 통보에 포함될 수 있는

내용을 개략적으로 종합·정리하여 90.9.20. 까지 당부로 보내

주시기 바라며 각 조치 내용과 관련하여 작성된 영문자료가 있으면

첨부하여 주시기 바랍니다. 끝.

수신처 : 경제기획원장관, 재무부장관, 농림수산부장관, 상공부장관

0018

1505-25(2-2) 일(1)을
85. 9. 9. 승인   "내가아낀 종이 한장 늘어나는 나라살림"

190㎜×268㎜ 인쇄용지 2 급 60g/㎡
가 40-41 1989. 11. 14

1. 주요쟁점

가. TNC앞 의장 보고서 상의 쟁점

   1) SS/RB 공약 이행

      ◦ 의장 보고서는 지금까지의 SS/RB 실적이 지조하므로 각국의
        계속적인 SS/RB 공약 이행을 촉구

      ◦ 또한 갓트 규정 합치 여부와 상관없이 각국의 UR이후의 R/B실적
        및 UR 종료시 까지의 R/B 계획을 90.10.12까지 제출토록 규정

   2) SS/RB 공약이행 강화 방안

      ◦ 호주는 TNC가 갓트 불법 판정된 모든 조치를 철폐토록 결정할 것을
        제의

      ◦ 뉴질랜드는 R/B 조치를 아래 기준으로 분류하여 UR 협상 종료시까지
        R/B 일정표를 재시토록 할 것을 제의
        1) 자발적 R/B
        2) UR 협상결과 합의될 결정에 의한 R/B(회색조치 의미)
        3) 패널에 의해 불법 판정된 조치의 R/B

      ◦ 이해 대해 이씨는 R/B 자발적 성격이어야 함을 들어 반대의사 표명

   3) SS/RB 공약의 시한

      ◦ 푼타선언에 S/S 공약에 대한 시한을 명시되어 있지 않으나 R/B
        공약이행의 시한은 UR 협상 종료시로 규정되어 있음.

73   0013

θ 이와 관련, 일부국가는 S/S 공약은 UR 협상이후에도 계속하며, R/B 공약은 갓트 규정 불일치 어부의 근거가 될 새로운 갓트 규범틀이 UR 협상 종료시 확정될 것이므로 UR 협상 종료후에도 R/B 공약을 계속 유효토록 해야 한다는 점을 언급함.

나. TNC 의장 요약문에 포함된 내용

θ 10.15까지 R/B 실적 통보

θ UR협상 종료시 갓트 불법조치에 대한 조치(action)가 가능토록 대비

2. 향후 협상 계획 및 전망

가. 협상 계획

θ 다음 감시기구 회의는 10.30. 개최 예정이며 각국의 TNC앞 SS/RB 현황 보고서를 마지막으로 일단 활동을 종료할 것으로 전망.

나. 협상 전망

θ 다만, R/B 공약이행 강화 방안, SS/RB 공약의 UR 협상이후의 연장 문제등에 관한 관심이 커질 경우애는 TNC 과정과 병행하어 이문제들을 협의할 가능성이 있음.

3. 아국입장 및 협상 대책

가. 입장 점검 사항

1) R/B 공약이행 실적 통보

θ 갓트 규정 합치 어부에 관계없이 R/B 실적을 10.12까지 통보토록 되어 있으므로 아국도 UR 협상에의 기어를 위해 UR 협상 개시이후 UR 종료시점까지의 자발적 자유화 조치와 쇠고기 패닐 보고서 권고 이행 사항을 통보하는 것이 좋을 것으로 사료되는바, 이에 대한 입장 검토

74

0020

2) SS/RB 공약 이행시한

0 SS/RB 공약을 UR 협상이후에도 계속 적용하는 방안이 검토될 경우,
아국도 무역환경 악화방지라는 차원에서 이를 지지하는 것이 좋을
것으로 사료되는바, 이에 대한 입장 검토

나. 본부 준비 사항

0 상기 R/B 공약이행 실적 통보 결정시 동 통보 사항을 10.12까지
사무국에 제출할 수 있도록 늦어도 10.5(금) 까지는 당관에 자료 송부

0021

발 신 전 보

분류번호	보존기간

번   호 : WGV-1284   900929 1339 DY 종별 : 암호송신

수   신 : 주 제네바   대사. 총영사

발   신 : 장 관   (통기)

제   목 : UR/RB 이행실적 통보

대 : 제네(경) 20644-30(90.8.3 UR 중반대책)

1. 감시기구와 관련, 대호 건의대로 지난 7월 TNC 의장보고서에 따라 갓트규정
   합치여부에 관계없이 UR 협상 개시이후 아국의 자발적 자유화 조치실적 및
   계획을 UR 협상에서의 기여로 10.12 시한까지 통보하는 것이 바람직함.

2. 상기 통보내용에는 그간 아국의 각종 비관세장벽 자유화 실적과 쇠고기
   패널보고서 이행사항이 포함되어야 할 것임.

3. 비관세장벽 자유화 실적 자료에 관한 영문초안을 10.8경 FAX 송부키 위해
   준비중인바, 쇠고기 패널보고서 이행사항이 추가될 수 있도록 7.11 이사회
   보고한 내용에 따라 적절한 문안을 준비해 두기 바람.

4. 특히 비관세장벽 자유화 실적은 갓트규정 합치여부와는 관계없는 자발적 조치
   임을 명시 바람. 끝.

(통상국장 김삼훈)

0022

대 한 민 국
상 공 부

국 협 28140-562   503-9446   1990. 9. 21

수 신 외무부장관

참 조 통상국장

제 목 RB 공약 이행 실적 통보

　　1. 통기 20644 - 40472 ('90.8.22)와 관련임.

　　2. 위호와 관련하여 우리나라의 비관세 장벽의 자발적 자유화 실적을
별첨과 같이 통보합니다.

첨 부 : 비관세 장벽의 자발적 자유화 실적 1부.

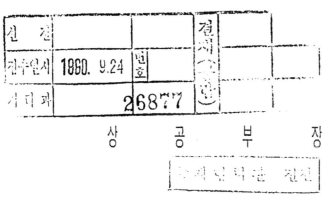

상 공 부 장

0023

비관세장벽의 자발적 자유화 실적

1. 수출입공고상 수입자유화 실적

o 85.9 확정된 '86-'88 간 수입자유화계획에 의거 자유화실시

- 그러나 일부품목은 조기개방되거나 개방연기가 불가피하게 조정된 경우도 있음
- 88년에 이르러 화학제품, 철강금속, 기계류, 전자전기등의 공산품과 일부 섬유류를 제외한 나머지 공산품은 모두 개방됨

o 89.6월에 '89-'91 간 수입자유화계획 확정

- 총규제품목중 약 절반정도인 273개품목이 개방대상임

	규제품목 수	자유화 계획				유보품목 수
		89	90	91	계	
품목수	547	84	98	91	273	279

- 90년 9월 현재 376개품목이 수입규제대상품목이나 대부분이 농축수산물로서 개방의 어려움이 많은 품목들임

o 각년도별 수입자유화 품목수

년도별	86.7	87.7	88.4	88.7	89.1	89.7	90.1
품목수	298	170	262	71	21	84	98

※ 86.7-87.7 : CCCN 8단위 기준
88년 이후 : HS 10단위 기준

- 년도별 자유화품목 내역 : 별첨참조

0024

2. 개별법상 수입규제제도 개선

가. 운영현황

o 개별법에 의한 수입규제제도는 수입을 제한하기 위한 것이 아니라
   인체의 보건. 위생 및 안전이나 환경보호등을 위한 절차적인 규제
   제도로서 예를 들어 전기용품의 안전을 확보하기 위한 형식승인,
   인체 유해제품의 수입 유통을 방지하기 위한 의약품. 화장품등에
   대한 검정. 허가, 폐기물. 독극물등에 대한 수입자격제한등을 하고
   있음.

o 이러한 수입관리는 GATT 등 국제관행상으로도 정당성이 인정되는
   제도로서 세계각국이 모두 시행하고 있으며 선진국일수록 이러한
   규제가 엄격한 것이 관례임.

o 개별법에 의한 규제는 그 내용이 객관적으로 명백하게 공시되어
   있으며 공시된 이외의 음성적인 규제는 없음

나. 주요 개선 사례

o 지난 '87년 이래 수차에 걸쳐 개별법상 각종 수입규제제도중 국제
   관행에 비추어 까다로운 절차등에 대해서는 이를 대폭 개선함으로서
   우리나라의 수입제도를 국제화해 나가고 있으며

o 앞으로도 국제관행으로 보아 특별히 까다로운 일부 수입절차에
   대해서는 계속해서 개선해 나갈 계획임

❋ 주요 개선 실적

- 공산품품질관리법 : 해외유명규격에 대한 상호인증
                  (CSA,UL 등 9개규격)

- 양곡관리법, 사료관리법 : 수량규제적인 수입추천품목의 대폭 축소
                       (예 : 이집트콩, 들깨유박등 31 개품목)

- 약사법 : 복잡한 수입절차 및 구비서류등 간소화등
          (화장품검정 : 색소만 상이한 경우 검정절차 면제등)

0025

3. 수입감시품목의 축소 및 제도폐지

가. 총 괄

(단위 : HS10 단위)

구 분	'86 이전	'86.7.1	'87.7.1	'88.4.1	'88.12.31
품목수	(111)	(106)	96(48)	36	제도폐지

주 : ( ) 내는 CCCN 8 단위기준 품목수임

나. 주요개선실적('86년 이후)

o '86.7.1 감시품목 축소(111개 -> 106 개)
- 해제품목 : 토마토, 양배추, 당근등 13 개 (CCCN 4단위기준)
- 추가품목 : 프레스가공 다이스 및 펀치등 10 개 (CCCN 4단위기준)

o '87.7.1 감시품목 축소(106개 -> 48개)
- 해제품목 : 육류 스우프, 혼합 스우프등 58 개

o '88.4.1 감시품목 축소(HS10 단위 96 개 -> 36개)
- 해제품목 : 대리석, 화강암등 60 개

o '88.12.31 수입감시제도 폐지
- 해제품목 : 고사리, 염장양송이등 22 개품목 수입자유화
- 제한품목 : 마늘, 생강등 12 개품목은 수출입공고에 편입 계속 제한

0026

년도별 자유화품목 내역

1) 86년 주요수입자유화품목

o 화학, 제지제품

  - 소다회, 카본블랙, 초산, 가성소다(액체), 테레프탈산, 카프
    로락탐, 폴리스티렌, 고밀도폴리에틸렌
  - 크라프트라이너, 골판지원지등

o 섬유제품

  - 합성장섬유사, 모직물, 아크릴방적사, 나이론카페트등

o 철강, 금속제품

  - 합금철, 강구, 동괴, 석도강판등

o 기계류

  - 냉동기계, 디젤엔진, 플레인사프트베아링, 식품포장 및 충전기계,
    적하 및 하역기계, 공작기계일부, 타자기등
    . 화물자동차(4톤초과), 고속버스 및 일반버스, 특장차등
      자동차, 260cc 이상의 모터사이클
    . 윈드스크린와이퍼, 점화코일, 스파크플러그등 자동차부품

o 전자, 전기제품

  - 전동공구, 알칼리건전지, 용접기, 스피커 및 앰프, 칼라TV,
    TV브라운관등

o 농수산물, 식품등

  - 칠면조고기, 기타 가금류의 고기, 가금류의 식용설육, 루풀린,
    소라, 건조대구등
  - 토마토소스, 인스탄트카레등

0027

2) 87 년 주요수입자유화품목

o 농수산물
  - 동물의 방광, 소시지유사식품, 돼지고기통조림, 가금고기통조림

o 화학제품
  - PVC 수지, LDPE수지, 석유수지, HDPE필름, PP필름,

o 섬유류
  - 나일론단섬유, 비스코스단섬유, 아세테이트토우, 아크릴단섬유

o 철강제품
  - 스테인레스봉강, 스테인레스강판(두께 3~4.75미리)

o 기계류
  - 차량엔진부문품, 건설중장비, 압연기, 공작기계, 승용차, 마이크로
    버스, 트럭, 펌프트럭, 오토바이등

o 전기. 전자제품류
  - 브라운관유리, 아날로그컴퓨터, 하이브리드컴퓨터, 중소형컴퓨터,
    발전기, 전동기, 유선통신기기, 무선통신기기, 비데오테이프등

o 잡화
  - 면도날 및 면도기, 지퍼, 필기구, 수입인지등

3) 88 년 주요수입자유화품목

가. 1 차 자유화품목('88.4.1)

  o 1 차산품
   - 마프멜로, 과일칵테일, 기타 조제과일등

  o 화학제품
   - 석탄산, 고체가성소다, 파라크실렌, PVC 필름, TDI, DOP.
     PPG 필프등

0028

o 철강·금속

   - 스텐레스강, 합금강등

o 기계류

   - 중소형자동차, 엔진, 기중기차, 베어링, 금속공작기계, 아날로그
     손목시계, 공업용미싱, 드릴, 선박등

o 전자·전기

   - 컴퓨터기기, VTR, TV 카메라, 전축, 발전기등

o 섬유제품

   - 폴리에스테르계 단섬유 및 토우 4개

o 기 타

   - 세공품, 동식물표본, 공업용진주

나. 2차 자유화품목('88.7.1)

   o 생활용품 수출입자유화 확대추진

   o 주요자유화 품목

   o 1차산품

      - 연어, 바다가재, 통조림
      - 들기름, 살구통조림, 멸치통조림, 전갱이, 통조림, 실지렁이,
        해덕, 어류간장, 검정대구등

   o 잡화류

      - 진주, 진주제품 신변장식용품(금박.은박등 보조신변
                                    장식용품)

0023.

4) 89 년 주요수입자유화품목

  o 농산물

    - 피스타치오, 대추야자, 과아버, 맹고, 포포우, 딸기, 커피크리머,
      럼, 진, 보드카등

  o 축산물

    - 산양고기, 말고기, 오리고기 육류조제품, 육즙등

  o 수산물

    - 연어, 대구, 꽁치, 대구 피젯트 , 어류간장, 달팽이, 다시마등

  o 공산품

    - 다이아몬드 원석, 옥수, 기타 귀석, 골동품, 신변장식용품등

4) 90 년 주요수입자유화품목

  o 농산물

    - 페칸. 메카다미아 저피, 파인애플, 토마토쥬스, 파인애플쥬스,
      연뿌리, 역상요구르트, 포도주, 위스키, 사과주등

  o 축산물

    - 산양고기, 소세지, 닭, 말. 당나귀, 노새와 버새고기,
      오리. 거위. 기니아새의 절단육

  o 수산물

    - 송어 다랭이 명태 닭고기 바다가재 홍합, 해삼, 게살,
      새우와 보리새우등

  o 기 타

    - 다이아몬드, 신변장식용품, 전자계산 조직용 대리프, 조각등

0030

Voluntary liberalization of Non-Tariff Barrier

1. Import liberalization by the Export and Import Public Notice.

    o Import liberalization schedule from 1986 to 1988 was confirmed on september, 1985.
       - There are some items that was early liberalized and some items that liberalization was postponed.
       - In 1988, the chemical products, steel, machinery, electronic products and texiles except some items was completely liberalized.

    o Confirmation of import liberalization schedule from 1989 to 1991 on June, 1989.
       - The 273 items of total restriction was liberalized

	restrictive items	liberalization schedule				remaining restrictions
		89	90	91	total	
items	547	84	98	91	273	279

       - 376 items are import restriction on september,1990. Most of them are agricultural items.

    o Number of Import liberalization items by year

Year	'86.7	'87.7	'88.4	'88.7	'89.1	'89.7	'90.1
Number of item	298	170	262	71	21	84	98

       ÷ '86.7 - '88.7 : CCCN 8 digit
         After 1988   : HS   10 digit

       - Detailed items are attached.

0031

2. Improvements to Individual Laws

A. The operation contents of individual laws

o The purpose of these laws is not to restcict import quantities but
  mainly to restrict import procedures with a view to maintain quality
  levels and to ensure safety and health standards, to protect environ
  -ment

o This import restrictive measures are internationally granted by GATT
  regulations, etc, and most of advanced countries take advantage of
  these measures

o Also, the import restrictive measures are clearly published, and there
  are not any invisible restrictive measures which are not published.

B. Key improvements to individual laws.

o Largely improving some restrictive measures not consistent with GATT
  regulations, etc., Korea has internationalized his import systems many
  times,

o Furthermore, Korea plans to improve some complicated import systems
  as compared international practice.

0032

* Key measures improved are as follow ;

      - Industrial goods quality control act.

         • 9 standards which are world-widely well- known are mutually
           admitted (CSA, UL, JIS, etc)

      - Grain management act, Animal feed management act.

         • 31 items subject to recommendation requirement were reduced.

      - Pharmaceuticals act.

         • About 160 items subject to recommendation system were simplified
           as reporting system

3. Elimination of import surveillance system

o Import surveillance system was abolished, on Dec. 31. 1988.

0033

[Apendix]

1) Import liberalization products in '86

o Chemical paper products
   - Soda-lime, other carbon black, acelic acid, solid sodium hydroxide,
     6-Hexanelactam(epsilon caprolactam), terephthalic acid, polystyrene,
     polyethylene having a specipic gravity of 0.94 or more, etc.
   - kraftliner, etc.

o Textile Products
   - Synthetic filaments of nylon or ther polyaimides woven fabrics, acrylic
     or modacrylic staple, capet of nylon etc.

o Iron products
   - Other articles of iron or steel, refined copper of cathodes and sections
     of cathodes, flat-rolled products of iron or non-ally steel of plated
     or coated with tin, etc.

o Machinery
   - Spark-ignition reciprocating or rotary internal combustion piston
     engines, plain shaft bearings. non-electric other type writers, etc.

o Electrical machinery
   - Alkalimanganese batteries, colour TV, Audio-frequency electric
     amplifiers, loudspeakers, etc.

o agriculture products
   - meat of turkeys, meat and edible offal of other poultry, lupulin,
     frozen top shells dried cod, tomato sauces etc.

2) Import liberalization products in '87

o Agriculture products
   - bladders, sausages similar prducts, swine in airtight containers,
     meat of poultry in airtight containers, etc.

o Chemical products
   - O-Xylene, Acetone, LDPE chloride, HDPE film, PP film, etc.

0034

o Textile products.
  - Synthetic staple fibres, fibres for spinning of viscose, Acrylic of
    polyesters, filament tow of cellulose acetate, etc.

o Iron products
  - Bars and rods of stainless steel, flat-rolled products of stainless
    steel, etc.

o Machinery
  - metal-rolling mills, motor cars for the transport of persons, truck,
    motorcycles, micro-bus, dumperstruck, etc.

o Electronical machinery
  - Electric generating set, teleprinters, image telegraphic,
    silicon didodes, video tape, etc.

o Others
  - fountainpens, ball point pens, razors, etc.

3) Import liberalization products in '88

  A) 1st liberalization products('88.4.1)

    o Agriculture products
      - quinces, fruit cockfail, fruitsalad, etc.

    o Chemical products
      - Caustic soda, P-Xylene, ethylacetate, pvc film, TDI, DOP,
        chemical wood pulp, etc.

    o Iron products
      - Stainless steel, bars and rods of silico-manganese steel, etc.

    o Machinery
      - engines, sewing machines, machine-tools for drilling. boring.
        milling. ----- grinders, motor car for the transport of persons,
        etc.

o Electronical machinery
  - electric generating sets, recordplayers, turntables, VTR, T.V
    camera, etc.

o Textile products
  - Synthetic filament tow of polyesters, Polyesters of special section
    face, etc.

o Others
  - Articles of goldsmiths or silversmiths, etc.

B) 2nd liberalization products('88.7.1)

  o agriculture products
    - Other live animals, haddock, coalfish, ivory of elephant, avocados,
      poppy seeeds, anchovies in airtight containers, etc.

  o Others
    - natural pearls, cultured pearls, articles of jewellery, imitation
      jewellery, worked ivory and articles of ivory, etc.

4) Import liberalization products in '89

  o agriculture products and fish
    - Pistachios, dates, guavas, mangoes, papaws, strawberries,coffee creamer,
      rum and tafia, gin and geneva, vodka, hake, salmon, cod,saury, fish
      fillets, livers of fish, snails, sea tangle, meat of goats, meat of
      horses.mules or hinnies, other meat-preparations, etc.

  o Others
    - Pegine, unworked diamonds, chakedony, other jewel, antiques, etc.

5) Import liberalization products in '90

  o Agriculture liberalization products
    - Pecan. macadimia of other muts, bark of paper mulberry, pineapple,
      tomato juice, pineapple juice, lotus roots, fluid yoguest, wine,
      whisky, meat of goats, sausages, trout, albacore, jorn dory, mussels,
      sea-cucumbers, etc.

0036

o Others
  - woven fabrics wholly of silk, shibori, diamonds, tapes recorded with
    data for E.D.P.S, sculptures, etc.

0037

외 무 부

종 별 :

번 호 : GVW-1971

일 시 : 90 0104 1200

수 신 : 장 관 (통기, 경기원, 재무부, 상공부)

발 신 : 주 제네바 대사

제 목 : UR/ 감시기구

10.30 개최 예정인 표제회의 의제를 별첨 송부함.

첨부: GATT/AIR/3111. 1부(GVW (F)-380). 끝

(대사 이상옥-국장)

통상국   경기원   재무부   상공부

90.10.05   03:32 FC

외신 1과 통제관

0038

GATT/AIR/3111

2 OCTOBER 1990

SUBJECT   URUGUAY ROUND - SURVEILLANCE BODY

1.   THE SURVEILLANCE BODY WILL HOLD ITS NEXT MEETING ON TUESDAY,
30 OCTOBER 1990, AT 10 A.M. IN THE CENTRE WILLIAM RAPPARD.

2.   THE FOLLOWING AGENDA IS PROPOSED:

   (A)   STANDSTILL

      (I)   EXAMINATION OF STANDSTILL NOTIFICATIONS
            (MTN.SB/SN/SERIES) SUBMITTED IN ACCORDANCE WITH THE
            AGREED PROCEDURES (MTN.TNC/W/10/REV.1).

            UNDER THESE PROCEDURES, NOTIFICATIONS ON STANDSTILL
            RECEIVED BY THE SECRETARIAT BY FRIDAY, 5 OCTOBER CAN BE
            EXAMINED AT THE MEETING.

      (II) CONSIDERATION OF ANY STATEMENTS BY PARTICIPANTS
            CONCERNING OTHER ASPECTS OF THE STANDSTILL COMMITMENT.

   (B)   ROLLBACK

         CONSIDERATION OF STATEMENTS CONCERNING THE ROLLBACK COMMITMENT,
         IN THE LIGHT OF THE AGREED PROCEDURES (MTN.TNC/W/10/REV.1) AND
         THE DECISION ON REPORTS ON ROLLBACK AT THE LAST SURVEILLANCE
         BODY MEETING (MTN.SB/13).

   (C)   OTHER BUSINESS, INCLUDING REVIEW OF THE SITUATION IN THE
         CONTEXT OF THE MEETING OF THE TRADE NEGOTIATIONS COMMITTEE IN
         DECEMBER AND CONSIDERATION OF THE CHAIRMAN'S REPORT TO THE TNC.

3.   NOTES ON THE PREVIOUS MEETINGS ARE CONTAINED IN MTN.SB/1-13

4.   GOVERNMENTS PARTICIPATING IN THE MULTILATERAL TRADE NEGOTIATIONS,
WHICH WISH TO BE REPRESENTED AT THIS MEETING, ARE INVITED TO INFORM ME OF
THE NAMES OF THEIR REPRESENTATIVES AS SOON AS POSSIBLE.

                                        A. DUNKEL

90-1377

WGV(F) - 201   DATE : 1/10 2022

수신 : 주 제네바 대사

발신 : 장 관 (통기)

제목 : UR/RB 이행실적 통보

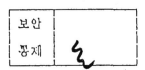

연 : WGV - 1284

연호 감시기구에 제출할 아국의 비관세장벽 자유화실적 자료를 별첨

송부하니 귀관에서 검토후 적절히 제출하기 바랍니다.

(통상국장 김 삼훈)

			담 당	과 장	국 장	차관보	차 관	장 관
안 고 재	통상기구과	90년 10월 10일						

심의관 :

Voluntary Liberalization of Non-Tariff Barriers

1. Import Liberalization by Export and Import Public Notice.

   o The import liberalization schedule from 1986 to 1988 was announced in September, 1985.

      - Some items were liberalized ahead of schedule while the liberalization of others was postponed.

      - In 1988, chemical products, steel, machinery, electronic products and texiles, with a few exceptions, were completely liberalized.

   o The import liberalization schedule from 1989 to 1991 was announced in June, 1989.

	restricted items	liberalization schedule				remaining restrictions
		89	90	91	total	
items	547	84	98	91	* 273	279

   * including 5 items which are partially liberalized

   - 376 items remain under import restriction as of September, 1990, most of which are agricultural items.

   o As a result of the above liberalization programme, total 1,004 products were liberalized between July 1986 and January 1990.

   The number of yearly import liberalization items are as follows :

Year	'86.7	'87.7	'88.4	'88.7	'89.1	'89.7	'90.1
Number of items	298	170	262	71	21	84	98

   * '86.7-'88.7 : CCCN 8 digit

     After 1988 : HS 10 digit

   - Detailed items are attached.

0041

2. Improvements in Individual Laws

A. Contents of individual laws
   ○ The purpose of these laws is not to restrict import quantities but mainly to regulate import procedures with a view to maintaining quality levels, ensuring safety and health standards, and protecting the environment
   ○ These measures are permissable under international arrangements including GATT provisions.
   ○ These measures are duly published.

B. Key improvements in individual laws.
   ○ Korea has substantially improved import regimes and plans to further improve the systems.
   ○ Key improvement measures are as follow :
      - Industrial Goods Quality Control Act.
         · Introduction of 9 internationally acknowledged standards (CSA, UL, JIS, etc)
      - Grain Management Act and Animal Feed Management Act.
         · 31 items which were under the requirement of import recommendation were abolished
      - Pharmaceuticals Act.
         · Import recommendation system applied to around 160 items were simplified to a reporting system

3. Elimination of Import Surveillance System
   ○ The Import Surveillance System was abolished, on Dec, 31. 1988.

0042

[Appendix]

Main import liberalized products

1986

o Chemical paper products
  - soda-lime, other carbon black, acetic acid, solid sodium hydroxide,
    6-Hexanelactam(epsilon caprolactam), terephthalic acid, polystyrene,
    polyethylene having a specific gravity of 0.94 or more, etc.
  - kraftliner, etc.

o Textile products
  - synthetic filaments of nylon or other polyaimides woven fabrics, acrylic
    or modacrylic staple, carpet of nylon etc.

o Iron products
  - other articles of iron or steel, refined copper of cathodes and
    sections of cathodes, flat-rolled products of iron or non-ally steel
    of plated or coated with tin, etc.

o Machinery
  - spark-ignition reciprocating or rotary internal combustion piston
    engines, plain shaft bearings, non-electric other type writers, etc.

o Electric and electronic machinery
  - alkalimanganese batteries, colour TV, audio-frequency electric
    amplifier, loudspeakers, etc.

o Agricultural products
  - meat of turkeys, meat and edible offal of other poultry, lupulin,
    frozen top shells, dried cod, tomato sauces etc.

0043

o   Agricultural products

    - bladders, sausages similar prducts, swine in airtight containers,
      meat of poultry in airtight containers, etc.

o   Chemical products

    - O-Xylene, acetone, LDPE chloride, HDPE film, PP film, etc.

o   Textile products.

    - synthetic staple fibres, fibres for spinning of viscose, acrylic
      of polyesters, filament tow of cellulose acetate, etc.

o   Iron products

    - bars and rods of stainless steel, flat-rolled products of stainless
      steel, etc.

o   Machinery

    - metal-rolling mills, motor cars for the transport of persons, truck,
      motorcycles, micro-bus, dumperstruck, etc.

o   Electric and electronic machinery

    - electric generating set, teleprinters, image telegraphic, silicon
      didodes, video tape, etc.

o   Others

    - fountainpens, ball point pens, razors, etc.

0044

○ Agricultural products

    - quinces, fruit cockfail, fruitsalad, other live animals, haddock, coalfish, ivory of elephant, avocados, popy sceds, anchovies in airtight containers, etc.

○ Chemical products

    - caustic soda, P-Xylene, ethylacetate, pvc film, TDI, DOP, chemical woodpulp, etc.

○ Iron products

    - stainless steel, bars and rods of silico-manganese steel, etc.

○ Machinery

    - engines, sewing machines, machine-tools for drilling, boring, milling, grinders, motor car for the transport of persons, etc.

○ Electronic machinery

    - electric generating sets, recordplayers, turntables, VTR, T.V camera, etc.

○ Textile products

    - synthetic filament tow of polyesters, polyesters of special section face, etc.

○ Others

    - articles of goldsmiths or silversmiths, natural pearls, cultured pearls, articles of jewellery, imitation jewellery, worked ivory and articles of ivory, etc.

0045

<u>1989</u>

o   Agricultural and fishery products

- pistachios, dates, guavas, mangoes, papaws, strawberries, coffee creamer, rum and tafia, gin and geneva, vodka, hake, salmon, cod, saury, fish fillets, livers of fish, snails, sea tangle, meat of goats, meat of horses, mules or hinnies, other meat-preparations, etc.

o   Others

- pegine, unworked diamonds, chakedony, other jewel, antiques, etc.

<u>1990</u>

o   Agricultural products

- pecan, macadimia of other nuts, bark of paper mulberry, pineapple, tomato juice, pineapple juice, lotus roots, fluid yoguest, wine, whisky, meat of goats, sausages, trout, albacore, jorn dory, mussels, sea-cucumbers, etc.

o   Others

- woven fabrics wholly of silk, shibori, diamonds, tapes recorded with data for E.D.P.S, sculptures, etc.

외 무 부

종 별 :

번 호 : GVW-2131 　　　　　　　　　　　일 시 : 90 1018 1900

수 신 : 장 관 (봉기, 경기원, 재무부, 농림수산부, 상공부)

발 신 : 주 제네바 대사

제 목 : UR/ 감시기구 비공식 협의

대: WGV-1284, WGV(F)-201

표제 비공식 회의가 10.18(목) 오전 MATHUR의장 사회로 개최된바 요지 아래
보고함. (오참사관 참석)

1. 의장은 TNC 에 제출기 위해 자신이 작성한 SS/RB 이행 현황에 관한 요약 보고서
초안을 제출함. (동 초안 파편 송부)

- 동 초안에 따른면 TNC 가 합의할 권고사항으로써 UR 협상경과에 따라
각국이푼타선언에 따른 RB 조치를 어느정도 이행할수 있을지를 검토하여 CP 에
보고토록 하며, 각료들이 CP 가 상기 각국의 보고서를 검토하여 RB이행을 위해
필요하다고 보는 적절한 추가조치에 관해 합의할 것을 권고하는 내용이 포함됨.

2. 상기 의장초안과 관련 각국은 아래와 같은 입장을 포함함.

- 뉴질랜드는 푼타선언에서 UR 협상 종료이전에 일정한 시한을 두어 RB 를
이행토록 한것은 현재 이행이 실질적으로 어렵게된 점을 감안, (UR 협상이 진행중이며,
특히 세이프가드 협상이 종료되어야 회색조치등 개념이 명확해진다는 점) UR 종료후
91.10 까지 각국이 모든 갓트 불법조치를 봉보하고 92.10 까지 철폐토록 할것을 제안

- 이씨는 푼타선언은 정치적인 약속이며, 분쟁해결 절차에 관한 교섭이
진행중에있어(특히 상소제도 도입문제등) 패널 보고서 이행문제와 관련 상기
뉴질랜드의 제의가 적절치 않다는 입장을 표명

- 홍콩은 푼타선언의 이행을 위해 좀더 확실하고 이행가능한 방안의 하나로 시한을
명시하도록 한 뉴질랜드의제안을 지지함.

- 일본은 기본적으로 RB 에 관한 푼타선언은 정치적인 약속이며, RB
협상종료로각종 규정이 명확히 된 이후에도 RB 문제를 별도로 다루어야 하느냐에
의문을 표시함.

통상국　　경기원　　재무부　　농수부　　상공부

PAGE 1　　　　　　　　　　　　　　　　　　　　90.10.19　06:26 FC

　　　　　　　　　　　　　　　　　　　　　　외신 1과 통제관

　　　　　　　　　　　　　　　　　　　　　　　　　　0047

3. 의장은 의장초안이 분쟁해결절차와 관련 문제가 없다는 생각에서 제출한 것이나 상기논의에 비추어 수일내 적절한 표현을 검토해서 내주중 다시 협의할수 있도록대안을 마련해 보기로함.

4. 대호의 아국 UR/RB 이행실적은 UR협상문서(MTN.SB/RBN/5)로 금일 회의자료로배포됨.끝

(대사 이상옥-국장)

민감토: 의장초안에대한
아국입장 통보.

주 제 네 바 대 표 부

제네(경) 20644-//0/   1990.10.19

수 신 : 장 관

참 조 : 통상국장

제 목 : UR/감시기구

            대 : WGV-1284

               WGV(F)-201

        대호, 감시기구에 제출한 아국의 Rollback 통고 관련 갓트

문서를 별첨 송부합니다.

        첨 부 : 통고문서 1부. 끝.

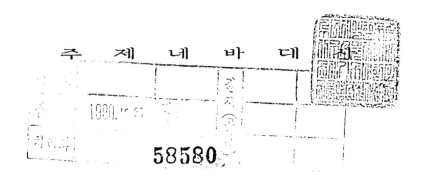

58580

0043

RESTRICTED

MTN.SB/RBN/5
October 1990

Special Distribution

Surveillance Body

Original: English

ROLLBACK

Notification

The following notification, dated 12 October 1990, has been received from the Permanent Mission of the Republic of Korea.

Pursuant to the commitment on rollback made by Ministers at Punta del Este and also to the agreement reached in the 5 July meeting of the Surveillance Body on the provision of further information to the TNC, the Korean government is communicating to the Surveillance Body its trade liberalization measures taken since inception of the rollback commitment as shown in the attachment.

This communication is made without prejudice to the question of consistency of the measures listed in the attachment with the General Agreement.

GATT SECRETARIAT

0050

A.   Autonomous Import Liberalization

1.   Korea has been implementing voluntarily ambitious liberalization
programmes from the early 1980s. This process has been accelerated since
1985 and the Korean government announced two sets of three-year
liberalization programmes for the period 1986-1991.

2.   As a result of these two programmes a total of 1,004 products have
been liberalized as of January 1990:

Year	July '86	July '87	Apr. '88	July '88	Jan. '89	July '89	Jan. '90
No. of items	298	170	262	71	21	84	98

*   July 1986-July 1988: CCCN 8 digit
    From January 1989:   HS 10 digit

*   A list of main items is attached in the Appendix.

B.   Elimination of Import Surveillance System

3.   On 31 December 1988, Korea voluntarily eliminated its import
surveillance system, which had been in place since 1977. The system was
similar in purpose to the Safeguards mechanism provided in Article XIX of
the General Agreement.

C.   Improvement of Import Procedures under Special Laws

4.   Since 1988, Korea has substantially improved import procedures under
its special laws. The purpose of these laws is not to restrict import
quantities but to regulate import procedures with a view to maintaining
quality levels, ensuring safety and health standards, and protecting the
environment.

5.   Key features of these improvements are as follows:

   (a)   Industrial Goods Quality Control Act:
         -     Introduction of nine internationally-acknowledged
               standards (CSA, UL, JIS, etc.).

   (b)   Grain Management Act and Animal Feed Management Act:
         -     Thirty-one items which required import recommendation
               were liberalized.

   (c)   Pharmaceuticals Act:
         -     The import recommendation system applied to around
               180 items was substituted with a reporting system.

D.   Implementation of Panel Reports on Korea's Beef Import Restrictions

6.   In accordance with recommendations in the Panel Reports (L/6503,
L/6504 and L/6505), Korea held consultations with the three complainants
and reached agreements in April, May and July 1990.

7.   The agreements, which, among other things, set forth Korea's
undertakings concerning its remaining import restrictions on beef, and
certain market access measures, were reported to the CONTRACTING PARTIES on
9 July 1990 (for details, see L/6697).

Appendix: List of Main Items Liberalized 1986-1990

0052

APPENDIX

LIST OF MAIN ITEMS LIBERALIZED 1986-1990

1986

Chemical paper products
-     soda-lime, other carbon black, acelic acid, solid sodium hydroxide,
      6-Hexanelactam(epsilon caprolactam), terephthalic acid, polystyrene,
      polyethylene having a specific gravity of 0.94 or more, etc.
-     kraftliner, etc.

Textile products
-     synthetic filaments of nylon or other polyaimides woven fabrics,
      acrylic, or modacrylic staple, carpet of nylon, etc.

Iron products
-     other articles of iron or steel, refined copper of cathodes and
      sections of cathodes, flat-rolled products of iron or non-alloy steel
      plated or coated with tin, etc.

Machinery
-     spark-ignition reciprocating or rotary internal combustion piston
      engines, plain shaft bearings, non-electric other typewriters, etc.

Electric and electronic machinery
-     alkalimanganese batteries, colour TVs, audio-frequency electric
      amplifiers, loudspeakers, etc.

Agricultural products
-     meat of turkeys, meat and edible offal of other poultry, lupulin,
      frozen top shells, dried cod, tomato sauces, etc.

1987

Agricultural products
-     bladders, sausages similar products, swine in airtight containers,
      meat of poultry in airtight containers, etc.

Chemical products
-     O-Xylene, acetone, LDPE chloride, HDPE, film, PP film, etc.

Textile products
-     synthetic staple fibres, fibres for spinning of viscose, acrylic of
      polyesters, filament tow of cellulose acetate, etc.

Iron products
-     bars and rods of stainless steel, flat-rolled products of stainless
      steel, etc.

0053

Machinery
- metal-rolling mills, motor cars for the transport of persons, trucks, motorcycles, micro-buses, trucks, etc.

Electric and electronic machinery
- electric generating sets, teleprinters, image telegraphics, silicon didodes, video tapes, etc.

Others
- fountain pens, ballpoint pens, razors, etc.

1988

Agricultural products
- quinces, fruit cocktail, fruit salad, other live animals, haddock, coalfish, ivory of elephant, avocados, poppy seeds, anchovies in airtight containers, etc.

Chemical products
- caustic soda, P-Xylene, ethylacetate, pvc film, TDI, DOP, chemical woodpulp, etc.

Iron products
- stainless steel, bars and rods of silico-manganese steel, etc.

Machinery
- engines, sewing machines, machine-tools for drilling, boring, milling, grinders, motor cars for the transport of persons, etc.

Electronic machinery
- electric generating sets, record players, turntables, VTR, TV cameras, etc.

Textile products
- synthetic filament tow of polyester, polyesters of special section face, etc.

Others
- articles of goldsmiths or silversmiths, natural pearls, cultured pearls, articles of jewellery, imitation jewellery, worked ivory and articles of ivory, etc.

1989

Agricultural and fishery products
- pistachios, dates, guavas, mangoes, papaws, strawberries, coffee creamer, rum and tafia, vodka, hake, salmon, cod, saury, fish fillets, livers of fish, snails, sea tangle, meat of goats, meat of horses, mules or hinnies, other meat preparations, etc.

0054

Others
-    unworked diamonds, chakedony, other jewels, antiques, etc.

<u>1990</u>

Agricultural products
-    pecans, macadamia or other nuts, bark of paper mulberry, pineapples,
     tomato juice, pineapple juice, lotus roots, fluid yogurt, wine,
     whisky, meat of goats, sausages, trout, albacore, mussels,
     sea-cucumbers, etc.

Others
-    woven fabrics wholly of silk, shibori, diamonds, tapes recorded with
     data for E.D.P.S., sculptures, etc.

0055

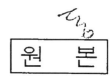

외 무 부

종　별 :

번　호 : GVW-2200　　　　　　　　　일　시 : 90 1023 1700

수　신 : 장관(통기, 경기원, 재무부, 농림수산부, 상공부)

발　신 : 주 제네바 대사

제　목 : UR/ 감시기구

연: GVW-1971

표제 그룹은 연호 10.30. 공식 회의 개최에 앞서10.24(수) 오전 갓트 위배조치의
<u>ROLLBACK</u> 에 관한결정문안 (<u>DRAFT DECISION</u>) 에 대해 비공식협의를 실시할 예정임을
통보하여 온바, 동결정문 초안 별첨 송부함.

　　(첨부: 상기문안 (90.10.19 자) 끝

　　(GVW(F)-448)

　　(대사 이상옥-국장)

통상국　　경기원　　재무부　　농수부　　상공부

PAGE 1　　　　　　　　　　　　　　　　　　　90.10.24　　22:14 CT

외신 1과 통제관

0056

GVW(乃)-448 010231700

GVW-2200 전무

ANNEX I

ROLLBACK OF GATT-INCONSISTENT MEASURES

(Draft Decision)

Ministers,

본 FAX 의 HEAD 전문은 화선고장으로
추후 재벌부 하겠습니다. 통계관: 가

Recalling the commitment on rollback in the Punta del Este
Ministerial Declaration and the agreed procedures adopted by the Trade
Negotiation Committee on 28 January 1987;

Recalling that the rollback commitment was to be implemented within
an agreed time-frame as provided for in the Punta del Este Ministerial
Declaration;

Having regard to the Surveillance Body Chairman's Summary on the
Implementation of the Standstill and Rollback Commitments ((MTN.SB/14)];

Recognizing that there are a number of measures still in place which
have been ruled GATT-inconsistent by Panel reports adopted by the
CONTRACTING PARTIES;

Recognizing that it has, so far, not been always feasible for
participants to determine the extent to which measures maintained by them
were inconsistent with the provisions of the General Agreement or
Instruments negotiated within the framework of GATT or under its auspices
since this could be determined only when account be taken of multilateral
agreements reached at the conclusion of the Uruguay Round;

Reaffirming the decisions taken in individual negotiating areas of
the Uruguay Round with respect to measures inconsistent with the provisions
of the General Agreement or Instruments negotiated within the framework of
GATT or under its auspices;

0057

A:C5-SB3

448-)-1

<u>Agree as follows:</u>

1. Without prejudice to the decisions on dispute settlement procedures taken in the Uruguay Round, contracting parties maintaining measures which have been ruled to be GATT-inconsistent by the CONTRACTING PARTIES, following Panel recommendations, shall communicate, not later than [1 October 1991], to the CONTRACTING PARTIES their programs for the phasing out of such measures, or for bringing them into conformity with the provisions of the General Agreement or Instruments negotiated within the framework of GATT or under its auspices, [within a timeframe not extending beyond 30 September 1992, unless otherwise agreed].

2. In the light of the results of the Uruguay Round, contracting parties shall also review trade policy measures other than those described in paragraph 1 above, that are being maintained by them, with a view to determining the extent to which their rollback commitments under the Punta del Este Declaration are met. Contracting parties shall communicate the result of such a review, including any further action that they intend to take in this matter, to the CONTRACTING PARTIES by no later than [1 October 1991].

3. The CONTRACTING PARTIES, at their session of 1991, shall review the situation in the light of the communications received by them. Without prejudice to the existing rights and obligations of contracting parties under the GATT or Instruments negotiated within the framework of GATT or under its auspices, they shall recommend such action as may appear appropriate for facilitaing the phasing-out of, or the bringing into conformity, measures inconsistent with the provisions of the General Agreement or Instruments negotiated within the framework of GATT or under its auspices.

A:C5-SB3

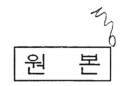

외 무 부

종 별 :

번 호 : GVW-2210　　　　　　　　　일 시 : 90 1024 1800

수 신 : 장 관(통기,경기원,재무부,농림수산부,상공부)

발 신 : 주 제네바 대사

제 목 : UR/ 감시기구

　　연: GVW-2200 표제그룹은 10.29(수) 오전 MATHUR 의장 사회로연호 결정문안에 대한 비공식 협의를 실시한바 주요 토의내용 아래 보고함(오참사관 참석)

　1. 결정문 초안 내용에 대한 각국 반응

　- 호주는 동 초안이 협의의 유용한 기초가 되나, 1항의 경우 일정시한 도입 문제에 대해서는 융통성이 필요하며 2항의 경우 다른 협상 그룹의협상 내용과 연계되어 있으므로 타 협상그룹의 협상 결과를 본후 동 결과를 보충하는 방향으로 작성되어야 할것이라고 함.

　- 아국은 패널보고서 이행문제는 사안에 따라 이행시한이 다를수 있고, 경우에 따라서는 관련국의 양자협의도 필요한 만큼 일률적인 철폐시한을 설정할 경우 서로 상충 될 가능성이있어 철폐시한 도입에 동의하기 어렵다는 입장을 표명함.

　- 미국은 철폐시한 도입에 문제가 있음을 지적하고, 2항의 경우 이미 합의한 TPRM 하에서도 UR 결과 이행사항을 검토하게 될것임에 비추어 감시기구 차원에서 이중적으로 다룰 필요가 있는지 여부에 의문을 제기함.

　- 이씨도 1.2항에 어려움을 표시하고 타협상 그룹의협상 결과를 본후 논의되어야 할 것이라고 함.다만 RB 공약의 정치적 중요성에 비추어 감시기구차원에서 어떤 형태로든 TNC 에 보고 문안을 작성해야 할 필요성에 대하여는 동감이라고 말함.

　- 북구, 멕시코, 우루과이, 칠레등은 철폐시한 도입에 찬성하면서 푼타선언에서 UR 협상종료 이전에 시한을 정해 철폐키로 한 점을 강조하고, 각료선언을 수정할 수는 없다는 입장을 견지함.

　- 뉴질랜드는 푼타선언 채택시에는 일정 시한내 철폐문제와 관련 당초 부터 문제가 없었던것은 아니나 일단 채택되었고, 지난 4년간 RB분야에서 전혀 진전이 없는 상태에 있음에 비추어 철폐시한 문제를 전혀 도외시할 수는 없는상황에 있고 한편 철폐시한

ㅡㅡㅡㅡㅡㅡㅡㅡㅡㅡㅡㅡㅡㅡㅡㅡㅡㅡㅡㅡㅡㅡㅡㅡㅡㅡㅡㅡㅡㅡ

통상국　　2차보　　경기원　　재무부　　농수부　　상공부

도입문제와 관련한 많은 국가의 우려도 충분히 이유가 있는만큼 공식회의 이전에 좀더 협의할 것을희망함.

　　2. 의장은 상기 제기된 문제점에 비추어 UR감시기구가 취할수 있는 대응 방안은 아래3방안으로 요약될 수 있으나 10.30 공식회의 이전에 이해 관계국과 좀더 절충을 시도하여 합의할 수 있는 방안을 강구해 보겠으며, 필요시 공식회의를 연기하는 문제도 검토해 보겠다고하였음.

　　- 타협상 그룹회의 결과가 나오기까지 협의를 보류함.

　　- 감시기구 차원에서 가능한 해결방안 강구

　　- 감시기구는 R.B 이행 현황과 문제점을단순히 열거하고 추후 해결책을 각료들이 결정토록하는 방안.끝.

　　(대사 이상옥-국장)

외 무 부

종 별 :

번 호 : GVW-2264　　　　　　　　　　일 시 : 90 1029 1520

수 신 : 장관(통기, 경기원, 재무부, 농림수산부, 상공부)

발 신 : 주 제네바 대사

제 목 : UR/ 감시기구

연: GVW-1971

당초 10.30 (화) 개최 예정이던 표제회의가 11.9(금) 연기 되었으니 참고 바람. 끝
(대사 이상옥-국장)

통상국　　경기원　　재무부　　농수부　　상공부

PAGE 1　　　　　　　　　　　　　　　　90.10.30　　06:51 DA

외신 1과 통제관

0061

AIRGRA_   AÉR●GRAMME ﾐ(ºﾚ)

GATT/AIR/3111/CORR.1   26 OCTOBER 1990

SUBJECT: URUGUAY ROUND - SURVEILLANCE BODY

    THIS IS TO INFORM YOU THAT THE NEXT MEETING OF THE SURVEILLANCE BODY
WILL BE HELD ON FRIDAY, 9 NOVEMBER 1990 AT 10 A.M. IN THE COUNCIL ROOM, NOT
ON 30 OCTOBER 1990 AS INDICATED IN GATT/AIR/3111.

                                       A. DUNKEL

OBJET: NEGOCIATIONS D'URUGUAY - ORGANE DE SURVEILLANCE

    CONTRAIREMENT A CE QUI ETAIT INDIQUE DANS L'AEROGRAMME GATT/AIR/3111,
LA PROCHAINE REUNION DE L'ORGANE DE SURVEILLANCE SE TIENDRA LE VENDREDI
9 NOVEMBRE 1990, A 10 HEURES, DANS LA SALLE DU CONSEIL, ET NON LE
30 OCTOBRE.

                                       A. DUNKEL

ASUNTO: RONDA URUGUAY - ORGANO DE VIGILANCIA

    EL PRESENTE ES PARA INFORMARLE QUE LA PROXIMA REUNION DEL ORGANO DE
VIGILANCIA SE CELEBRARA EL VIERNES 9 DE NOVIEMBRE A LAS 10 H EN LA SALA DEL
CONSEJO Y NO EL 30 DE OCTUBRE DE 1990 COMO SE INDICABA EN EL AEROGRAMA
GATT/AIR/3111.

                                       A. DUNKEL

90-1538

0062

SENT BY: Director-General, GATT, Tel. address: GATT GENEVA

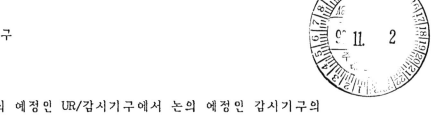

주 제 네 바 대 표 부

제네(경) 20644-*11*$1*$ 1990. 11. 1

수신 : 장 관

참조 : 통상국장

제목 : UR/감시기구

　　　　11. 9 개최 예정인 UR/감시기구에서 논의 예정인 감시기구의

TNC 앞 보고서 초안을 별첨 송부합니다.

　　첨 부 : 감시기구 보고서 초안 1부. 끝.

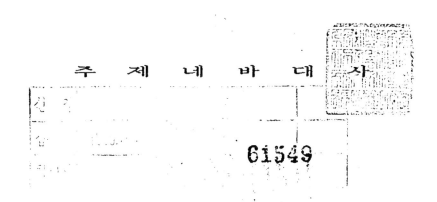

주 제 네 바 대 사

61549

0063

외 무 부

종 별 :

번 호 : GVW-2453

일 시 : 90 1109 1720

수 신 : 장 관(봉기, 경기원, 재무부, 농림수산부, 상공부)

발 신 : 주 제네바 대사

제 목 : UR/ 감시기구

1. 표제회의가 11.9(금) 10:00 MATHUR 의장 사회로 개최되어, 감시기구로서의 마지막 회의를 갖고 TNC앞 보고서를 채택한 바, 회의 경과는 아래임 (오참사관, 홍서기관 참석)

가. STANDSTILL 통고 검토

- 미국의 기존 통고 사항과 관련한 통고 (MTN.SB/SN/21) 외에 신규 통보는 없었음

나. STANDSTILL 관련 사항 검토(조기 경보적 사안포함)

- 칠레는 미국의 MARKETING ORDER 에 의한 포도, 키위, 자두, 사과등 과일과 채소류에 대한 품질 검사규정이 실행될 경우 내국민 대우, 최혜국 대우원칙에 위배되고, 칠레의 수출에 영향을 미칠수 있음을 지적함. 뉴질랜드가 이에 동조함.

- 멕시코는 미국의 참치 수입 규제 동향에 우려를 표시한바, 이씨가 이에 동조함.

- 미국은 이씨, 일본간 자동차 쿼타 협상에 일본외에서 생산되는 일본제 자동차에도 영향을 미칠 것인지 대해 관심을 표시함.

다. ROLLBACK 관련 사항 검토

- 알젠틴, 콜롬비아, 아국, 핀란드, 인도네시아, 홍콩, 미국의 신규 통고를 TAKE NOTE 함.

라. TNC 관련 사항 협의

1) 의장 언급사항

- 의장은 11.8 자 TNC 앞 감시기구 의장 보고서초안 (파편 송부)을 소개하고, 이는 TNC 가 SS/RB공약 이행 상황을 검토할 수 있도록 돕기위한 순수한 사실 보고라고 설명함. 또한 ROLLBACK공약 이행 방안과 관련한 결정안은 비공식협의에서도 합의되지 않았다고 설명함.

2) TNC 앞 보고서 검토

통상국 2차보 경기원 재무부 농수부 상공부

90.11.10 09:50 WG

외신 1과 통제관

0064

- 미국은 미국 통상법 337조와 관련, 동 법을 특정적으로 지칭하는 표현들은 완화해 줄것을요청함.

- SS/RB 공약의 종료시한 (ANNEX 36 항) 과 관련, 칠레, 유고, 우루과이등은 푼타선언의 해석상 동 공약은 UR 협상의 종료시까지 완수되어야 하므로 보고서를 이러한 방향으로 수정할 것을 주장하였으며, 이씨, 카나다는 이에 반대함. 의장은 36항의 첫 문장만 푼타선언을 그대로 인용수정키로 함

- ROLLBACK 공약이행 방안 (본문 16항) 과 관련, 이씨는 ' WHAT FURTHER ACTION IS NEEDED' 를 'WHETHER FURTHER ACTION IS NEEDED' 로 수정할 것을 제의하였으나, 뉴질랜드, 홍콩, 호주등이 반대함

- 상기 미국 337조 관련사항 및 ANNEX 36 항을 의장 책임하에 수정키로 하고, TNC 앞 보고서를 채택함.

마. 기타

- 호주, 뉴질랜드, 칠레등은 불법조치들을 철폐 또는 갓트에 일치시키기 위한 ROLLBACK 공약 이행방안이 UR 협상 종료시까지 합의되어야 한다는 입장에 변함이 없다하고, 이에대한 계속적인 협의를 희망한바, 미국, 카나다가 이에 반대의사를 표시함.

- 의장은 관심국가끼리 협의를 하고, 필요한 경우 사무국이 지원할 수 있을 것이라고 함

2. 관찰 및 평가

- UR/ 감시기구의 공식회의는 일단 TNC 앞보고서 채택으로 종료되었는바, 그동안 문제가 되어온 ROLLBACK 공약 이행방안은 계속 미결과제로 남게됨.

- 그간의 비공식 협의에서 뉴질랜드, 호주, 칠레, 홍콩등은 UR 협상 종료와 동시에 갓트 불법조치들을 시한을 정하여 철폐한다는 내용의 ROLLBACK 공약 관련 결정안을 감시 기구가 TNC 에 권고할것을 주장하였으나, 미국, 이씨, 카나다등의 반대에 의해합의되지 못함.

- 금일 회의에서 뉴질랜드, 호주등이 동 결정안을 계속 추진할 것임을 밝힘에 따라 앞으로 그린룸협의 과정 또는 브랏셀 각료회의에서 거론될 것으로 예상되는바, 미국, 이씨, 카나다등 주요 국가가모두 결정안에 반대하고 있어 합의가 어려울 것으로 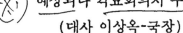예상되나 각료회의시 주요쟁점의 하나가 될것으로 예상됨.끝.

(대사 이상옥-국장)

주 제 네 바 대 표 부

제네(경) 20644-*1183*   1990. 11. 9

수신 : 장   관

참조 : 통상국장

제목 : UR/감시기구

       연 : GVW-2453

연호, UR/감시기구가 TNC에 제출할 보고서 초안을 별첨 송부합니다.

첨부 : 11. 8자 보고서 초안 1부.   끝.

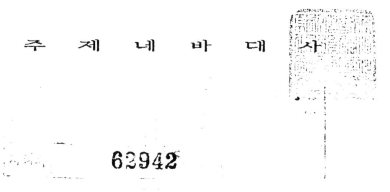

주 제 네 바 대 사

63942

0066

2792

8 November 1990

..... Attached is the **revised** draft Report by the Chairman of the Surveillance Body to the TNC meeting at Ministerial level in Brussels, for consideration at the meeting of the Surveillance Body on 9 November 1990.

The revised parts are shown in heavy type.

0067

<u>DRAFT</u>

<u>REPORT BY THE CHAIRMAN OF THE SURVEILLANCE BODY</u>
<u>TO THE TNC MEETING AT MINISTERIAL LEVEL IN BRUSSELS</u>

1.   The aim of this note is to provide the TNC with a brief summary of the implementation of the standstill and rollback commitments. It also contains a more detailed account of the implementation of the commitments (ANNEX).

(1)   <u>Standstill</u>

2.   Since the standstill commitment took effect in September 1986, a total of 25 notifications, by 11 participants against 8 participants, were submitted to the Surveillance Body. These notifications covered 23 cases, as two measures were, each, subject to two notifications.

3.   Twenty-four notifications were made during the period October 1986 to November 1988. One notification was submitted in 1990.

4.   According to the information provided to the Surveillance Body, in six of the 23 cases participants have taken action with a view to ensuring the withdrawal of measures contrary to the standstill commitment. Three of these actions were in response to recommendations of GATT Panel reports adopted by the CONTRACTING PARTIES; in the other three cases, the measures concerned were lifted autonomously. In a seventh case, a participant expressed its intention to act upon the notified measure in the light of the outcome of the Uruguay Round.

A:N-SB3

0068

5.   The remaining 16 cases notified under standstill were also discussed at meetings of the Surveillance Body. Some actions were reported concerning the measures in question. However, the views of the participants remained divided as to the consistency or inconsistency of the measures with the standstill commitment.

6.   Participants also engaged in "early warning" discussions on proposed legislation and other actions affecting trade. Altogether 34 cases were subject to discussions, some being discussed at several meetings. The discussion in the Surveillance Body served to ensure that the concerns brought up by participants were duly shared and transmitted, in an appropriate fashion, to the authorities concerned.

(2) Rollback

   (a)   Rollback consultations

7.   A total of twenty rollback requests covering a wide range of measures were made by eight participants, addressed to seven participants. In some cases, there was some overlap of the measures notified. Most requests concerned quantitative restrictions considered by the notifying participant to be inconsistent with the General Agreement.

8.   Nineteen requests were made during the period June 1987 to October 1988. One request was made in 1990.

9.   Fifteen requests were the subject of consultations. A total of twenty-one consultations were held. There have been no notifications concerning consultations on the remaining five requests.

10.   Three participants to which requests were addressed (the EC, Japan and the United States) notified undertakings already implemented or intended. In all cases, the undertakings covered only part of the measures contained in the rollback requests made by other participants.

A:N-SB3

0069

The other **four** participants addressed have not submitted any information on undertakings in response to the rollback requests.

11. In one case, the requesting participant indicated that the measure notified had been removed.

(b)   Implementation of Panel recommendations

12. Four participants (Canada, Japan, the Republic of Korea and the United States) notified the Surveillance Body of their actions on certain measures which had been ruled GATT-inconsistent by the CONTRACTING PARTIES, following Panel recommendations.

(c) Autonomous trade liberalization measures

13. Some participants (Australia, Argentina, Canada, Colombia, the EC, Finland, Indonesia and the Republic of Korea) informed the Surveillance Body of autonomous trade liberalization measures. Most of these measures had not been subject to rollback requests from other participants. The actions included measures such as the elimination of discriminatory import restrictions or changes in import licensing régimes. Most of these notifications were made without prejudice to the question of GATT-consistency of the measures concerned. In discussing these autonomous actions, the point was made that the rollback commitment was only related to GATT-inconsistent measures and therefore a distinction should be made between the autonomous liberalization of GATT-inconsistent and that of GATT-consistent measures. However, many participants recognized the difficulties in determining the GATT-inconsistency of the measures concerned.

(3)   Considerations for the full implementation of the rollback commitment

14. The Surveillance Body has given active attention to the development of procedures for promoting rollback action and to proposals made by individual participants to this end. The Surveillance Body has also made

an effort to assess the extent to which GATT-inconsistent measures continue
to be maintained by individual contracting parties. Upon request of the
Surveillance Body, the Secretariat prepared a note on measures which,
following Panel findings, had been found by the CONTRACTING PARTIES to be
inconsistent with the General Agreement. Forty-two cases were listed,
covering the period 1951-90. In general, full information on the follow-up
action taken to implement Panel findings is not available. It was found
that in many of the more recent cases implementation of the Panel
recommendations remained pending.

15.   Participants identified two difficulties in establishing the full
picture of outstanding GATT-inconsistent measures. First, in a strict
legal sense, the GATT-inconsistency of a particular measure maintained by a
participant can only be determined by a ruling of the CONTRACTING PARTIES.
Second, the Punta del Este Ministerial Declaration requires that each
participant implement the rollback commitment, taking into account
multilateral agreements, undertakings and understandings reached in the
Uruguay Round. However, before completion of the Uruguay Round, it has
been difficult for participants to determine what measures should be
considered to be GATT-inconsistent since agreements, undertakings and
understandings with respect to GATT provisions were still under
negotiation.

16.   Against this background, the Surveillance Body has considered ways by
which the full implementation of the rollback commitment could be
facilitated. However, without knowledge of final agreements or decisions
in individual negotiating areas of the Uruguay Round, including agreements
on procedures to phase out or bring into conformity measures henceforth
inconsistent with the provisions of the General Agreement or Instruments
negotiated within the framework of GATT or under its auspices, it was
difficult for the Surveillance Body to come to consensus in this matter, as
these agreements or decisions would affect the implementation of the
rollback commitment. The Surveillance Body therefore concluded that in the
light of multilateral agreements, undertakings and understandings,
including strengthened rules and disciplines, reached in the Uruguay Round,
Ministers meeting at the TNC in Brussels may wish to consider what further
action is needed to ensure that the rollback commitment be fully met.

A:N-SB3

0071

ANNEX

1.   The Punta del Este Ministerial Declaration contains the following commitments on standstill and rollback:

"Standstill

(i)   not to take any trade restrictive or distorting measure inconsistent with the provisions of the General Agreement or the instruments negotiated within the framework of GATT or under its auspices;

(ii) not to take any trade restrictive or distorting measure in the legitimate exercise of its GATT rights, that would go beyond that which is necessary to remedy specific situations, as provided for in the General Agreement and the Instruments referred to in (i) above;

(iii) not to take any trade measures in such a manner as to improve its negotiating positions."

"Rollback

(i)   that all trade restrictive or distorting measures inconsistent with the provisions of the General Agreement or Instruments negotiated within the framework of GATT or under its auspices, shall be phased out or brought into conformity within an agreed time-frame not later than by the date of the formal completion of the negotiations, taking into account multilateral agreements, undertakings and understandings, including

A:N-SB3

0072

strengthened rules and disciplines, reached in pursuance of the Objectives of the Negotiations;

(ii) there shall be progressive implementation of this commitment on an equitable basis in consultations among participants concerned, including all affected participants. This commitment shall take account of the concerns expressed by any participant about measures directly affecting its trade interests;

(iii) there shall be no GATT concessions requested for the elimination of these measures."

2. A consolidated text of the Ministerial commitments on standstill and rollback, and of the procedures agreed by the TNC and by the Surveillance Body, is contained in document MTN.TNC/W/10/Rev.1.

3. The Surveillance Body held thirteen meetings to examine and monitor the implementation of the standstill and rollback commitments. Detailed reports of its activities are contained in MTN.SB/1-15. The latest list of notifications and communications on standstill and rollback is contained in MTN.SB/W/3/Rev.9.

(1) Standstill

4. Since the standstill commitment took effect on 20 September 1986, a total of 25 notifications, by 11 participants against eight participants, were submitted to the Surveillance Body. Twenty-four notifications were made during the period October 1986 to November 1988. There was no notification in 1989. In 1990, one notification was submitted.

5. The 25 standstill notifications covered a total of 23 cases, as two measures were, each, subject to two notifications.

A:N-SB3

0073

6.　　Ten notifications, referring to nine different subjects, were addressed to the United States; six notifications, referring to five different subjects, to the European Communities; three notifications were addressed to Canada; two to Brazil; and one each to Greece, Indonesia, Sweden and Switzerland. The notifications covered quantitative restrictions, tariffs, import levies, import controls and prohibitions, export restrictions, internal taxes, production and export subsidies, and government procurement.

7.　　Sixteen notifications cited violations of paragraph (i) of the standstill commitment. Two notifications cited violations of both paragraphs (i) and (ii). Eleven notifications referred to paragraph (iii) of the commitment, three to paragraphs (i) and (iii), and one to paragraphs (ii) and (iii). One notification did not specify any particular paragraph.

8.　　In two cases, concerning a ban on imports of almonds into Greece (MTN.SB/SN/10) and Brazil's expansion of the list of products for which the issue of import licences was temporarily restricted (MTN.SB/SN/2), the notifying participant (United States) withdrew its notifications, following the lifting of the ban by Greece and the abolition of the practices in question by Brazil.

9.　　Seven notifications under standstill addressed a total of five measures which, at the same time, were subject to Article XXIII:2 Panel proceedings. These measures were the United States customs user fee (there were two notifications on the issue), the United States Superfund tax, the EC apple import quota system (there were two notifications), Canada's import controls on dairy products, and United States restrictions on imports from Brazil. As for the last case, the United States measures reflected in the notification were terminated effective 2 July 1990 and Brazil withdrew its complaint under Article XXIII:2 before the Panel proceeding was completed. In the other four cases, the measures were found by the Panels to be inconsistent with the General Agreement. The Council adopted the Panel reports. The EC measures concerning imports of apples

A:N-SB3
0074

had expired before the adoption of the Panel report. The United States
amended the Superfund tax in accordance with the Panel recommendations.
The United States also revised the customs user fee to bring it into
conformity with the GATT. With respect to Canada's restrictions on some
dairy products, Canada expressed its intention to implement the Panel
recommendation in the light of the outcome of the Uruguay Round.

10.   The decision taken by the TNC at its Mid-Term Review in April 1989
emphasized the need to take appropriate action to ensure withdrawal of all
measures contrary to the standstill commitment, taking into account that
there were a number of measures which had been ruled GATT-inconsistent by
Panel reports adopted by the CONTRACTING PARTIES. There have been two
notifications of actions to bring measures into conformity with the General
Agreement (the United States amendment of the Superfund tax, MTN.SB/RBN/2;
and the United States revision of the customs user fee, MTN.SB/RBN/8).

11.   According to the information provided to the Surveillance Body,
participants have taken action with a view to ensuring the withdrawal of
measures contrary to the standstill commitment with respect to six of the
23 cases covered by the 25 notifications; in a seventh case, it was
indicated that action would be taken in the light of the outcome of the
Uruguay Round. The remaining 16 cases were discussed at the meetings of
the Surveillance Body. Some actions were reported concerning these
measures. However, no consensus was achieved as to the inconsistency of
the measures concerned with the standstill commitment.

12.   In the Surveillance Body's "early warning" discussions on proposed
legislation and other actions affecting trade, 34 cases were subject to
discussions, some being discussed at several meetings. Sixteen cases were
related to actions by the United States, including the Omnibus Trade and
Competitiveness Act of 1988, and the "Super 301" and "Special 301"
provisions under the Act (MTN.SB/1-7, 9-13). Twelve cases concerned EC
actions, including the "Television without Frontiers" Directive, and
increases in certain agricultural aids (MTN.SB/2-5, 7, 10-13). Other

A:N-SB3

0075

countries concerned were Australia (MTN:SB/6), Finland (MTN.SB/9), Brazil (MTN.SB/11), and the Republic of Korea (MTN.SB/13).

13. The Surveillance Body has limited information on the current situation with respect to the proposed measures. Among actions known to the Surveillance Body are that the 1988 Textile, Apparel and Footwear Trade Bill of the United States was vetoed; that the President of the United States vetoed again a textile and footwear bill in October 1990; and that the EC's proposed measures on oils and fats were not pursued.

(2) Rollback

(a) Rollback consultations

14. In accordance with the agreed procedures and arrangements on rollback consultations, a total of twenty rollback requests covering a wide range of measures were notified. These requests were made by eight participants and addressed to seven participants. Nineteen requests were made during the period June 1987 to October 1988. There was no request in 1989. One request was made in February 1990.

15. One half of the requests came from developed participants (seven from Canada, two from the United States, and one from Japan), and the other half from developing participants (four from Argentina, three from Uruguay, and one each from Chile, Hong Kong, and Romania). Five requests each were addressed to the European Communities, Japan and the United States, two to Sweden, and one each to Brazil, Finland and Norway.

16. Most requests concerned quantitative restrictions considered by the notifying participant to be inconsistent with Articles XI and XIII of the General Agreement. Other measures covered by the requests included import licensing systems, sanitary and phytosanitary regulations, prohibition of imports, export subsidies, and voluntary export restraints.

A:N-SB3

- 10 -

17. Fifteen requests were the subject of consultations. Altogether, twenty-one consultations took place. There have been no notifications concerning consultations on the remaining five requests (RBC/5, 10, 15, 20, and 21).

18. The Surveillance Body had agreed on a target of 30 days for beginning the process of consultations following receipt of requests. In many cases, this target was not met. The frequency of consultations greatly diminished after 1988 (five consultations in 1987, thirteen in 1988, three in 1989 and no consultation in 1990).

19. The decision taken by the TNC at its Mid-Term Review in April 1989 emphasized the need for timely action on rollback, and prompt response to rollback requests, so as to ensure progressive implementation of the rollback commitment on an equitable basis. The Surveillance Body, at its meetings of March and July 1990, agreed that reports on the status and outcome of the rollback consultations should be submitted by participants within an agreed time limit.

20. In response, the Surveillance Body received written notifications from the EC, Japan **and the United States** on undertakings resulting from, or relating to, their rollback consultations or **on the status of their consultations**. The other **four** participants addressed have not submitted any information on undertakings in response to the rollback requests. As for participants requesting rollback action, Canada, Hong Kong, **Japan and the United States** reported on the status and outcome of their rollback consultations.

21. The European Community reported on its consultations with Japan (RBC/17/Add.2). As a result, the EC had eliminated a range of quantitative restrictions notified by Japan under RBC/17.

22. In its communication (RBC/22), Japan reported on the termination of import allocation systems for eight categories of agricultural products, which were subject to rollback consultations with Argentina, Hong Kong, the United States and Uruguay. Japan also reported that some measures subject

A:N-SB3

0077

to rollback consultations with the United States had been removed through
other autonomous market-opening measures contained in document L/6370.
With respect to consultations with the EC requested by Japan, Japan noted
the measures taken by the EC (see paragraph 21 above) and stated that
bilateral contacts were continuing with regard to the EC's remaining
quantitative restrictions maintained against Japan.

23.   In its communication (MTN.SB/RBN/8), the United States reported on
the status of rollback consultations which had been requested by other
participants (RBC/4, 7, 15, 16 and 20) or had been requested by the United
States (RBC/1 and 18). With respect to Section 337 legislation (RBC/15),
the United States indicated that it would take steps to make the necessary
modifications in domestic legislation. With respect to other United States
measures concerned, the United States reported that, in most cases, it
considered the consultations completed with participants concerned. As
regards requests to Japan and the EC, the United States took note of the
actions announced by these participants and looked forward to further
action. However, the United States did not seek additional consultations
on the remaining items.

24.   Canada informed orally the Surveillance Body of the outcome of
rollback consultations with other participants, which Canada had requested
(MTN.SB/13). In Canada's view, the original cause for Canada's
communication on Brazil's "law of similarity" (RBC/9) appeared to have been
removed by recent changes in Brazil's international trade régime. With
respect to Japan's import quotas on fish products notified by Canada in
1987 (RBC/12), Canada considered that the current conditions of access to
Japan permitted Canadian products to be exported to Japan. According to
the statement of Canada, other issues contained in Canada's rollback
requests had not been resolved.

25.   In its communications (RBC/8/Add.5 and 6), Hong Kong reported the
outcome of its consultations with Japan concerning Japan's import quota
system on 13 items and the Prior Confirmation System on imports of silk
fabrics. Hong Kong accepted Japan's justification in respect of the import

A:N-SB3

0078

quota system on six items, noted that Japan was implementing Panel recommendations on three items, and received further information and clarification from Japan for restrictions on the four remaining items. Hong Kong did not intend to follow up consultations on these remaining items. Consultations remained inconclusive on the question of the GATT-consistency of the Prior Confirmation System maintained by Japan on imports of silk fabrics.

(b)   Implementation of Panel recommendations

26.   Some participants considered the implementation of GATT Panel reports adopted by the CONTRACTING PARTIES an integral part of the rollback process. In their view, the rollback commitment provided an additional means of encouraging participants to fully and speedily implement Panel reports. Some other participants thought that the implementation of Panel reports adopted by the CONTRACTING PARTIES had no direct relevance to the rollback commitment, as it should follow the normal GATT dispute settlement procedures.

27.   Three notifications by Canada, Japan and the Republic of Korea (MTN.SB/W/6, MTN.SB/RBN/1 and MTN.SB/RBN/5) contained the liberalisation of some measures which had been ruled GATT-inconsistent by Panel reports. [Sentence deleted]. The United States made rollback notifications on legislation to amend the Superfund tax and the customs user fee in pursuance of Panel recommendations (MTN.SB/RBN/2 and MTN.SB/RBN/8). These United States measures were the subject of standstill notifications from other participants.

(c)   Autonomous trade liberalization measures

28.   Some participants informed the Surveillance Body of autonomous trade liberalization measures. These measures had not been subject to rollback requests from other participants. In most cases, the notifications were made without prejudice to the question of GATT-consistency of the measures concerned, and the notifying participants did not specify whether the

A:N-SB3

0079

measures constituted undertakings of the rollback commitment on GATT-inconsistent measures.

29.   A notification of the European Community (RBC/19/Rev.1) contained autonomous rollback measures related to the elimination of specific quantitative restrictions and the suspension of non-specific quantitative restrictions on imports from Hungary and Poland. Seven other participants (Argentina, Australia, Canada, Colombia, Finland, Indonesia and the Republic of Korea) submitted written notifications on autonomous trade liberalisation measures which they had recently implemented (MTN.SB/RBN/3 and Rev.1, MTN.SB/W/7, MTN.SB/W/6, MTN.SB/RBN/4, 6, 7 and 5, respectively).

30.   In the context of these autonomous actions, the point has been made that the rollback commitment was only related to GATT-inconsistent measures. Therefore, a distinction should be made between the autonomous liberalization of GATT-inconsistent and that of GATT-consistent measures. However, many participants recognized the difficulties in determining the GATT-inconsistency of the measures concerned.

(3)   Proposals for implementation of rollback action

31.   On the whole, with respect to rollback consultations, only a few undertakings have been reported to the Surveillance Body. Some participants reported the implementation of Panel recommendations as rollback undertakings; but a number of measures have remained in force which have been ruled to be GATT-inconsistent by the CONTRACTING PARTIES, following Panel reports. As noted above, while some participants have notified autonomous trade liberalization measures without prejudice to the question of GATT-inconsistency of the measures concerned, views have been divided whether these actions should be considered rollback measures as provided for in the Punta del Este Ministerial Declaration.

32.   The Surveillance Body has given active attention to the development of procedures for promoting rollback action and to proposals made by individual participants to this end. Following the Mid-Term Review,

A:N-SB3

0080

Australia (MTN.SB/W/7) and New Zealand (MTN.SB/W/8) put forward proposals on ways to ensure the fulfilment of the rollback commitment. Australia proposed that the TNC agree on the full implementation of all outstanding Panel reports adopted by the CONTRACTING PARTIES. New Zealand proposed that the Surveillance Body should agree on the following ways in which the rollback commitment might be evaluated:

(i) through the implementation of individual offers to roll back measures;

(ii) through the implementation of any multilateral agreements, undertakings and understandings reached in the course of the multilateral negotiations which established that certain types of measures, the present GATT status of which was not necessarily agreed, would henceforth be inconsistent with GATT provisions; and

(iii) through the phasing-out of measures ruled inconsistent with the GATT by Panel reports adopted by the CONTRACTING PARTIES.

33. The Surveillance Body discussed these proposals on a number of occasions. While there was considerable support for these proposals, there was no consensus on their adoption. Views remained divided about the ways in which autonomous trade liberalisation measures and the implementation of Panel reports should be evaluated.

34. The Surveillance Body has also made an effort to assess the extent to which GATT-inconsistent measures continue to be maintained by individual contracting parties. In this connection, the Secretariat was asked to prepare a list of measures which, following Panel findings, had been found by the CONTRACTING PARTIES to be inconsistent with the General Agreement. The Secretariat also added available information regarding actions taken in response to such findings (MTN.SB/W/11). In general instances, full information on the follow-up action taken to implement Panel findings is not available. In the majority of the 42 cases listed (covering the period

A:N-SB3

0081

1951-90), actions appear to have been taken in response to the recommendations. However, in many of the more recent cases, implementation of the Panel recommendations remained pending.

35.   Participants identified two difficulties in establishing the full picture of outstanding GATT-inconsistent measures. First, in a strict legal sense, the GATT-inconsistency of a particular measure can only be determined by the CONTRACTING PARTIES and, therefore, there are no other means available for participants to definitively determine the GATT-inconsistency of measures maintained by other participants. Second, the Punta del Este Ministerial Declaration requires that each participant implement the rollback commitment, taking into account multilateral agreements, undertakings and understandings reached in the Uruguay Round. However, it has been difficult for participants to determine, before the formal completion of the Uruguay Round, what measures should be considered to be GATT-inconsistent since agreements, undertakings and understandings with respect to GATT provisions were still under negotiation.

36.   The Punta del Este Ministerial Declaration requires that the implementation of the rollback commitment be made within an agreed time-frame. In this respect, the view has been advanced that agreement on a time-frame does not necessarily imply that all measures subject to the commitment should be phased out, or brought into conformity with the provisions of the General Agreement or Instruments negotiated within the framework of GATT or under its auspices, before the end of the Uruguay Round. This view is based on the consideration that the full details of multilateral agreements, undertakings and understandings might emerge only towards the end of the Uruguay Round.

A:N-SB3

0082

1903

<u>DRAFT</u>

1 August 1990

    Attached is a draft note by the Secretariat on actions taken regarding measures which were found by the CONTRACTING PARTIES to be inconsistent with the GATT. The Secretariat intends to submit the final version of the note to the October meeting of the Surveillance Body. Any comments on the contents of the draft note are requested to be passed on to the Secretariat (Mr. Akasaka, tel: 739 5149; or Mr. Adlung, tel: 739 5436) by Friday, 14 September 1990.

0083

DRAFT
1.8.90

Surveillance Body

ACTIONS TAKEN REGARDING MEASURES WHICH WERE
FOUND BY THE CONTRACTING PARTIES
TO BE INCONSISTENT WITH THE GATT

Note by the Secretariat

As the Chairman's Summary of the Current Situation on Implementation
of the Standstill and Rollback Commitments (MTN.SB/13, Annex II) noted in
paragraph 21, the Secretariat was requested to examine whether it could
supply, for the October meeting of the Surveillance Body, a list of
measures which have been found by the CONTRACTING PARTIES, following Panel
findings, to be inconsistent with the General Agreement, and any
information available regarding actions taken in response to such findings.

The present note has been prepared by the Secretariat in response to
this request. It is based on information contained in GATT documents,
particularly a Note by the Secretariat for the Negotiating Group on Dispute
Settlement (MTN.GNG/NG13/W/4/Rev.1) and another Note by the Secretariat for
the Negotiating Group on Non-Tariff Measures (MTN.GNG/NG2/W/70). It is
also supplemented in some cases by information supplied directly to the
Secretariat by the parties concerned.

0084

Complaint against/by, and date of adoption of Panel report	Measure	Product coverage	Reference	Information provided to GATT on actions taken
1. United States/ Netherlands 26 October 1951	Import restrictions	Dairy products	II/16, 1S/31,32,62, 2S/28,3S/46, 4S/31,99, 5S/28,142, 6S/14,157, 7S/23,128	In 1952, the CONTRACTING PARTIES, noting that import restrictions continued to be applied by the United States, adopted a decision to authorize the Netherlands to suspend the application to the United States of their obligations under the General Agreement. Concessions were suspended by the Netherlands on wheat flour, on the basis of the CONTRACTING PARTIES' annual resolutions, during the period 1952 to 1959.
2. Greece/ United Kingdom 3 November 1952	Increase of bound import duties (coefficients for currency conversion)	A number of products included in Schedule XXV	1S/23,51, SR.8/7	At the Eight Session, the Greek delegation informed the CONTRACTING PARTIES that the measures in question had been rescinded on 20 July 1953 (SR.8/7).
3. Belgium/Norway and Denmark 7 November 1952	The levy of a charge on foreign goods purchased by public bodies when these goods originated in a country whose system of family allowances did not meet specific requirements		1S/59, 7S/68, L/187	At the Ninth Session the CONTRACTING PARTIES were informed that the discriminatory application of the tax had been terminated by a new law which entered into force on 6 March 1954 (L/187).

Complaint against/by, and date of adoption of Panel report	Measure	Product coverage	Reference	Information provided to GATT on actions taken
4. France/Italy 17 January 1955	Special temporary compensation tax on imports		3S/26, 4S/20, 5S/27, 7S/68	It was reported at the Twelfth Session that the tax had been abolished on 10 August 1957 and replaced by other measures. The CONTRACTING PARTIES therefore considered this matter as having been settled (SR.12/5).
5. France/Australia 21 November 1958	Assistance to exports	Wheat and wheat flour	7S/22,46, L/1323, L/1548, SR.13/8	In October 1960, the Governments of France and Australia notified that an agreement had been reached between the two Governments on 20 April 1960 following discussions held, as a result of the Recommendation of 21 November 1958 of the CONTRACTING PARTIES, on the question of exports of French flour to South East Asian countries (L/1323).
6. France/ United States 14 November 1962	Import restrictions		11S/55,94, L/3744, C/M/80,81,83	In September 1972, the United States proposed to suspend tariff concessions on articles of French origin on grounds that the Government of France had not withdrawn restrictions inconsistent with Article XI, in conformity with the recommendation of the CONTRACTING PARTIES. The Council, at its meeting of December 1972, noted that bilateral consultations had been carried out between the United States and France, and deferred discussions on the item (C/M/83).

Complaint against/by, and date of adoption of Panel report	Measure	Product coverage	Reference	Information provided to GATT on actions taken
7. Canada/ United States 16 November 1962	The application of values for duty	Potatoes	11S/55,88, L/1968, L/2682	In January 1963, the Canadian Government advised the Secretariat that the Minister of National Revenue had ordered the cancellation of the value for duty on potatoes, effective on 2 January 1963 (L/1968). In July 1966, the Canadian Government informed the Secretariat of the decision to establish values for duty on imports of potatoes until 31 August 1966 (L/2682).
8.[1] a. Austria/ Uruguay	Import permit requirements and mixing regulations	Meat, edible oils, yarn of combed wool, wool textiles, and wheat	11S/102, 13S/38,50	The report of the Panel (L/2278), adopted on 3 March 1965, noted that all the items had been liberalized, or brought into conformity with the General Agreement, in response to the Panel recommendations.
b. Belgium/ Uruguay	Import permit requirements and quotas	Meat, linseed oil, edible oils, oilcake and meal, and combed wool	11S/105, 13S/40,50	The above-mentioned Panel report (L/2278) noted that some items had been liberalized, and that the Belgian authorities maintained their position that the measures relating to all the other items was purely administrative and not restrictive or incompatible with GATT. The representative of Belgium noted, at the Council meeting on 30 October 1964, that his Government considered that the items in question were de facto liberalized (L/2278/Add.1).

[1]The countries listed here were part of the fifteen countries against which complaints were brought to the CONTRACTING PARTIES by Uruguay. The Panel report with recommendations addressed to these seven countries was adopted on 16 November 1962.

Complaint against/by, and date of adoption of Panel report	Measure	Product coverage	Reference	Information provided to GATT on actions taken
c. France/ Uruguay	Import permit requirements and quotas	Meat, combed wool, yarn of combed wool, and woollen textiles	11S/120, 13S/41,51	The above-mentioned Panel report (L/2278) noted that the measures applying to combed wool and meat had been, or were to be, removed in 1963 to 1964. The report also noted that imports of yarn of combed wool and woollen fabrics had been liberalized for OECD countries, and the liberalization would be extended to other countries, including Uruguay. It was pointed out by the French delegation that there was no known case in which a licence application had been denied for imports of these products from Uruguay.
d. Germany, Fed. Rep./ Uruguay	Import permit requirements and quotas	Meat, leather, woven fabrics of wool or of fine animal hair, and yarn of combed wool	11S/125, 13S/41,52	The above-mentioned Panel report (L/2278) noted that the discriminatory quota applying to meat had been replaced by a global quota in 1962, and that the import permit quota on leather had been removed in 1964. Some of the remaining items were liberalized in 1965 (L/2278/Add.1), while the recommendations of the CONTRACTING PARTIES were outstanding on certain other measures.

Complaint against/by, and date of adoption of Panel report	Measure	Product coverage	Reference	Information provided to GATT on actions taken
e. Italy/ Uruguay	Quotas	Meat, linseed oil	11S/128, 13S/43,53	The above-mentioned Panel report (L/2278) noted that by November 1964, all the Italian restrictions covered by the recommendations of the CONTRACTING PARTIES would have been removed.
f. Norway/ Uruguay	Import permit requirements	Meat	11S/136, 13S/43,54	The above-mentioned Panel report (L/2278) noted that the Norwegian Government had initiated a study to determine whether the restrictions in question should be considered as consistent with the General Agreement; on the basis of this study, the Norwegian Government was to take a position as to possible changes in the import system for agricultural goods. The report noted that up to then, the Government had not acted on the report by the officials.
g. Sweden/ Uruguay	Import permit requirements	Meat	11S/139, 13S/44	The Panel report (L/2074), adopted on 3 March 1965, noted that the Panel considered that, by removing the import permit requirement in respect of frozen and chilled bovine meat of Uruguayan origin, the Government of Sweden had complied with the relevant recommendation of the CONTRACTING PARTIES.

0090

Complaint against/by, and date of adoption of Panel report	Measure	Product coverage	Reference	Information provided to GATT on actions taken
9. EC/ United States 14 March 1978	Requirements for the compulsory purchase of skimmed milk powder for use in animal feed	Skimmed milk powder	25S/49	
10. EC/ United States 18 October 1978	Minimum import price and ass:ciated additional security system	Certain processed fruits and vegetables	25S/68	
11. Norway/ United Kingdom on behalf of Hong Kong 18 June 1980	Import restrictions	Certain textile products	27S/119, C/M/141,144	At the meeting of the Council held in November 1980, the representative of Norway stated that his Government would take a decision on Norway's import régime for 1981 on 17 November 1980, taking into account the Council decision of 18 June 1980, as Norway understood it (C/M/144).
12. EC/Chile 10 November 1980	Import restrictions	Apples	27S/98, C/M/144	At the Council meeting of November 1980, on the occasion of the adoption of the Panel report, the EC representative expressed willingness to enter into bilateral consultations with Chile in pursuance of the Panel recommendation (C/M/144).

Complaint against/by, and date of adoption of Panel report	Measure	Product coverage	Reference	Information provided to GATT on actions taken
13. EC/Canada 10 March 1981	Tariff quota	Beef	28S/92, C/M/146	At the Council meeting of March 1981, on the occasion of the adoption of the Panel report, the EC representative stated that his authorities had taken note of the report and were examining its consequences (C/M/146).
14. Spain/Brazil 11 June 1981	Tariff treatment	Unroasted coffee	28S/102, C/M/151	Spain informed the Council at its meeting of October 1981 that, following high level discussions in Brazilia, Spain had informed Brazil of the Spanish decision to take the necessary steps prior to 31 December 1981 so that equal tariff treatment would be accorded by Spain to unwashed Arabica and other unroasted coffees. Accordingly, Spain had already started the necessary legislative procedures to modify the Royal Decree 1764/79 (C/M/151).
15. United States/ EEC 7-8 December 1981	Tax benefits for a US corporation qualified as a DISC (Domestic International Sales Corporation)		23S/98, 28S/114, L/5716,5723, L/5774, C/M/183,185	In December 1981, the Council adopted the Panel report on the understanding that economic processes (including transactions involving exported goods) located outside the territorial limits of the exporting country need not be subject to taxation by the exporting country and should not be regarded as export activities in terms of Article XVI:4 of the General Agreement.

362 우루과이라운드 제도 및 기타 분야 협상 2

0092

Complaint against/by, and date of adoption of Panel report	Measure	Product coverage	Reference	Information provided to GATT on actions taken
				In July 1984, the United States Congress enacted the Foreign Sales Corporation Act (FSCA), which replaced the DISC legislation (L/5723). At the Council meeting of November 1984, the United States stated that the FSCA had removed the offending trade practice (C/M/183). Subsequently, the European Communities requested consultations with the United States under Article XXII on the GATT compatibility of the FSCA legislation, including the provision for forgiveness of taxes deferred earlier under DISC (L/5774). At the Council meeting of January 1985, the United States expressed its preparedness to consult on the issue under Article XXII with the Community and any other contracting parties (C/M/185).
16. France/ United States 7-8 December 1981	Income tax practices		23S/114, 28S/114	In December 1981, the Council adopted the Panel report on the understanding that economic processes (including transactions involving exported goods) located outside the territorial limits of the exporting country need not be subject to taxation by the exporting country and should not be regarded as export activities in terms of Article XVI:4 of the General Agreement.

Complaint against/by, and date of adoption of Panel report	Measure	Product coverage	Reference	Information provided to GATT on actions taken
17. Belgium/ United States 7-8 December 1981	Income tax practices		23S/127, 28S/114	In December 1981, the Council adopted the Panel report on the understanding that economic processes (including transactions involving exported goods) located outside the territorial limits of the exporting country need not be subject to taxation by the exporting country and should not be regarded as export activities in terms of Article XVI:4 of the General Agreement.
18. Netherlands/ United States 7-8 December 1981	Income tax practices		23S/137, 28S/114	In December 1981, the Council adopted the Panel report on the understanding that economic processes (including transactions involving exported goods) located outside the territorial limits of the exporting country need not be subject to taxation by the exporting country and should not be regarded as export activities in terms of Article XVI:4 of the General Agreement.
19. United States/ Canada 22 February 1982	Import prohibition	Tuna and tuna products	29S/91, C/M/155,156, 159	Before the Panel report was adopted, the United States had lifted the prohibition on imports of tuna and tuna products from Canada, and in July 1981, the two parties had ratified a treaty on Pacific Coast Albacore Tuna Vessels and Port privileges. At the Council meetings of 1982, Canada expressed concern about the possibility of further embargoes by the United States on other Canadian

0093

Complaint against/by, and date of adoption of Panel report	Measure	Product coverage	Reference	Information provided to GATT on actions taken
				fishery products, and sought the Council's recommendations in this matter. In reply, the United States stated that Canada's apprehension would be speculative in nature and not appropriate for consideration by the Council (C/M/155, 156, 159).
20. EC/ United Kingdom on behalf of Hong Kong 12 July 1983	Quantitative import restrictions	Knitwear, clothing, umbrellas, radios, boats, microscopes, toys, and electronic watches	31S/129, C/M/210	In 1983 and 1984, quantitative restrictions on some product categories were removed. At the Council meeting of November 1986, the EC reported that imports of toys had been liberalized, that there had already been a substantial increase in the quota for imports of radios and that further moves were being examined (C/M/203). At the June 1987 Council meeting, Hong Kong reported that the restrictions on imports of toys and radios had been liberalized with effect from 1 January 1987 and that this had brought the dispute to an end (C/M/210).
21. Canada/ United States 7 February 1984	Local purchase requirements in the administration of the Foreign Investment Review Act		30S/140, C/M/194	At the Council meeting of November 1985, Canada informed the Council that the monitoring of existing undertakings had been altered, and this alteration had brought purchase undertakings in existence in February 1984 into conformity with Canada's GATT obligations. Canada had therefore fulfilled the Panel's recommendation (C/M/194).

Page 12

0095

Complaint against/by, and date of adoption of Panel report	Measure	Product coverage	Reference	Information provided to GATT on actions taken
22. United States/ Nicaragua 13 March 1984	Import quotas	Sugar from Nicaragua	31S/67, C/M/178,183	At the Council meetings of 1984, the United States stated that the measure in question had been taken for broader reasons than trade considerations, and that to lift the measure would first require a resolution of the broader dispute. The United States recognized that Nicaragua had certain rights under Article XXIII which it had reserved and could continue to exercise (C/M/178,183).
23. United States/EC 15/16 May 1984	Import prohibition under the Manufacturing Clause	Copyrighted work consisting preponderantly of non-dramatic literary material in the English language, the author of which is a United States domiciliary	31S/74, C/M/201	At the Council meeting of July 1986, the Unites States informed the Council that the Manufacturing Clause had expired as of 1 July 1986 and had not been extended by Congress (C/M/201).
24. Japan/ United States 15-16 May 1984	Quantitative import restrictions	Leather	31S/94, L/5978	In a communication dated 11 March 1986, Japan notified that, as from 1 April 1986, the Government of Japan had eliminated quantitative restrictions on leather imports in accordance with the Panel report while introducing a tariff quota system for these products (L/5978).

366 우루과이라운드 제도 및 기타 분야 협상 2

Complaint against/by, and date of adoption of Panel report	Measure	Product coverage	Reference	Information provided to GATT on actions taken
25. EC/Canada 20 November 1984	Tariff quotas	Newsprint from Canada	31S/114, C/M/183	At the Council meeting of November 1984, on the occasion of the adoption of the Panel report, the European Communities stated that, on 1 November 1984, it had submitted a notification that it was ready to begin negotiations on this matter under Article XXVIII, as had been recommended by the Panel (C/M/183).
26. New Zealand/ Finland 18 July 1985	The imposition of anti-dumping duties	Electrical transformers from Finland	32S/55, C/136	New Zealand had decided to implement the report before its adoption and has in the meantime carried out the Panel's recommendations (C/136).
27. United States/ Canada, EC and Mexico 17 June 1987	Discriminatory taxation	Petroleum and petroleum products	MTN.SB/RBN/2	The United States notified the Surveillance Body that on 22 December 1989, President Bush signed legislation to amend the superfund tax in compliance with the Panel's recommendation to apply uniform taxes on imported and domestic petroleum products.
28. Japan/EC 10 November 1987	Discriminatory taxation	Whiskies, brandies, other distilled spirits, liqueurs, still wines, sparkling wines	34S/83, L/6465	Japan informed the Council at its meeting of 8-9 February 1989 that legislation had been passed by the Diet to: (i) abolish the ad valorem tax on whiskies/brandies, wines and certain alcoholic beverages, the "grading" system for these beverages as well as taxation according to the extract content of "liqueurs", etc.

Complaint against/by, and date of adoption of Panel report	Measure	Product coverage	Reference	Information provided to GATT on actions taken
				(ii) reduce considerably existing differences between taxes on whiskies/brandies and "shochu" by reducing the rate of the specific tax, based on quantity, on whiskies/brandies, and by raising that on "shochu" (C/M/228). Detailed information was provided in L/6465.
29. United States/ Canada and EC 2 February 1988	Customs user fee (customs service processing fee)		35S/245, SR.45/2	The United States reported to the 45th Session of the CONTRACTING PARTIES, meeting on 4 December 1989, that the fees were due to expire in October 1990 and that the United States administration was committed to bringing them into conformity with GATT, should they be renewed (SR.45/2). Conferees of the United States Senate and House of Representatives are currently finalizing legislation to bring the fees into conformity with GATT.
30. Japan/ United States 2 February 1988	Import allocation system	Processed cheese, other sugars and sugar syrups, fruit purée and paste, fruit otherwise prepared or preserved, non-citrus fruit juices, tomato juice, ketchup and sauce, food preparations mainly	35S/163, L/6370, L/6389, L/6489, C/M/243	In communications circulated in July and September 1988 (L/6370 and L/6389), Japan notified that the import allocation system for the products in question was to be terminated between 1 October 1988 and 1 April 1990, with transitional measures being taken in the intervening period. At the meeting of the Council held on 14 June 1990, Australia reserved

0098

Complaint against/by, and date of adoption of Panel report	Measure	Product coverage	Reference	Information provided to GATT on actions taken
		consisting of sugar, prepared and preserved meat and meat products of bovine animals or pigs		its rights with respect to implementation of the recommendation of the CONTRACTING PARTIES concerning dairy products (C/M/243).
31. Canada/ United States 22 March 1988	Export restrictions	Unprocessed herring and salmon	35S/98, C/M/232	At the Council meeting in May 1989, Canada informed the Council that it had taken steps to remove the export prohibitions on Pacific salmon and herring, in compliance with the Panel's recommendations, and had introduced a GATT-consistent landing requirement (C/M/232).
32. Canada/EC 22 March 1988	Operation of provincial monopolies for supply and distribution ("listing/delisting" requirement, availability of points of sale, mark-ups greater than additional costs necessarily associated with marketing of imported products)	Alcoholic beverages	35S/37, C/W/590, DS/17/1	The Canadian Minister for International Trade announced on 20 December 1988, that a settlement had been reached with the European Communities on implementation of the GATT Panel Report that found Provincial liquor board practices which discriminated against imported alcoholic beverages to be inconsistent with the GATT. The Canada/EC agreement, formally signed on 28 February 1989, provides: (a) national treatment for EC products including pricing, listing and distribution of spirits;

9300

Complaint against/by, Measure and date of adoption of Panel report	Product coverage	Reference	Information provided to GATT on actions taken
			(b) national treatment on the listing and distribution of EC wines; (c) phasing-out of discriminatory mark-ups on wine over seven years, with some exceptions for 100 per cent Canadian wines and some blended wines; (d) national treatment in the listing of EC beer, as well as a cap on the maximum differential mark-up charged on beer. Canada has confirmed that products of other countries would be treated on an m.f.n. basis. A letter exchanged at the time of the agreement affirmed that Canada would bring measures on pricing of beer into conformity with its GATT obligations following a successful conclusion of negotiations on the reduction or elimination of inter-Provincial barriers to trade in alcoholic beverages (C/W/590, page 8). In a communication dated 29 June 1990, the United States stated that most of the discriminatory practices of provincial liquor boards in Canada affecting beer imports, which had been found to be inconsistent with

0100

Complaint against/by, and date of adoption of Panel report	Measure	Product coverage	Reference	Information provided to GATT on actions taken
				the GATT, remained in place. These practices, including discriminatory price mark-ups and restrictions on the points of sale and on listing, nullified and impaired benefits accruing to the United States under the GATT. According to the United States, Canada had not taken such reasonable measures as may be available to it to ensure observance of the provisions of the GATT by the provincial liquor boards, and the United States was therefore requesting consultations under Article XXIII:1 on this matter (DS17/1).
33. Japan/EC 4 May 1988	Monitoring of costs and prices of exports to markets other than the United States	Semi-conductors	35S/116, C/M/234	At the Council meeting of June 1989, Japan stated that it had implemented necessary measures to comply with the Panel's recommendations effective on 1 June 1989 (C/M/234).
34. Norway/ United States 21-22 June 1989	Import restrictions	Apples and pears	L/6474, L/6651, C/M/240, DS16/1	In a communication dated 2 March 1990, Norway stated that a new import régime would be introduced to bring the measures applying to imports of apples and pears into conformity with GATT obligations (L/6651). The United States subsequently advised the Council that it questioned whether the replacement measures were consistent with the GATT. Consultations under Article XXIII:1 are continuing (C/M/240, DS16/1).

0101

Complaint against/by, and date of adoption of Panel report	Measure	Product coverage	Reference	Information provided to GATT on actions taken
35. EC/Chile 21-22 June 1989	Import restrictions	Dessert apples	L/6491, C/M/232,234	The measure examined by the Panel had expired on 31 August 1988 before the adoption of the Panel.
36. EC/ United States 21-22 June 1989	Import restrictions	Apples	L/6513, C/M/234	The measure examined by the Panel had expired on 31 August 1988 before the adoption of the Panel.
37. United States/ Australia 21-22 June 1989	Imports restrictions	Sugar	L/6514, C/M/234,238, 241	Consultations are continuing on implementation of the recommendations of the Panel (C/M/234,238,241).
38. United States/ EC 7 November 1989	Section 337 of the Tariff Act (enforcement of patent laws in respect of imported products)		L/6439, C/M/237	At the meeting of the Council held on 7 November 1989, the United States stated that the US Administration's ability to obtain legislation amending Section 337 would be maximized should the latter be in the context of legislation implementing the results of the Uruguay Round. The United States was committed to seeking to bring itself into compliance with GATT rules. However, it hoped and expected that broad recognition by contracting parties of the benefits of adequate and effective enforcement of intellectual property rights would lead to a multilateral agreement providing for stronger disciplines in this area (C/M/237).

Complaint against/by, and date of adoption of Panel report	Measure	Product coverage	Reference	Information provided to GATT on actions taken
39. Korea, Rep. of/ United States, Australia and New Zealand 7 November 1989	Import restrictions	Beef	L/6503, L/6504, L/6505, C/M/237, L/6697	In a communication dated 4 July 1990, the Republic of Korea circulated the texts of agreements it had concluded with Australia, the United States and New Zealand for the implementation of the recommendations contained in the Panel reports (L/6697).
40. Canada/ United States 4 December 1989	Import restrictions	Ice-cream and yoghurt	L/6568, C/M/243, L/6694	At the meeting of the Council held on 14 June 1990, Canada reiterated that implementation would be considered in the context of the outcome of the Uruguay Round. The United States reserved its rights on this question (C/M/243). In a communication dated 27 June 1990, the United States stated that it continued to seek agreement with Canada on a time-frame during which Canada would comply with its obligations under the General Agreement, but that, if no mutually satisfactory solution could be reached, the United States would submit to the Council a detailed request for authorization to suspend concessions (L/6694).
41. EC/ United States 25 January 1990	Subsidies	Oilseeds and animal-feed proteins	L/6627, L/6636, C/M/238	In a communication dated 25 January 1990, the Community stated that it would engage in the process for complying with the recommendations and would adopt the Community regulations in question in the context of the implementation of the results of the Uruguay Round (L/6636).

Complaint against/by, and date of adoption of Panel report	Measure	Product coverage	Reference	Information provided to GATT on actions taken
42. EC/Japan 16 May 1990	Anti-circumvention duties	Parts and components	L/6657, C/M/241	At the meeting of the Council held on 16 May 1990, the Community stated that it would examine the changes which might be brought to its present regulations only when negotiations in the Uruguay Round on the ways and means, which would enable contracting parties to combat the circumvention of anti-dumping duties, had led to results which were satisfactory from a contractual point of view (C/M/241).

2639

26 October 1990

.....   Attached is the draft Report by the Chairman of the Surveillance Body
to the TNC meeting at Ministerial level in Brussels, for consideration at
the meeting of the Surveillance Body on 9 November 1990.

0104

DRAFT

REPORT BY THE CHAIRMAN OF THE SURVEILLANCE BODY
TO THE TNC MEETING AT MINISTERIAL LEVEL IN BRUSSELS

1.   The aim of this note is to provide the TNC with a brief summary of
the implementation of the standstill and rollback commitments. It also
contains a more detailed account of the implementation of the commitments
(ANNEX I).

(1)   Standstill

2.   Since the standstill commitment took effect in September 1986, a
total of 25 notifications, by 11 participants against 8 participants, were
submitted to the Surveillance Body. These notifications covered 23 cases,
as two measures were, each, subject to two notifications.

3.   Twenty-four notifications were made during the period October 1986 to
November 1988. One notification was submitted in 1990.

4.   According to the information provided to the Surveillance Body, in
four of the 23 cases participants have taken action with a view to ensuring
the withdrawal of measures contrary to the standstill commitment. Three of
these actions were in response to recommendations of GATT Panel reports
adopted by the CONTRACTING PARTIES; in the fourth case, the measure
concerned was lifted autonomously. In a fifth case, a participant
expressed its intention to act upon the notified measure in the light of
the outcome of the Uruguay Round.

0105

A:N-SB3

- 2 -

5.   The remaining 18 cases notified under standstill were also discussed at meetings of the Surveillance Body. Some actions were reported concerning the measures in question. However, the views of the participants remained divided as to the consistency or inconsistency of the measures with the standstill commitment.

6.   Participants also engaged in "early warning" discussions on proposed legislation and other actions affecting trade. Altogether 34 cases were subject to discussions, some being discussed at several meetings. The discussion in the Surveillance Body served to ensure that the concerns brought up by participants were duly shared and transmitted, in an appropriate fashion, to the authorities concerned.

(2)   Rollback

  (a)   Rollback consultations

7.   A total of twenty rollback requests covering a wide range of measures were made by eight participants, addressed to seven participants. In some cases, there was some overlap of the measures notified. Most requests concerned quantitative restrictions considered by the notifying participant to be inconsistent with the General Agreement.

8.   Nineteen requests were made during the period June 1987 to October 1988. One request was made in 1990.

9.   Fifteen requests were the subject of consultations. A total of twenty-one consultations were held. There have been no notifications concerning consultations on the remaining five requests.

10.   Two participants to which requests were addressed (EC and Japan) notified undertakings. In both cases, the undertakings covered only part of the measures contained in the rollback requests made by other participants. The other five participants addressed have not submitted any information on undertakings in response to the rollback requests.

A:N-SB3

0106

11. In one case, the requesting participant indicated that the measure notified had been removed.

(b)   Implementation of Panel recommendations

12. Four participants (Canada, Japan the Republic of Korea and the United States) notified the Surveillance Body of their actions on certain measures which had been ruled GATT-inconsistent by the CONTRACTING PARTIES, following Panel recommendations.

(c)   Autonomous trade liberalization measures

13. Some participants (Australia, Argentina, Canada, Colombia, the EC, Finland, Indonesia and the Republic of Korea) informed the Surveillance Body of autonomous trade liberalization measures. Most of these measures had not been subject to rollback requests from other participants. The actions included measures such as the elimination of discriminatory import restrictions or changes in import licensing régimes. Most of these notifications were made without prejudice to the question of GATT-consistency of the measures concerned. In discussing these autonomous actions, the point was made that the rollback commitment was only related to GATT-inconsistent measures and therefore a distinction should be made between the autonomous liberalization of GATT-inconsistent and that of GATT-consistent measures. However, many participants recognized the difficulties in determining the GATT-inconsistency of the measures concerned.

(3)   Considerations for the full implementation of the rollback commitment

14. The Surveillance Body has given active attention to the development of procedures for promoting rollback action and to proposals made by individual participants to this end. The Surveillance Body has also made an effort to assess the extent to which GATT-inconsistent measures continue to be maintained by individual contracting parties. Upon request of the Surveillance Body, the Secretariat prepared a note on measures which,

A:N-SB3

0107

following Panel findings, had been found by the CONTRACTING PARTIES to be inconsistent with the General Agreement. Forty-two cases were listed, covering the period 1951-90. In general instances, full information on the follow-up action taken to implement Panel findings is not available. It was found that, in many of the more recent cases, implementation of the Panel recommendations remained pending.

15. Participants identified two difficulties in establishing the full picture of outstanding GATT-inconsistent measures. First, in a strict legal sense, the GATT-inconsistency of a particular measure maintained by a participant can only be determined by a ruling of the CONTRACTING PARTIES. Second, the Punta del Este Ministerial Declaration requires that each participant implement the rollback commitment, taking into account multilateral agreements, undertakings and understandings reached in the Uruguay Round. However, before completion of the Uruguay Round, it has been difficult for participants to determine what measures should be considered to be GATT-inconsistent since agreements, undertakings and understandings with respect to GATT provisions were still under negotiation.

16. Against this background, the Surveillance Body has considered ways by which the full implementation of the rollback commitment could be facilitated. However, without knowledge of final agreements or decisions in individual negotiating areas of the Uruguay Round, including agreements on procedures to phase out or bring into conformity measures henceforth inconsistent with the provisions of the General Agreement or Instruments negotiated within the framework of GATT or under its auspices, it was difficult for the Surveillance Body to come to consensus in this matter, as these agreements or decisions would affect the implementation of the rollback commitment. The Surveillance Body therefore concluded that in the light of ministerial agreements, undertakings and understandings, including strengthened rules and disciplines, reached in the Uruguay Round, Ministers meeting at the TNC in Brussels may wish to consider what further action is needed to ensure that the rollback commitment be fully met.

A:N-SB3

<u>ANNEX I</u>

1.   The Punta del Este Ministerial Declaration contains the following commitments on standstill and rollback:

"<u>Standstill</u>

(i)   not to take any trade restrictive or distorting measure inconsistent with the provisions of the General Agreement or the instruments negotiated within the framework of GATT or under its auspices;

(ii)   not to take any trade restrictive or distorting measure in the legitimate exercise of its GATT rights, that would go beyond that which is necessary to remedy specific situations, as provided for in the General Agreement and the Instruments referred to in (i) above;

(iii) not to take any trade measures in such a manner as to improve its negotiating positions."

"<u>Rollback</u>

(i)   that all trade restrictive or distorting measures inconsistent with the provisions of the General Agreement or Instruments negotiated within the framework of GATT or under its auspices, shall be phased out or brought into conformity within an agreed time-frame not later than by the date of the formal completion of the negotiations, taking into account multilateral agreements, undertakings and understandings, including

A:N-SB3

0103

strengthened rules and disciplines, reached in pursuance of the
Objectives of the Negotiations;

(ii) there shall be progressive implementation of this commitment on
an equitable basis in consultations among participants
concerned, including all affected participants. This
commitment shall take account of the concerns expressed by any
participant about measures directly affecting its trade
interests;

(iii) there shall be no GATT concessions requested for the
elimination of these measures."

2.   A consolidated text of the Ministerial commitments on standstill and
rollback, and of the procedures agreed by the TNC and by the Surveillance
Body, is contained in document MTN.TNC/W/10/Rev.1.

3.   The Surveillance Body held thirteen meetings to examine and monitor
the implementation of the standstill and rollback commitments. Detailed
reports of its activities are contained in MTN.SB/1-15. The latest list of
notifications and communications on standstill and rollback is contained in
MTN.SB/W/3/Rev.9.

(1)   Standstill

4.   Since the standstill commitment took effect on 20 September 1986, a
total of 25 notifications, by 11 participants against eight participants,
were submitted to the Surveillance Body. Twenty-four notifications were
made during the period October 1986 to November 1988. There was no
notification in 1989. In 1990, one notification was submitted.

5.   The 25 standstill notifications covered a total of 23 cases, as two
measures were, each, subject to two notifications.

A:N-SB3

0110

6.   Ten notifications, referring to nine different subjects, were
addressed to the United States; six notifications, referring to five
different subjects, to the European Communities; three notifications were
addressed to Canada; two to Brazil; and one each to Greece, Indonesia,
Sweden and Switzerland. The notifications covered quantitative
restrictions, tariffs, import levies, import controls and prohibitions,
export restrictions, internal taxes, production and export subsidies, and
government procurement.

7.   Sixteen notifications cited violations of paragraph (i) of the
standstill commitment. Two notifications cited violations of both
paragraphs (i) and (ii). Eleven notifications referred to paragraph (iii)
of the commitment, three to paragraphs (i) and (iii), and one to
paragraphs (ii) and (iii). One notification did not specify any particular
paragraph.

8.   In one case, concerning a ban on imports of almonds into Greece, the
notifying participant (United States) withdrew its notification, following
the lifting of the ban by Greece.

9.   Seven notifications under standstill addressed a total of five
measures which, at the same time, were subject to Article XXIII:2 Panel
proceedings. These measures were the United States customs user fee (there
were two notifications on the issue), the United States Superfund tax, the
EC apple import quota system (there were two notifications), Canada's
import controls on dairy products, and United States restrictions on
imports from Brazil. As for the last case, Brazil withdrew its complaint
under Article XXIII:2 before the Panel proceeding was completed. In the
other four cases, the measures were found by the Panels to be inconsistent
with the General Agreement. The Council adopted the Panel reports. The EC
measures concerning imports of apples had expired before the adoption of
the Panel report. The United States amended the Superfund tax in
accordance with the Panel recommendations. The United States also revised
the customs user fee to bring it into conformity with the GATT. With
respect to Canada's restrictions on some dairy products, Canada expressed

A:N-SB3

0111

its intention to implement the Panel recommendation in the light of the outcome of the Uruguay Round.

10.   The decision taken by the TNC at its Mid-Term Review in April 1989 emphasized the need to take appropriate action to ensure withdrawal of all measures contrary to the standstill commitment, taking into account that there were a number of measures which had been ruled GATT-inconsistent by Panel reports adopted by the CONTRACTING PARTIES.   There has been one notification of such withdrawal (the United States amendment of the Superfund tax, MTN.SB/RBN/2).

11.   According to the information provided to the Surveillance Body, participants have taken action with a view to ensuring the withdrawal of measures contrary to the standstill commitment with respect to four of the 23 cases covered by the 25 notifications;   in a fifth case, it was indicated that action would be taken in the light of the outcome of the Uruguay Round.   The remaining 18 cases were discussed at the meetings of the Surveillance Body.   Some actions were reported concerning these measures.   However, no consensus was achieved as to the inconsistency of the measures concerned with the standstill commitment.

12.   In the Surveillance Body's "early warning" discussions on proposed legislation and other actions affecting trade, 34 cases were subject to discussions, some being discussed at several meetings.   Sixteen cases were related to actions by the United States, including the Omnibus Trade and Competitiveness Act of 1988, and the "Super 301" and "Special 301" provisions under the Act (MTN.SB/1-7, 9-13).   Twelve cases concerned EC actions, including the "Television without Frontiers" Directive, and increases in certain agricultural aids (MTN.SB/2-5, 7, 10-13).   Other countries concerned were Australia (MTN:SB/6), Finland (MTN.SB/9), Brazil (MTN.SB/11), and the Republic of Korea (MTN.SB/13).

13.   The Surveillance Body has limited information on the current situation with respect to the proposed measures.   Among actions known to the Surveillance Body are that the 1988 Textile, Apparel and Footwear Trade

A:N-SB3

0112

Bill of the United States was vetoed; that the President of the United States vetoed again a textile and footwear bill in October 1990; and that the EC's proposed measures on oils and fats were not pursued.

(2) Rollback

(a) Rollback consultations

14. In accordance with the agreed procedures and arrangements on rollback consultations, a total of twenty rollback requests covering a wide range of measures were notified. These requests were made by eight participants and addressed to seven participants. Nineteen requests were made during the period June 1987 to October 1988. There was no request in 1989. One request was made in February 1990.

15. One half of the requests came from developed participants (seven from Canada, two from the United States, and one from Japan), and the other half from developing participants (four from Argentina, three from Uruguay, and one each from Chile, Hong Kong, and Romania). Five requests each were addressed to the European Communities, Japan and the United States, two to Sweden, and one each to Brazil, Finland and Norway.

16. Most requests concerned quantitative restrictions considered by the notifying participant to be inconsistent with Articles XI and XIII of the General Agreement. Other measures covered by the requests included import licensing systems, sanitary and phytosanitary regulations, prohibition of imports, export subsidies, and voluntary export restraints.

17. Fifteen requests were the subject of consultations. Altogether, twenty-one consultations took place. There have been no notifications concerning consultations on the remaining five requests (RBC/5, 10, 15, 20, and 21).

18. The Surveillance Body had agreed on a target of 30 days for beginning the process of consultations following receipt of requests. In many cases,

A:N-SB3

0113

this target was not met. The frequency of consultations greatly diminished after 1988 (five consultations in 1987, thirteen in 1988, three in 1989 and no consultation in 1990).

19.   The decision taken by the TNC at its Mid-Term Review in April 1989 emphasized the need for timely action on rollback, and prompt response to rollback requests, so as to ensure progressive implementation of the rollback commitment on an equitable basis. The Surveillance Body, at its meetings of March and July 1990, agreed that reports on the status and outcome of the rollback consultations should be submitted by participants within an agreed time limit.

20.   In response, the Surveillance Body received written notifications from the EC and Japan on undertakings resulting from, or relating to, their rollback consultations. The other five participants addressed have not submitted any information on undertakings in response to the rollback requests. As for participants requesting rollback action, Canada and Hong Kong reported on the status and outcome of their rollback consultations at meetings of the Surveillance Body.

21.   The European Community reported on its consultations with Japan (RBC/17/Add.2). As a result, the EC had eliminated a range of quantitative restrictions notified by Japan under RBC/17.

22.   In its communication (RBC/22), Japan reported on the termination of import allocation systems for eight categories of agricultural products, which were subject to rollback consultations with Argentina, Hong Kong, the United States and Uruguay. Japan also reported that some measures subject to rollback consultations with the United States had been removed through other autonomous market-opening measures contained in document L/6370.

23.   Canada informed orally the Surveillance Body of the outcome of rollback consultations with other participants, which Canada had requested (MTN.SB/13). In Canada's view, the original cause for Canada's communication on Brazil's "law of similarity" (RBC/9) appeared to have been

A:N-SB3

0114

removed by recent changes in Brazil's international trade régime. With respect to Japan's import quotas on fish products notified by Canada in 1987 (RBC/12), Canada considered that the current conditions of access to Japan permitted Canadian products to be exported to Japan. According to the statement of Canada, other issues contained in Canada's rollback requests had not been resolved.

24. In its communications (RBC/8/Add.5 and 6), Hong Kong reported the outcome of its consultations with Japan concerning Japan's import quota system on 13 items and the Prior Confirmation System on imports of silk fabrics. Hong Kong accepted Japan's justification in respect of the import quota system on six items, noted that Japan was implementing Panel recommendations on three items, and received further information and clarification from Japan for restrictions on the four remaining items. Hong Kong did not intend to follow up consultations on these remaining items. Consultations remained inconclusive on the question of the GATT-consistency of the Prior Confirmation System maintained by Japan on imports of silk fabrics.

(b)   Implementation of Panel recommendations

25. Some participants considered the implementation of GATT Panel reports adopted by the CONTRACTING PARTIES an integral part of the rollback process. In their view, the rollback commitment provided an additional means of encouraging participants to fully and speedily implement Panel reports. Some other participants thought that the implementation of Panel reports adopted by the CONTRACTING PARTIES had no direct relevance to the rollback commitment, as it should follow the normal GATT dispute settlement procedures.

26. Three notifications by Japan, Canada, Japan and the Republic of Korea (MTN.SB/W/6, MTN.SB/RBN/1 and MTN.SB/RBN/5) contained the liberalisation of some measures which had been ruled GATT-inconsistent by Panel reports. The Canadian notification did not refer to these measures as rollback undertakings. The United States made a rollback notification on

A:N-SB3

legislation to amend the Superfund tax in pursuance of Panel recommendations (MTN.SB/RBN/2). The tax was the subject of standstill notifications from other participants.

(c) Autonomous trade liberalization measures

27. Some participants informed the Surveillance Body of autonomous trade liberalization measures. These measures had not been subject to rollback requests from other participants. In most cases, the notifications were made without prejudice to the question of GATT-consistency of the measures concerned, and the notifying participants did not specify whether the measures constituted undertakings of the rollback commitment on GATT-inconsistent measures.

28. A notification of the European Community (RBC/19/Rev.1) contained autonomous rollback measures related to the elimination of specific quantitative restrictions and the suspension of non-specific quantitative restrictions on imports from Hungary and Poland. Seven other participants (Argentina, Australia, Canada, Colombia, Finland, Indonesia and the Republic of Korea) submitted written notifications on autonomous trade liberalisation measures which they had recently implemented (MTN.SB/RBN/3 and Rev.1, MTN.SB/W/7, MTN.SB/W/6, MTN.SB/RBN/4, 6, 7 and 5, respectively).

29. In the context of these autonomous actions, the point has been made that the rollback commitment was only related to GATT-inconsistent measures. Therefore, a distinction should be made between the autonomous liberalization of GATT-inconsistent and that of GATT-consistent measures. However, many participants recognized the difficulties in determining the GATT-inconsistency of the measures concerned.

(3) Proposals for implementation of rollback action

30. On the whole, with respect to rollback consultations, only a few undertakings have been reported to the Surveillance Body. Some participants reported the implementation of Panel recommendations as

A:N-SB3

rollback undertakings; but a number of measures have remained in force which have been ruled to be GATT-inconsistent by the CONTRACTING PARTIES, following Panel reports. As noted above, while some participants have notified autonomous trade liberalization measures without prejudice to the question of GATT-inconsistency of the measures concerned, views have been divided whether these actions should be considered rollback measures as provided for in the Punta del Este Ministerial Declaration.

31.   The Surveillance Body has given active attention to the development of procedures for promoting rollback action and to proposals made by individual participants to this end. Following the Mid-Term Review, Australia (MTN.SB/W/7) and New Zealand (MTN.SB/W/8) put forward proposals on ways to ensure the fulfilment of the rollback commitment. Australia proposed that the TNC agree on the full implementation of all outstanding Panel reports adopted by the CONTRACTING PARTIES. New Zealand proposed that the Surveillance Body should agree on the following ways in which the rollback commitment might be evaluated:

(i)   through the implementation of individual offers to roll back measures;

(ii)   through the implementation of any multilateral agreements, undertakings and understandings reached in the course of the multilateral negotiations which established that certain types of measures, the present GATT status of which was not necessarily agreed, would henceforth be inconsistent with GATT provisions; and

(iii)   through the phasing-out of measures ruled inconsistent with the GATT by Panel reports adopted by the CONTRACTING PARTIES.

32.   The Surveillance Body discussed these proposals on a number of occasions. While there was considerable support for these proposals, there was no consensus on their adoption. Views remained divided about the ways

A:N-SB3

- 14 -

in which autonomous trade liberalisation measures and the implementation of Panel reports should be evaluated.

33.   The Surveillance Body has also made an effort to assess the extent to which GATT-inconsistent measures continue to be maintained by individual contracting parties. In this connection, the Secretariat was asked to prepare a list of measures which, following Panel findings, had been found by the CONTRACTING PARTIES to be inconsistent with the General Agreement. The Secretariat also added available information regarding actions taken in response to such findings (MTN.SB/W/11). In general instances, full information on the follow-up action taken to implement Panel findings is not available. In the majority of the 42 cases listed (covering the period 1951-90), actions appear to have been taken in response to the recommendations. However, in many of the more recent cases, implementation of the Panel recommendations remained pending.

34.   Participants identified two difficulties in establishing the full picture of outstanding GATT-inconsistent measures. First, in a strict legal sense, the GATT-inconsistency of a particular measure can only be determined by the CONTRACTING PARTIES and, therefore, there are no other means available for participants to definitively determine the GATT-inconsistency of measures maintained by other participants. Second, the Punta del Este Ministerial Declaration requires that each participant implement the rollback commitment, taking into account multilateral agreements, undertakings and understandings reached in the Uruguay Round. However, it has been difficult for participants to determine, before the formal completion of the Uruguay Round, what measures should be considered to be GATT-inconsistent since agreements, undertakings and understandings with respect to GATT provisions were still under negotiation.

35.   The Punta del Este Ministerial Declaration requires that the implementation of the rollback commitment be made within an agreed time-frame. In this respect, the view has been advanced that agreement on a time-frame does not necessarily imply that all measures subject to the commitment should be phased out, or brought into conformity with the

A:N-SB3

0118

provisions of the General Agreement or Instruments negotiated within the framework of GATT or under its auspices, before the end of the Uruguay Round. This view is based on the consideration that the full details of multilateral agreements, undertakings and understandings might emerge only towards the end of the Uruguay Round.

A:N-SB3

0119

1. Standstill

    가. Standstill 통고사항 검토

        0 기존 및 신규 통고 사항 검토

        0 아국 해당사항 없음.

    나. Standstill 관련 검토 (조기경보사항 포합)

        0 90. 7. 회의시 미국이 아국의 사치품 과소비 자제 조치의
           수입재한적, 차별적 성격에 대해 우려 표명

           - 미측의 재언급시 별첨 아국의 갓트 이사회에서의
              발언문에 의거 반박

2. Rollback

    가. Rollback 관련 검토

        0 Rollback 공약위배사항에 대한 각국 Statement 검토

           - 아국해당사항 없음.

    나. 아국의 자발적 R/B 통고에 대한 예상 질문

        1) 아국 통고의 성격

            - 수입 자유화는 아국의 장기적 구조조정 정책 수행의 일환

- 1 -

0120

이며, 금번 통보된 조치들은 UR 협상기간동안의 자유화 조치들을 포함합.

- 자발적 수입 자유화, 수입감시제도 철폐, 특별법하의 수입 제한 완화는 갓트 규정 위배 여부와는 관계없이 통보된 것이며 쇠고기 패널 권고의 이행은 권고의 내용과 이해 당사국과의 협의 결과에 따른 것임.

- 일부 품목은 과거 갓트 18조 B항에 의거 수입제한되던 것도 있으나, 자유화 조치는 대아국 BOP 협의 이전부터 계획, 추진 되어옴

2) 자발적 자유화에 대한 credit 추구 여부

- UR 협상의 진전상황을 보아 결정할 것임.

- R/B 사항에 대하여는 상응하는 양허를 요구치 않는다는 푼타선언의 내용은 갓트 규정 위배 조치에만 적용되는 것으로 해석함

3) 잔여 수입제한 계속 품목에 대한 처리 방안

- 수입자유화 잔존 품목, 특별법하의 수입 제한 계속 품목은 전반적인 자유화 정책의 일환으로 계속 자유화될 것으로 보며, 특히 UR 협상 결과를 고려할 것으로 전망됨.

- 상세한 자료가 없으므로 관련 언급을 take note 본부에 전달하겠음.

다. Rollback 관련 결정안

- 필요시 아국은 시한을 설정하여 처리하는데 반대한다는 기존 입장 재표명

- 2 -

0121

3. TNC 앞 보고서

  0 특별한 사항 없음. 끝.

0122

SS/RB 감시기구

1. 협상배경 및 목표

가. 협상배경

○ UR 협상의 성공적 타결 및 협상 여건 개선을 위한 보호주의
  무역조치의 억제 필요성 인식

나. 협상목표 (PDE 선언)

○ GATT 및 관련 규정에 위배되는 무역제한 조치의 억제(Standstill)

○ GATT 및 관련 규정에 위배되는 모든 무역제한 조치를 UR 협상종료
  이전까지 합의되는 시한내에 철폐 또는 GATT규정 합치(Rollback)

○ 본공약 이행 확보를 위한 감시기능 수행(Surveillance)

2. 진전 상황

가. 주요 협상 경과

○ 중간 평가 합의사항(88.12. 몬트리올)

- SS/RB 공약 이행을 위한 결의 확인

- SS 위배 조치의 철폐를 위한 행동 필요성 강조

- SS 공약에 영향을 줄 입안중인 법안에 대한 검토 필요성 인식

- RB 공약의 시의 적절한 이행 및 RB 요청에 대한 신속한 반응 필요

- RB 공약 이행 방법 및 시기를 감시기구에 통보할 것을 각국에 촉구

- RB 공약 이행을 위한 조치를 신중히 검토할 것을 각국에 촉구

- 각국은 상기 검토 결과를 신속히 감시기구에 통고할 것에 합의

0123

ㅇ 협상 경과 종합 (의장보고서 요지)

　1) Standstill

　　- 86.9. 이후 25건의 SS notification이 제출됨 (상세)

　　- 감시기구는 각국 통고사항을 논의하였으나 해당조치들의
　　　SS 공약 위배 여부에 대해 의견 일치를 보지 못함.

　　- 감시기구에서 미통상법 301조등 각국 국내 입법사항에 대한
　　　"early warning"이 논의 되었으며, 이를 통해 해당국에
　　　적절한 우려를 전달함.

　2) Rollback

　　(a)RB 협의

　　　- 총 20건의 RB request 가 제출되었으며, 대부분 GATT 규정
　　　　위배 여부가 문제되는 수량제한 조치 사항임

　　　- 2건에 대해서만 해당국이 undertaking을 통보

　　(b)패널 권고사항 이행

　　　- 한국, 카나다, 일본, 미국등 4개국이 패널권고사항 이행실적 통보

　　(C)자발적 자유화 조치

　　　- 한국, EC, 호주, 카나다등 일부국가가 GATT 위배여부에 관계없이
　　　　자국의 자발적 자유화 실적을 통보

　　　- 자발적 조치는 GATT 위배조치 철폐와는 구별되어야 한다는
　　　　지적이 있으나 다수국가가 위배여부 판단에 어려움이 있음을 인정

나. 합의 사항

　ㅇ 특기사항 없음.

0124

다. 미합의 사항

　ㅇ Rollback 공약 완전 이행 방안 검토

　　- 이행상의 문제점

　　　1) GATT 규정 위배여부는 체약국단 결정에 의해서만 가능

　　　2) 판정 기준이될 GATT 제반 규정이 현재 UR 에서 논의중

　　- 이에 따라 감시기구는 브랏셀 각료회의에서 RB 공약 이행을
　　　위해 필요한 사항을 검토하도록 결정

3. 브랏셀 회의에서 논의할 사항

가. 쟁점별 주요국 입장

　ㅇ GATT 위배 판정 조치의 RB이행 방안 (철폐시한 포함)

　　- 북구, 호주, 뉴질랜드, 홍콩 및 개도국

　　　; 푼타선언에 의거, UR 협상 종료전에 철폐시한등 구체적인
　　　　RB 공약 이행 방안 합의 필요

　　- 미국, EC, 일본, 카나다

　　　; 푼타선언의 RB공약은 정치적 선언에 붙과하여, 분쟁해결에
　　　　관한 별도의 협상이 있으므로 시한설정등 감시기구에서의
　　　　구체적 이행 방안 마련은 부적절

나. 아국 입장 및 반영 우선 순위

　ㅇ RB이행 방안

　　- 이행방안 마련 필요성 지지

　　- 단, 사안에 따라 이행기간이 다를 수 있고, 관련국의 양자
　　　협의가 필요한 경우도 있으므로 일률적인 철폐시한 도입은
　　　부적절

　　- 아국은 중도적 입장 견지 (양보 가능 분야)

0125

다. 협상 전략

   ○ RB 공약 이행은 대상조치가 대부분 미국, EC 등 주요선진국들의
     무역조치로서 이들이 수용하기는 어려울 것임.

   ○ 따라서 아국이 이를 적극 주장할 필요성은 없음.

4. 브랏셀회의 협상 전망

   ○ 개도국들은 RB 공약 이행 문제를 거론할 것으로 예상되나 직접 이해
     당사자인 미국, EC등의 반대로 철폐시한등 구체적 방안 합의는
     어려울 것으로 전망.

   ○ 단, 원칙적 성격의 RB공약 계속 이행 필요성은 합의 가능할 것임.

5. 협상 타결이 아국에 미치는 영향과 대책

   ○ 쇠고기 패널 결과가 유일한 패널 판정 사항이나 아국으로서는 패널
     권고사항을 이행 완료하였다고 보며, 또한 쇠고기 수입제한 조치는
     향후 UR 농산물 협상 결과에 따를 것이므로 특별한 연관성은 없을
     것으로 봄

   ○ 아국 수출과 관련된 미관세법 337조등 여타국의 패널 판정 조치도
     궁극적으로 UR 협상 결과에 합치하게 될것임.

6. 발언 요지 (필요시)

   ○ UR 협상결과 이행 및 국제무역 환경 악화 방지차원에서 SS/RB 공약의
     정신이 계속유지되기를 희망함.

   (○ 그러나 기존 패널판정 결과의 이행 문제는 사안의 다양성, 필요시 이해
     당사국간 양자협의 가능성등에 비추어 일률적인 철폐시한을 설정하는
     것은 적절하지 못함)

0126

2. 1991 년도

RESTRICTED

MTN.SB/SN/22/Rev.2
19 July 1991
Special Distribution

Surveillance Body

Original: Spanish

STANDSTILL

Notification

1. **Participant notifying**: Brazil, Colombia, Costa Rica, Cuba
    El Salvador, Guatemala, Honduras, Mexico,
    Nicaragua, Peru and Venezuela

2. **Participant maintaining the measure**: Italy

3. **Description of the measure** (including date of entry into force and
    reference to any relevant legislation or other document):

    Substantial increase in selective internal taxes on coffee,
    cocoa and products thereof.

    The measure was established by a Decree of the Council of
    Ministers of the Italian government, dated 31 December 1990, entitled
    "Imposti di Consumo su Caffe e cacao", published in the Official
    Gazette of 31 December 1990, with effect as of 1 January 1991. See
    Annex 1.

    It should be noted that the selective internal taxes have
    increased by 400 per cent in respect of green coffee, and
    700 per cent in respect of unroasted cocoa. Furthermore, their
    ad valorem incidence increased from 15 per cent in 1989 to
    62 per cent in 1991 in respect of green coffee; and from 7 per cent
    in 1989 to 59 per cent in 1991 in respect of cocoa beans. See
    Annex 3.

4. **Products covered, including tariff headings** (CCCN where applicable,
    otherwise national tariff lines):

    See Annex 2.

5. **Country or countries to which the measure applies**:

    All developing countries exporting coffee, cocoa and products
    thereof.

GATT SECRETARIAT
UR-91-0086

0128

6. Relevance of the measure to the standstill commitment:

    Paragraphs (ii) and (iii).

7. Comments by the participant maintaining the measure:

    -   the increase of the value of the specific internal taxes on
        coffee and cacao in Italy have been made within the general
        regulations applicable in Italy for the adjustment of specific
        taxes to the relevant price indices, to guarantee the
        ad valorem incidence of a specific tax;

    -   the adjustment has in fact been made to a lesser extent than
        justified by the development of the relevant price indices;

    -   neither the adjustment as such, nor its incidence therefore is
        in any way inconsistent with the European Community's
        standstill commitment.

0129

ANNEX 1

CONSUMPTION TAX ON COFFEE AND COCOA

	Up to 31.12.90 Lire/Kg.	From 1.1.91 Lire/Kg.
COFFEE		
Raw	500	2,050
Roasted, whether or not ground	625	2,562.50
Raw, decaffeinated	525	2,152.50
Roasted, decaffeinated	656.50	2,260.125
Instant	1,500	6,150
COCOA		
Cocoa beans, not roasted	180	1,260
Beans, roasted, not shelled	200	1,400
Beans, roasted, shelled, broken	225	1,575
Hulks and waste	0	1,280
Paste	225	1,575
Powder	225	1,575
Defatted powder (less than 1 per cent fat)	170	1,190
Butter	280	1,960

0130

ANNEX 2

PRODUCTS AFFECTED, INDICATING TARIFF HEADINGS

COFFEE

0901.11	Not roasted
0901.21	Roasted
0901.12	Not roasted, decaffeinated
0901.22	Roasted, decaffeinated
2101.10	Instant coffee

COCOA

1801.00	Cocoa beans, raw
	Cocoa beans roasted, not shelled
	Cocoa beans, roasted, shelled, broken
1802.00	Shells, husks, and waste
1803.10.20	Cocoa paste
	Cocoa powder
1805.00	Cocoa powder, defatted (less than 1 per cent fat)
1804.0	Cocoa butter

0131

ANNEX 3

INCIDENCE OF TAX ON COFFEE AND COCOA BEANS

	Incidences of previous tax rates						New Rates
	1969	1971	1975	1979	1985	1989	1991
Coffee beans	109%	97%	60%	17%	10%	15%	62%
Cocoa beans	31%	42%	17%	6%	4%	7%	59%

0132

ANNEX 4

Statement by the Delegations of Brazil, Colombia, Costa Rica,
Cuba, El Salvador, Guatemala, Honduras, Mexico,
Nicaragua, Peru and Venezuela

By a Decree of the Council of Ministers dated 21 December 1990 and published in the Official Gazette of 31 December 1990, the Government of Italy increased the consumption tax on coffee and cocoa.

This measure entered into force on 1 January 1991, and is of general application for all countries exporting those products.

The products concerned by this measure are the following:

HS	COFFEE
0901.11	Raw
0901.21	Roasted
0901.12	Raw, decaffeinated
0901.22	Roasted, decaffeinated
2101.10	Instant

HS	COCOA
	Cocoa beans, raw
1801.00	Beans roasted, not shelled
	Beans, roasted, shelled, broken
1802.00	Shells, husks and waste
1803.10.20	Cocoa paste
18.05.00	Cocoa powder, defatted (less than 1% fat)
18.04.00	Cocoa butter

The increase amounted to 400 per cent in the case of coffee and 700 per cent in the case of cocoa. These taxes have an ad valorem equivalent of 61.5 per cent for raw coffee and 58.5 per cent for cocoa beans.

At the end of the Tokyo Round, in 1979, some EEC member countries made statements on their policy with respect to the application of internal taxes on tropical products (document MTN/TP/(Secret)/2/(Rev.3).

In the case of Italy, the statement reads: "The Government of Italy, underlining the link with current economic policy in the present situation

0133

of that country, indicates that it will take this problem into consideration in a sympathetic manner."

In the GATT Ministerial Declaration on the Uruguay Round in 1986, with regard to standstill, member countries undertook, <u>inter alia</u>: "... not to take any trade-restrictive or distorting measure in the legitimate exercise of [their] GATT rights, that would go beyond that which is necessary to remedy specific situations as provided for in the General Agreement ...".

With regard to tropical products, the Ministerial Declaration also establishes that "negotiations shall aim at the fullest liberalization of trade in tropical products, including in their processed and semi-processed forms, and shall cover both tariff and all non-tariff measures affecting trade in these products. The CONTRACTING PARTIES recognize the importance of trade in tropical products to a large number of less-developed contracting parties and agree that negotiations in this area shall receive special attention ...".

Bearing in mind that Italy produces neither coffee nor cocoa, the taxes in question are a direct restriction on imports of these tropical products originating in developing countries.

Consequently, the increase, moreover the excessive increase, in selective taxes on coffee and coffee products and cocoa and cocoa products constitutes a breach of the standstill commitment of the Punta del Este Declaration entered into by all GATT member countries. In addition, this measure is not in keeping with the agreed negotiating objectives of the Negotiating Group on Tropical Products as set out in the Ministerial Declaration.

0134

R̶E̶STRICTED

MTN.SB/W/12
30 July 1991

Special Distribution

Surveillance Body

COMMUNICATION FROM THE CHAIRMAN OF THE SURVEILLANCE BODY
TO THE TNC MEETING IN JULY 1991

The Surveillance Body held its first meeting since Brussels on 1 July this year. The record of this meeting is contained in document MTN.SB/16.

As the record shows, there have been very few new developments in relation to the standstill and rollback commitments during the past seven months. One new notification on standstill was made by a number of Latin American and Caribbean countries, concerning an increase in Italy's selective internal taxes on coffee, cocoa and their products (MTN.SB/SN/22/Rev.2). A discussion of this measure was the main point on the agenda at the last meeting of the Body.

As regards rollback, there have been notifications on autonomous trade liberalization measures by one participating country (Colombia), but no further communications on the implementation of the rollback commitment. At the recent meeting of the Surveillance Body, one participating country (New Zealand) indicated its intention to pursue, in future meetings of the Body, its proposal to expedite rollback implementation on measures which have been found GATT-inconsistent by Panels. The Ministerial TNC meeting in December had, in document MTN.SB/14, a comprehensive report on the status of proposals for rollback action.

The Surveillance Body proposes to hold its next meeting in October of this year.

GATT SECRETARIAT
UR-91-0096

0135

ANNEX I

REPORT BY THE CHAIRMAN OF THE NEGOTIATING GROUP ON AGRICULTURE
TO THE CHAIRMAN OF THE GROUP OF NEGOTIATIONS ON GOODS

The Negotiating Group on Agriculture has met four times since the last meeting of the Trade Negotiations Committee on 7 June 1991.

At each of the four meetings the Chairman informed the Group of the results of the intensive informal consultations that he had conducted. This information has been made available to participants in the negotiating group. The consultations have led the Chairman to circulate on his own responsibility a Note on Options in the Agriculture Negotiations (document MTN.GNG/AG/W/1).

Progress continues to be made on a range of technical issues in each of the three areas of Domestic Support, Market Access and Export Competition. Important political issues, however, remain outstanding and will have to be addressed urgently in order to move the negotiations to the final phase.

While all options remain on the table until common ground on the modalities for negotiation has been established, the Chairman intends to circulate, on his own responsibility but basing himself on the consultations which have taken place so far, further notes aimed at exploring various options in more detail. These notes will cover the following topics:

Product Coverage

Domestic Support
- Green Box
- Definition of the AMS
- Definition of Equivalent Commitments
- Special and Differential Treatment

Market Access
- Policy Coverage and Guidelines for Tariffication
- Minimum Access Commitments
- Special and Differential Treatment

Export Competition
- Export Subsidies to be Subject to the Terms of the Final Agreement
- Special and Differential Treatment

0136

ANNEX II

REPORT BY THE CHAIRMAN OF THE NEGOTIATING GROUP ON INSTITUTIONS
TO THE CHAIRMAN OF THE GROUP OF NEGOTIATIONS ON GOODS

The Negotiating Group on Institutions was established as a part of the new negotiating structure replacing the previous Negotiating Groups No. 13 on Dispute Settlement and No. 14 on Functioning of the GATT System. The responsibilities of the Group fall essentially into three areas:

- the elaboration of rules and procedures for dispute settlement;

- the drafting of the final instruments to embody the results of the Uruguay Round negotiations;

- the elaboration of a new organizational structure to be implemented after the Round.

The Group has not yet met but it is envisaged that the Group will meet on 26 September to discuss dispute settlement issues.

The two main outstanding issues in this area - the commitment not to use unilateral measures and the counterpart: the automaticity in the Council's decisions on the establishment of panels, the adoption of reports and the authorization or retaliation - are not likely to be settled until the main results of the Uruguay Round are known.

There are, however, three areas where technical discussions at this stage may be useful:

- The provisions dealing with non-violation complaints. Some participants argue that the more automatic and legalistic procedures contained in the proposed Uruguay Round rules are not suitable for non-violation cases. The main points for further negotiations concern the definition of the types of cases that could fall under such special non-violation procedures and what such special procedures should be.

- The so-called "consolidated dispute settlement text". It has been tentatively agreed that at the end of the negotiations there shall be prepared a single text, consolidating into one all the various GATT dispute settlement texts (e.g. the 1966 text on cases involving developing countries, the 1979 Understanding, the 1982 Ministerial Declaration, and the new Uruguay Round text).

- The provisions concerning the maximum length of dispute settlement proceedings. There is general agreement on a twenty-one month limit but it is not agreed whether this limit should be absolute, or subject to a _force majeure_ provision.

0137

Another matter to be considered by the Group is the incorporation into the dispute settlement text, as it appears in document MTN.TNC/W/35/Rev.1, of some improvements that were discussed in Brussels but not formally approved there.

The Group will also consider what can be done in order to ensure that dispute settlement texts negotiated in various sectors of the Uruguay Round are harmonized as far as possible.

The Negotiating Group will at a later date consider other matters falling within the competence of the Group, inter alia concerning the final instruments and a new organizational structure.

Julio Lacarte-Muró
Chairman, Negotiating Group on Institutions

0138

ANNEX III

REPORT BY THE CHAIRMAN OF THE NEGOTIATING GROUP ON MARKET ACCESS
TO THE CHAIRMAN OF THE GROUP OF NEGOTIATIONS ON GOODS

As you requested, and further to my letter of 24 June 1991
(MTN.GNG/MA/W/1), I am setting out below the status of the negotiations in
the Market Access Group at this time, and the work which will have to be
pursued in this autumn. Our work continues to proceed on the assumption
that the negotiations should be concluded by the end of 1991.

1. Status of the negotiations

There have been two meetings of the Market Access Negotiating Group
since the restructuring of the negotiating groups at the beginning of May.
These were on 13-14 June and 26 July. Although participants have renewed
efforts to develop a substantial and broad based package of liberalization
results and are engaged in good faith bilateral negotiations, the problems
identified in my letter of 24 June have not yet been resolved.

The situation in each of the areas covered by the mandate of the
Negotiating Group is as follows:

On tariffs, participants are actively pursuing bilateral and
plurilateral negotiations to reduce, harmonize or eliminate tariffs on a
vast range of specific products. They have also started to address the
problem of high tariffs and tariff peaks, the possibility of eliminating or
substantially reducing or harmonizing tariffs in certain products groups,
and the issue of tariff bindings. However, only limited progress has been
made to date and I am concerned that unless some major bilateral
negotiations make concrete progress soon, it will be difficult to accelerate
the pace of other market access negotiations.

Participants at this stage have engaged in little result-orientated
negotiations on non-tariff measures (NTMs), and there has been no
substantial progress on product specific non-tariff measures. This is a
matter of increasing concern to many participants. While it seems clear
that certain NTMs are being addressed in other negotiating groups dealing
with agriculture, textiles and rule-making, the elimination or
liberalization of product specific non-tariff measures in the market access
negotiations remains important to ensure that the value of tariff
reductions is not eroded.

At present, the negotiations on tropical products are not making
progress because many participants are still unwilling to offer further
commitments beyond the results achieved in the Mid-Term Review until the
agricultural negotiations progress. Achieving the Montreal ministerial
objectives on tropical products remains a major element of a successful
market access package for many participants.

0139

The negotiations have made little progress to date on natural resource-based products because of the issue of the scope of the market access negotiations. Certain participants continue to consider that a number of these products should be dealt with in the agricultural negotiations.

The negotiations so far have resulted in the draft text of a Protocol (MTN.TNC/W/35/Rev.1, page 7) to which the results of the market access negotiations will be annexed. Two points in the Protocol remain to be settled: the application of Article XXVIII to the modification or withdrawal of non-tariff concessions, and the period of implementation of tariff concessions. In addition, the questions of credit for bindings and recognition for autonomous liberalization measures have been addressed on the basis of plurilateral consultations held by participants which have put forward proposals in this regard. However, these discussions have not yet resulted in a common understanding.

2. Future work

A new urgency has been given to completing the Uruguay Round by the end of this year. If that is to be done, however, a great deal of work needs to be accomplished from September onward in the market access negotiations.

- bilateral and plurilateral negotiations to reduce, harmonize or eliminate tariffs must not only be intensified, but the time has come when participants should begin to reach concrete ad referendum packages of results on the basis that the overall MTN will be completed as a single global undertaking. This is essential if participants are to narrow down the range of issues for resolution when the decisive push to conclude comes. This would also help to take account of limited resources available to many participants.

- even if the major outstanding issues were substantially narrowed down in the early fall, ways will need to be found to deal with the various substantive linkages established by many participants between different sectors of trade. In particular there are continuing constraints imposed on progress in the Market Access Group by the differences on scope of the negotiations. For example, the situation in agriculture impacts on progress in tropical products, natural resource-based products and product specific NTM's.

- the question of how to evaluate bindings and apply credit for them will need to progress concurrently with the substantive barrier reduction negotiations themselves. However, a solution to the related but separate question of recognition of autonomous trade liberalization measures still remains to be found.

Accomplishing these tasks means, of course, that the problems identified in my 24 June letter will have to be resolved. I intend to hold another meeting of the Market Access Negotiating Group in September and further meetings as required throughout the autumn.

0140

At my July 26 meeting, I have stressed the urgency for participants to begin to achieve concrete results on an <u>ad referendum</u> basis. I have also stressed the need for participants to be prepared to play all their cards in the access negotiations after the summer break so that the shape of the overall market access package will reflect the interests of all participants.

If the Market Access Negotiating Group makes substantial progress in narrowing down the issues before it, and substantive negotiating linkage issues can be addressed, then I would envisage that comprehensive and intensive exchange of tariff and NTM's concessions at the bilateral and plurilateral level will be necessary in mid-autumn.

Germain Denis
Chairman
Negotiating Group on Market Access

0141

ANNEX IV

REPORT BY THE CHAIRMAN OF THE NEGOTIATING GROUP
ON RULE MAKING AND TRIMS
TO THE CHAIRMAN OF THE GROUP OF NEGOTIATIONS ON GOODS

In preparation for the TNC meeting of 30 July 1991, I am writing to inform you of the status of work in the Negotiating Group on Rule Making and trade-related investment measures.

In assessing the status of the negotiations in this Group, it has to be borne in mind that in some areas covered by the Group a point has been reached where major political decisions are necessary to complete the negotiations. As such decisions can be expected only in the context of the final package of the Uruguay Round, the work in these areas at this stage is, necessarily, of a limited nature. My report should, therefore, be seen from this perspective.

The Negotiating Group met on 10-12 June and on 22-26 July 1991. At its first meeting the Negotiating Group noted the importance attached by participants to this area of the Uruguay Round negotiations and reviewed the progress made so far in the subject-areas covered by its mandate. In the light of the results achieved so far (both before and during the Brussels Ministerial Conference) in a number of these subject-areas where texts were in a very advanced stage, it was agreed that the Group should concentrate its attention on subsidies and countervailing measures, anti-dumping, trade-related investment measures, balance-of-payments measures, and safeguard measures and that the Group could revert at a later stage to certain issues (including questions of a purely technical nature) which remain to be settled with respect to the other subject-areas.

At its meeting held on 22-26 July 1991 the Negotiating Group evaluated the state of play in the areas of anti-dumping, subsidies and countervailing measures, trade-related investment measures and balance-of-payments measures and agreed how to proceed in these subject-areas in the near future. The Group also agreed to postpone, for the time being, any further examination of the draft text on safeguards.

Regarding anti-dumping I was encouraged by the fact that participants agreed on the importance of an agreement on anti-dumping as part of the overall package of results of the Uruguay Round negotiations. It would appear that, given the intensive discussions which have already taken place on anti-dumping during the course of 1990 and the draft texts prepared in the context of these discussions, the absence at this time of a single text as an agreed basis for the final phase of the negotiations is not perceived to constitute an important obstacle to the successful conclusion of the negotiations in this area.

It was agreed that, starting at the meeting of the Negotiating Group in the week of 30 September the Group will hold a discussion which will

0142

address the relevant outstanding issues as a whole and serve to provide an opportunity for delegations to develop a sense of direction as to how an overall balance in the outcome of the negotiations on anti-dumping might be achieved.   Furthermore, whenever necessary during the course of these discussions I shall call on experts from various delegations to give me advice on specific technical points.   I hope that this process will help participants to prepare themselves for the political decisions which will have to be taken on a number of major matters.

With respect to the status of the negotiations on subsidies and countervailing measures I have noted that the draft text appearing in document MTN.TNC/W/35/Rev.1 continues to be accepted as the basis for the final phase of negotiations in this subject-area but that there are certain basic questions which will have to be resolved through political decisions at the appropriate point in time.

The consultations which I have conducted have given me a better idea of issues in respect of which further efforts are necessary in order to prepare these political decisions and find the basis for possible compromise solutions.   At the same time, however, it has been confirmed to me that delegations do not intend to unravel the draft text or propose another basis for the work of the Negotiating Group in this area.

I intend to continue consultations on some of these issues during the meeting of the Negotiating Group in the week of 30 September 1991.   While some of these issues can probably be resolved only through political decisions it would seem to me that some others could benefit from further technical work.

With regard to Trade-Related Investment Measures (TRIMs), my informal consultations with participants have enabled me to arrive at a better understanding of the status of work and of the major difficulties confronting the Group. As I indicated in this week's formal meeting of the Group, although important divergences remain on some very basic points of approach and substance, I think we can be reasonably optimistic about the prospects of intensifying the negotiations after the summer break. It was agreed that the intensification of the negotiating process would be based on a detailed consideration of the following list of issues, including those appearing in the commentary on TRIMS in the document sent to the Brussels Ministerial Meeting (MTN.TNC/W/35/Rev.1), which I presented to the Group: (i) Coverage of the agreement; (ii) Disciplines; (iii) Treatment of Developing Countries; (iv) Transition Periods; (v) Restrictive Business Practices; (vi) Other Issues. It is my hope that such a discussion would greatly assist me in the presentation, at the appropriate time, of a draft text which could form the basis of further negotiations on this subject.

With reference to the balance-of-payments provisions, I have held informal consultations with a number of delegations which I found helpful and constructive.   Participants explained their current positions and their negotiating objectives and a number of them drew my attention to the changes that had taken place in the economic environment relating to these

0143

provisions, and the need to take these into account in the future work of the Group on this subject. As I informed the Group at its meeting last week, the consultations have encouraged me to undertake a further round of informal consultations at the time of the next meeting of the Group in September with a view to seeking common ground on which to base further work on this subject.

George A. Maciel
Chairman
Negotiating Group on Rule-Making
and Trade-Related Investment
Measures

0144

ANNEX V

REPORT BY THE CHAIRMAN OF THE NEGOTIATING GROUP
ON TEXTILES AND CLOTHING
TO THE CHAIRMAN OF THE GROUP OF NEGOTIATIONS ON GOODS

1.   The first meeting of the Negotiating Group on Textiles and Clothing, since the establishment of the formal structure for conducting the negotiations in the final phase, was held on 5 July 1991.

2.   The Chairman informed the Group of consultations he had conducted in March and April, in pursuance of the work programme adopted by the TNC in February. This had resulted in a paper compiling trade data provided by some participants; it was suggested at the July meeting that similar data be provided by others as well. The Group went on to discuss a programme for its work in the coming weeks and months with the objective of advancing the negotiation process in an orderly and constructive manner. The Group reaffirmed that the basis for further negotiations remained the draft text of an agreement as contained in document MTN.TNC/W/35/Rev.1, and the commentary attached thereto which identified the main points of divergence. It was also agreed that the objective of future work should be arriving at an agreement which was as clear and predictable as possible. In this context, it was decided that, in the first instance, a number of key topics like product coverage (Annex II) and the transitional safeguard mechanism (Article 6) should be taken up for technical level discussions through a combination of informal consultations and formal meetings.

3.   On this basis, informal consultations were held on 15 and 16 July at which questions relating to the trade data provided and the proposal for additional data as well as aspects relating to the composition of Annex II were examined in detail. These discussions were held in an atmosphere of cooperation and good-will. The discussions also made it clear that these subjects should be re-visited for further examination before proceeding to the substantive negotiations.

4.   The Negotiating Group was re-convened on 19 July, to receive the Chairman's report and to discuss the progress achieved thus far in the informal process. It was agreed that informal technical discussions should continue in July and in the early Autumn. One more such consultation was held on 22 July on the transitional safeguard mechanism (Article 6), and a number of specific points were raised by participants which could provide the basis for future works in this area.

5.   The Negotiating Group itself will meet on or about 30 September.

ANNEX VI

REPORT BY THE CHAIRMAN OF THE NEGOTIATING GROUP ON TRIPS
TO THE CHAIRMAN OF THE GROUP OF NEGOTIATIONS ON GOODS

    In preparation for the TNC meeting of 30 July 1991, I am writing to
inform you of the developments in the TRIPS negotiations since the new
negotiating structure was put into place on 7 June 1991.

    The Negotiating Group on Trade-Related Aspects of Intellectual
Property Rights including Trade in Counterfeit Goods met on 27-28 June.
This meeting was devoted to both formal sessions and informal
consultations. As I informed the Group at the end of the meeting, I was in
general encouraged by the meeting and the consultations. All participants
demonstrated a cooperative and positive spirit and reaffirmed their
commitment to the negotiating process for which the Group is responsible.
The meeting enabled: first, participants to take stock of the status of
the TRIPS negotiations in the context of the state of play in the Uruguay
Round as a whole; secondly, the re-establishment of the Group as a
functioning negotiating unit; and, thirdly, the taking of necessary
decisions on the organisation of the further negotiations.

    I was in particular encouraged by the general emphasis on the
importance of basing the further work on the text sent to the Brussels
Ministerial meeting in document MTN.TNC/W/35/Rev.1 and also of ensuring
that the work done in Brussels would be taken into account. In this
regard, it was agreed that a detailed description on a point by point basis
of the work undertaken in Brussels should be made available, in oral form
at least, indicating the subjects discussed, any new ideas or proposals
that had emerged and, where possible, any convergence of views or apparent
common understanding or agreement. This is one of the tasks that the Group
plans to undertake at its next meeting, scheduled for the week of
16 September.

    Another common perception was that the rapidity of the progress that
could be made in the TRIPS negotiations would depend on developments in
other areas of the negotiations, since for the most part the work on TRIPS
had been carried to a point where what remained were those decisions on key
issues that could only be expected to be taken in the final phase of the
Uruguay Round. There was nevertheless a general appreciation that the
Group has the responsibility to ensure that all necessary preparations are
made for these decisions, though their timing will be largely a function of
considerations of globality.

    In the light of what I have said, the Group has agreed on a work
programme for its September meeting, account being taken of the need for
flexibility so that the Group can act very quickly when the need arises.
This work programme has three main elements. The first two consist of
questions that, even though closely related to rather key political
decisions, can be usefully further discussed so as to clarify further the

0146

options, even if it proves too early in September to attempt to take those decisions. These two questions are, first, Article 73 of the draft Agreement on Trade-Related Aspects of Intellectual Property Rights including Trade in Counterfeit Goods (page 228 of MTN.TNC/W/35/Rev.1) concerning the extent to which the obligations in a TRIPS agreement would apply to existing intellectual property and, secondly, the issue of dispute settlement. It will be recalled that the draft Agreement on Trade-Related Aspects of Intellectual Property Rights including Trade in Counterfeit Goods sent to Brussels contains in an Annex three draft texts on dispute settlement, indicating the range of options before the Group. The reason for this is that the issue of dispute settlement is closely related to that of the institutional arrangements for the implementation of the results of the negotiations, on which there are different views, and which question has been specifically left for decision by Ministers when the results of the negotiations are established. Nevertheless, it is important, before these decisions can be taken, to clarify the technical implications of the options available.

The third item on the work programme for September is the remaining outstanding issues in the texts sent to Brussels as listed in the commentary to those texts (pages 193-195 of MTN.TNC/W/35/Rev.1). As mentioned above, one major purpose of this work will be to recall in some detail the work done in Brussels. It will also provide an opportunity for any further clarification of positions that participants feel necessary. It is my hope that it will be possible to go further than this and to start settling these outstanding issues; but, given that they are issues on which it is essentially a matter of taking key decisions rather than conducting technical work, the extent to which this will be possible will depend very much on perceptions of participants of progress in the Uruguay Round as a whole.

Since the Group met in June, the delegation of the Republic of Korea has tabled a proposal on the establishment of a Dispute Prevention System in respect of the Transfer of Technologies. This, then, will also be an item for consideration at the Group's September meeting.

As I have informed the Negotiating Group, I plan to circulate informally somewhat nearer the time of the Group's September meeting more detailed suggestions on the organisation of the work at that meeting, so as to help participants prepare for the meeting and thus maximise its utility. In these suggestions, I plan to include, for example, a checklist of the issues that have to be decided in connection with Article 73.

In conclusion, I am confident that, in line with progress in other areas of negotiations, it will be possible for the Group to complete the negotiations on TRIPS so that the results in this area can make their full contribution to the final Uruguay Round package.

Lars Anell
Chairman
Negotiating Group on Trade-Related
Aspects of Intellectual Property Rights
including Trade in Counterfeit Goods

0147

15 October 1991

<u>Surveillance Body</u>

  Attached is the draft of the revised report by the Chairman of the Surveillance Body to the TNC. The draft will be the subject of discussion at the formal meeting on 16 October 1991.

0148

RⅢ̶ICTED

MTN.SB/14/Rev.1
15 October 1991

Special Distribution

Surveillance Body

DRAFT

<u>REPORT BY THE CHAIRMAN OF THE
SURVEILLANCE BODY TO THE TNC</u>

1.   In December 1990, a report by the Chairman of the Surveillance Body (MTN.SB/14) was transmitted to the TNC meeting at Ministerial level in Brussels. The aim of this note is to update that report, taking into account what has happened since then. The note provides the TNC with a brief summary of the implementation of the standstill and rollback commitments. It also contains a more detailed account of the implementation of the commitments (ANNEX).

(1)   <u>Standstill</u>

2.   Since the standstill commitment took effect in September 1986, a total of 26 notifications, by 11 individual participants and a group of participants against 9 participants, were submitted to the Surveillance Body. These notifications covered 24 cases, as two measures were, each, subject to two notifications.

3.   Twenty-four notifications were made during the period October 1986 to November 1988. One notification was submitted in 1990 and one in 1991.

4.   According to the information provided to the Surveillance Body, in nine of the 24 cases participants have taken action with a view to ensuring the withdrawal of measures contrary to the standstill commitment. Three of these actions were in response to recommendations of GATT Panel reports adopted by the CONTRACTING PARTIES; in the other six cases, the measures concerned were lifted autonomously. In a tenth case, a participant expressed its intention to act upon the notified measure in the light of the outcome of the Uruguay Round.

5.   The remaining 14 cases notified under standstill were also discussed at meetings of the Surveillance Body. Some actions were reported concerning the measures in question. However, the views of the participants remained divided as to the consistency or inconsistency of the measures with the standstill commitment.

6.   Participants also engaged in "early warning" discussions on proposed
·legislation and other actions affecting trade. Altogether 35 cases were
subject to discussions, some being discussed at several meetings.   The
discussion in the Surveillance Body served to ensure that the concerns
brought up by participants were duly shared and transmitted, in an
appropriate fashion, to the authorities concerned.

(2)   Rollback

      (a)   Rollback consultations

7.   A total of twenty rollback requests covering a wide range of measures
were made by eight participants, addressed to seven participants. In some
cases, there was some overlap of the measures notified. Most requests
concerned quantitative restrictions considered by the notifying participant
to be inconsistent with the General Agreement.

8.   Nineteen requests were made during the period June 1987 to
October 1988. One request was made in 1990.

9.   Fifteen requests were the subject of consultations. A total of
twenty-one consultations were held. There have been no notifications
concerning consultations on the remaining five requests.

10.   Three participants to which requests were addressed (the EC, Japan
and the United States) notified undertakings already implemented or
intended.   In some cases, the undertakings covered only part of the
measures contained in the rollback requests made by other participants.
The other four participants addressed have not submitted any information on
undertakings in response to the rollback requests.

11.   In one case, the requesting participant indicated that the measure
notified had been removed.

      (b)   Implementation of Panel recommendations

12.   Four participants (Canada, Japan, the Republic of Korea and the
United States) notified the Surveillance Body of their actions on certain
measures which had been ruled GATT-inconsistent by the CONTRACTING PARTIES,
following Panel recommendations.

      (c)   Autonomous trade liberalization actions

13.   Some participants (Australia, Argentina, Canada, Colombia, the EC,
Finland, Indonesia and the Republic of Korea) informed the Surveillance
Body of autonomous trade liberalization actions. Most of the measures

0150

affected by these actions had not been subject to rollback requests from other participants. The actions included the elimination of discriminatory import restrictions and changes in import licensing régimes. Most of these notifications were made without prejudice to the question of GATT-consistency of the measures concerned. In discussing these autonomous actions, the point was made that the rollback commitment was only related to GATT-inconsistent measures and therefore a distinction should be made between the autonomous liberalization of GATT-consistent measures and that of GATT-inconsistent measures. However, many participants recognized the difficulties in determining the GATT-inconsistency of the trade measures concerned.

(3)   Considerations for the full implementation of the rollback commitment

14.   The Surveillance Body has given active attention to the development of procedures for promoting rollback action and to proposals made by individual participants to this end. The Surveillance Body has also made an effort to assess the extent to which GATT-inconsistent measures continue to be maintained by individual contracting parties. Upon request of the Surveillance Body, the Secretariat prepared a note on measures which, following Panel findings, had been found by the CONTRACTING PARTIES to be inconsistent with the General Agreement. Forty-two cases were listed, covering the period 1951-90. In general, full information on the follow-up action taken to implement Panel findings is not available. It was found that in many of the more recent cases implementation of the Panel recommendations remained pending.

15.   Participants identified two difficulties in establishing the full picture of outstanding GATT-inconsistent measures. First, in a strict legal sense, the GATT-inconsistency of a particular measure maintained by a participant can only be determined by a ruling of the CONTRACTING PARTIES. Second, the Punta del Este Ministerial Declaration requires that each participant implement the rollback commitment, taking into account multilateral agreements, undertakings and understandings reached in the Uruguay Round. However, before completion of the Uruguay Round, it has been difficult for participants to determine what measures should be considered to be GATT-inconsistent since agreements, undertakings and understandings with respect to GATT provisions were still under negotiation.

16.   Against this background, the Surveillance Body has considered ways by which the full implementation of the rollback commitment could be facilitated. However, without knowledge of final agreements or decisions in individual negotiating areas of the Uruguay Round, including agreements on procedures to phase out or bring into conformity measures henceforth inconsistent with the provisions of the General Agreement or Instruments

0151

negotiated within the framework of GATT or under its auspices, it was difficult for the Surveillance Body to come to consensus in this matter, as these agreements or decisions would affect the implementation of the rollback commitment. The Surveillance Body therefore concluded that in the light of multilateral agreements, undertakings and understandings, including strengthened rules and disciplines, reached in the Uruguay Round, the TNC may wish to consider what further action is needed to ensure that the rollback commitment be fully met.

0152

ANNEX

1.   The Punta del Este Ministerial Declaration contains the following commitments on standstill and rollback:

"Standstill

(i)   not to take any trade restrictive or distorting measure inconsistent with the provisions of the General Agreement or the instruments negotiated within the framework of GATT or under its auspices;

(ii)   not to take any trade restrictive or distorting measure in the legitimate exercise of its GATT rights, that would go beyond that which is necessary to remedy specific situations, as provided for in the General Agreement and the Instruments referred to in (i) above;

(iii) not to take any trade measures in such a manner as to improve its negotiating positions."

"Rollback

(i)   that all trade restrictive or distorting measures inconsistent with the provisions of the General Agreement or Instruments negotiated within the framework of GATT or under its auspices, shall be phased out or brought into conformity within an agreed time-frame not later than by the date of the formal completion of the negotiations, taking into account multilateral agreements, undertakings and understandings, including strengthened rules and disciplines, reached in pursuance of the Objectives of the Negotiations;

(ii)   there shall be progressive implementation of this commitment on an equitable basis in consultations among participants concerned, including all affected participants.   This commitment shall take account of the concerns expressed by any participant about measures directly affecting its trade interests;

0153

(iii) there shall be no GATT concessions requested for the elimination of these measures."

2.   A consolidated text of the Ministerial commitments on standstill and rollback, and of the procedures agreed by the TNC and by the Surveillance Body, is contained in document MTN.TNC/W/10/Rev.1.

3.   The Surveillance Body held fifteen meetings to examine and monitor the implementation of the standstill and rollback commitments. Detailed reports of its activities are contained in MTN.SB/1-17. The latest list of notifications and communications on standstill and rollback is contained in MTN.SB/W/3/Rev.11.

(1)   <u>Standstill</u>

4.   Since the standstill commitment took effect on 20 September 1986, a total of 26 notifications, by 11 individual participants and a group of participants against 9 participants, were submitted to the Surveillance Body. Twenty-four notifications were made during the period October 1986 to November 1988. There was no notification in 1989. In 1990 and in 1991, one notification was each submitted.

5.   The 26 standstill notifications covered a total of 24 cases, as two measures were, each, subject to two notifications.

6.   Ten notifications, referring to nine different subjects, were addressed to the United States; six notifications, referring to five different subjects, to the European Communities; three notifications were addressed to Canada; two to Brazil; and one each to Greece, Indonesia, Italy, Sweden and Switzerland. The notifications covered quantitative restrictions, tariffs, import levies, import controls and prohibitions, export restrictions, internal taxes, production and export subsidies, and government procurement.

7.   Sixteen notifications cited violations of paragraph (i) of the standstill commitment. Two notifications cited violations of both paragraphs (i) and (ii). Twelve notifications referred to paragraph (iii) of the commitment, three to paragraphs (i) and (iii), and two to paragraphs (ii) and (iii). One notification did not specify any particular paragraph.

8.   In two cases, concerning a ban on imports of almonds into Greece (MTN.SB/SN/10) and Brazil's expansion of the list of products for which the issue of import licences was temporarily restricted (MTN.SB/SN/2), the notifying participant (United States) withdrew its notifications, following

0154

the lifting of the ban by Greece and the abolition of the practices in question by Brazil.

9.   Seven notifications under standstill addressed a total of five measures which, at the same time, were subject to Article XXIII:2 Panel proceedings. These measures were the United States customs user fee (there were two notifications on the issue), the United States Superfund tax, the EC apple import quota system (there were two notifications), Canada's import controls on dairy products, and United States restrictions on imports from Brazil. As for the last case, the United States measures reflected in the notification were terminated effective 2 July 1990 and Brazil withdrew its complaint under Article XXIII:2 before the Panel proceeding was completed. In the other four cases, the measures were found by the Panels to be inconsistent with the General Agreement. The Council adopted the Panel reports. The EC measures concerning imports of apples had expired before the adoption of the Panel report. The United States amended the Superfund tax in accordance with the Panel recommendations. The United States also revised the customs user fee to bring it into conformity with the GATT. With respect to Canada's restrictions on some dairy products, Canada expressed its intention to implement the Panel recommendation in the light of the outcome of the Uruguay Round.

10.   The decision taken by the TNC at its Mid-Term Review in April 1989 emphasized the need to take appropriate action to ensure withdrawal of all measures contrary to the standstill commitment, taking into account that there were a number of measures which had been ruled GATT-inconsistent by Panel reports adopted by the CONTRACTING PARTIES. There have been two notifications of actions to bring measures into conformity with the General Agreement (the United States amendment of the Superfund tax, MTN.SB/RBN/2; and the United States revision of the customs user fee, MTN.SB/RBN/8).

11.   According to the information provided to the Surveillance Body, participants have taken action with a view to ensuring the withdrawal of measures contrary to the standstill commitment with respect to nine (MTN.SB/SN/1 (i) and (ii), 2, 3, 7, 10, 12 (and 15), 17, and 19) of the 24 cases covered by the 26 notifications; in a tenth case (MTN.SB/SN/9), it was indicated that action would be taken in the light of the outcome of the Uruguay Round. The remaining 14 cases were discussed at the meetings of the Surveillance Body. Some actions were reported concerning these measures. However, no consensus was achieved as to the inconsistency of the measures concerned with the standstill commitment.

12.   In the Surveillance Body's "early warning" discussions on proposed legislation and other actions affecting trade, 35 cases were subject to discussions, some being discussed at several meetings. Seventeen cases were related to actions by the United States, including the Omnibus Trade

0155

and Competitiveness Act of 1988, and the "Super 301" and "Special 301" provisions under the Act (MTN.SB/1-7, 9-13). Twelve cases concerned EC actions, including the "Television without Frontiers" Directive, and increases in certain agricultural aids (MTN.SB/2-5, 7, 10-13). Other countries concerned were Australia (MTN:SB/6), Finland (MTN.SB/9), Brazil (MTN.SB/11), and the Republic of Korea (MTN.SB/13).

13. The Surveillance Body has limited information on the current situation with respect to the proposed measures. Among actions known to the Surveillance Body are that the 1988 Textile, Apparel and Footwear Trade Bill of the United States was vetoed; that the President of the United States vetoed again a textile and footwear bill in October 1990; and that the EC's proposed measures on oils and fats were not pursued.

(2) Rollback

    (a) Rollback consultations

14. In accordance with the agreed procedures and arrangements on rollback consultations, a total of twenty rollback requests covering a wide range of measures were notified. These requests were made by eight participants and addressed to seven participants. Nineteen requests were made during the period June 1987 to October 1988. There was no request in 1989 and in 1991. One request was made in February 1990.

15. One half of the requests came from developed participants (seven from Canada, two from the United States, and one from Japan), and the other half from developing participants (four from Argentina, three from Uruguay, and one each from Chile, Hong Kong, and Romania). Five requests each were addressed to the European Communities, Japan and the United States, two to Sweden, and one each to Brazil, Finland and Norway.

16. Most requests concerned quantitative restrictions considered by the notifying participant to be inconsistent with Articles XI and XIII of the General Agreement. Other measures covered by the requests included import licensing systems, sanitary and phytosanitary regulations, prohibition of imports, export subsidies, and voluntary export restraints.

17. Fifteen requests were the subject of consultations. Altogether, twenty-one consultations took place. There have been no notifications concerning consultations on the remaining five requests (RBC/5, 10, 15, 20, and 21).

18. The Surveillance Body had agreed on a target of 30 days for beginning the process of consultations following receipt of requests. In many cases, this target was not met. The frequency of consultations greatly diminished

after 1988 (five consultations in 1987, thirteen in 1988, three in 1989 and no consultations in 1990 or in 1991).

19.   The decision taken by the TNC at its Mid-Term Review in April 1989 emphasized the need for timely action on rollback, and prompt response to rollback requests, so as to ensure progressive implementation of the rollback commitment on an equitable basis.   The Surveillance Body, at its meetings of March and July 1990, agreed that reports on the status and outcome of the rollback consultations should be submitted by participants within an agreed time limit.

20.   In response, the Surveillance Body received written notifications from the EC, Japan and the United States on undertakings resulting from, or relating to, their rollback consultations or on the status of their consultations.   The other four participants addressed have not submitted any information on undertakings in response to the rollback requests.   As for participants requesting rollback action, Canada, Hong Kong, Japan and the United States reported on the status and outcome of their rollback consultations.

21.   The European Community reported on its consultations with Japan (RBC/17/Add.2).   As a result, the EC had eliminated a range of quantitative restrictions notified by Japan under RBC/17.

22.   In its communication (RBC/22), Japan reported on the termination of import allocation systems for eight categories of agricultural products, which were subject to rollback consultations with Argentina, Hong Kong, the United States and Uruguay.   Japan also reported that some measures subject to rollback consultations with the United States had been removed through other autonomous market-opening measures contained in document L/6370. With respect to consultations with the EC requested by Japan, Japan noted the measures taken by the EC (see paragraph 21 above) and stated that bilateral contacts were continuing with regard to the EC's remaining quantitative restrictions maintained against Japan.

23.   In its communication (MTN.SB/RBN/8), the United States reported on the status of rollback consultations which had been requested by other participants (RBC/4, 7, 15, 16 and 20) or had been requested by the United States (RBC/1 and 18).   With respect to Section 337 legislation (RBC/15), the United States had indicated at the time of adoption of the Panel report on the issue that it would take steps to make the necessary modifications in domestic legislation and that it regarded the Uruguay Round implementing legislation as the most appropriate legislative vehicle for accomplishing such modifications.   An active consultative process was on-going in the United States to seek the comments of all interested parties on implementation issues and interested foreign governments had been able to

0157

participate in this process. With respect to other United States measures concerned, the United States reported that, in most cases, it considered the consultations completed with participants concerned. As regards requests to Japan and the EC, the United States took note of the actions announced by these participants and looked forward to further action. However, the United States did not seek additional consultations on the remaining items.

24. Canada informed the Surveillance Body orally of the outcome of rollback consultations with other participants, which Canada had requested (MTN.SB/13). In Canada's view, the original cause for Canada's communication on Brazil's "law of similarity" (RBC/9) appeared to have been removed by recent changes in Brazil's international trade régime. With respect to Japan's import quotas on fish products notified by Canada in 1987 (RBC/12), Canada considered that the current conditions of access to Japan permitted Canadian products to be exported to Japan. According to the statement of Canada, other issues contained in Canada's rollback requests had not been resolved.

25. In its communications (RBC/8/Add.5 and 6), Hong Kong reported the outcome of its consultations with Japan concerning Japan's import quota system on 13 items and the Prior Confirmation System on imports of silk fabrics. Hong Kong accepted Japan's justification in respect of the import quota system on six items, noted that Japan was implementing Panel recommendations on three items, and received further information and clarification from Japan for restrictions on the four remaining items. Hong Kong did not intend to follow up consultations on these remaining items. Consultations remained inconclusive on the question of the GATT-consistency of the Prior Confirmation System maintained by Japan on imports of silk fabrics.

(b) Implementation of Panel recommendations

26. Some participants considered the implementation of GATT Panel reports adopted by the CONTRACTING PARTIES an integral part of the rollback process. In their view, the rollback commitment provided an additional means of encouraging participants to fully and speedily implement Panel reports. They drew attention in this regard to MTN.SB/W/11, dated 26 October 1990, which contained a note by the Secretariat on actions taken regarding measures which were found by the CONTRACTING PARTIES to be inconsistent with the GATT. Some other participants thought that the implementation of Panel reports adopted by the CONTRACTING PARTIES had no direct relevance to the rollback commitment, as it should follow the normal GATT dispute settlement procedures.

27.   Three notifications by Canada, Japan and the Republic of Korea
(MTN.SB/W/6, MTN.SB/RBN/1 and MTN.SB/RBN/5) referred to the liberalization
of some measures which had been ruled GATT-inconsistent by Panel reports.
The United States made rollback notifications on legislation to amend the
Superfund tax and the customs user fee in pursuance of Panel
recommendations (MTN.SB/RBN/2 and MTN.SB/RBN/8). These United States
measures were the subject of standstill notifications from other
participants.

(c)   Autonomous trade liberalization actions

28.   Some participants informed the Surveillance Body of autonomous trade
liberalization actions with respect to certain trade measures earlier
maintained by them. These measures had not been subject to rollback
requests from other participants. In most cases, the notifications were
made without prejudice to the question of GATT-consistency of the measures
concerned, and the notifying participants did not specify whether the
actions constituted undertakings of the rollback commitment on
GATT-inconsistent measures.

29.   A notification by the European Community (RBC/19/Rev.1) contained
autonomous rollback measures related to the elimination of specific
quantitative restrictions and the suspension of non-specific quantitative
restrictions on imports from Hungary and Poland. Seven other participants
(Argentina, Australia, Canada, Colombia, Finland, Indonesia and the
Republic of Korea) submitted written notifications on autonomous trade
liberalization actions which they had recently taken (MTN.SB/RBN/3 and
Rev.1, MTN.SB/W/7, MTN.SB/W/6, MTN.SB/RBN/4, 5, 6 and 7, L/6868 and L/6869
respectively).

30.   In the context of these autonomous actions, the point has been made
that the rollback commitment was only related to GATT-inconsistent
measures. Therefore, it was suggested that a distinction should be made
between the autonomous liberalization of GATT-inconsistent measures and
that of GATT-consistent measures, such as autonomously reducing an applied
m.f.n. tariff further below its bound rate. However, many participants
recognized the difficulties in determining the GATT-inconsistency of the
measures concerned.

(3)   Proposals for implementation of rollback action

31.   On the whole, with respect to rollback consultations, only a few
undertakings have been reported to the Surveillance Body. Some
participants reported the implementation of Panel recommendations as
rollback undertakings; but a number of measures have remained in force
which have been ruled to be GATT-inconsistent by the CONTRACTING PARTIES,

following Panel reports. As noted above, while some participants have notified autonomous trade liberalization actions without prejudice to the question of GATT-inconsistency of the measures concerned, views have been divided whether these actions should be considered rollback measures as provided for in the Punta del Este Ministerial Declaration.

32. The Surveillance Body has given active attention to the development of procedures for promoting rollback action and to proposals made by individual participants to this end. Following the Mid-Term Review, Australia (MTN.SB/W/7) and New Zealand (MTN.SB/W/8) put forward proposals on ways to ensure the fulfilment of the rollback commitment. Australia proposed that the TNC agree on the full implementation of all outstanding Panel reports adopted by the CONTRACTING PARTIES. New Zealand proposed that the Surveillance Body should agree on the following ways in which the rollback commitment might be evaluated:

> (i)   through the implementation of individual offers to roll back measures;
>
> (ii) through the implementation of any multilateral agreements, undertakings and understandings reached in the course of the multilateral negotiations which established that certain types of measures, the present GATT status of which was not necessarily agreed, would henceforth be inconsistent with GATT provisions; and
>
> (iii) through the phasing-out of measures ruled inconsistent with the GATT by Panel reports adopted by the CONTRACTING PARTIES.

33. The Surveillance Body discussed these proposals on a number of occasions. While there was considerable support for these proposals, there was no consensus on their adoption. Views remained divided about the ways in which autonomous trade liberalization actions and the implementation of Panel reports should be evaluated.

34. Mexico proposed that the burden of proof concerning the GATT-consistency of particular measures notified under the rollback procedures should be shifted to the participant applying such measures.

35. The Surveillance Body has also made an effort to assess the extent to which GATT-inconsistent measures continue to be maintained by individual contracting parties. In this connection, the Secretariat was asked to prepare a list of measures which, following Panel findings, had been found by the CONTRACTING PARTIES to be inconsistent with the General Agreement. The Secretariat also added available information regarding actions taken in response to such findings (MTN.SB/W/11). In general instances, full

information on the follow-up action taken to implement Panel findings is not available. In the majority of the 42 cases listed (covering the period 1951-90), actions appear to have been taken in response to the recommendations. However, in many of the more recent cases, implementation of the Panel recommendations remained pending.

36. Participants identified two difficulties in establishing the full picture of outstanding GATT-inconsistent measures. First, in a strict legal sense, the GATT-inconsistency of a particular measure can only be determined by the CONTRACTING PARTIES and, therefore, there are no other means available for participants to definitively determine the GATT-inconsistency of measures maintained by other participants. Second, the Punta del Este Ministerial Declaration requires that each participant implement the rollback commitment, taking into account multilateral agreements, undertakings and understandings reached in the Uruguay Round. However, it has been difficult for participants to determine, before the formal completion of the Uruguay Round, what measures should be considered to be GATT-inconsistent since agreements, undertakings and understandings with respect to GATT provisions were still under negotiation.

37. The Punta del Este Ministerial Declaration requires that the implementation of the rollback commitment be made within an agreed time-frame not later than by the date of the formal completion of the negotiations, taking into account multilateral agreements, undertakings and understandings, including strengthened rules and disciplines, reached in pursuance of the Objectives of the Negotiations. In this respect, the view has been advanced by some participants that agreement on a time-frame does not necessarily imply that all measures subject to the commitment should be phased out, or brought into conformity with the provisions of the General Agreement or Instruments negotiated within the framework of GATT or under its auspices, before the end of the Uruguay Round. This view is based on the consideration that the full details of multilateral agreements, undertakings and understandings might emerge only towards the end of the Uruguay Round. Some other participants did not share this view.

0161

외 무 부

종 별 :

번 호 : GVW-2035   일 시 : 91 1017 1830

수 신 : 장관(통기,경기원,재무부,농수산부,상공부)

발 신 : 주 제네바 대사

제 목 : UR/감시기구

　　　연: GVW-1234

　　　1. 표제 회의가 10.16(수) 10:00 개최된바, 회의 결과를 아래 보고함.(당관 이성주 참사관,위성락 서기관 참석)

　　　가. STANDSTILL 통고 검토

　　　0 91.7 공식회의 이후 신규 통고는 없었으나, 남미 국가들이 연호 이태리의 커피 및 코코아에 대한 소비세 인상 문제를 계속 제기함(혼두라스가 기조발언을 하고콜럼비아, 코스타리카, 니카라과, 엘살바돌, 베네주엘라, 브라질등이 동조 발언)

　　　0 남미 제국의 주요 논거와 동 조치 철회 요구는 종래와 동일하였으나 다음 사항이 다소 새로운점이었음.

　　　- 혼듀라스가 동 소비세 인상과 관련한 통계자료(수입량 및 소비량 변화등 관련)를 요구

　　　- 콜럼비아, 코스타리카등이 동 품목 관련, 자국의 대 이태리 수출이 실제 감소하였음을 언급(91.7회의시 EC 측이 실제 영향이 거의 없으리라는견해를 피력한데 대한 반론)

　　　- 니카라과, 베네주엘라, 콜럼비아등은 영향 여부에관계없이 SS 위배 사항은 철회되어야 함을주장

　　　- EC 는 종래 입장을 반복하고 통계자료 제시를통한 사실관계 규명에 응하겠다고함.

　　　나. SS 관련 사항(조기경보) 검토

　　　0 카나다는 91.9.1 부터 적용되는 이스라엘의 신무역정책(주로 비관세 장벽등을관세화 하는내용)에 대해 언급, 카나다측의 검토가 완료되지 않았으나, 일부측면(예컨데 자국관심 품목에대한 막대한 관세부과등)에 큰 관심을 갖고있으며,

---

통상국　　2차보　　정와대　　안기부　　경기원　　재무부　　농수부　　상공부

PAGE 1

91.10.18　　08:30 DU

외신 1과 통제관 0162

추후 문제를 제기하겠다고 함.

0 이스라엘 대표는 참석치 않은바, 의장은 이를 TAKE NOTE 함.

다. ROLLBACK 관련사항

1) EC 의 일본 자동차 수입 제한 완화 및궁극적 철폐 봉보

0 EC 와 일본이 공동으로 (91.10.11 부) EC 의 일본 자동차 수입 제한 완화 및궁극적 철폐를 봉보함.(상세내용 별전 보고)

0 이와 관련 지난 회의시 EC/일본간 자동차 수입협의에 대한 자료를 요청한바 있는 미국은 금번 자료에 사의를 표하고, 추후 미국 입장 표명 권리를유보함.

2) 베네주엘라의 무역 자유화 조치

0 베네주엘라는 자국의 AUTONOMOUS LIBERALIZATIONPOLICY 를 봉보함.

(관세 인하 및 대상 품목 축소, 수량제한 완화및 궁극적 철폐등)

3) PANEL 판정 조치의 ROLLBACK

0 한편 뉴질랜드는 PANEL 에서 GATT 불법 조치로 판정된 조치들을 시한을 정하여 ROLLBACK 시키는 프로그램의 중요성을 재강조함.

0 이에 대하여 호주는 뉴질랜드를 적극 지지하면서, GATT 불법 조치 시행과 UR시 한을 연계해서는 안되며, 불법조치는 즉시 ROLLBACK해야 함이 원칙임을 강조함.또한 호주는사무국이 작성한 TNC 앞 보고서 초안(90.11 브랏셀 TNC 앞 보고와 대동소이)중 관련부분이 과거와 동일함을 지적하고(초안에는 TNC MAY WISH TOCONSIDER WHAT FURTHER ACTION IS NEEDED,......로 되어있음) 거의 막바지에 이른 UR 협상의ㅎ 현단계에서 감시기구가 보다 진전된 입장을 제시해야 한다고 주장, 이를 위한 협의 필요성을제기함.(알젠틴, 스위스, 헝가리, 홍콩, 우루과이가동조)

0 EC, 미국, 일본, 카나다는 PANEL 의 불법판정과 UR 협상 최종 결과에 따른 판단이 반드시 일치하지 않을수 있으므로 이 문제를 신중히 다루어야 하며, UR 의 분쟁해결 절차가 별도로 협상되고 있으므로 이와 중복될 가능성도 염두에 두어야 한다고 함. 그러나 동 제국들은 협의에는 참가할 의향을 표함.

(특히 일본은 지난번 회의시 집중적 논의 결과로 나온 것이 브랏셀 TNC 앞 문구와 대동소이한 문구였음을 지적하고 현시점에서 그 이상 진전이 있을지에 대해 회의적 견해를 표명)

0 결국 의장은 동 문제 협의를 위하여 추후 비공식협의를 열기로 하고 이에 따라차기 감시기구 회의를 개최할 여지도 남겨둔다고 결정함.

PAGE 2

0163

2. 사무국 작성 TNC 앞 보고서 초안(미채택)등 관련 자료 파편 송부함. 끝
(대사 박수길-국장)

외 무 부

원 본

종   별 :

번   호 : GVW-2036   일   시 : 91 1017 1830

수   신 : 장관(봉기,봉삼,경기원,재무부,상공부,사본;주EC대사-직송필)

발   신 : 주 제네바대사

제   목 : UR/감시기구-EC의 일본 자동차 수입

연: GVW-2035

연호 10.16 감시기구 회의시 EC 와 일본이 공동으로 제출한 EC 의 일본 자동차 수입제한완화 및 철폐 관련 통보 요지(91.10.11 자)를 아래보고함.

1. 목적

0 EC 의 자동차 수입 체제를 점진적으로 완화,궁극적으로 자유화

- 시장 교란 방지, 적절한 과도기 부여, EC생산자의 경쟁력 확보를 위한 구조조정촉진등을 배려

2. 내용

0 지금부터 EC 의 국별 규제를 완화, 늦어도93.1.1 까지 철폐

0 93-99.12.31. 간을 과도기로 설정하고 동 기간중 일본은 대 EC 수출 전체와 대 불란서, 이태리,폴튜갈, 스페인, 영국 수출을 계속 감시(MONITOR)

- 년 2회 양자 협의 실시

3. 감시 대상

0 일본으로 부터 EC 에 수출되는 승용차, 험지용차량(OFF-ROAD VEHICLES)상업용소형차, 5톤 이하소형 트럭 및 동종 차량의 완전 해체형태(COMPLETE KNOCKED DOWN SETS)

4. 기타

0 일본의 EC 내 투자는 계속 제한없으며, 동투자에 따른 생산품은 EC 내에 자유로이 유통

0 1999 년의 EC 자동차 수요를 1510 만대로 보고, 동시점에서 일본의 수출을 123만대로 예측. 끝

(대사 박수길-국장)

통상국   2차보   통상국   경기원   재무부   상공부

외 무 부

종 별 :

번 호 : GVW-2237　　　　　　　　　일 시 : 91 1101 2030

수 신 : 장 관(통기, 경기원, 재무부, 농수산부, 상공부)

발 신 : 주 제네바대사

제 목 : UR/감시기구

　　연: GVW-2035, 제네(경) 20644-883

　　1. 감시기구 의장은 그간 비공식 협의과정에서개진된 각국 의견을 반영하여 작성한안을 배포하였음(동문안 FAX 송부)

　　2. 상기 내용은 기존 초안을 바탕으로 패널판정조치의 ROLLBACK 문제관련, 일부국가들의 문제 제기 사실을 적시하고(동 문안 15항으로서 신설됨), 17항 후반의 문구를 TNC로 하여금 ROLLBACK이 충분히 시행되도록 필요한 조치를 고려할 것을 요청한다(CONSIDER ... THE FURTHER ACTIONTHAT MAY BE NEEDED TO ENSURE ..)는 표현으로 수정한것인바, 연호 뉴질랜드, 호주등의 강한 문제제기를 반영한 것임

　　3. 사무국측에 의하면 의장은 동 문안이 감시기구회의에서 공식통과 된것은 아니라, 그간의 협의과정에서 제기된 바를 적절히 반영한 내용이라고 보고, 특기할 이의가 없는한 TNC 에 보고할것이라고 함.

　　첨부: GVW(F)-0475

　　끝

　　(댓 박수길-국장)

통상국　　2차보　　경기원　　재무부　　농수부　　상공부

PAGE 1　　　　　　　　　　　　　　　　91.11.02　　09:10 WH

　　　　　　　　　　　　　　　　　　외신 1과 통제관

　　　　　　　　　　　　　　　　　　　　　0166

─VベL/1)- V 千7J ─//°/ 2─ฮ3 ๐

MULTILATERAL TRADE NEGOTIATIONS
THE URUGUAY ROUND

// GUW-2237詩박

RESTRICTED
MTN.SB/18
30 October 1991
Special Distribution

Surveillance Body

REPORT BY THE CHAIRMAN OF THE SURVEILLANCE BODY TO THE TNC

1.   In December 1990, a report by the Chairman of the Surveillance Body (MTN.SB/14) was transmitted to the TNC meeting at Ministerial level in Brussels. Following consultations with participants, the Chairman has updated the report to take account of the developments and discussions held since Brussels. The report provides the TNC with a brief summary of the implementation of the standstill and rollback commitments and views expressed in the matter. A more detailed account is provided in the Annex.

(1)   Standstill

2.   Since the standstill commitment took effect in September 1986, a total of 26 notifications, by 11 individual participants and a group of participants against 9 participants, were submitted to the Surveillance Body. These notifications covered 24 cases, as two measures were, each, subject to two notifications.

3.   Twenty-four notifications were made during the period October 1986 to November 1988. One notification was submitted in 1990 and one in 1991.

4.   According to the information provided to the Surveillance Body, in nine of the 24 cases participants have taken action with a view to ensuring the withdrawal of measures contrary to the standstill commitment. Three of these actions were in response to recommendations of GATT Panel reports adopted by the CONTRACTING PARTIES; in the other six cases, the measures concerned were lifted autonomously. In a tenth case, a participant expressed its intention to act upon the notified measure in the light of the outcome of the Uruguay Round.

5.   The remaining 14 cases notified under standstill were also discussed at meetings of the Surveillance Body. Some actions were reported concerning the measures in question. However, the views of the participants remained divided as to the consistency or inconsistency of the measures with the standstill commitment.

GATT SECRETARIAT
UR-91-0143

0167

4 -1

MTN.SB/18
Page 2

6.   Participants also engaged in "early warning" discussions on proposed legislation and other actions affecting trade. Altogether 35 cases were subject to discussions, some being discussed at several meetings. The discussion in the Surveillance Body served to ensure that the concerns brought up by participants were duly shared and transmitted, in an appropriate fashion, to the authorities concerned.

(2)   Rollback

    (a)   Rollback consultations

7.   A total of twenty rollback requests covering a wide range of measures were made by eight participants, addressed to seven participants. In some cases, there was some overlap of the measures notified. Most requests concerned quantitative restrictions considered by the notifying participant to be inconsistent with the General Agreement.

8.   Nineteen requests were made during the period June 1987 to October 1988. One request was made in 1990.

9.   Fifteen requests were the subject of consultations. A total of twenty-one consultations were held. There have been no notifications concerning consultations on the remaining five requests.

10.   Three participants to which requests were addressed (the EC, Japan and the United States) notified undertakings already implemented or intended. In some cases, the undertakings covered only part of the measures contained in the rollback requests made by other participants. The other four participants addressed have not submitted any information on undertakings in response to the rollback requests.

11.   In one case, the requesting participant indicated that the measure notified had been removed.

    (b)   Implementation of Panel recommendations

12.   Four participants (Canada, Japan, the Republic of Korea and the United States) notified the Surveillance Body of their actions on certain measures which had been ruled GATT-inconsistent by the CONTRACTING PARTIES, following Panel recommendations.

    (c)   Autonomous trade liberalization actions

13.   Some participants (Australia, Argentina, Canada, Colombia, the EC, Finland, Indonesia, the Republic of Korea and Venezuela) informed the Surveillance Body of autonomous trade liberalization actions. Most of the

0168

measures affected by these actions had not been subject to rollback requests from other participants. The actions included the elimination of discriminatory import restrictions, changes in import licensing régimes, progressive liberalization of import restrictions and removal of other non-tariff measures. Most of these notifications were made without prejudice to the question of GATT-consistency of the measures concerned. In discussing these autonomous actions, the point was made that the rollback commitment was only related to GATT-inconsistent measures and therefore a distinction should be made between the autonomous liberalization of GATT-consistent measures and that of GATT-inconsistent measures. However, many participants recognized the difficulties in determining the GATT-inconsistency of the trade measures concerned.

(3) Considerations for the full implementation of the rollback commitment

14. The Surveillance Body has given active attention to the development of procedures for promoting rollback action and to proposals made by individual participants to this end. The Surveillance Body has also made an effort to assess the extent to which GATT-inconsistent measures continue to be maintained by individual contracting parties. Upon request of the Surveillance Body, the Secretariat prepared a note on measures which, following Panel findings, had been found by the CONTRACTING PARTIES to be inconsistent with the General Agreement. Forty-two cases were listed, covering the period 1951-90. In general, full information on the follow-up action taken to implement Panel findings is not available. It was found that in a number of the more recent cases implementation of the Panel recommendations remained pending.

15. In this connection, the Surveillance Body has considered proposals by some participants for action on the rollback of measures inconsistent with GATT or related instruments. Particular reference was made to measures found inconsistent by the CONTRACTING PARTIES following panel reports, and in this context, to a timeframe for the phasing out of such measures.

16. Participants identified two difficulties in establishing the full picture of outstanding GATT-inconsistent measures. First, in a strict legal sense, the GATT-inconsistency of a particular measure maintained by a participant can only be determined by the CONTRACTING PARTIES. Second, the Punta del Este Ministerial Declaration requires that each participant implement the rollback commitment, taking into account multilateral agreements, undertakings and understandings reached in the Uruguay Round.

17. Against this background, the Surveillance Body has considered ways by which the full implementation of the rollback undertaking could be facilitated. The Surveillance Body notes that it is difficult for it to proceed further, in view of the fact that final agreements or decisions in

K-3

0169

MTN.SB/18
Page 4

individual negotiating areas of the Uruguay Round, including agreements on
procedures to phase out, or bring into conformity, measures henceforth
inconsistent with the provisions of the General Agreement or Instruments
negotiated within the framework of GATT or under its auspices, have yet to
be reached. In the circumstances, the Surveillance Body requests the TNC
to consider, including in the light of all information regarding agreements
or decisions reached in the Uruguay Round Negotiating Groups, the further
action that may be needed to ensure that the rollback undertaking is fully
met.

0170

외교문서 비밀해제: 우루과이라운드2 10

우루과이라운드 제도 및 기타 분야 협상 2

초판인쇄 2024년 03월 15일
초판발행 2024년 03월 15일

지은이 한국학술정보(주)
펴낸이 채종준
펴낸곳 한국학술정보(주)
주 소 경기도 파주시 회동길 230(문발동)
전 화 031-908-3181(대표)
팩 스 031-908-3189
홈페이지 http://ebook.kstudy.com
E-mail 출판사업부 publish@kstudy.com
등 록 제일산-115호(2000. 6. 19)

ISBN   979-11-7217-112-4 94340
        979-11-7217-102-5 94340 (set)